Northern Ireland

MERLYN REES

NORTHERN IRELAND

A Personal Perspective

Methuen . London

First published 1985

Printed in Great Britain
for Methuen London Ltd
11 New Fetter Lane, London EC4P 4EE
by Robert Hartnoll (1985) Ltd

British Library Cataloguing in Publication Data

Rees, Merlyn
Northern Ireland: a personal perspective.
1. Northern Ireland——History——1969–
I. Title
941.60824 DA990.U46

ISBN 0–413–52590–2

To Colleen Faith

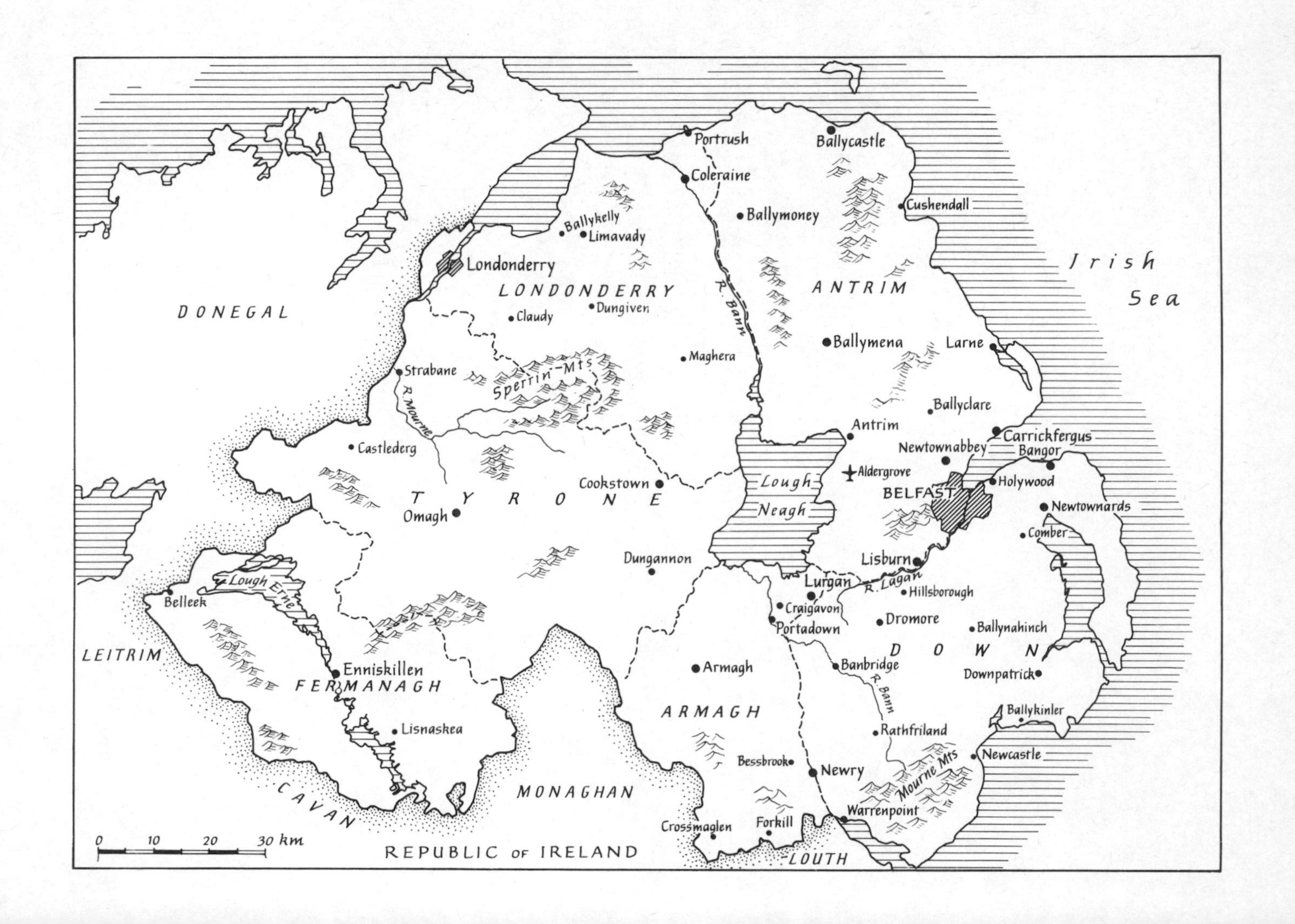
Irish Sea
DONEGAL
LONDONDERRY
ANTRIM
TYRONE
FERMANAGH
ARMAGH
DOWN
LEITRIM
CAVAN
MONAGHAN
LOUTH
REPUBLIC OF IRELAND
Portrush
Ballycastle
Coleraine
Ballymoney
Cushendall
Ballykelly
Limavady
Londonderry
Claudy
Dungiven
Maghera
Ballymena
Larne
Strabane
Sperrin Mts
R. Mourne
R. Bann
Ballyclare
Antrim
Carrickfergus
Newtownabbey
Bangor
Aldergrove
Holywood
BELFAST
Newtownards
Castlederg
Cookstown
Omagh
Lough Neagh
Comber
Dungannon
Lisburn
Lurgan
R. Lagan
Hillsborough
Craigavon
Portadown
Dromore
Ballynahinch
Lough Erne
Belleek
Enniskillen
Banbridge
Armagh
Downpatrick
Lisnaskea
Ballykinler
Rathfriland
Bessbrook
Newry
Newcastle
Mourne Mts
Warrenpoint
Crossmaglen
Forkill
0 10 20 30 km

CONTENTS

Abbreviations

CLF	Commander Land Forces
DUP	Democratic Unionist Party
GOC	General Officer Commanding
INLA	Irish National Liberation Army
IRA	Irish Republican Army
IRSP	Irish Republican Socialist Party
LAW	Loyalist Association of Workers
NICICTU	Northern Irish Committee of the Irish Congress of Trade Unions
NIES	Northern Ireland Electricity Service
NILP	Northern Ireland Labour Party
OUP	Official Unionist Party
RTE	Radio Telefis Eireann
RUC	Royal Ulster Constabulary
SDLP	Social Democratic and Labour Party
TD	Teachta Dala; Member of the Dail
UDA	Ulster Defence Association
UDR	Ulster Defence Regiment
UFF	Ulster Freedom Fighters
ULCC	Ulster Loyalist Central Co-ordinating Committee
UPNI	Unionist Party of Northern Ireland
UUUC	United Ulster Unionist Council (or Coalition)
UUUM	United Ulster Unionist Movement
UUUP	United Ulster Unionist Party
UVF	Ulster Volunteer Force
UWC	Ulster Workers' Council
VPP	Volunteer Political Party
VUPP	Vanguard Unionist Progressive Party

INTRODUCTION

My first interest in Ireland came from my father who, as a private soldier, had been sent there from the Western Front during the Easter Rising. He often talked about places where he had been billeted in Cork, Fermoy, Kingstown and, of course, Dublin. He thought it a comment on the whole affair that afterwards he fought on the Somme alongside men from the North and South. I still have the certificate recording his gallant conduct on the field on 7 June 1917 while serving in the Irish Brigade. He was gassed in France, which permanently damaged his health and finally caused his death.

The effects of the war lingered on in our household longer than they did in the pages of the newspapers. My father was left with strong views on 'army brass' and the flag-waving politicians who supported them, but with fraternal feelings for all those fellow soldiers who had actually been in battle. Although he had passed the first 11-plus in 1906–7 and gone to the local grammar school, when he left there he almost inevitably went into the pit and on his demobilisation he returned to the Albion Colliery in Cilfynydd, South Wales, joining my grandfather, the checkweigher and miners' representative. The economic and social distress was great in our valleys and my father and grandfather, who had long been involved in labour politics, both became founder members of the new Labour Party after 1918. Thus it was that I became involved in it at an early age.

I grew up being told about the explosion in our colliery on 23 June 1895 when nearly three hundred men were killed, including my mother's grandfather; his twelve-year-old son was one of the few survivors. The House of Commons with a Liberal majority had preferred to send regrets to France on the death of its president rather than to the relatives of the Cilfynydd dead. This was long remembered in our community and explained why at the time Keir Hardie, MP for nearby Merthyr, opposed the motion of congratulation to Queen Victoria on the birth of a great grandson – the future Duke of Windsor.

From such a background I inherited not only an interest in politics but also a scepticism about the old political parties and their politicians. The new Labour Party was going to be different and not subservient to the newspaper proprietors: one of my earliest memories is being taken from door to door in the village selling Lansbury's *Daily Herald*.

In my teens the early spark of interest in Ireland was stimulated by a brilliant teacher at my grammar school who guided us through the cycles of concession and coercion in nineteenth-century Irish history. Only later did I come to read with more perception about the Gaelic League, the Civil War, Connolly and Larkin, and the work of the Land League and Michael Davitt. I found that I had more in common with him than with Gladstone, whose sepia picture looked gravely down from the bedroom wall in my maternal grandmother's home. Davitt also spent more years in prison than Parnell spent months, and without the latter's special treatment: there was obviously an earlier version of 'special category status'.

As I grew more active in politics in the late 1930s, I read about General Eoin O'Duffy and his fascist blue shirts. This is radical, revolutionary Ireland, I thought! I had much to learn about the South. I also read of Harry Midgley in Belfast, which showed that to be Labour there did not mean support for a united Ireland. Clearly, I had much to learn about the North too.

My first practical realisation of the consequences of a divided Ireland came as a young RAF officer in the 1940s. Without the Northern Irish coastal command bases more seamen would have died in the Battle of the Atlantic and the blockade on Britain would have been more severe. Recognising this did not, however, mean that I accepted the argument put by Admiral Beresford in his book *Against Home Rule*, published in 1912, that 'Ireland under Home Rule must in the event of war be regarded as a potentially hostile country'. The Admiral had gone on to write that 'naval officers are accustomed to deal with facts rather than words', which may well be true but removes any chance of understanding the Irish question.

I wonder what he would have made of the fact that my wife's uncle Robert – from an Irish Catholic family and named after the Irish patriot Robert Emmet – served in the Royal Navy and was drowned in the waters of Scapa Flow early in the First World War; we still have his patriotic letters. An understanding of Ireland defies mere facts.

When I became a Member of Parliament in 1963, the affairs of Ireland were far from my mind, though I listened with interest to the tussles with the Speaker of a group of young Labour MPs – Stan Orme, Paul Rose and Kevin McNamara – who were trying to break the convention that Stormont was the place to discuss the affairs of Northern Ireland. The first time that I became really aware of the political problems of the province was in 1969 when as a junior Home Office minister I saw at first hand how Jim Callaghan, the Home Secretary, had to involve the government urgently in Stormont affairs. In the early seventies, out of office, I became Opposition Spokesman on Northern Ireland and then, from 1974 to 1976, the Secretary of State for Northern Ireland. In this time the province and all its problems entered my bloodstream.

In 1979, after our defeat in the General Election of that year, I began preparations for writing a book about my experiences in the province. My main aim was to pass on my views of the nature of the Ulster problem, which I hoped would help in understanding it. Above all, I wanted to emphasise that there were no solutions to it lying around on the shelves of a government department or in the eagle mind of some journalist. At the same time I hoped to clarify the processes of government, which from the outside and in the pages of constitutional text books seem far more logical than they really are.

Given the nature of the sources that I needed to consult, all the research had to be done by me alone. The first couple of years were consequently taken up with note-taking from my own papers in the Northern Ireland Office and from Cabinet sub-committee papers in the Cabinet Office. I am grateful to the staff in both places for producing this archive material for me, and also to the staff in the House of Commons Library, particularly the late Stan Gothard, who ferreted out every mention of Ireland in parliamentary papers between 1969 and 1977.

The book also draws on my diary, in the form of twenty-four tapes on which I recorded my thoughts on people and events in the province from 1971 to September 1976. The tapes have proved invaluable as a basis for my research and I have sometimes quoted from them, although I have deliberately omitted passages that might compromise individuals and also some late-night soliloquies spoken in ill temper that do not bear the passage of even a short period of time.

I am grateful to Christopher Falkus of Methuen who understood that the first fruits of my research were only pattern-making and not the first draft of the book, and who encouraged me over the years. I thank Ann Wilson, who edited the book in its later stages and asked the questions that forced me to explain more clearly the events which I had too easily assumed were common knowledge.

Finally, of course, my thanks and love go to my wife who typed the millions of words in the research papers I prepared and then the many drafts of the book. Nobody else could, or would, have done it!

Eventually, there emerged my perspective of Northern Ireland based on my experience as Secretary of State for the province. I always followed the road that I believed was right while not forgetting the words of that great Ulster poet, Louis McNeice:

> And if the world were black or white entirely
>   And all the charts were plain
> Instead of a mad weir of tigerish waters,
>   A prism of delight and pain,
> We might be surer where we wished to go
>   Or again we might be merely
> Bored but in brute reality there is no
>   Road that is right entirely.

Part I

INITIATION

1971–1974

Chapter 1

SHADOW SECRETARY OF STATE

I was a junior minister at the Home Office in Harold Wilson's government when the recent history of troubles in Northern Ireland began in the late 1960s. Since the Ireland Act of 1920 and the division of the country that followed, Northern Ireland had been left very much to its own devices, a part of the United Kingdom that Westminster preferred to forget. For Dublin governments also, it had been preferable to turn a blind eye to the six counties of the North after the bitter fighting involved in establishing the Irish Republic. The province had a devolved government, with its own parliament at Stormont, and a representation by twelve MPs at Westminster. For international affairs it was of course part of the United Kingdom and it needed Whitehall support in, for example, financial and agricultural matters, but otherwise Ulster affairs played little part in Westminster thinking over the years up to the late sixties.

The underlying grievances in the divided community of Northern Ireland then surfaced in widespread civil rights protests. They were the culmination of the Roman Catholic minority's resentment at discrimination in jobs and housing, and the inequitable voting system in local elections, which reflected the power held by the Protestant majority and the unbroken years of government by the Unionist Party. In the summer of 1969 the civil rights disturbances reached a head. Clashes with the police in the Catholic Bogside district of Londonderry were followed by serious communal riots there and in Belfast, where the B Specials – the loyalist Protestant auxiliary of the Royal Ulster Constabulary – had been called in. Several people were killed and many injured; it was clear that the RUC could not cope with the situation. The Catholic communities had little protection from the loyalist mobs, increasingly fearful of the implications of reform. Protestant fears for their future were heightened when in August Jack Lynch, Taoiseach of the Irish Republic, warned that the South could no longer stand idly by in the face of the violence.

In the same month, James Callaghan, the Home Secretary, together with the Prime Minister, decided to send in British soldiers to help the civil power preserve law and order, and the General Officer Commanding assumed overall responsibility for security operations, including those conducted by the RUC. At the same time Northern Ireland's position within the UK was reaffirmed in a declaration from Downing Street, as a reassurance to the Protestant majority that Irish unity could not be forced on them. A UK government representative, Oliver Wright from the Foreign Office, was appointed to Belfast. His role was to liaise between the UK and Northern Ireland governments; he could also be in day-to-day contact with the GOC and thus keep abreast of the security situation.

It was the Home Office that had retained residual responsibility for the province and it was now galvanised into action by Jim. He visited Northern Ireland and put pressure on the Stormont government to make changes. The recommendations of the Hunt report – commissioned as a result of the problems – were implemented: the B Specials so distrusted by the Catholics were disbanded to be replaced by the Ulster Defence Regiment, and the RUC was disarmed. A Police Authority was set up whose task was to maintain an efficient police force in the province. A Commission for Complaints Office was established and an Ombudsman and a Community Relations Commission came into existence. Changes took place in the allocation of houses, and in the electoral system – one man one vote was to apply to the next elections following local government reorganisation; Londonderry, where the Catholics were in the majority and where the worst gerrymandering had taken place, was to be administered by specially appointed commissioners. The UK government representative was instructed to ensure that the Stormont government be kept aware of Whitehall's objectives for reform in the province and to brief the UK government on political developments there.

It was unfortunate for Northern Ireland that the General Election of June 1970 came so soon after reforms had been initiated. Edward Heath's Conservative government came to power and Reginald Maudling was appointed Home Secretary. I became number two to Jim Callaghan, now the Shadow Home Secretary, and I know that in his view Heath and Maudling 'disengaged' from the province at the wrong time. Jim had been the driving force behind change, bringing those involved to face the reality of the situation; now, as the violence continued, his initiatives were not followed up.

The IRA, which had been of little significance up to and including the civil rights movement – its initials had even been claimed by Catholics to stand for 'I Ran Away' – had belatedly started to respond to the unrest in Northern Ireland. In early 1970 there was a split in the leadership, with the more militant members breaking off from the 'Official' and so-called Marxist organisation to form the Provisional IRA. The Provisionals were able to take advantage of fears in the Catholic communities to present themselves as protectors against loyalist extremists despite the presence of the British troops.

The bombings and shootings increased and soon in Belfast and Derry there were Catholic areas where the writ of the security forces did not run. By the summer of 1971 the security situation had seriously deteriorated and Protestant demands for action became increasingly vociferous. On 9 August, Northern Ireland's Prime Minister, Brian Faulkner, introduced with the agreement of the Heath government internment without trial.

The overnight arrest of suspects was followed immediately by riots and further killings, and by large-scale civil disobedience in the Catholic community. The Social Democratic and Labour Party, which largely represented the Catholics and which had already withdrawn from Stormont in protest at events, now declared its refusal to talk with either a British or Northern Ireland government while internment lasted. The problem of Northern Ireland was back in earnest on the political agenda of Britain and the Irish Republic after a gap of fifty years.

It was from this time onwards that the affairs of the province became entwined in my daily life, for in October 1971 I became the Opposition spokesman on Northern Ireland. My first visit to the province as an MP took place that autumn, following the introduction of internment. Allegations had been made about the conditions in the new prison camp set up at the old airfield at Long Kesh near Lisburn and the British government had decided to send an all-Party delegation to visit it and also the Crumlin Road prison in Belfast where some internees were also being kept. Bill Deedes, then Conservative MP for Ashford and later editor of the *Daily Telegraph*, led the delegation and I headed the Labour Party element.

At this time there were only two compounds at Long Kesh, which was later to be known as the Maze. They held a total of 180 men, who were housed in Nissen huts equipped with television and radio and with wash-houses attached that included showers and flush toilets. The men in the compound visited by my half of the delegation had divided themselves into three groups – the Provisional IRA, the Official IRA and the rest, which seemed to include those who were straightforward civil rights protesters. The first group was drawn up in three lines abreast and was called to attention by an adjutant who addressed them as the Belfast Brigade. One man then broke off and told me that they were not prepared to meet representatives of the 'imperialist power'. I replied that nevertheless my group was going into the hut and was prepared to talk with those who wished to talk to us.

Peter Archer, the Shadow Solicitor General, Tony Buck, Tory MP for Colchester, and I sat down with a group of men whom I assumed, from the way they spoke, were members of the Official IRA. At issue was the working of the Brown Commission, set up by Brian Faulkner's government under the Special Powers Act, to which internees could put their case for release. Few were apparently prepared to use this procedure so I asked Peter Archer to explain this legal 'Brown' aspect of their internment. He started off with an advocate's preamble: 'I assume none of you has been involved in violence?' There was silence, but two of the men turned to me and winked! He did not convince them or anyone else to use their right of appeal.

We afterwards visited the Crumlin Road prison, a forbidding nineteenth-century building, where the internees who were housed in 'C' block refused to allow us in. Three representatives did, however, come to the prison governor's room to make allegations against the police and the army during the arrest operation.

Later we met the wives and mothers of some of the internees at the home of Gerry Fitt, leader of the Social Democratic and Labour Party and its Westminster MP. As we sat in the front room of his Antrim Road house in West Belfast, we could feel the 'crump crump' of explosions nearby. The women made allegations of ill treatment, which included complaints that prison officers were telling their men 'behind the wire' that they were 'carrying on' with soldiers. We passed on the allegations to the Northern Ireland government. We did not hear the grievances of the prison officers because it was ruled that they had their own procedures, but it was not hard to appreciate the kind of stress and danger they faced.

That first visit to Long Kesh affected me greatly. It was not that the physical conditions as such were bad but that this kind of imprisonment could have been considered necessary at all. What sort of United Kingdom province was it that needed internment without trial? I did not realise then the incompetence of the Northern Ireland Department of Home Affairs nor the hearsay nature of the information that had led to the very inaccurate list of people to be picked up.

The formal decision to introduce internment had been taken by the Northern Ireland government. There may have been a Joint Security Committee chaired by Brian Faulkner and consisting of Northern Ireland ministers, the GOC, the Chief Constable of the RUC, the government security adviser and the UK representative in Belfast but, as Reginald Maudling stated in response to my questioning, it was for the Northern Ireland authorities to take decisions on matters which were their responsibility. It was all part of a 'leave it to Northern Ireland' policy, the drift that had begun in June 1970. On many political matters in the province I can see the virtue of listening to Northern Ireland advice but on fundamental matters of security where the army is involved – no! and certainly not at that stage.

Some of the interrogation procedures authorised then were to lead to a world outcry and, at the instigation of the Irish government, to the appearance of the United Kingdom government before the European Commission and Court of Human Rights. Allegations against the security forces of physical brutality during the arrest operation of 9 August led to the Compton Commission, which reported in November 1971. Mr Maudling stated in the House of Commons that the 'government rejected any suggestion that the methods currently authorised contain any element of cruelty'; the Compton Report, in his view, confirmed this opinion. I found this a difficult judgment to accept: wall-standing, hooding, noise, deprivation of food and sleep, were surely cruelty. There was widespread criticism of the report and Maudling subsequently announced that there would be a further commission, under Lord Parker, to investigate interrogation procedures of detainees in Northern Ireland.

The Parker Commission reported in March 1972, with a majority view that 'the procedures should be used under stronger controls and better machinery of complaint'. It was to the credit of the Prime Minister, Edward Heath, that he accepted the minority view of Lord Gardiner, who wrote that the blame 'lies with those who many years ago decided to abandon the legal, well-tried, and highly successful wartime interrogation methods and replace them by procedures which were secret, illegal, not morally justifiable and alien to the traditions of what I believe still to be the greatest democracy in the world'.

Brian Faulkner wrote later that the procedures had already been cleared with the appropriate authorities in London and he had seen no reason to object to the proposal if it had received political clearance. He added: 'The possibility that HMG would do anything of dubious propriety did not, given the background of exaggerated caution on security, occur to me.'

Such authorisation should never have been given on the basis of the inadequate information received, let alone on moral grounds. It was a ministerial decision and, again in the words of Lord Gardiner, 'No minister could lawfully or validly have authorised the use of the procedures. Only Parliament can alter the law. The proceedings were and are illegal.'

When I came to know Brian Faulkner from my visits to the province, I was impressed by his professionalism. It was from him that I began to see how Northern Ireland, whatever the intention had been in 1920, had developed as an independent part of the United Kingdom. It had a governor, a privy council, a separate judiciary, a Senate (with red leather furniture as in the House of Lords), a House of Commons (with blue leather furniture unlike, for obvious Irish reasons, the green of Westminster), a Cabinet, and a separate Northern Ireland civil service working for individual departments of state. The Finance Minister attended meetings of international and Commonwealth organisations, and the Department of Commerce had set up offices to promote industry in various capitals of the world. I often felt after I became Secretary of State for Northern Ireland and was studying constitutional possibilities that the Ireland Act of 1920 had been drafted in the same spirit as the Southern Rhodesian Act of 1924.

But if I was impressed by Brian Faulkner, I was frightened by some of the Unionist Party officials whom I met at the Glengall Street headquarters in Belfast – they were simply anti-Catholic and anti-republican. It was a measure of the state of the Party, which after nearly fifty years of power was cracking under the strain of the violence in the province; it was losing its public support and splinter groups were emerging.

Many of its working-class supporters – members of British trade unions – had formed themselves into the Loyalist Association of Workers under the leadership of Billy Hull, a member of the Amalgamated Union of Engineering Workers. LAW had close ties with William Craig, Stormont MP and a former Northern Ireland minister who was strongly opposed to the Unionist government's reforming measures, and it also had ties with the Orange Order and with the local vigilante groups, which drew together in September 1971 to form the Ulster Defence Association. Their demand was for stronger security measures, a demand also being loudly voiced by the Rev Ian Paisley, who with fellow Stormont MPs Desmond Boal and John McQuade, had formed the ultra-loyalist Democratic Unionist Party. In early September Paisley and Craig, who both played on loyalist fears of Catholic subversion, had succeeded in organising a rally of 15,000 Belfast industrial workers in support of a tougher security policy.

Fear of a Protestant backlash had been behind the decision to introduce internment, which had met with the approval of most Unionists, although Paisley had opposed it on the grounds that it might be turned to use against loyalists. Its immediate effect, however, had been dramatically to alienate the Catholic community, and in the months that followed the incidents of violence had increased. By early 1972 there were constant rumours circulating in Belfast and Westminster, and reported in the media, that a government initiative was in the offing. The guessing game went on and then, as so often in the affairs of Northern Ireland, the scene was transformed by a single event: Bloody Sunday. In Londonderry, on 30 January, thirteen civilians were shot dead by British soldiers at the end of an 'illegal' march from the Bogside.

Understandably, all hell was let loose. The Irish ambassador to London was withdrawn, and the British embassy in Dublin was burned down. The world's press was critical. In the highly charged debate in the House of Commons, Bernadette McAliskey (then Devlin), the young Independent MP for Mid-Ulster, struck Reginald Maudling in the face. The government had already announced an official enquiry, under Lord Widgery – a demand for which had been made by Cardinal Heenan of Westminster as well as the Labour Party. On Labour's behalf, I asked for the transfer of security policy to Westminster; it was obvious that the split control with the Northern Ireland government simply could not be allowed to continue. I wanted to know whether the decision had been made at Westminster before Sunday that troops should go into the Bogside, where there had been practically no movement by security forces for some time. Was the opportunity of the march taken to try to deal with the Bogside in the way that similar areas had already been dealt with in Belfast? There was no clear answer and the issue of split security was felt so strongly by the Labour Party that although we favoured the enquiry, we voted against the government in the division that followed.

The events of Bloody Sunday raised fundamental questions about the government's overall policy in Northern Ireland. In its aftermath came the Official IRA's bombing of the Parachute Regiment Depot in Aldershot on 22 February, when a Catholic army chaplain and five women domestic staff were killed. The questioning was further increased with the March publication of the Parker Report on interrogation procedures.

The same month Harold Wilson received a message from the Provisional IRA via Dr John Connell, a Labour Party member of the Dail. The Provisionals had, apparently, been impressed by a speech made by Harold in his Huyton constituency, in which he had said that a ceasefire might begin in April if the government released internees whom it did not intend to bring to trial. The message contained their terms for a truce: immediate withdrawal of British troops from Ulster's streets, and eventual evacuation; abolition of the Stormont Parliament; and a total amnesty for all political prisoners and those on the 'wanted list' in both Northern Ireland and Britain. No British government could agree to such terms and Harold indicated this, but he agreed to go to Dublin to meet 'friends of the IRA' – the IRA was officially an illegal organisation in the Republic as in the North.

Harold asked me to accompany him and on 13 March I flew into Dublin. Harold had already arrived and had talked over lunch with Taoiseach Jack Lynch, the Fine Gael Opposition leader Liam Cosgrave, and the Irish Labour Party leader Brendan Corish. I joined him at the television studios where he was being interviewed. During the programme he repeated the need to end internment in Northern Ireland and to transfer security powers to Westminster – but he added that the Provisional IRA's terms should be discussed in any talks about the future.

The broadcast upset people in both the North and South. Harold had referred to the Provisional IRA as being 'well-disciplined', which he meant as a reference to the organisation's chain of command that extended down to active service units all over Northern Ireland, but it was a phrase that stung many people in the North given the atrocities perpetrated there by the IRA. It was also understandable that the proposal to include the Provisionals' terms in any future discussions on Northern Ireland would upset the Unionists, but neither was it welcome to the elected Dublin politicians.

To the latter, the IRA of any variety was a sensitive subject, for it recalled the Dublin Easter Rising of 1916 and the Civil War of the 1920s, from which the main Irish parties – Fianna Fail and Fine Gail – had emerged. The IRA's intermittent military activities since then had led to it being declared illegal; it was regarded as an irrelevant remnant from the past, but the recent troubles in Northern Ireland were stirring old memories and loyalties. The Dublin political parties were committed to the idea of Irish unity by consent and at some vague future date; the events in the North were focussing attention on what they preferred to ignore.

The Irish government's stance on security had not been helped by the charges of arms smuggling brought in 1970 against Finance Minister Charles Haughey and other members of Jack Lynch's government. Their contacts with the IRA were shown in the subsequent 'Arms Trial', which found the accused not guilty – Haughey was later to become Taoiseach.

Dublin's attitude to IRA activities was something I wondered about when, after Harold's broadcast, we were driven to John Connell's home to meet with three 'friends of the IRA', all members of the Provisional Sinn Fein – the legal political wing of the Provisional IRA. I was deputed to enter the room first and to proceed in such a way that there would be no hand-shaking! I duly introduced myself and, with a backward wave of the hand, my colleagues. Harold sat down at one end of the table, I at the other, with Joe Haines, Harold's press officer, and

Tony Field, his secretary, on one side. On the other side sat the Sinn Fein members. They certainly had other membership claims, for here were David O'Connell, soon to become Chief of Staff of the Provisionals, Joe Cahill, the Provisionals' Belfast Commander before his move to Dublin, and John Kelly, also active in the North and one of those charged with Haughey in the Arms Trial.

The meeting lasted some four hours. Drinks and sandwiches were provided but no alcohol was consumed. It was obvious that O'Connell was the boss, and he did much of the talking. We were told that the IRA wanted peace; it was the Unionists who had started the current round of violence. What the Provisionals wanted was a declaration of intent that the British were going to leave Northern Ireland. Apparently the Irish people, North and South, were to work out their own destiny.

Harold made it clear that there could be no question of amnesties for convicted prisoners, political or otherwise. He instanced the recent killing at the Aldershot barracks, for which the perpetrators would have to serve their sentences. O'Connell indicated that Aldershot was not the Provisionals doing – the Official IRA had claimed responsibility.

A major concern of ours was the present withdrawal from Stormont politics of the Social Democratic and Labour Party. Harold asked if the SDLP could negotiate for the Catholics of the North since a British government could not negotiate with the Provisionals. Joe Cahill responded briefly: 'Those who do the fighting do the talking.' If, Harold asked, the SDLP leaders were to talk with the British government, would they be shot by the friends of our visitors? Out of the confused dialogue that followed, the answer seemed to be 'No', but O'Connell observed that the SDLP could not anyway talk without an end to internment; their Catholic electors would see to that. It was a pertinent observation, if hardly remarkable.

O'Connell was reputed to have acute political judgment but at this meeting none of the three men seemed to me to show much sign of it. They may have understood the politics of the South, where in electoral terms they anyway counted for little, but they showed little comprehension of the Protestant working class of the North or of politics in Great Britain. These were hard men who talked and looked like soldiers. They thought solely in terms of military victory; there was no sign of compromise.

At midnight, Kelly told us that it was too late to continue talking of a truce; time was up and operations were already under way. After this chilling statement we all felt that the quicker the meeting was over the better. As we returned to the hotel, I wondered if the Garda had followed the men back to their Dublin homes, as they had followed us on our way to the meeting. It was common knowledge that the

Provisionals' 'Army Council' met in Dublin and organised from there the strategy of the Northern campaign. The Dublin government surely knew that weapons and ammunition were being routed to the North by these paramilitaries.

Our meeting had achieved nothing. There was little doubt that after the weeks of rumours of impending change, the British government now had to act to restore Catholic confidence. Lives would depend on the decision, yet we in the Opposition had been told nothing during this time of speculation. It was no way to proceed. We had already shown that we were not unhelpful when in the previous month, on 23 February, the government had asked Parliament to rush through an emergency one-clause bill to bring the activities of British soldiers in Northern Ireland within the law. This had suddenly proved necessary after a decision by the Northern Ireland High Court that some of the army's activities under the Special Powers Act were illegal, and Harold Wilson and the Labour Party had then responded to Edward Heath's call for co-operation.

To Brian Faulkner, the lack of consultation with his government and the subsequent Conservative government decision was 'pure Westminster perfidy'. On 22 March he was invited to Downing Street, there to be faced with what he regarded as, in effect, an ultimatum and one that was presented to him in less than civilised fashion. Heath's main proposals to Faulkner were: periodic plebiscites on the question of the border; the beginning of a phasing out of internment; and the transfer of all responsibility for law and order to Westminster. Faulkner and his Unionist colleagues agreed to the first two proposals but could not agree to the third. They were not prepared to run, as Brian Faulkner put it, a county council. So, on 24 March 1972, two and a half years after British troops went into Northern Ireland, direct rule from Westminster was announced.

Stormont was not to be dissolved but to stand prorogued. All legislative and executive powers vested in it were to be transferred to the United Kingdom Parliament. The new office of Secretary of State for Northern Ireland was to be created, with William Whitelaw, then Leader of the House of Commons, as its first holder. There was to be a Northern Ireland Commission 'of persons resident in Northern Ireland to advise and assist him in the discharge of his duties'.

I do not believe that a Labour government could have acted as Edward Heath had just done without provoking a political crisis at Westminster. In those circumstances, the Tories would not have been able to ignore the strength of Protestant feelings in Northern Ireland, nor the atavism that would have broken through in their own party – which was after all a Conservative and Unionist party. As it was, the government legislation introducing direct rule, with Labour Party support, went through Parliament without serious problems. Gerry Fitt of the SDLP supported it cautiously. The Ulster Unionists at Westminster of course voted against it, as – for different reasons – did Bernadette Devlin and Frank McManus, the Independent Republican MP for Fermanagh.

Dick Crossman, speaking from the Labour back-benches during the debate on 28 March, made some comments on the attitude of the South which were to seem particularly relevant to me the more I learned of Ireland:

> If the Irish are left with the delusion that they can have the convenience of having us in Northern Ireland taking all the blame and all the kicks and paying for it for ever, they will never do anything to settle it. Southern Ireland sits pretty without any settlement. It is doing very well. It has every advantage in Britain although it is outside the Commonwealth. It has it both ways in every kind of way, and it does not want the burden of Northern Ireland.

Certainly I had detected no signs that the South was preparing itself to take over Northern Ireland and deal with its pressing problems, such as the running of Harland and Wolff shipyard or the urban renewal of Belfast. The fact of one million loyalists who would not be governed from Dublin had put all such problems out of mind.

By the time the direct rule decision was taken, the UK government representative in Belfast, successor to Oliver Wright and Ronald Burrows, was Howard Smith, formerly ambassador in Prague. The representative's office had moved in 1971 to Laneside, along Belfast Lough, a secluded location close to Stormont which made it easier for visitors to come and go away from the glare of publicity. Howard Smith had followed closely the events of the previous year, briefing the Westminster government accordingly. He also briefed me on the political situation in the province when I visited it as Opposition spokesman. His analysis was clear and concise, and I admired his political common sense.

When I later became Home Secretary, I appointed him head of MI5 since I thought it wise at that time to have someone from outside the service. Some commentators then drew the wrong conclusion from his Northern Ireland past, suggesting that, since the British government did not need diplomatic representation in Northern Ireland, the real purpose of the post had been the security co-ordination job later publicly assigned to Sir Maurice Oldfield, former director of MI6.

That this conclusion was wrong was shown by the fact that, after the introduction of direct rule, there was no need for a UK government representative. Laneside became the home of the Political Affairs Division, an integral part of the Northern Ireland Office now set up by William Whitelaw. The Division's role was to develop contacts with Northern Ireland politicians, political organisations, community groups, churches and grass roots opinion generally. The Secretary of State and the security forces could thus be given a constant flow of advice on the attitudes of all parts of the community to government policy and on likely reactions to proposed initiatives. Equally important, Laneside could act as a medium through which to put across the government's policy to politicians and influential groups in the community, informally and without publicity, so that people could feel free to talk without taking up entrenched positions.

The new Department of State for Northern Ireland was created by Willie Whitelaw with commendable speed. In practice the old Northern Ireland Cabinet Office was expanded to become the Northern Ireland Office, but the main staffing came from the Home Office in London. It was split in two geographically, on the lines of the Scottish Office, with one part in Whitehall and the other in Stormont Castle. Like the Chief Secretary for Ireland in the nineteenth century, the Secretary of State concentrated on the overall political and security problems; junior ministers were appointed with direct and personal responsibilities for departments – education, agriculture, etc. They had a heavy work load; and so too did the Shadow ministers.

At first I was on my own as Shadow Secretary of State but shortly afterwards Stan Orme, MP for Salford West, was appointed as my number two. Since 1966 Stan had been part of a small group of Labour MPs with a particular interest in Ireland who had defied the convention that Northern Irish affairs could not be discussed on the floor of the House. Others had joined after 1969 and now, with direct rule, a backbench Northern Ireland Committee was set up. It was an informal group, including MPs with an Irish background – Kevin McNamara, Pat Duffy, Maurice Foley, Jock Stallard – leavened by Dick Douglas and Hugh Brown from Scotland, and Peter Archer, Paul Rose, Jack Mendelson and Russ Kerr from England. Their advice and support proved extremely valuable to me then and in the years ahead.

Stan Orme became a firm friend and I always listened to him with respect. He spoke with personal knowledge of the province in the 1960s and had close ties with the SDLP and also, through his membership of the AUEW, with his fellow union members in Northern Ireland – all ardent loyalists. I learned in those days of Opposition to keep closely in touch with the trade unions in Britain. Most of them had members in Northern Ireland and were consequently realistic about affairs there. It was no surprise to them that in Northern Ireland the political levy was worked on a basis of contracting in rather than out – a Labour Party in Northern Ireland would have to be a loyalist party to succeed, for that is what most trade unionists there are by background and instinct.

One personal difficulty for me as Shadow Secretary was travel arrangements. The problems of Northern Ireland can only be understood by visiting the province, talking to the people there and seeing for oneself the realities of day-to-day life; it was a lesson I had learned from Jim Callaghan. At this time, however, there was no House of Commons members' allowance to cover such travel expenses, and I made visits to the North about once a fortnight and also occasional visits to the South. Since I had no income outside my parliamentary salary, plus a little extra brought in from teaching a few hours a week, the cost of visits became increasingly impossible to sustain.

Willie Whitelaw, helpful as ever, arranged for me to 'hitch' a lift if a spare seat was available on RAF flights to and from Belfast's Aldergrove airport. In practice I would fly out by RAF and return civil, paying for my hotel accommodation, though on security grounds it was agreed that car transport would be provided by the Northern Ireland Office. Without these concessions I could not have continued with my job – but it was a strange way to have to operate as a Shadow spokesman. One did not visit Northern Ireland for fun!

I had a lot to learn about the Republic as well as the North. On my visits to the South I met whenever possible with members of the Irish Labour Party – Brendan Corish, Frank Cluskey, Conor Cruise O'Brien, Brendan Halligan. I talked with Jack Lynch and his successor as Taoiseach in 1973, Liam Cosgrave, and also with Garret Fitzgerald who became Foreign Minister in Cosgrave's new government. Meeting with officials of the Irish Congress of Trade Unions in Dublin and with employers gave me an idea of industrial developments in the South. Emigration was slowing down even before the Republic entered the Common Market in 1973. When I spoke at Trinity College and at University College, Dublin, I learned particularly about middle-class republicanism. The strength of feeling that the North would one day have to come into the Republic was clear, but there was little understanding of working-class Belfast.

On one visit with Stan Orme, we met the Archbishop of Dublin, Dr Dermot Ryan, who politely but firmly was reluctant to concede anything of consequence. The Catholic Church of Ireland was part and parcel of the republican ethos and it would be impossible to convince the people of the Shankhill that in an Irish Republic they could carry on exactly as before.

The extra workload of my job brought with it extra secretarial work, and it was shouldered by my wife Colleen, who already acted as my secretary and had intimate knowledge of my Leeds constituency. I also had the services of Roger Darlington – one of the 'chocolate soldiers' paid for by the Rowntree Trust. He had worked previously for Jim Callaghan, but it had not been the best of relationships. He was a researcher, not a political adviser, and his value to me was in keeping in contact with the trade unions in Northern Ireland and with the Labour Party research department and the Northern Ireland Office.

I received large numbers of letters from Northern Ireland as well as many from Britain, the Irish Republic and much further afield. Northern Ireland loyalists would write in protest that Harold Wilson was, as they believed, committed to Irish unification 'at a stroke'; others, from the other side of the divide, wanted William Craig and his fellow leader of the Ulster Loyalist Association, the Rev Martin Smyth, to be interned – internment was evidently acceptable if applied to 'the other lot'. In an answer to one letter from a woman in the Republic who wanted 'the British out', I replied that we were not occupying Northern Ireland and that there was nothing that the British would like better than to have the army out eventually; the Provisional IRA later quoted this letter as evidence of my real view on Northern Ireland and the London *Times* quoted it in turn!

From within Britain, people with family connections in Ireland wrote in predictable terms. The United Ireland Association and the Gaelic Athletic Association were hardly objective in their analyses. Those with no connections wanted to pull out and let the Irish kill themselves; others wanted to teach the Protestants a lesson by withdrawing subsidies to the province.

From outside the UK, I had letters from the National Council of Irish Americans; to their view that Ulster was 'Britain's Vietnam' I replied, 'If it was that simple, our solution would be equally simple.' Also unsurprising in their views were the letters from the Ulster American Loyalists; one came from Los Angeles, which seemed a suitable distance from which to pronounce with certainty on the problems of Northern Ireland.

There were also of course the letters from cranks. Some of the threatening letters which gave no address were passed to the police, but in practice those who are intending violence do not write, with or without addresses.

However large my postbag, it would be nothing compared to William Whitelaw's. He faced a formidable task in his new appointment. The minority feeling of alienation which had flared up in 1969 had been compounded by the deaths in Derry on Bloody Sunday; the announcement of direct rule was not going to soften it. The response of the

Provisional IRA to the announcement was to escalate the violence. The majority was bitterly angry at the loss of Stormont and were shattered at being, as they saw it, sold down the river by the Tories, their fellow Unionists. Immediately direct rule was announced, there was a two-day loyalist strike in protest.

I was already beginning to learn that the Ulster loyalists were loyal to a Protestant Northern Ireland, not to the United Kingdom. Their political arithmetic was bounded by the six counties and twelve parliamentary constituencies. Harold Wilson felt very strongly about this and described the use of the word 'loyalist' in the House of Commons on one occasion as 'nauseating' and on another as a euphemism for 'disloyalty'. It went along with something that I began to call Ulster Nationalism. Jim Callaghan had noted it when visiting Portadown in 1971. 'You have no right to come here,' he was told, and in the same breath came the assertion that Northern Ireland was an integral part of the United Kingdom. Loyalty was to things Northern Irish and to a type of monarchy that had long since ceased to exist.

I set out to meet representatives of the loyalist community, both in order to learn and because they were suspicious of the Labour Party. I talked with Ian Paisley, educated theologically at the Bob Jones Academy in North Carolina, who was now emerging into the public consciousness not only as a fundamentalist but also as one of the new Unionist politicians. On one visit, he introduced me to his Democratic Unionist Party colleague, John McQuade. He was representative of a hardline Unionism which was far from my own political persuasion but I preferred him to some of the middle-class Unionists I had met at the main party's Glengall Street headquarters.

I met Mrs McQuade at their terraced back-to-back house – where a photograph of the Queen was prominently displayed – in Belfast's Shankill, and we walked down the street to talk to Johnny's constituents; the women in their blue pinnies out sweeping the pavements in front of their homes took me back to my own childhood. When I was introduced to one as 'Mr Whitelaw's opposite number', the reply came, 'If he's against that man, that's good enough for me'! I saw bullet marks on the walls of people's homes and met children injured by bomb and gun. How, I asked myself, could the Provisionals be stupid enough to believe that they could win in this manner? Even now, after the part they had played in ending Stormont, they were not prepared to involve themselves politically. There was still the same blinkered outlook that had been shown at the Dublin meeting with Harold and me.

I also met William Craig, who led the Unionist pressure group, Ulster Vanguard, which was prominent in opposing direct rule and had organised the forty-eight-hour loyalist protest strike on its announcement. The Vanguard Unionist Progressive Party was formed from this movement in March 1973 and at the Party's first meeting in Lisburn Craig arrived with a motorcycle escort and reviewed a quasi-military formation of five hundred men. He read out a pledge to maintain Northern Ireland and asked those present to endorse this by a shout of 'I do' and a raising of arms three times. When I talked to him, I found him full of ideas but deeply sceptical of all UK political parties. His idea for 'independence' included hiving off some border areas – including Derry – to the Republic.

It was not only the Unionist Party which had been torn asunder by the problems in the province. The Catholic Nationalist Party had virtually disappeared with the formation in 1970 of the Social Democratic and Labour Party. The new party's leader, Gerry Fitt, was a former Republican Labour politician and he and Paddy Devlin – a former chairman of the Northern Ireland Labour Party – formed the 'L' in the SDLP. Both were Belfast politicians, though the Party was strongest west of the River Bann where the other SDLP founders were from – Austin Currie in East Tyrone and John Hume in Londonderry. The SDLP was neither Social Democratic in the European sense nor Labour in the British sense, but its leaders were a group of able young men who endeavoured to attract people to a modern Irish nationalist party which questioned both the North and the South, believed in civil liberties and, in the short run at least, wished to work within Northern Ireland. Its political role was far from easy, for it had to operate in the context of the Provisionals' 'military' activities in the Catholic community.

The formation of the SDLP added to the difficulties of the small Northern Ireland Labour Party, which consequently lost most of the Catholic votes that had come its way. Its link with the Northern Ireland Committee of the Irish Congress of Trade Unions also became less meaningful when the vast majority of trade union members voted and worked for the new Unionist parties. The NILP was further weakened by another new party which had emerged in the late 1960s – the Alliance Party, which aimed to cut across sectarian lines and appeal to both unionists and nationalists of liberal persuasion. It was led by a Belfast Catholic, Oliver Napier, and though smaller than the SDLP and the Unionist parties – it commanded about ten per cent of the vote – it had a steady if largely middle-class following.

These new political groupings reflected the changes that had taken place in the province but it was not politics but the escalation of violence that William Whitelaw had first to deal with in the months following direct rule. There was an outbreak of sectarian killings, the majority by loyalists. The usual pattern was for one of the loyalist paramilitary groups – the Ulster Volunteer Force or the Ulster Freedom Fighters – to carry out what was considered an avenging exercise: the Provisionals, it was argued, had won a victory by killing in bringing about direct rule, and the balance needed to be corrected. I have no doubt, from later experience, that some of those killed had been involved in violence, but many were simply Catholics, the victims of plain sectarian murder.

On 22 April, the Loyalist Association of Workers held a great rally in protest against direct rule outside Londonderry Guildhall. The crowd could not be contained by the security forces, and the protesters crossed over the bridge into the Catholic Waterside and the Gobnascale housing estate. Loyalist disagreement with government policy continued on a threatening scale and on 14 May the Ulster Defence Association, in military-style denims and face masks, went on to the streets of Belfast. For the first time there were road blocks in the Shankill. The Secretary of State was told that the road blocks would increase unless the Catholic no-go areas were ended. What the IRA could do, the UDA could do also!

On 20 May the army tried to bulldoze the barricades in East Belfast, but with the large numbers of loyalists around, the job proved too much. On 27 May there was a mass march of several thousand members of the UDA in Belfast, again wearing military-style uniforms and in dark glasses.

In the same month William Whitelaw tried to give some boost to Northern Ireland's economy by announcing extra money for Belfast's Harland and Wolff shipyard, manned traditionally by loyalist workers. It was only part of the province's fundamental economic problems. Unemployment was worse than in any other UK region. There had been a decline in the three staples of the Northern Ireland economy – agriculture, textiles and shipbuilding. Although, with government intervention and the arrival of British, American and German firms, the rate of growth in output per head from 1966–70 had been the highest in the UK, it was still in absolute terms the lowest – in 1972 it was only seventy-three per cent of the UK average, and earnings were also lower on average.

Social conditions too were worse than in other parts of the UK, with poorer housing, a shorter life expectancy and a higher infant mortality rate – though the population was growing fast. The province had, however, benefited from the social welfare legislation of the late 1940s, changes that increased the divide between the North and South.

When I visited secondary schools in the province, I found both the 'state' and Catholic schools authoritarian in outlook. I quickly learned that the Catholic Church was satisfied with the government grants it received and would in no way give in to demands for integrated schools. However, there was, in effect, a sort of integration at higher levels of education, for a large number of Catholics had benefited from the 1947 Northern Ireland Education Act, which provided secondary educational opportunities for the minority on a par with those in Britain – and beyond those in the South, and some of these Catholics had proceeded to university. The young Catholic politicians of the 1960s and 1970s were in part the creation of this Act. However, when at this time I visited the Polytechnic and Queen's University in Belfast, and the new University in Coleraine, it was pointed out to me that political discussion among the students was marked by its absence. The murders and bombings had frozen the attitudes of young people as much as those of the old.

The record of violence in 1972 was worse than any in the previous or following years. The Provisional IRA violence went on escalating despite, as I learned later, a mood for 'peace' in parts of the Belfast Brigade, and the Official IRA was responsible for several incidents in Belfast in April, including attacks on the RUC. In May it claimed responsibility for the killing of Ranger Best, a Catholic soldier in the Royal Irish Regiment of the British army who was home on leave in Derry. The outraged reaction of the Bogside and Creggan communities helped bring about the Official IRA's announcement of a ceasefire on 29 May. This fundamental change speeded their move towards community politics and since then the ceasefire has largely been kept to as far as the security forces are concerned.

The Provisionals did not follow suit, but they could not ignore the feeling of war-weariness in the province. On 22 June they announced a suspension of military activities from 26 June if the UK government would do likewise – by which they meant a stop to 'searching and harassing' by the security forces. William Whitelaw announced in the House of Commons that 'if offensive operations by the IRA in Northern Ireland cease on Monday night, Her Majesty's forces will obviously reciprocate'.

I had not been involved in any of the preliminaries to the ceasefire, although there had been stories to that effect and on 8 June I had denied in the House of Commons being an 'intermediary' in talks with the Provisionals. A few days later, on 13 June, I did in fact have strong wind of the Provisionals' intentions because I happened to be on a visit to Derry at the same time, as it turned out, as Sean MacStiofain, the Provisionals' Chief of Staff.

John Hume, the SDLP's deputy leader, lived in the Bogside and he had taken me to his home, a car journey which had in itself been instructive. He and a doctor friend had met me outside Ebrington barracks and as we drove down the hill towards 'Free Derry Corner' with its barricades and armed masked men, John and the doctor agreed that as usual they were not going to stop. We drove straight through and as I looked back I could see a Provisional with a gun raised in aim at the car. He did not fire!

At John's home I met his family and local SDLP members; a few reporters were there but, much to my surprise, I was informed that most of them were with MacStiofain and Martin McGuinness, Derry's Provisional IRA leader, at a press conference where a ceasefire was to be announced. It did not of course happen then but clearly discussions were under way.

As we left the Bogside later, the barricades again provided a glimpse into the realities of Northern Ireland life. John did not drive straight through this time but wound the window down and, addressing the masked armed guard by his first name, asked him about the ceasefire. 'There's no bloody ceasefire!' came the reply. I only discovered later that John Hume and Paddy Devlin were at least marginally involved in the talks that led finally to the announcement on 22 June.

William Whitelaw, trying to ensure the continuation of the truce, arranged for a secret meeting with six Provisional leaders in London on 7 July. As Sean MacStiofain revealed in his book, the leaders who attended were, apart from MacStiofain himself, McGuinness, David O'Connell, the Belfast commander Seamus Twomey, and two other Belfast Provisionals, Ivor Bell and Gerry Adams, the last specially released from internment for the talks.

Whitelaw had just announced the introduction of 'special category status' for republican and loyalist paramilitary prisoners for offences related to 'civil disturbances'. Such prisoners were not to be required to work, could wear their own clothes and were allowed extra visits and food parcels. They were to be housed in compounds because of the shortage of cell accommodation.

This was done in the context of the precarious truce and a hunger strike by republicans in a Belfast prison. There was indeed a problem in the prisons and some precedent in Irish history to give the move a certain credence. The Labour Party did not oppose it, and some members were actively in favour of it, as were the SDLP. Willie stated in the Commons on 6 July, 'I have made it perfectly clear that the status of political prisoner is not being granted.' In practice it was, and it was a grave mistake – as Willie Whitelaw himself later admitted. Those who are convicted of criminal offences should not be treated differently because of a difference of motive. Murder is murder.

It was internment and special category status that came to concern me more than other policy matter. The compounds housing internees and special category prisoners became like military staff colleges, something I saw for myself when I visited the Shankill loyalist hero, Gusty Spence, in the Maze prison. He was serving a life sentence for murdering a Catholic in a bar in 1966 and, as leader of the Ulster Volunteer Force, presided over the special category UVF members in the prison. Interestingly, when I later met Billy McKee, a Provisional IRA leader in the Maze, he told me that he would have been prepared to meet Gusty Spence if I had arranged it. Both the paramilitary organisations these men represented were in contact with their fellow members inside the prison.

It was Billy McKee who, during a discussion on the nature of violence, said that in the RAF you (meaning me) did not flinch at bombing Germany, with its consequent thousands of civilian casualties, and nor did the Provisional IRA flinch today. This was a view that might have had some logic if the Provisional IRA had been the government of the South, but it was another example of the political blindness I was regularly to find in the province. Willie Whitelaw was facing it now.

Following his secret talks with the Provisionals, he reported their demands to the House. They called on the British government to 'recognise publicly that it is the right of the whole people of Ireland acting as a unit to decide the future of Ireland'; 'to declare their intention to withdraw all British forces from Irish soil' – the withdrawals to be immediate from sensitive areas and the whole to be completed by 1 January 1975; and to declare a general amnesty for all political prisoners in Irish and British gaols, for all internees and detainees, and for all persons on the wanted list. At the same time, they recorded their dissatisfaction that internment had not been ended in response to their ceasefire initiative.

They were impossible demands but there was hardly time to consider them for, two days after the meeting, the Provisionals claimed that the British government had broken the truce in an incident on the Lenadoon estate in Belfast, which involved the allocation of housing between Protestants and Catholics. In a later article in the *Observer*, Mary McGuire, who was associated with the Provisionals at the time, described the disagreements in the organisation over the truce, and named the hawks and the doves.

> That the truce broke down after only thirteen days was a real tragedy. It was the result of a lack of understanding by both sides of the explosive situation in Belfast over the Lenadoon housing dispute. Whitelaw's civil servants just didn't seem to grasp how deadly serious it was. Dave [O'Connell], who was still doing most of the negotiating, made desperate

last-minute attempts to save the situation, but Whitelaw didn't return his last telephone call.

I have serious doubts about these revelations, not least because in the same article Mary McGuire reported that Harold Wilson, at the March meeting with the Provisionals in Dublin, 'swore a lot and generally seemed to be behaving in the way he imagined Provos behave'. Since, as I pointed out in a letter to the *Observer*, I was present at the meeting, I could vouchsafe that Miss McGuire's second-hand allegation was completely untrue.

The evening of the breakdown of the truce, Harold Wilson and I had gone round to Willie Whitelaw's flat to discuss matters. He was very emotional about what had happened, and did not demur when Harold said that he was thinking of meeting the Provisional leaders to try to get the temporary ceasefire restored; after all, in his House of Commons statement Willie had already asked the Provisionals to reconsider.

I was with a Labour Party delegation in Dublin on 17 July when I received a message from Harold to fly back for a secret meeting in Britain with the Provisionals. Once again it had been arranged by Dr John Connell. He picked me up from my Dublin hotel in his car, and alongside him was a stranger who was dropped off shortly afterwards and who, I then heard to my surprise, was Rory O'Brady of the Provisional Sinn Fein. My Labour Party colleagues walking back to the hotel did not see us pass but it was a cloak-and-dagger situation that I found very unpleasant.

Edward Heath sent a message to Harold stressing that the meeting was purely our responsibility and there was to be no suggestion that the government was in any way part of it. Jack Lynch also knew about it from Harold, and from me since I had had to leave for England midway through a luncheon arranged by him. That morning Northern Ireland radio had in fact suggested that I was in touch with the IRA in Dublin! There are few secrets in Ireland.

The meeting took place at Harold's Buckinghamshire home. The Provisionals were represented by Joe Cahill and Myles Shevlin, a Dublin lawyer, and another Belfast man whom I did not recognise. They basically repeated the demands already made to Whitelaw. Harold emphasised that a leader of the Opposition could give no commitment, and he castigated them for putting the Secretary of State in an impossible position by having revealed their talks with him. I disliked Shevlin intensely, and made it clear. When Harold remarked to the effect that I might in the future become Secretary of State for Northern Ireland, the lawyer remarked, 'He is worse than Whitelaw'!

The aim of the meeting had been to try to get the Provisionals to see political reality, to get them back to a ceasefire. On any terms it was a failure; we were wasting our time. The 'secret' meeting was reported on the news that night, but whatever media interest it might have had was killed by the report at the same time of the resignation of the Home Secretary, Reginald Maudling, over the Poulson affair.

Three days later, on 21 July, twenty-two bombs went off in the Oxford Street bus station of Belfast. Nine civilians and two soldiers were killed, seventy-seven women and girls, fifty-three men and boys, were injured. All who saw the remains of what had been human beings were sickened. Bloody Friday had entered the annals of Irish history alongside Bloody Sunday. The world was horror-stricken; the whole of Ireland was shattered. I was told of a Provisional in Long Kesh who, seeing the carnage on television, got up out of his seat and announced, 'That's me finished.' The organisers – one involved in politics today – gloried in it.

It was another of those turning points in the history of Northern Ireland. All attempts to 'talk down' the barriers in the republican no-go areas had failed and now, with the strong feelings aroused in the province by Bloody Friday, Whitelaw decided to send in the army. The number of soldiers was increased to 21,000 and on 31 July they finally and successfully breached the no-go areas in 'Operation Motorman'.

Whitelaw had signalled his intending action in a broadcast of 28 July and had talked freely of it in the corridors of Westminster. This was deliberate: he wanted the Provisionals to know that resistance would be useless, and to avoid any possibility of another Bloody Sunday. They took note and did not attempt a set battle with the British army but, in response, on the same day eight people were killed by car bombs in the small Londonderry village of Claudy.

One important result of the ending of the republican no-go areas was that it removed the immediate threat of unilateral action by the loyalist paramilitary groups to achieve the same end. Another, on the political side, was that the Unionist MPs at Westminster and their followers in the province were delighted. Brian Faulkner was now in a position to meet and talk formally with Whitelaw – whatever the hardline Unionists represented by Paisley and Craig did.

There was not much hope from that quarter but for some time the Alliance Party and the Northern Ireland Labour Party had made it clear that they were willing to enter into formal talks. To make any progress, what mattered now was to involve the SDLP, and messages came from the South urging them to be helpful. I happened to be in Belfast on 7 August at a dinner with the Secretary of State and civil servants, during which I noted that Willie arrived late from a 'historic meeting' with the SDLP and left early to continue the discussions. It was characteristic, I was to learn, of the way such affairs were conducted in Northern Ireland.

The log-jam seemed as if it might be broken, and on 11 August the Secretary of State invited the Unionist Party, the SDLP, and the Alliance, Democratic Unionist, Republican Labour and Northern Ireland Labour parties to attend a conference on the political future of the province, not with the aim of reaching agreement but to review the possibility of progress. It was too much to hope that all those invited would turn up at the conference – arranged to take place in Darlington on 25–27 September. The SDLP were willing to participate but they were faced by the problem that internment was still in use. Internment was an emotive word in the Catholic community and the SDLP were unable to risk playing into the hands of the Provisionals.

Willie tried to ease their position and on 22 September he announced the setting up of the Diplock Commission to consider alternative arrangements to internment for dealing with terrorist activities. Harold Wilson and I also tried to help. We met the SDLP leaders twice in London; they would have been happier, they said, with our idea of a commission of British, Commonwealth and Irish jurists working to broader terms of reference than those given to Diplock. The date of the Darlington conference was, however, far too near to give the SDLP room for manoeuvre and despite a last-minute appeal from Edward Heath, their representatives did not attend, and neither did Paisley's Democratic Unionists or the Republican Labour Party.

As a result Darlington was attended only by the Faulkner Unionists, the Alliance Party and the Northern Ireland Labour Party. There could be no practical progress but it was a beginning and on 30 October the government published a green paper setting out the proposals for the future of Northern Ireland put forward by all the parties and groups in Northern Ireland and Great Britain. Basically, the Unionists wanted a return to the old Stormont system; the Alliance and NILP wanted a system of proportional representation with a power-sharing executive; the SDLP wanted Northern Ireland to be governed initially by a condominium of the UK and the Irish Republic, which would lead to eventual unification. The government made it clear that Northern Ireland would remain in the United Kingdom as long as a Northern Ireland majority wished it, but it took into account an 'Irish dimension' – new institutions of government would have to be based on consensus and any new assembly be capable of involving all its members.

In the following month Willie pressed on with changes in the method of internment. The old system under which the Secretary of State held full powers to intern was replaced by a new system in which there was an 'interim custody order'; once a twenty-eight-day period was up, the detainee had either to be released or the case referred to quasi-judicial commissioners for detention. In the spring of 1973 Willie went further and introduced legislation to set up juryless courts to deal with certain terrorist offences. The move towards the courts would, it was hoped, help the SDLP participate in discussions on constitutional changes, though the lack of a jury and the continuing existence of some form of detention remained as stumbling blocks.

To help the position of the Faulkner Unionists Willie emphasised once more the guarantee that the status of the North would not be changed without the approval of the majority there, and he also pressed ahead with the plebiscite on the border question which had been promised at the introduction of direct rule. The issue for the loyalists was, as always, the link with Britain. I understood this but, on behalf of the Labour Party, I spoke in the Commons against the poll. It was a numbers game. The future of Northern Ireland was never going to be determined arithmetically by a ten-yearly border poll. Nevertheless, on 8 March the plebiscite was held, with the Catholics boycotting it, and we learned what we all knew: there was a majority in Northern Ireland for staying in the UK.

On 20 March the government published its White Paper on proposals for the future of Northern Ireland. There was to be an Assembly elected by proportional representation, with an Executive but not a Cabinet; the Assembly would have a strong committee system. A large number of the powers of the old Stormont were to be returned but legal matters, elections, taxation, and law and order were to remain the responsibilities of Westminster. The Executive could no longer be based solely on any single party if that party drew its support and its elected representatives virtually entirely from only one section of a divided community. In other words power sharing was now part of the constitutional vocabulary.

Particularly significant was the section which said there was a need to facilitate the 'establishment of institutional arrangements for consultations and co-operation between Northern Ireland and the Republic of Ireland'. This, coming from a Tory government, was a radically different approach. The procedures for setting up these 'institutional arrangements' would come after the election in Northern Ireland for a new Assembly, when the British government would invite representatives of Northern Ireland and the Republic of Ireland to take part in a conference. At the time, though I was concerned about the Paper's vagueness on power sharing and how the Executive was to be chosen, I did not foresee the future importance of this conference – the first reference to what was to become Sunningdale.

In the period following the White Paper, Willie Whitelaw and his staff constructed a Constitution Bill which, with the full support of the Labour Party, went through Parliament during the early summer of 1973. The elections by proportional representation took place for the new Assembly on 28 June, an earlier date than that which the government first proposed and which had been brought forward at my suggestion in the House of Commons. The results did not augur well for the future: of the 78 seats, 22 were won by Faulkner Unionists, 10 by 'unpledged' Unionists, 18 by Paisley/Craig Unionists, 8 by the Alliance Party, 19 by the SDLP and 1 by the Northern Ireland Labour Party. Brian Faulkner's Unionists, plus the Alliance, SDLP and NILP, made up a majority that supported or at the least did not oppose the new Constitution Act, but the twenty-eight Unionists outside the Faulkner group raised an obvious problem – Brian Faulkner was in a minority in the loyalist community.

The behaviour of the new members in the Assembly also cast doubts on the future. It was boorish and vulgar, and there was little consensus at its meetings. But talks outside the Assembly between the Faulkner Unionists, the SDLP and the Alliance Party went on, and as I listened to the news of their progress – first- and second-hand – my mood fluctuated between hope and despair. I wrote in my diary: 'The whole process has little in common with the usual post-colonial conferences at Lancaster House. It is quite a different scene, with newly emerging politicians leading new or fractured parties. They are disparate groups who have to look over their shoulders to their electorate.'

On 22 September Gerry Fitt gave me a rundown of the talks he had had with William Whitelaw and in the South, and was very hopeful that the SDLP was going to be able to make the new constitution work. When I talked with John Hume and Paddy Devlin they were equally positive. All of them wanted to play a part in the Assembly but what they did not want was to get into the Executive only to find that the whole set-up broke down in a matter of weeks.

Only a few days later, on 27 September, I spoke with Willie and my mood changed. 'The SDLP had overplayed their hand on the matter of the Council of Ireland,' I was told. The more I listened to him, the more gloom filled me. I just did not see, as I commented in my diary, 'how these people were going to work together. We would have to face up to the fact that the new constitution could not work.'

But by 5 October the Faulkner Unionists, the SDLP and the Alliance formally accepted the Constitution Act and set about forming an Executive. It nearly foundered as a result of an error of judgment by Edward Heath when he spoke at a press conference at the conclusion of a visit to the Taoiseach. He was asked what would happen if an Executive was not formed before March 1974, as laid down in the Act, and after answering, quite properly, that there would be direct rule, he added, 'I think this time people would feel that we cannot have continuing uncertainty and it is much better that the whole thing should be arranged on an integrated United Kingdom basis. And then we shall be able to produce an efficient and fair government for the whole of the United Kingdom.'

The fat was in the fire. Brian Faulkner felt that the ground had been cut from beneath his feet. He had been told that integration was not on. William Whitelaw had told him this, and so had I. His Unionist opponents gloated. The SDLP also felt let down, for the last thing that they wanted was integration.

Harold wrote a letter to Edward Heath on my prompting, asking for the matter to be straightened out. Ted testily replied, 'I have never sought to advocate integration,' etc. More letters followed and in the end, weeks later, the issue died. It all showed that Willie, or at least someone with a knowledge of Ireland, should have been with the Prime Minister in Dublin.

Agreement was eventually reached by the Northern Ireland parties on 21 November after long-drawn-out discussions on power sharing, policing and detention. A power-sharing Executive was formed but only after the Constitution Act was amended in the Commons at short notice, and with Labour Party agreement, to increase the size of the administration to fifteen members with only eleven having voting rights. Willie needed to be able to appoint more members so that he could get a 'better' proportion between the parties. It was a price worth paying to get agreement in the short run but in the long run, as I was to realise when I became Secretary of State, it meant that there were too many ministers and too many departments.

I congratulated Willie in the House of Commons for his role in bringing about a power-sharing administration. He had shown, I said, an understanding of the Irish situation and a realistic flexibility in all the negotiations he undertook. This was not parliamentary flannel. He is a man of complete integrity. Throughout his period as Secretary of State he used the House of Commons intelligently; despite his heavy load at Stormont he made sure that the House was informed on issues both large and small. Misunderstandings arose anyway, but without an openness at Westminster they would have been worse. I commented in the House, 'I wish other ministers would do the same. It is something to have the press listening to what is said in the House rather than Members of Parliament finding out what the press has learnt before them.'

It was easy to work with Willie. He kept me in the picture on developments in government policy, and we always spoke bluntly to each other, making no false promises. Both the main parties at Westminster were in favour of a power-sharing Executive and a Council of Ireland – and no one wanted to repeat the story of the nineteenth century when the problem of Ireland had profoundly affected the structure of British politics – but the bipartisan approach to Northern Ireland that developed after direct rule, helped by the good personal relationship between Willie and me, did not mean that there was no public disagreement. The Labour Party had, for example, been against the border plebiscite and I had said so plainly, but I accepted implicitly that policy in Northern Ireland was too important for normal inter-party wrangles. The wrong word at Westminster could lead to injury and death in Northern Ireland.

Given that agreement on a power-sharing administration had now been reached, it remained for the final conference to take place, which was fixed to happen at Sunningdale in Berkshire on 6 December 1973. At this juncture Willie was returned – foolishly in my view – to London to become Minister of Labour, and Francis Pym was pitched into a field he knew little about.

I was not present at Sunningdale but I felt the chance of agreement was far greater than all the cliff-hanging reports suggested. Dublin ministers, Westminster ministers and the Executive members wanted power sharing, and the Southern representatives had long expressed support for 'consent' as the password for unification. Compromise was the order of the day – no change in the status of Northern Ireland until a majority of the people in the province wanted it.

A legal commission was to be set up, four members from the North and four from the South, to report on methods for dealing with crimes of violence in all parts of Ireland; a Police Authority would be constituted in the South to match the one in the North; and there was to be a Council of Ireland with seven members for the North and seven for the South 'acting in unanimity on a harmonising and consultative role in the fields of natural resources, agriculture, trade and industry, tourism, roads and transport, public health, and culture and arts. The Council would be serviced by a secretariat. A second-tier Consultative Assembly would also be set up consisting of thirty members of the Northern Ireland Assembly and thirty from the Dail – chosen by their fellows on the basis of the single transferable vote.'

The new Executive took over on 1 January 1974 and all the reports from within Stormont Castle and the Northern Ireland Civil Service were complimentary. The loyalist community was not, however, concerned about that aspect of the change; it was the Council of Ireland – the 'Trojan horse' – that concerned them. Protest marches and meetings against Sunningdale followed; there was rioting, with the

Ulster Defence Association in the background. The rows in the Assembly grew worse. Brian Faulkner had to tread carefully and he spoke publicly of not proceeding with the proposals for a Council of Ireland until there was 'clarification' of speeches made by Irish government ministers which had emphasised the Council's implications for eventual unification.

The mood in Britain, in the media generally, and at Westminster was, however, jubilant. Praise came from all sides and I expressed my full support willingly, but with a nagging doubt. Like Jim Callaghan, who had said in the Commons that in Ireland 'the extremist always wins', I was concerned by the outcry in the loyalist community. The Council of Ireland was seen by them as yet another betrayal, and I noted the historical allusion of a UDA spokesman who recalled that it was on 6 December 1921 that the Anglo/Irish Treaty had been signed by Michael Collins who, like Brian Faulkner, had been 'conned' by the British. Yet another clash of anniversaries!

Brian Faulkner was in political trouble. It was no good preening ourselves at Britain's reaction. It was Northern Ireland that mattered and there, on 4 January, the Ulster Unionist Council, the Unionist Party's executive, rejected the Council of Ireland. Everything went sour; there were defections from the Faulkner Unionists and a declaration by the 'unpledged' Unionists that they would oppose the proposals in the Assembly. Brian Faulkner resigned as the party leader.

If Sunningdale was to have a chance of success, time was needed for both sides to see that no one was being 'sold down the river'. But that was not to be. Towards the middle of February, Ted Heath, faced by a coalminers' strike, called a General Election. As I noted in my diary just before the announcement, 'I should feel extremely angry if Sunningdale was thrown into the melting pot just because the hawks or whatever you choose to call them – the suburbans? – in the British Cabinet brushed it aside in order to win an election victory on the basis of an anti-trade union vote.'

My view was nothing to do with normal British politics. It was nothing to do with who might win or lose – and I certainly did not realise that Labour would win because the Liberal vote would harm us less than the Tories. It was to do with my involvement in Northern Ireland, perhaps over-involvement. Sunningdale was not the major issue of the day in Great Britain but when I looked at the possible scenario for Northern Ireland in the event of a General Election, I could see no good reason for going to the country.

When the results were announced, all my fears of what we would end up with at Westminster were realised: of the twelve Northern Ireland seats, eleven were won by anti-Faulkner Unionists, including Ian

Paisley and William Craig, leaving only one – won by Gerry Fitt – occupied by an MP in favour of Sunningdale.

At first it was not clear which party was going to form a government at Westminster. The Shadow Cabinet met at Labour Party headquarters on the day after the Election and in the light of the confused situation we agreed to say nothing while Edward Heath attempted to build a coalition with the Liberals. Harold did, however, take Denis Healey and me aside as we were leaving and told us that if he did form a government, we were to take it as read that we would be offered the portfolios we had been shadowing.

Ted Heath, much to my surprise, sent a telegram to Harry West, the leader of the 'Official' Unionists and now a Westminster MP, offering his party the Tory Whip. In his reply Harry said that there could be no decision until he had consulted Paisley's Democratic Unionist Party and Craig's Vanguard Unionist Progressive Party. It anyway made no difference because the Tory/Liberal coalition ran into the ground, and on Monday 4 March Harold went to the Palace to 'kiss hands'.

Shortly afterwards I became Secretary of State for Northern Ireland. After three years' involvement with the affairs of the province, I was to have ministerial responsibility for it. I would not have wanted any other job.

Part II

FIRST PERIOD OF OFFICE

March–October 1974

Chapter 2

THE EARLY MONTHS

My first job as Secretary of State was to agree on junior ministers with the Prime Minister. Stan Orme was the obvious choice as Minister of State, though his appointment was not initially well received in the loyalist community because of his involvement with the civil rights campaign of the minority Catholics in the 1960s. 'Apprehension' was the word used by Brian Faulkner. The feeling did not last long for Stan soon showed that he fully understood Protestant working-class feelings and that, as Brian Faulkner later observed, he 'cared about people and their living conditions'.

The other appointment to the Northern Ireland Office was Lord Donaldson as Parliamentary Under-Secretary. On paper it might not seem that Stan Orme, trade unionist and member of the Tribune Group, would find it easy to work with old Etonian peer Jack Donaldson, but it was a fruitful partnership and they became close friends. They complemented each other. Jack's particular knowledge of prison reform was to be of great value to me and he added to our team strength with his general attitude of calm and a keenness and energy that belied his age – he was now in his late sixties.

I of course knew the UK civil servants in the Northern Ireland Office from my days in Opposition, though my relationship with Frank Cooper, the Permanent Under-Secretary, went back much further than his time working under Whitelaw and Pym. He and I had served together in the RAF in Italy during the war and because of this we did not always play in public the usual 'Yes, minister' game. It sometimes caused raised eyebrows, particularly from a few Northern Ireland politicians, who preferred the old 'Yes, sir, no sir, three bags full' relationship. There even arose a piece of gossip that Frank had been my commanding officer, which was completely false. Not quite as untrue was another war story that when Frank had been forced to bale out north of Rome, he had walked back through the lines to be greeted by me as operations officer with the words 'Where the hell have you been?'!

Frank's career as a civil servant had been mainly in the Ministry of Defence, a background which helped prevent the incipient disagreements between the police and army in Northern Ireland from erupting. He was swift and incisive in thought and action, keenly aware of what was happening in the province, and he had an able group of civil servants working under him. The Deputy Secretary, Philip Woodfield, I knew from the Home Office. His sardonic turn of phrase and Whiggish pose hid a deep feeling for Northern Ireland; he could always be depended on to see the main point in a confused tangle of events.

I quickly learned to appreciate the unusual relationship between ministers and civil servants in the Northern Ireland Office. We were operating far from the Whitehall scene, living cheek by jowl and dealing with a tense political situation. It created a working opportunity that a Secretary of State could use if he wished. I did, and I hope improved on it.

The new pattern of life began for me immediately on my appointment. On 6 March I made my first journey to Belfast as Secretary of State, a journey I recall vividly. Once landed at Aldergrove airport, we flew by helicopter into the city. The aerial view of the river, of the well-known dividing streets and landmarks, formed a black-and-white patchwork that matched the orange-and-green demographic map on my office wall. The detached feeling from the air was very different to the one I had had in Opposition when driving into Belfast from Aldergrove: the straight road from the airport, then round the sharp bend to receive the first view of Belfast's terraced streets, on into Ligoniel, Ballysillan and down the Cliftonville or Crumlin Road to the city centre; then, if the ultimate destination was Stormont, over one of the bridges into East Belfast, dominated by the Harland and Wolff shipyard, past Ballymacarrett and Sydenham and through the suburban fastnesses of Holywood and Belmont.

Belfast is a city unto itself – the only British city in Ireland. A few weeks after my appointment, I commented on it in an interview with Jimmy Kelly of the *Irish Independent*: 'The more I read about the origins of the sectarian rioting in Belfast and the reaction of the 'Sandy Row boys' to the movement of the Catholic population from the rural areas into the very 'British' city of Belfast in 1830 (and the years that followed), the more I realised the basic historical nature of the problem ahead.' As always, a knowledge of history matters in Ireland.

The flights to and from Belfast formed a regular weekly routine: Monday to Wednesday in Northern Ireland; Thursday in London for the Cabinet meeting before returning to Belfast; Friday evening in Leeds; and back to London or Belfast on Saturday. The journeys were rarely wasted; it was a good opportunity to catch up on paperwork and for reading and discussions with fellow ministers and civil servants. On one occasion as we landed in Belfast, my protection officer remarked, 'Here we go through the looking-glass again'. Mad Hatter's tea party Northern Ireland is not, but it is another world. If the English Channel explains the insular attitude of the British to Europe, then the Irish Sea – or, as the loyalists would have it, St George's Channel – is a similar divide for Ireland and Great Britain.

Although so much of my time was taken up in Northern Ireland, I was determined that my constituency work should not be adversely affected. The day-to-day problems of the people in South Leeds were of major concern and I made sure never to miss the General Management Committee meeting of the local Party. It was typical of the co-operation I received from them that the day of the meeting was changed from Sunday to Friday to make it easier for me to attend. A similar kind of understanding was shown by my constituents in general. I noted in my diary after attending a function in Leeds in the early days of my ministerial appointment that 'it is a pleasure to be so well received and to be back at home among one's own people'. Little effect seemed to have been made by the small Liberal organisation in the area, which had put leaflets about saying that they wanted someone to concern themselves with South Leeds instead of Belfast and Northern Ireland. Kitchen sink politics were all the rage with grass-roots Liberals at this time; the trouble was the sink proved to be too near the sewer.

My indebtedness to my wife Colleen was now greater than ever. An active Labour Party member since the immediate post-war years, she had always supported my work in South Leeds and now, because of my constant travels between Belfast, London and Leeds, she had to step in to take my place at official functions. We were frequently apart but we kept in touch by phone every evening and as soon as Colleen was able to make arrangements for the care of our three sons, she made regular visits to Northern Ireland. She and Peggy Cooper, Frank Cooper's wife, played an active part in the province, travelling round it to meet people from all walks of life, and I was gratified to read later the words of Michael Cudlipp, for a time Consultant on Public Relations at the Northern Ireland Office, who said of Colleen: 'She must have been frightened and worried, but she never showed it. She was smashing.'

The Culloden Hotel at Holywood was the place where I and the UK ministers and top civil servants lived in 1974. We would invite groups to dine with us there or nearby, making sure that they came from both sides of the community: politicians of course but also educationalists, doctors, industrialists, etc. From the time of my appointment, I began a series of visits to prisons, factories, farms, schools, local authorities and, above all, the police and the army. I was determined not to stick in the office but to be out and about, seeing the trouble spots for myself, talking to as many people as possible and forming my own opinion as Secretary of State. I soon came to appreciate the value of the helicopter in enabling me to visit all parts of the province at short notice.

It became obvious early on that the arrangements at the Culloden were not adequate for our special purposes. Our official headquarters were of course at Stormont Castle but so much in Northern Ireland affairs happened at night that the hotel room often had to act as a cramped operational headquarters. Shortly into my period of office it was therefore decided to convert the old Speaker's House at Stormont into sleeping quarters and offices for the UK staff. I had dismissed the idea of personally using Hillsborough House, the former home of the Governor, south of Belfast. It was too much of an identification with the old order and, above all, I felt that the Secretary of State must be available at any time of the day or night in the place where decisions were taken.

At the Culloden and later at Stormont – the Speaker's House was ready by January 1975 – we would talk round ideas with the security advisers and others late at night and early in the morning. In Northern Ireland decisions have to be taken quickly and often it was only my final conclusions that the civil servants would commit to paper. In some instances the archives consequently have little background material for the historian to mull over.

I was outside the Westminster swim but I had to make sure that my Cabinet colleagues and their departments, as well of course as the House of Commons itself, were fully informed on events and policies in the province. It was for this reason that I determined to use to the full the Cabinet sub-committee set up and chaired by the Prime Minister. Its aim was to keep under review the government's policy on Northern Ireland, including relations with the Republic, particularly in the context of the Council of Ireland and the countering of violence. Other than myself, the main members were the Foreign Secretary, the Home Secretary, the Secretary of State for Defence and the Attorney General. From time to time officials would attend from the Northern Ireland Office and the Foreign Office, together with senior army officers. It was to this committee that I submitted detailed memoranda either direct or via the Prime Minister on all aspects of the problems of the province.

My Parliamentary Private Secretary, Dr Edmund Marshall, kept me in touch with the affairs of the House of Commons and I kept in close contact with the Labour Party back-bench committee, now headed by Kevin McNamara in succession to Stan Orme. Despite Kevin's strong feelings in favour of a unified Ireland, he did not try to manipulate the committee in that direction and I was to find his advice valuable and down to earth.

Willie Whitelaw's policy of keeping the official Opposition informed on developments in the province was something I was determined to follow and while Willie remained involved in the affairs of Northern Ireland, there would, I told my colleagues, be no problem about bipartisanship. I was more sceptical about the future. There were Tories in the background who disapproved of the Heath government's policy – the policy that we were carrying on where our predecessor had left off.

On my first day in the province I met the leaders of the Executive and emphasised that our aim was to implement Sunningdale. After the meeting I issued a statement assuring the Executive of my support and making it clear that despite loyalist demands there would be no Assembly elections in the immediate future. I wanted the Executive to have time to show the fruits of its work. I took the opportunity to reassure the people of Northern Ireland of my determination to deal with terrorism and I also referred to the economic problems facing both communities. Once again I emphasised our commitment to an equal and fair society in which the minority would have the opportunity to play a full part, while I also returned to the theme I had used constantly, without much success, over the past three years to allay the majority's fears about Labour Party intentions: 'You cannot be pushed into the Republic either now or by stealth in the long run.'

The Queen's speech laying down the government's programme for the forthcoming parliamentary session included the words: 'My ministers will give their support to the constitutional arrangements which now offer to Northern Ireland the prospect of healing its political and social divisions and of achieving prosperity and security for all its people. They will play their part, together with the Northern Ireland Executive and the Government of the Republic of Ireland, in developing co-operation in matters of mutual interest and in bringing violence to an end.' In other words, Sunningdale.

This was the keystone of our policy in Northern Ireland but, keystone or not, Westminster or not, I soon found that there was little support for Sunningdale in the majority community. The General Election results had meant only one thing to them – their rejection of Sunningdale. I had tried to put the results in perspective at my first meeting with the leaders of the Executive: 'The eleven loyalist Westminster MPs will soon find out the views of the over six hundred representatives of the rest of the people in the United Kingdom. There will be opportunities for debate at Westminster and they will find overwhelming support for the general constitutional approach set by the previous administration. I am always available to meet with Westminster MPs and this, of course, includes the Members for Northern Ireland.'

But the truth was that Westminster did not matter. Great Britain was 'across the water'; it was Northern Ireland that counted. There, the United Ulster Unionist Council – a coalition of anti-Sunningdale Unionist Party groups – had done well in the Election and Faulkner's 'Unionist Pro-Assembly' group had done badly. On 4 March, just before my arrival in the province, this latter group, despite its involvement in the Sunningdale agreement, had decided that no further steps should be taken towards its ratification. The Irish government, it was argued, had not honoured the commitments it had made on the status of Northern Ireland, nor done enough to deal with terrorism. The group knew that its support was being eroded and felt that it would get worse. The Council of Ireland in particular was at risk.

I was concerned about the responses to the whole Sunningdale package that I was picking up throughout the loyalist community. Even on social occasions among the establishment, anti-Whitelaw remarks were made to me; they were probably meant to ingratiate – and I gave them short shrift – but it all added to my mood. Away from Britain I was getting a different view of how Sunningdale was going and from my talks with people in the province, from television, radio, the newspapers there, it was not going well.

The situation in the South was also deteriorating after the initial euphoria over Sunningdale in December 1973. The main Opposition party, Fianna Fail, led by Jack Lynch, was only half-hearted in support and to counteract this, senior ministers in the Fine Gael government began making far more of the Council of Ireland than was warranted – forgetting presumably that their remarks were read and listened to closely in the North.

The detailed reports of the Boland case caused particular concern in Northern Ireland. Kevin Boland, a Fianna Fail politician, had resigned from the Lynch government in 1970 as a protest against the dismissal of his colleagues, Charles Haughey and Neil Blaney, because of their alleged implication in the importation of arms into Northern Ireland. After Sunningdale Boland tried to get the agreement declared unconstitutional through the Irish courts. The clause at issue was that which said: 'The Irish government fully accepted and solemnly declared that there could be no change in the status of Northern Ireland until a majority of the people of Northern Ireland desired a change in that status.' Boland's argument hinged on the fact that the Irish Republic had a written constitution under which Northern Ireland was part of the Republic.

Boland lost his case but it was of little help in the North. The court ruled, impeccably, that Sunningdale did not acknowledge that Northern Ireland was part of the UK; and the Irish government, equally impeccably, made a statement to the court that under the Irish constitution Northern Ireland was part of the Irish Republic. To the Protestant majority in the North it was all taken as proof once again of the double-dealing of Irish republicans. They said one thing at Sunningdale and another at home.

I had made contact early on with the Irish government and on 7 March Garret Fitzgerald, the Foreign Minister, visited me in my London office. He knew of the problems facing Brian Faulkner on the question of Northern Ireland's status in general and the Boland case in particular. A statement from the Irish government would, he said, appear soon. It was made in the Dail by Liam Cosgrave on 13 March: 'The factual position of Northern Ireland is that it is within the United Kingdom and my government accepts this as a fact.' He solemnly reaffirmed that Northern Ireland's position within the UK could not be changed except by a decision of a majority of the people in the North, and declared that all democratic parties in the Republic were resolved that 'the unity of Ireland is to be achieved only by peaceful means and by consent'.

I welcomed this with a statement of my own from Stormont Castle and told my Cabinet colleagues at our first sub-committee meeting that the Irish Prime Minister had gone as far as was possible in his statement without an amendment of the Irish constitution. It would not of course satisfy the anti-Assembly Unionists. Indeed, William Craig said that he took more notice of the Irish government's statement to the court in the Boland case than its subsequent statement; Harry West stated that he thought it made no change in the position at all; and Ian Paisley called it a piece of 'political gymnastics'.

There was, however, a heartening side to the post-Sunningdale scene. Reports from all sides, and particularly from those working closely with its members, were that the power-sharing Executive was working well. I was advised that most of the members were making impressive progress and that a close personal relationship was developing between Brian Faulkner and Gerry Fitt. As the weeks went on I saw the workings of the Executive for myself at first hand and I felt that there was a future for the arrangement.

Important departments had been allocated to the SDLP, and John Hume, Paddy Devlin and Austin Currie took to their work as if born to it. The Party showed political courage in its decisions; for example, on 3 April, Austin Currie announced that there could be no amnesty for those on rent and rates strike, and the SDLP supported Basil McIvor, one of Brian's men, when he proposed a scheme for beginning integrated education.

Other members were also doing well. Leslie Morrell, another pro-Assembly Unionist, showed a quick grasp of the needs of Northern Irish agriculture. The Alliance Party was represented by two able men in Oliver Napier and Bob Cooper, who by the nature of their Party could and did speak out on the issues that divided the community, in a way denied to most Unionists and SDLP members.

There were, inevitably, some problems. Roy Bradford, on paper a Faulkner Unionist, seemed to spend much of his time setting himself up as Brian's successor; and Paddy Devlin and he got on badly in private and public. But such differences were not of major importance and I felt that there was no reason why the power-sharing Executive should not show the world, and above all the people of Northern Ireland, that it could govern the province well.

It was, however, the Council of Ireland that continued to bother the loyalists in the province. I was therefore more than glad to learn in early March that the leaders of the Executive were considering changes in the timetable of the Council. Confidential discussions had already begun with a view to a longer-term phasing. This issue was important, but there was no way that I could or should be involved; any change had to come from within Northern Ireland.

While the Executive was responsible for the government of the province – industry, agriculture, education, etc. – I and my colleagues were concerned not only with constitutional matters but also with the wider field of security – the army, police, prisons. It was one thing to look at security procedures when in Opposition; now they were my immediate responsibility. The questions concerning me were: how did the army co-operate with the RUC? What changes would have to be made for the police to take over more of the work of the army outside the republican areas? In what ways did my staff co-operate on policy matters with the security forces, including intelligence? I looked again at the work done at Laneside and agreed that the Political Affairs Division still had a job to do even though the Executive was now in existence.

On my first days in the province I had met and talked with Frank King, the General Officer Commanding Northern Ireland, and Jamie Flanagan, Chief Constable of the RUC. I assured them of my complete support for their actions in implementing government security policy. There would be no repeat of the interrogation procedures and events of 1971. I told the GOC of my concern about army information policy: there had been too much talk in the press of division between the politicians and the security forces in the days of my predecessor. I knew this had come from army headquarters at Lisburn but, as I was to discover, it stemmed not from the top but from those lower down the line in the information service who were not aware of the evolving discussions and agreements reached with senior officers.

I told them that I wanted to end detention but that while the Provisional IRA and some of the loyalist paramilitaries continued a deliberate campaign of violence, action had to be taken. My view remained as I had expressed it in the debate on the Detention of Terrorists Order in December 1972: 'We must not close our eyes in a nice liberal fashion to the realities of the situation on the other side of the water. Even the European Convention on Human Rights recognises the right of society to take special action by derogation. The Convention recognises that in modern society there are those who will seek to achieve their political ends by military means.'

The Provisionals had a vested interest in keeping detention going. To end it was not going to be easy and meanwhile it would have to continue to be used. Releases would take place under the procedures already laid down in the legislation, but those who engaged in violence or its organisation would be picked up again. All authorisation for detention would have to be approved by me personally; arrangements involving Stan Orme and Jack Donaldson were made for dealing with warrants when I was in Britain.

Initially I was the only person with the right of access to highly secret information on events and people involved in violence in the province. This was a problem and after the Prime Minister had been alerted to it Stan Orme was made a Privy Councillor so that he too had similar access. It made our discussions on security policy more worthwhile.

My security advisers gave me a full briefing on the situation. Supplies of arms for the Provisional IRA were coming in from the Middle East, with about a fifth of the money arriving from the United States, just as money for the loyalists came from Canada. Most of the money came in fact from bank and post office robberies in both the North and South, which were difficult to deal with since it was not possible to have members of the security forces posted at the entrances to hundreds of banks and post offices. They would anyway make sitting targets in the North, and the civilian staff and their families would be put at risk. The materials to make the explosives – the commercial nitrate to add to the agricultural nitrate – were coming at this time from the South, as were the detonators.

I was given details of the paramilitary and associated organisations in Northern Ireland, which amounted to over thirty groups with a membership running into many thousands. The main republican organisation was of course the Provisional IRA, with its allied groups using pseudonyms such as the Irish Freedom Fighters and the South Armagh Action Force. Its origins lay in the fighting of the 1920s, when it had been organised into brigades and battalions, using military-type ranks – volunteer, captain, etc. As I, and presumably also the Irish government, already knew, its leaders – the Army Council – met in Dublin on Thursdays, and it was from the South that the violence in the North was orchestrated. In the same way, the activities of its political wing, the Provisional Sinn Fein, were planned in the South.

Similarly, too, the Official IRA and its Sinn Fein political counterpart organised activities in the North from its Southern base, although since its declared ceasefire in the summer of 1972, the accent had been on political activities apart from internecine warfare with the Provisional IRA.

The numbers involved in these republican groups could only be roughly estimated, particularly as the gap between political and military membership was narrow or non-existent. The Provisionals probably had an active force of some five hundred men, as did the Officials, though in a crisis the numbers would greatly increase. I was advised that the results of the Provisionals' activities were likely to be obvious very shortly, for the indications were that the leadership was planning to welcome me and warn the exultant Unionists with a show of their strength.

The main loyalist group, the Ulster Defence Association, with its associated groups which used the pseudonym of the Ulster Freedom Fighters or the Young Militants, was a much larger group overall than either the Provisional or Official IRA, but its military wing was smaller – though, again, in a crisis its numbers would swell. The Ulster Volunteer Force, whose folk-hero leader was Gusty Spence, the sentenced special category prisoner whom I had earlier met in the Maze, did not have the membership of the UDA but its murdering activities often loomed larger. Like the UDA, it was a working-class organisation, as was the Red Hand Commandos, whose small numbers were active from time to time in East Belfast, Bangor and North Down generally.

The many other groups on both sides of the divide included, for example, Saor Eire – the so-called left-wing republican group active in Derry and Belfast – and the Ulster Special Constabulary Association, consisting of former members of the B Specials. A loyalist group that particularly concerned me was Tara, which after ceasing to be an anti-ecumenical ginger group inside the Orange Order had gone paramilitary. In a province where evil abounds, this group, although very small, was evil-plus.

The existence of these many groups may not have been foreign to the social history of Ireland but it was clear that by now, in 1974, terrorism had become a traditional way of life for them in some parts of the North. I soon learned the names of many of those involved because of my role in the detention procedures, and I became increasingly aware of the fringe involvement of a number of loyalist politicians with the loyalist paramilitaries. Such a connection did not apply to the SDLP.

Given the existence of the paramilitary organisations, I early had to consider the matter of proscription, by which they were put outside the protection of the law. Before I went to Northern Ireland and in the context of the Emergency Provisions Act of 1973, I had expressed reservations about the efficiency of this concept. I thought that proscription could be sidestepped by, for example, the organisation changing its name, or was irrelevant because membership was difficult to prove. Once I arrived in Northern Ireland, however, I came to the conclusion that proscription was necessary for those organisations which engaged in military activities. To deproscribe would condone murder and in any event I found that the charge of membership of an illegal organisation, although not of prime importance, was at least useful in getting suspected terrorists through the courts.

The list of proscribed bodies would therefore remain but I looked carefully at the names on it. I considered including the UDA but since most of its activities were not terrorist in nature and at that time it did not have a separate political wing, I left it unproscribed. Anyway, its undercover group, the Ulster Freedom Fighters, was on the list and there were already UDA members who were serving sentences in the Maze for crimes of violence.

To meet my concern, also expressed in Opposition, that those who supported the so-called political aims of the paramilitary groups should have freedom of expression and the opportunity to work through political channels, I decided to remove both Sinn Fein and the Ulster Volunteer Force from the proscribed list. There was a problem here because the UVF did not have a political wing as such, but I was informed of strong political aspirations in this group and I particularly wanted to encourage these if at all possible.

After all the briefings I had been given, I needed to report to the House of Commons and I therefore presented two papers to the Cabinet sub-committee in preparation for a debate. The first was on the deteriorating political situation since the General Election. The results – 422,000 for anti-Sunningdale candidates compared with 246,000 for those pro-Sunningdale – had come at a time when it was too easy for the loyalists to focus on the emotive issue of the Council of Ireland as a first step towards unification. The issue brought together both moderates and extremists in the Protestant community and there had been a sharp drop in the morale and credibility of the Executive and increasing criticism of the South by Unionists of all persuasions.

I saw no possibility of a strong mainstream Unionist Party forming in the future and warned of the likelihood of further defections to the United Ulster Unionist Council. Ian Paisley's attempt to dominate this body was causing some internal unease and there were signs of possible disruption but, though there were differing views on detention in these Unionist groups, all sides were united in wanting increased representation at Westminster, a regional parliament with responsibility for internal security, and the renegotiation of the constitutional issue and of Sunningdale.

Brian Faulkner and his Pro-Assembly Unionist Party wanted action against terrorists sheltering in the South and a far more gradualist approach on the Council of Ireland. The Party's problems would not, I warned my Cabinet colleagues, be alleviated by the forthcoming recommendations of the Law Enforcement Commission set up under the Sunningdale agreement. From the soundings taken, it seemed that the Commission's proposals to deal with all-Ireland terrorist crime would not be strong enough to counter the growing criticism of the South for the ineffectiveness of their security measures.

Liam Cosgrave's government was keen to ratify Sunningdale and was, I felt sure, sincere in its good will, but in the North there was deep distrust. The escape of Provisional leader Seamus Twomey from a Dublin gaol the previous October had provoked ridicule; nor had it since helped that there were reports of IRA suspects being arrested only to be released, and that a ship was searched in Dublin Bay for illegal arms, which were found to be 'supplies for the Irish army'.

The Alliance Party, like the Faulkner Unionists, was setting great store by the Law Enforcement Commission's forthcoming proposals on security. It wished to go forward on the Council of Ireland but did not believe that the idea could be sold to Northern Ireland at this time.

The SDLP was, I reported, looking for movement on detention and a Council of Ireland in its full sense, which included full executive responsibility. They were seeking to bargain support for the RUC in return for implementing Sunningdale in full.

The new Assembly clearly faced major problems but my response to the loyalist demands for new elections to it was to give reassurances from the UK government that the Assembly would run its term and that power sharing would not be abandoned.

The second and more important paper that I presented to my Cabinet colleagues was on future policy and dealt mainly with security. It was the result of much thought and discussion in the Northern Ireland Office and with the RUC and army. I wanted first of all to set up a security review committee to consider in detail the role of the security forces. I emphasised the view of my military advisers that the problem in Northern Ireland could not be solved by the use of increased military force. It was not possible at present to proceed with the Sunningdale ideas on policing but in the short run we would reconstitute the Police Authority so that it included members of the Assembly and I would ask Brian Faulkner to set up an Assembly Police Committee to consider how best to introduce effective policing. On a local level, there would be liaison committees, involving the elected district councils, to exchange views with the police on their problems.

The recommendations for the RUC itself included a streamlined command structure, with three operational divisions – based in Londonderry, Belfast and the border – each with an Assistant Chief Constable in charge. In effect, other than Belfast, the province would be divided administratively into two areas, with the dividing line running East to West. A non-residential cadet scheme, based on technical colleges, was also proposed, plus changes in the complaints procedure and more effort to improve community relations. Derry was to have more police, which would allow troops to be withdrawn from the area.

A long-term reduction in troops was a policy inherited from the Heath government with which I totally concurred, and an immediate reduction of three army units between April and July 1974 was now proposed by the Ministry of Defence. It was an army view held for operational reasons and Roy Mason as Minister of Defence pointed out that, with twenty-four hours' notice, reinforcements could arrive in the province. However, much as I agreed with him, I did not think that we should go too far before the proposed security review committee had examined the army's role, and I therefore recommended a reduction of only one unit at this time.

It was important too, I emphasised, that this reduction should not be presented as a political decision against the wishes of the army. As a junior army minister in the mid-sixties I recalled the row over the policy of ending the old Territorial Army, which had been the result of strong advice from army staff but had been landed firmly in the politicians' lap, with the press putting the blame on the 'wicked socialists'. I wanted no repeat in this case and at the end of the meeting I had a word with the Chief of the Defence Staff and of course with Roy Mason, repeating again that the army information people in Lisburn must be clearly briefed and it made very clear that the reduction in units was not in any way being forced on the army by the politicians.

Another of the proposals I made at the meeting was to introduce stronger controls on firearms. Harold had long been concerned about the number of legally held guns in the province, though as I pointed out the real problem came from stolen guns. I also put forward my proposal to remove Sinn Fein and the Ulster Volunteer Force from the list of proscribed organisations. I reminded my colleagues that I had argued for this in Opposition in order to give the major paramilitary organisations at least a chance of working through political channels. However hard it might be for those outside Ireland to understand the division between political and military wings, it was there and I wanted to use it. I was under no illusion that some people managed to operate on both sides of this very Irish divide, but deproscribing these organisations would not prevent arrest and sentence on those against whom evidence was available.

My major concern was, however, detention, and I proposed to set up an enquiry into the workings of the 1973 Emergency Provisions Act. I had promised this when in Opposition and I regarded it as the only way to begin the long-term process of changing the policy on detention. In the short term, the Emergency Provisions Act would have to be renewed in July, but I would also begin a phased release of detainees, linked with resettlement measures designed to bring released detainees back into society and to reduce recidivism. There was no intention of introducing an amnesty but I hoped that better police organisation would lead to more terrorists appearing before the courts.

Closer security liaison with the South was also important and one of the paper's proposals was for a conference of ministers and expert officials from each country. I provided a copy of my letter to Garret Fitzgerald following my meeting with him on 7 March. This detailed the subjects that we needed to discuss at the conference, which included co-operation through regular meetings between the Chief Constable of the RUC and the Commissioner of the Garda. (There had already been one meeting but I wanted them to be on a regular basis.) I suggested discussing the possibility of regular meetings also of the respective Army Chiefs of Staff, although I realised that this stood little chance. In particular, I put forward proposals for co-operation on the border itself.

It was urgent that we had early action on the report of the Law Enforcement Commission stemming out of Sunningdale. The legal complexities were considerable but until the report appeared – which would probably be after Easter – Brian Faulkner would find it extremely difficult to get the Assembly backing to ratify Sunningdale. The Attorney General, Sam Silkin, led the discussion on this issue and again reinforced my doubts about whether the Commission would come down in favour of extradition, as much as logic led that way and as much as the North might be pinning hopes on it. The stumbling block was that an extradition agreement with the North would conflict legally with the South's written constitution. We were going to have trouble on all this in Northern Ireland.

All the proposals that I put forward at the Cabinet sub-committee meeting, including the timing of army reductions, were agreed to by colleagues and I was ready for the first full-scale debate on Northern Ireland in Parliament since we took office. This was due to take place on 4 April and, knowing that it was imminent, the Provisional IRA now stepped up the campaign of violence which they had been waging since the General Election. The events meant that I had to make a report to the Commons on 1 April, before my major speech. I first outlined the facts:

> On Thursday 28th March a bomb of between 500 and 600 lb exploded outside a hotel in the centre of Belfast which is at present an army headquarters. On the following day there were more bombs outside Catholic bars in Belfast, and on Saturday 30th March the level of violence was further stepped up, with bomb and incendiary attacks in Armagh, Lisburn and Bangor, as well as more incidents in Belfast, and the violence continued on Sunday 31st March.
>
> In these four days six civilians were killed and sixty-five injured. The army had eight casualties and the RUC two, fortunately not serious. The pattern of these incidents shows a succession of acts of retaliation and revenge between one community and another.

I told the House that I had visited Belfast city centre on the Friday morning. I did not say that this was against the advice of my security advisers, nor that I went because I did not want to be seen simply issuing statements from on high at Stormont Castle. I was right to go but I had a difficult two or three hours from a hostile crowd and was grateful for the physical support of my protection officers.

Brian Faulkner was also out and about, and I heard that he too had a rough time. By some strange alchemy, Ian Paisley also appeared on the scene and was shown on television talking to me. On the Saturday I was again out and about in Belfast, and on the Sunday Stan Orme went over to Bangor and Lisburn to visit the scenes of the bombings there, which he described to me in graphic terms. It was particularly difficult for him in the predominantly Protestant territory, which the Provisionals had chosen for that reason, but he saw at first hand the effects of the small incendiary bombs, easily made from commonplace materials, secreted in books or cornflake packets and placed by apparently innocent shoppers. Both of us were left in no doubt about the strength of the public's feelings.

As ever there was a cry in the Commons and the media for more troops and I took the opportunity to put the counter-argument in perspective:

> It was a bad weekend, and it has led – and I fully understand this – to demands for increased action by the security forces. If violence on this scale occurred in cities in Great Britain, Hon Members would rightly be demanding that all available resources should be thrown against those responsible. As Hon Members will know, I have since I came into office four weeks ago been reviewing with the GOC and the Chief Constable the security situation. I can already say quite clearly that no increase in the number of troops in Northern Ireland would eliminate the sorts of incident which happened last weekend. For example, I was told on Saturday in Belfast by army commanders that the security forces are making about 100,000 searches a day at the Segment [the entrance to the Belfast shopping area].

I asserted, in view of allegations to the contrary, and Francis Pym agreed with me in his response, that there was 'no question whatsoever of the security forces being prevented by political directives from taking any necessary action against terrorists'. I told the House that if terrorist organisations had increased their acts of violence to test the present government, then 'I pledge this government to act resolutely to deal with terrorists from wherever they come'.

I always listened carefully to Northern Irish MPs and on this day I particularly noted the words of Gerry Fitt when he told the Commons that the Provisional IRA as well as the UDA were out to defeat Sunningdale. He also accused certain elected representatives of 'almost inciting these people to continue their acts of violence'. He was absolutely right on both assertions.

A possible cause of the bombings, I told the Commons, other than that of bringing down the Northern Ireland Constitution Act and the Sunningdale agreement, was 'that this is the spring offensive by members of the IRA to bomb themselves to the conference table. On behalf of the government, I say that we talk with those who act politically, because that is why the House is in business.'

Three days after my statement I was back in the Commons opening the full-scale debate on Northern Ireland. As in my first days in the province, I reiterated the government's support for Sunningdale; our policies were firmly based on those of our predecessors in office. I then unfolded the decisions agreed to at the Cabinet meetings, backing the policy for achieving the primacy of the police with a statement issued by the Executive:

> We all want to see normality in Northern Ireland – a normality in which detention will have ended and in which law and order can be preserved by a civilian police force and not by the presence of heavily armed troops.
>
> We now call upon all those in Northern Ireland who are appalled and disgusted by the recurrent violence to recognise that there are practical steps which they can take to create that situation of normality. If reliance on the army is to be reduced, the locally recruited security forces must be in a position to take on further responsibilities. This they can only do when they have the support of the whole community. This is our objective.
>
> The best way to deal with men of violence is through the effective operation of the ordinary processes of the law. But the law cannot be effective until each citizen accepts a personal commitment to see to it that his area, his housing estate, his street, is not used by the bomber or the gunman.

With regard to the security review, I told the Commons that we were looking afresh at the role of the army. 'The question of the number of troops and the degree of flexibility we can produce are closely bound together. What we are aiming for is the minimum number of troops actually in Northern Ireland which the needs of the situation require.' I then turned to the vexed issue of the Emergency Provisions Act which had been of so much concern to us in Opposition. I reminded the House that during the passage of the original Bill in 1973, we had stated our belief that the Diplock Report, on which the legislation was based, should have been given wider terms of reference. This was why I now proposed to set up a committee under the chairmanship of Lord Gardiner to investigate the Emergency Provisions Act and other measures to deal with terrorism. I hoped that its report would enable me to end the use of the powers of detention.

I had originally planned to announce to the House the names of the committee members but, although we had made good progress in a month, I had not yet received acceptances from all the people invited to sit on the committee. A few days later, however, I was able to announce a range of names of eminent people from Northern Ireland as well as Great Britain – Professor Alastair Buchan, Judge J. P. Higgins, Professor Kathleen Jones, Lord MacDermott, the former Lord Chief Justice of Northern Ireland, Michael Morland QC and Dr J. H. Whyte.

I expected adverse comments from the official Opposition in the Commons to my proposal to deproscribe both Sinn Fein and the UVF, but they were not forthcoming. I should have read more into the speech of Francis Pym on 16 February, made in his Cambridgeshire constituency during the General Election campaign, which had invited these organisations to advance their views through the democratic process. At least the two of us agreed that, whatever the double talk of the Provisional Sinn Fein and the UVF, political action must be given a chance. This was not the view of either Brian Faulkner, who said so forcibly, or of Gerry Fitt, who while more non-committal on deproscription than Brian had, with the SDLP as a whole, little time for the political aspirations of men of violence.

Francis Pym's response on this point typified the response of the Conservative front-bench to all the points in my speech. Both he and Ian Gilmour, now the Opposition spokesman on Northern Ireland, were positive and helpful, and responded acidly to some of their own back-benchers, as well as to the Unionist MPs. William Craig, in a generally critical speech, made an interesting reference to 'two nations' in Northern Ireland, a reinforcement of my incipient view on Ulster nationalism. Other Northern Ireland Unionists carped and criticised, with Harry West capping them all. How, I asked myself afterwards, could this man be a leader of a party?

When Gerry Fitt spoke, we had the usual historical section, which drew Tam Dalyell, Scottish Labour MP, to interject, protesting that we were becoming 'impatient and depressed at the Irish Members harking back to the past the whole time'. So be it. In Ireland, history matters.

I had left it to Stan Orme in his winding-up speech to outline the sponsorship scheme that had been put to us during office discussions. He and I had accepted the point that one of the main reasons for ex-detainees returning to violence was the lack of job opportunities, and that one way of reducing this recidivism was to introduce an unconventional scheme outside the established after-care agencies designed for the ODCs – ordinary decent criminals – to provide work for ex-detainees and special category prisoners.

Stan had looked at the practical problems involved and had set up a working party to recommend solutions to them. He emphasised to me that the scheme would have to operate within the Catholic areas, for it would be far too dangerous for the men concerned to move outside them. He therefore told the Commons: 'Perhaps the most important help that we could receive would be for courageous men and women in the hardline ghetto communities to come forward with offers of help in resettling detainees. We need that kind of help, and I know that members of the SDLP and other parties in Northern Ireland have offered to give such assistance.'

The announcement seemed to be well received in the Commons but the media treated it with a mixture of cynicism and heavy humour. 'Rent a terrorist' set the tone. I could not blame them, for we had not thought out the idea carefully enough. We had slipped up in other ways too, for no sooner was the announcement made than it was leaked from army headquarters at Lisburn that the staff there preferred a variant of the idea by which detainees would go through the resettlement scheme before being released. This was obviously a non-starter, since once detainees knew that they were to be released, they would not co-operate. I was, however, surprised because I had understood that the proposed scheme had come from the security forces. Only later did I realise that the idea had been around for some time before my arrival in the province, and Willie Whitelaw had talked approvingly of it in his valedictory speech. It was clearly one of those ideas that everybody thought sensible but nobody had taken a grip on with the change of government.

We should have been better prepared in those early days, and Stan and I learned a lesson from the whole affair that we never forgot. It made us realise too that, while the responsibility for security in the widest sense was ours, there was an additional problem of discussing such matters as sponsorship with the Executive. This could not be done until Parliament had approved such plans or at least had been informed, and when we spoke to members of the Executive about sponsorship, it was to find that support there was also minimal. For example, Ivan Cooper, the Minister of Community Relations, opposed it because it was 'independent' of government, and the Unionist members, predictably, were not enthusiastic either. However, after Stan had argued for the proposal, and John Hume and Paddy Devlin had weighed in behind it, reluctant acceptance was given. The plan had all gone too wrong, however, for us to proceed in the way envisaged and as early as 24 April Stan reported that the proposal was 'unacceptable and unworkable'. Later in the year he tried again with a variant of the scheme but that too had to be abandoned because of practical difficulties.

In his winding-up speech to the Commons, Stan also turned to the economic scene, which was to occupy much of his time in the province and which was high on the agenda of our responsibilities. Stan informed the House of his recent involvement with John Hume, the member of the Executive responsible for commerce, about the problem of Harland and Wolff. This large shipbuilding firm was already partially owned by the Northern Ireland Department of Commerce but even at this stage the money provided the previous December by Francis Pym was proving inadequate. Stan had kept closely in touch with the chairman, Lord Rochdale, and Hoppe, the Danish general manager, as well as shop stewards and union leaders, and it was clear that something was very wrong in the shipyard, even given the world depression in oil-tanker building.

Given the attitude of the loyalist working class in Belfast and the competing needs of British yards in the North East, Scotland and Merseyside, it was not easy to convince Cabinet colleagues of the urgency for more finance to keep going what the Catholics regarded as a 'Protestant soup kitchen'. However, in those early days we did obtain sufficient funds for the short-term, while we worked out a long-term strategy.

Financial provision for the province in general was also proving a troublesome issue in the Executive. Brian Faulkner, Sir David Holden, head of the Northern Ireland Civil Service, and I had discussed estimates for the following year, and though extra expenditure had been allowed for, there were limits to the number of projects that could be financed straight away. When the matter was discussed in the full Executive, Brian and David explained the need for priorities and that some of the SDLP's election promises would have to be shelved for the time being. It evidently led to an explosive confrontation with the SDLP in general and Paddy Devlin in particular. I was left to ponder on where this financial issue was going to lead us. Governments normally have to raise money by taxation, a discipline that was not applicable to the Executive.

This problem had not yet surfaced for me to report on to the Commons on 4 April but the policies that I did report then received almost complete support. There were, however, difficulties ahead. The ratifying of the Sunningdale agreement and the Council of Ireland in particular were as far off as ever, whatever the cosy views in London and Dublin. It all looked different in Belfast and an angry, disjointed meeting in the Cabinet room at Stormont on 8 April added to my disquiet. Here, Stan and I met with representatives of the Ulster Workers' Council, a body which had emerged in late 1973 in place of the Loyalist Association of Workers.

Their theme was clear: Sunningdale was undemocratic and had been shown to be so at the General Election. The Executive was forcing the North into the South and 'was instrumental in the appointment of an "IRA sympathiser", Frank Lagan, as Assistant Chief Constable in Londonderry'. This, of course, was not true, and neither was the next assertion that when I talked with ministers in the South, I was 'negotiating with terrorists' who were not averse to relaxing the laws on contraception merely as a device to encourage eventual unification! I was even told that this was the sort of 'dirty subject' that Catholics would be keen about.

I rejected once more the call for new Assembly elections and told them that the Executive should be given four years to prove itself. A desultory discussion followed on what would happen constitutionally if the Executive fell before then. The subject shifted to particular issues, such as the transfer of Londonderry loyalist detainees from the Maze to Magilligan prison nearer home, and the delay in providing telephones in the province. Throughout the meeting, voices were raised and tempers ran high. It all contributed to my overall scepticism about Sunningdale, and I expressed this in a confidential minute which I sent on the same day to the Prime Minister.

I told him that Brian Faulkner now felt that it was impossible for him to get Unionist support for the full implementation of the Council of Ireland proposal agreed at Sunningdale. Indeed, he had proposed in a letter to Liam Cosgrave a watered-down version, by which there would be a Council of Ireland with an equal number of ministers from North and South but with no headquarters, no secretariat and no second-tier consultative assembly. Only later on, with a fresh mandate from elections in the province, would he be prepared to expand the Council of Ireland to the full scope set out in the Sunningdale communiqué. I told Harold that I could not see the Southern government agreeing to this change but that Brian himself was hopeful that his revision – which he had discussed with the SDLP members of the Executive – would be accepted. I had asked to be kept informed, but in no way would I be involved.

I warned Harold that the danger was either that the Sunningdale agreement would break down and would not be ratified or that Unionist support in the Assembly for the Executive would disappear and power sharing collapse. Either way the consequences were serious and a crisis would hit unexpectedly – perhaps from a leak of Faulkner's talks with the SDLP about the Council of Ireland. I asked Harold to bear this in mind, for it could affect his proposed visit to Northern Ireland the following week. I did not want him to arrive in the middle of a constitutional crisis.

Two days afterwards, on 10 April, I expressed the same concern at the full Cabinet meeting. Without the Council of Ireland, the Irish government and the SDLP would find it impossible to continue with Sunningdale; with it, Brian Faulkner would be totally rejected. It was unwise to make confident predictions about developments in Northern Ireland, where the political climate can change unexpectedly, but I felt bound to warn colleagues that there was a danger of political collapse.

I instanced a loyalist petition against Sunningdale which was gathering support in the province. It was more meaningful than a BBC-commissioned poll which showed seventy-four per cent of the electorate supporting power sharing and ninety-six per cent disapproving of the use of violence. This disapproval did not apply to all loyalist leaders for at this time William Craig said on a Radio Telefis Eireann programme that he found sectarian murders 'unfortunate but understandable', and he was the man who in January had publicly pronounced that the loyalists would 'save' Ulster in 1974.

I did not recommend to my colleagues a change of policy; indeed I thought it essential that we showed confidence in our present policies and pressed ahead with them. Otherwise the danger of collapse would be even greater. However, I thought that we should prepare in the strictest confidence plans for alternative methods of government. The most likely solution if the Executive collapsed was a return to direct rule, which would not be introduced as in 1972 in a climate of hope but one of failure.

The prospect of reinstituting power sharing would be remote and there would be strong pressure for withdrawal, which would carry grave consequences for Great Britain as well as for Northern Ireland and the Republic. I advised that these consequences should be taken into account as part of the contingency planning. There was no question, I told my colleagues, of pulling out; I was simply alerting them, immersed as they were in the post-Heath situation in Britain, that we needed to be prepared for breakdown. It is always sensible for members of governments to lift their eyes above immediate preoccupations.

Harold Wilson asked a small group of ministers, mainly from the Northern Ireland Office and the Defence Department, to be involved in the contingency planning; options were not to be excluded on the grounds that they were unlikely to be adopted. Harold himself turned to one of his ideas, often expressed in Opposition, that there should be an all-party conference, which might lead to a joint conference with representatives from Northern Ireland and the Republic. I did not think much of this idea but I wanted to include all possibilities; the wider the discussion the better.

Harold was firm on existing policy when he visited the province on 18 April, the date originally agreed, and had talks with security chiefs, the Executive members, trade unionists and church leaders. At the subsequent press conference, he weighed in against the men of violence and pointed out the support at Westminster for power sharing. He added: 'Were this initiative to fail, or were any of us prepared to let it be destroyed or to founder, for whatever reason, then there would be little hope that we could once again reconstruct a fresh political initiative. . . . We stand by the Sunningdale agreement. We want to see it become a reality.'

He was absolutely right to talk in this way, for there was still a chance of success. It was not, however, helped when later in the month Roy Mason ruffled the dovecote with a speech in Newcastle under Lyme in which he warned that pressure was mounting in Great Britain to pull out the troops and to set a date for withdrawal so that 'the leaders of the "warring factions" could get together and hammer out a solution'. The Ministry of Defence promptly issued a statement, authorised of course by Roy, that there was no change in government policy and no suggestion of a time limit for the withdrawal of troops. I was left wondering why the speech had been made in the first place.

The denial did not quieten the furore in Northern Ireland. Gerry Fitt, as Deputy Chief Executive, at once came to London to see Harold, telling him that while the statement from the Ministry of Defence had 'eased the worry', the original speech might cause the Provisional IRA to think 'One more push and we've won'. Harold issued a Cabinet statement the following day making it clear that government policy in Northern Ireland was unchanged.

There was also concern in the South. As soon as Roy's speech was reported, I had been contacted by the Irish government, and I met Garret Fitzgerald in London, where I reassured him that there would be no withdrawal of troops. The Irish government was not, however, entirely convinced; it was not sure of a Labour government and there was always a lingering historical feeling in Dublin about perfidious Albion.

The 'warring factions' referred to by Roy were of course a reality, with the Provisional IRA principally involved in the continuing violence. There had earlier been stories of a possible Provisional IRA ceasefire emanating from the 'rumour factory' at the Europa Hotel in Belfast where many of the press stayed. I had known no more than that there was much 'twittering and chattering' going on about the Belfast Brigade and a 'settlement', but I did not think that anything was likely to come of it. I was anyway not willing to enter into any deals and wanted no repeat of Willie Whitelaw's experience in 1972.

The rumour had, however, been taken for real and was part of the withdrawal issue. It was enough to prompt Garret Fitzgerald to reject the idea that the IRA should be invited to sit at a conference table and he was obliquely supported in this by the Opposition leader, Jack Lynch.

On 22 April, a few weeks after the ceasefire rumour had begun to circulate, Frank McManus, the former Independent Republican MP for Fermanagh, asked to see me at Stormont. He was close to some members of the Provisional IRA and because we had met at Westminster, I thought that we might be able to talk to each other in terms that we both understood. At the least, Frank McManus sitting in an easy chair in the former Prime Minister's room at Stormont Castle was something for the history books.

We talked about the power-sharing Executive and Sunningdale, but he told me that neither he nor his friends were interested in this type of political settlement and they wanted the withdrawal of British troops to barracks immediately, and eventual total withdrawal. I gave the message loud and clear that the Provisionals would not bomb their way to the conference table. It was nonsense to believe that there could be a military victory for either side. Politics were going to win out, however much the Provisionals and people of their ilk disliked the SDLP.

Nothing came of the rumour of a ceasefire and the true nature of the Provisional IRA was shown to the world when in early May security forces found Provisional IRA papers in a Belfast flat. Harold Wilson reported on them to the Commons:

> These documents reveal a specific and calculated plan by the IRA, by means of ruthless and indiscriminate violence, to foment intersectarian hatred and a degree of chaos with the object of enabling the IRA to achieve a position in which it could proceed to occupy and control certain predesignated and densely populated areas in the city of Belfast and its suburbs. The plan shows a deliberate intention to manipulate the emotions of large sections of the people by inflicting violence and hardship on them in the hope of creating a situation in which the IRA could present itself as the protector of the Catholic population.
>
> It is also clear from the documents that the IRA did not expect, even if it was initially successful, to be able to continue to hold a number of strongpoints in parts of Belfast and that its intention would have been to carry out a scorched earth policy of burning the houses of the ordinary people as it was compelled to withdraw.

Jim Wellbeloved, then a Labour MP and representative of a school which thought that the Irish government were double dealers, asked if the documents might be submitted to the European Commission of Human Rights, which was still looking into the allegations of brutality by British troops brought by the Irish government after the events of 1971. The Republic's continuing complaint to the European Commission added to the North's distrust of the South's attitude and to the problems over Sunningdale. Indeed, the former Conservative Attorney General, Sir Peter Rawlinson, asked the Prime Minister on 7 May not to ratify Sunningdale while the case was being considered.

Much more immediately worrying was the report of the Law Enforcement Commission at the end of April, which as expected did not meet the hopes put on it by the Northern Ireland political parties, and the Unionists and loyalists in particular. The eight eminent jurists, four from the South and four from the UK, including the Lord Chief Justice of Northern Ireland, Sir Robert Lowry, and Lord Justice

Scarman from London, were evenly split on straight South/UK lines on the crucial issue of extradition. The South's opposition was based on Justice Henchy's view that extradition would probably be invalid under the written Irish constitution, which held the North to be part of Ireland.

As second best, the Commission recommended the 'extra-territorial method', under which jurisdiction would be conferred on courts in both parts of Ireland to try offences committed in another part. 'But we all recognise and emphasise that its efficacy depends upon the success of measures designed to bring before the court the relevant evidence, by encouraging witnesses, for both the prosecution and the defence, to cross the border to the place of trial or, where this is not practicable, by securing their attendance to give evidence on commission.' The weakness of the method was obvious and in Northern Ireland the report was seen as typical Southern evasion. The Unionist members in particular were bitterly disappointed and in the background was a row engendered by Roy Bradford, who claimed that the SDLP members had an advantage over the Unionists because they had been shown the proposals by the Irish government.

The report could only add to Brian Faulkner's gathering problems in the Assembly which since the middle of March had been indulging in a long, nasty and sometimes violent 'debate' on Sunningdale. It was made worse when at the Portrush conference of the UUUC at the end of April the delegates supported a motion calling for a complete renegotiation of the constitutional settlement and the setting up of a Northern Ireland regional parliament.

By early May it was announced that there was at last to be a vote on Sunningdale in the Assembly. This became the big talking point throughout the province and not just a subject for esoteric comment in the political pages of the British press. The trouble over Sunningdale was coming to a head. This was made even more clear by a statement issued on 10 May by the Ulster Workers' Council.

> We strongly advise the Unionist Assembly members at Stormont to vote cautiously in the crucial issue of Sunningdale. Assemblymen must remember that they were returned to Stormont to represent the views of the electorate and as such they should vote in line with the majority views within their constituencies. The mandate of many politicians in the Assembly expired as a result of the recent Westminster election and the UWC considers it unwise of the British government to ignore legitimate demands for a fresh election at Stormont.

Behind this statement lay the threat of strike action should the

Assembly ratify Sunningdale and, in particular, the Council of Ireland. In retrospect, it was a threat that should have been taken more seriously, yet at the time it was not only my security advisers who did not see the UWC as of major significance. Brian Faulkner in his memoirs said that 'few of us had heard much of this organisation before and assumed it was a successor to the short-lived and not very successful Loyalist Association of Workers which had in early 1973 called several strikes which rebounded on the organisers'. He was supported in this view by most other politicians in the province.

The final debate on Sunningdale in the Assembly mattered in Northern Ireland in a way that is almost inconceivable in Great Britain. On 14 May, the last day of it, the atmosphere was electric, yet all Brian Faulkner could do was insist, with the support of his Executive, that all the commitments entered into at Sunningdale should be honoured. He was unable to say anything about the talks taking place in the Executive about the long-term phasing of the Council of Ireland. As he wrote in his memoirs, 'It was frustrating to be put in this false political position but we could not do anything else until we had got a decision on the Executive.'

As long as his Unionist members remained loyal to him, there was no problem winning the final vote, and in the event the Executive won the debate by forty-four votes to twenty-eight to carry on with the original concept of the Council of Ireland. But all was far from well. It might have been if there had been time for the Executive to reach agreement on the Council and also for the new government to show the true worth of power sharing. As it was, the vote immediately provoked the Ulster workers' strike.

Chapter 3

THE ULSTER WORKERS' STRIKE

The fourteen-day strike that began on 15 May brought Northern Ireland to a standstill. It was led by the Ulster Workers' Council, whose twenty-one member executive was made up of active trade unionists. The chairman was Harry Murray, a boilermaker from Harland and Wolff, the treasurer Harry Patterson of the Sheet Metal Workers Union and among the members were power workers William Kelly and Tom Beattie, Jim Smyth from Rolls Royce and Glen Barr of the AUEW, who was also the Vanguard Party leader in Londonderry. Unlike the earlier Loyalist Association of Workers, its aim was not mass membership but the recruitment of key workers in the province's basic industries, particularly the power stations. Control and manipulation of these, it was argued, would be the best way to mount a successful strike.

The Co-ordinating Committee set up actually to run the strike showed, however, that the UWC also saw the need for political and paramilitary activity and support. Glen Barr was its chairman and as well as other UWC executive members, the Committee included politicians Harry West, Ian Paisley and William Craig, and such leading paramilitaries as Andy Tyrie of the Ulster Defence Association, Gibson and Hannigan of the Ulster Volunteer Force, Green of the Ulster Constabulary Specials, Marno of the Orange Volunteers and Colonel Brush of the Down Orange Welfare.

The politico-paramilitary influence was seen at a meeting with Stan Orme held at Stormont on the first day of the strike when I was in London. Members of the UWC were accompanied by Craig, Paisley and John Laird, former Stormont Unionist MP, together with three armed observers. Despite cool relations between the UWC and the loyalist politicians at a Portrush meeting a few weeks earlier, they were now very close, and the changed attitude of the politicians was to be made public on 20 May in a half-page advertisement in the loyalist newspaper, *The Newsletter*, when they called for support for the strike. Loyalty to the UK was supposed to be their creed but only as long as it suited them.

The strike strategy was made clear at the meeting with Stan: the UWC was going to force its political aims by limiting the supply of electricity and determining who should be supplied. Paisley had changed his tune since the unsuccessful strike called in 1973 by LAW, which he had condemned in the Commons to Willie Whitelaw: 'Is the Rt Hon Gentleman aware that the vast majority of workers were almost compelled to take part in the strike because power and electricity were cut off?' Now he thought differently. Indeed, at the meeting with Stan, he was not talking politics but arguing the technical case for switching industry off the electricity grid so that the sixty per cent load which had been set by the UWC could provide a service for the ordinary consumer. He also raised the case of William Kelly of the UWC who had, he said, been 'locked out' from Belfast East power station. Outside Stormont Castle afterwards Paisley threatened a complete blackout unless Kelly was reinstated.

The aim of the Co-ordinating Committee was, however, political and always at the forefront was the demand to end the Sunningdale agreement and have new elections at an early date. It made the stoppage different from the engineers' strike over the Heath government's Industrial Relations Act, with which Paisley taunted Stan, an AUEW-sponsored MP. There had been little public support for the engineers in Britain, or for the miners – as was shown by Labour's relatively poor showing in the February Election, when the Liberals had been the main electoral beneficiary of the policies of the Heath government. It was a point of difference I made to West, Barr and William Beattie, Paisley's deputy, when they came to see me on 17 May on my return from London, for it was not Paisley alone who voiced such views. Comparison with recent industrial disputes in Great Britain was part of the Ulster politicians' stock-in-trade at this time.

In view of the armed observers at the meeting with Stan, I asked a Lieutenant Colonel from 39 Brigade in Belfast to be present in the room for the meeting on the 17th, in battledress and fully armed. My armed personal detectives were also there. They were not needed, but should loyalist 'heavies' have turned up, we had to be able to deal with them. Indeed, when Frank Cooper and I had heard about Stan's earlier meeting, we instituted checks for arms at the front door even if senior loyalist politicians were present.

At the meeting, members of the UWC failed to appear. One reason, I was told, was because it was being claimed that we were going back on an 'agreement' reached on the sixty per cent electricity issue – though there had been no agreement. Another reason was that I was not prepared to negotiate with them over Sunningdale.

By this time, there were already roster systems for lighting homes, with predictable future effects on sewerage and water supplies, and the electricity cuts were accompanied by a limitation of petrol and food supplies – all organised from the Co-ordinating Committee's Hawthornden Road headquarters in Belfast. These activities prompted me to say later in the Commons: 'It is a matter of regret that certain Members of this House should attempt to set up a provisional government in Northern Ireland by issuing their own ration books and so on, and then come here and draw pay as democrats. That makes me a little sick.' Ian Paisley challenged me with a careful textual use of words, to which I told him:

> He meets daily organisations consisting of people who are seeking to bring down the system of government in Northern Ireland that was agreed by both sides of the House. The Hon Gentleman knows that permit cards are being issued in Northern Ireland by those with whom he associates. The Hon Gentleman cannot have double standards and be a democrat here and a demagogue in Northern Ireland. I find distasteful his attempt to stand up as a 'loyalist' and to use the words of the Queen.
>
> The Hon Gentleman and some of his friends are attempting to bring down the elected government which this country set up under the Constitution Act, and the Hon Gentleman now asks whether I will negotiate with his friends, whether I will negotiate about the supply of electricity, and whether I will give in to them about the Sunningdale agreement. My responsibility is to the House and not to the sort of people with whom the Hon Gentleman is associating, people who are backed by paramilitary groups with arms and ammunition. That is the sort of man the Hon Gentleman is. He is making a mockery of the Christianity that I learned.

I was not speaking merely from anger. I was deliberately attempting to make clear the nature of the strike. Moreover, this was not the full story. From the first day of the stoppage the paramilitary allies of these loyalists were being used to intimidate. On 15 May uniformed men had 'cut off' the town of Larne, and threats of car burning had quickly emptied the Harland and Wolff yard when it seemed that the strike call might not be obeyed. There were telephone calls to firms, visits to shops by strong-armed thugs, threats to genuine trade unionists, and bus hi-jackings. Catholic workers were beaten up in the Michelin Tyre factory and in Courtaulds. Intimidation was the order of the day. I was particularly angry when I saw representatives of the UWC – the men who bore a terrible responsibility for the violence – being lionised on BBC programmes. Due impartiality was apparently being shown.

The advice being freely given to me by local politicians in the early days of the strike was to sit tight. Once the population saw the intrinsic nastiness of it all and faced shortages, it would, I was told, react in the government's favour. There was little sign of this happening but my own view also was that the only approach was to take it slowly. I was not prepared to have a shooting match with unarmed civilians and a slip would have led to bloodshed.

In the office we had discussed the whole issue of the electricity supply with army staff and consulted the top management of the Northern Ireland Electricity Service. It was not clear what could be achieved if we brought technical personnel from the armed services to the province, and it was doubtful anyway if middle management would co-operate, but I asked the Ministry of Defence to bring the troops in just in case they were required. Meanwhile, officers in civilian clothes would look round the power stations to assess the position.

I asked the emergency committee which I had set up in the Castle to provide me with an estimate of the sort of electrical output we might be able to produce. With co-operation from within the Electricity Service it would be, I was told, about thirty per cent – half the percentage named by the UWC. John Hume, the minister responsible for electricity supply, disagreed with the figure. He was also at loggerheads with the general manager of the NIES over the power station at Coolkeeragh where the labour force was mainly Catholic and from which John believed that power supplies could be provided for the rest of the province, particularly Belfast. It was explained forcefully to him that for technical reasons there could never be any question of this. However capable John Hume was as a minister, the NIES had the technical expertise and it was helpful that the points put by their general manager were clear, concise and full of common sense.

The argument about percentages was still being pursued on Saturday, 18 May, when news came that the UWC was going for an all-out strike. We needed now to be able to restrict the use of electricity by industry if power on the grid dropped to a level that would seriously affect transport and food supplies. To do this required a proclamation under Section 40 of the 1973 Northern Ireland Constitution Act, and on the basis that the community would be deprived of the essentials of life, I issued the proclamation on Sunday. It had a predictable effect on the UWC, who made the statement: 'It's no use trying to use jackboot tactics. All we want are Assembly elections and for someone from the government to talk to us.'

I decided to go over to Chequers to speak to Harold and on the way I called in briefly to have a word with Jim Callaghan at the Foreign Secretary's Buckinghamshire home. Harold was, as ever, well briefed on the situation and after our discussion he issued a statement endorsing and authorising the measures I was taking. He always understood the loneliness of the Northern Ireland Secretary.

The decision of the UWC to go for an all-out strike meant that we in turn had to decide on the use of the technicians from the armed services. On my return to the province, I was advised firmly, and not by the army only, that without the help of middle management in the electricity industry, the technicians did not have the necessary experience to operate the complicated electricity system. Middle management refused point-blank to help, partly for reasons of self-preservation and partly because of their own anti-Sunningdale feelings. Nor was there any chance of getting middle managers from Britain. Stan Orme had had a word with the leader of the appropriate trade union in Britain and was given a dusty response.

I was advised of the confusion resulting from the lack of proper information on plant availability; the usual channels for information from the power stations had broken down and there was no forward planning or co-ordination. The aim of the Northern Ireland Electricity Service was, I was told, to keep the general public informed but the Board felt that to provide information on rota cuts in the way it would be provided in Great Britain in an industrial dispute would in Northern Ireland enable thugs to plan violence in the blackout areas. The information was consequently not being given.

The NIES chairman also decided, and I would be surprised if John Hume was informed, that senior directors should not appear on the media because it might seem that management were involved in the strike! The way people distanced themselves from the British throughout the stoppage was remarkable. The job of keeping the public informed was left to Hugo Patterson, the usual spokesman for the NIES and also a cricket commentator. He was a chatty man, an Ulster John Arlott, given to colourful phrases, and the role he was playing was not helpful.

My advisers also told me bluntly that because of problems about servicing generating plant, a complete shutdown was always a possibility and had been from the first day of the strike. A message from Harold Wilson asked me to have investigated the idea of anchoring a submarine in Belfast Lough to supply power, but I was advised by the army at Lisburn that for technical and security reasons any power generated could not be put ashore.

We were in fact beaten technically on all aspects of the strike, and the army also advised me that even if this were not the case, it could not guarantee to protect the power stations or pylons. The Provisional IRA had already shown the vulnerability of pylons, as I had seen for myself in the border areas, where sabotaged pylons were left lying on the ground; they could be replaced only at the risk of further bomb attacks.

When I met my Cabinet colleagues on 21 May, it was not therefore to ask to introduce technicians into the power stations but to give the facts and point out the impossibility of the task. I told them that the UWC had succeeded in enforcing a widespread stoppage of work, affecting factories, shops and services generally, and I reported on the number of road blocks and the intimidation being used. The security forces were heavily stretched and reinforcements were needed, though they would only keep the main roads free.

Despite what armchair theorists thought at the time, permanently to remove the road blocks that had been erected all over the province was impossible. Nor was it useful to compare, as Ted Heath did later, the role of the army in 1974 with that at the time of Operation Motorman: the UWC barricades were not localised and the circumstances now were quite different. At the beginning of the second week of the strike, we mounted a major effort to persuade the UDA to remove the barricades in West Belfast; it was more difficult in East Belfast, where human chains were formed across the roads. On one day a total of 2,000 men – 1,500 troops plus members of the RUC – was needed to keep the five main roads into Belfast open, and although these roads were kept open for most of the strike, it would obviously have taken many more men than could be made available to remove all the existing road blocks.

At the Cabinet sub-committee meeting I pointed out the political motive of the stoppage and the lack of influence of the trade unions. The leaders of the Northern Irish Committee of the Irish Congress of Trade Unions had continually spoken out publicly against the strike and had organised meetings of shop stewards to influence union members. The loyalist working class had not responded and the return-to-work march in Belfast led by Len Murray, General Secretary of the TUC, was an abject failure.

Len had come at the invitation of the NICICTU and not the government. We advised him of the danger he would be facing despite the battalion of soldiers that would be deployed, but bravely he decided to continue. He had strong feelings about the UWC: 'They are a body created to pursue a sectarian policy which is rejected by the trade union movement generally and their objectives and activities have no connection with the protection of working people or the promotion of their common interest.' That policy was, however, what the loyalist working class wanted, and they were supported by Protestants who normally would have rejected both the UWC and the UDA. Now they were 'our boys' defending the majority against the sell-out of Sunningdale.

This attitude was made clear to me in face-to-face meetings. On 22

May, for example, Sandy Scott, the leader of the boilermakers in Harland and Wolff, brought with him to London the Rev John Stewart and the Rev Derek McKalvey from loyalist areas of Belfast, and we had a long discussion about the situation. They put forward interesting ideas of constitutional conferences but basically they wanted me to talk with the UWC. In UK terms they were my kind of people, from a trade union, political and nonconformist point of view, but their proposals amounted to giving in on the existing constitutional position. I firmly told them, 'No', as I did an NILP delegation which came to put the same view.

Nor was it just the trade unionists who were in no mood to stand firm against the strikers. A delegation from the CBI, led by Sir Robin Kinahan, asked me to open discussions with them, after telling me that industry was being used as a hostage for the British government and that there was absolutely no chance that the strikers would give in. Farmers also demonstrated against me, and used their tractors to form road blocks in the province. Both the leaders of the farmers and the CBI regularly visited the Hawthornden Road strike headquarters to obtain passes and visas, though neither group would have responded in this way to an industrial dispute in Great Britain.

I recall going back to the Culloden Hotel very late one evening and as we walked through the lounge full of middle-class late-night drinkers, the cry of 'traitors' came in unison. It was not an example of the bad manners sometimes encountered by Labour ministers in Great Britain. It was a spontaneous response of anger: we, the Brits, were the outsiders, always ready to sell good loyalists down that mythical river into the Catholic South.

What was uniting all these diverse social and economic groups of loyalists in the province, from the paramilitaries to the CBI and the NILP, from the industrial workers to farmers and middle-class professionals, was opposition to Sunningdale. When it was seen that I was not prepared to capitulate on the agreement, the cement of Ulster nationalism hardened.

It was against this background that the Executive talks on Sunningdale and the phasing of the Council of Ireland had still been going on and at last, on 22 May, a new scheme was agreed. In essence it was for a first phase of a council of ministers from North and South acting only in complete unanimity on economic and social matters and on human rights and policing – which was as agreed at Sunningdale. However, the second phase, in which the council would have far greater powers, would only be implemented after a test of opinion at the Assembly election of 1977–78. The key words in the preamble to the proposal were:

> The Executive recognises the difficulty of securing general public support for the new constitutional arrangements in a situation of continuing violence; and it is for precisely that reason that those opposed to such arrangements continue to use violence. While there can be no instant solution to this problem, it is appreciated that in the long term the new arrangements are bound to be judged by the contribution which they make to peace and stability.

It was one thing for the SDLP leaders to agree to a revision of the Council of Ireland but a serious disagreement arose about it with their Assembly Party. At 2.15 pm on the day of the announcement, Gerry Fitt came down to the Castle and asked Stan Orme to go up to the Parliament buildings where the SDLP Assembly Party had voted eleven to eight against accepting the changes agreed by the working party. I reminded Gerry that the Council of Ireland was a matter for the Executive and the government of the South. The UK government could not be involved and had played no part in the secret discussions. Stan had no status except the high respect in which he was held by the SDLP and if personally he could help, he would attend. It was on this basis that he went up to the meeting.

Much of the discussion, it was reported to me afterwards, was related to the UK government action, or lack of it, against the UWC strike. On this Stan asked the Party not to bring the Executive down by rejecting the proposals, not to do the UWC job for it. A number of Assemblymen complained that the British government was forcing the SDLP to make a decision while the strike was on. A decision was not necessary, it was further argued, because the issue of Sunningdale was not related to the strike! Others argued that it would ruin the SDLP electorally!

Stan took pains to emphasise that the UK government had taken no active part in the Executive's negotiations. It was entirely a matter for them. John Hume said that it was Brian Faulkner's Party which had indicated that it could go no further without reaching some agreement on Sunningdale. This was the main issue and Gerry Fitt took it further when he asked what would happen if the Executive fell. Stan replied that he could not forecast what decision the British government would come to in this situation. It would be a matter for the Cabinet, but he doubted whether it would be possible to begin negotiations for another power-sharing Executive. He appealed to them to reconsider the whole matter in the light of the current situation and not to do anything which might precipitate the downfall of the Executive and give a victory to the UWC.

When he left the meeting the SDLP had a further discussion and voted again on the issue. First by fourteen votes to five, then unanimously, they agreed to the phasing of the Council of Ireland. If it had been known before 14 May when the vote on Sunningdale was at last taken that an amendment to the Council was under discussion, it may have made a difference. Now it was all too late. The Assembly decision looked like a victory for the UWC and now they wanted not a mere change to the Council of Ireland but fresh elections. The Westminster government would certainly have amended the Council of Ireland proposals earlier, and the Executive in general and the SDLP in particular must bear the major blame for that prime error.

The Irish government had leant on the SDLP to make the concession that they finally did, and it was perhaps for this reason that on 23 May the Taoiseach wrote to Harold Wilson. Garret Fitzgerald had already telephoned me on a number of occasions, concerned about a spillover of the troubles into the Republic, particularly after the terrible loyalist car bombings in Dublin and Monaghan on 17 May, when twenty-seven people were killed. Liam Cosgrave's personal message to Harold was mainly about our policy for dealing with the strike. His support for the phasing of the Council of Ireland, he recalled, had been motivated primarily by the importance of ensuring the survival of power sharing. He complained that the British government had not yet taken the necessary action to deal 'effectively' with the strike, and went on to ask that the government take immediate action with whatever forces prove necessary.

I had long believed that Dublin did not fully comprehend the true nature of the situation in the North, but this letter took the breath away. What, I wondered, would a Dublin government ever do with the Protestant community in general and the working class in particular if its long-term aim for a united Ireland was ever realised? Use the army to keep East Belfast down? The Irish government was also being hoisted with its own petard, for in the South successive governments had persisted in regarding the activities of the IRA as political and on the same terms the present actions of the UWC and their paramilitary supporters were political. The difference was that we in the British government would have acted against the power strike if we possibly could have.

Whatever the Assembly decision on 22 May, the mood of the community remained as hard as ever and our very position in the province was in question. I had personally been warned of an assassination attempt, and Stan Orme, Jack Donaldson and I, with our small Northern Ireland Office British staff, found it difficult to travel the roads. We had tried 'choppering' from the Culloden Hotel but working from there at night in the inadequate quarters had been proving more difficult than ever and we therefore decided to camp in the Speaker's House at Stormont. The conditions were elementary – camp beds, tinned food – and the atmosphere was reminiscent of periods in my war service. We were isolated, working long hours, and I do not think Westminster realised how difficult that time was for us. The bright spot was the loyalty of the small group of Northern Ireland civil servants, who worked hard and always got through to the Castle. We were in close contact, too, with Brian Faulkner, Gerry Fitt and John Hume through the emergency committee and it was clear that the authority of the Executive was cracking.

Every report we received showed the deteriorating situation, and the problem of fuel oil was particularly on our minds. The army had ensured its own supplies and made sufficient available to the police and the Post Office. I was informed that the BBC on their own initiative was obtaining supplies from the Republic! On Wednesday 22 May, John Hume brought out for discussion in the Executive a fuel oil plan left over from an old industrial dispute. It would provide supplies from selected garages but on a limited scale. We discussed it in detail on 23 May and I informed Harold because its implementation would involve the army. He decided that I should bring the three leaders of the Executive over to Chequers the following day so that he could listen to their views. He would be accompanied by the Secretary of State for Defence and the Attorney General.

At the meeting Brian Faulkner was clear that effective administration was in the hands of the strikers. He did not want me to talk with the UWC, and he was still of the view that if the UK government asserted its control, support for the strike would decline. Gerry Fitt also believed that in the face of effective action by the government, the strikers would back down, and he criticised the BBC for their pro-loyalist policy and the RUC for lack of arrests of those organising the road blocks.

Gerry was by no means alone in complaining about the BBC. I had no doubt that the UWC had been helped all along by the BBC's treatment of the strike as an industrial dispute and not a political stoppage. Individual members of the UWC had become overnight the stars of television and radio. Complaints had poured in from Brian Faulkner and the Executive members in particular, and from the SDLP and minority population in general. Stan Orme considered that the BBC acted as 'quislings', and I later learned that the Irish government had also reacted strongly to the BBC's policy, though that is perhaps understandable given its own policy of 'control' of RTE.

After the strike Gerry vented his feelings in the House of Commons:

> Why did the BBC, a national institution, allow itself to be used during the

> whole course of the strike by those engaged in disruption? I was amazed that an announcer said during a broadcast in Northern Ireland, 'I have just received word from the Ulster Workers' Council that if you go to such-and-such an address or ring a certain telephone number, you will get a pass which will enable you to go to a garage and obtain petrol'. That was a national institution acting as official spokesman for those who were engaged in the stoppage.

His conclusion was that 'with the BBC and the newspapers acting for those behind the strike, it is no wonder the vast majority of people in Northern Ireland began to think, "They're winning. We had better get on their side."'

Dick Francis, the BBC Controller during the strike, stated in a lecture given in February 1977 on his broadcasting experience in Northern Ireland that 'in seeking to report objectively, our task was not made easier by the fact that, throughout, the self-appointed UWC called the political tune and that, for long periods, the Northern Ireland Office and the Executive seemed to be powerless and speechless'. He was right. The UWC did call the political tune and our information organisation was weak. There was a lack of co-ordination between the RUC, the army and the Executive, and in particular a lack of co-ordination with the Northern Ireland Electricity Service. It was part of an overall lack of planning and thought about the consequences of a political stoppage in Northern Ireland in the months and years before. However, none of that excuses the BBC.

Dick Francis went on in his lecture to reiterate the BBC philosophy of impartiality, claiming that once it was clear that the strike was political, it would have been unthinkable to change the 'editorial posture' unless the strike had been declared illegal. That sort of legislative action was not possible but, even so, it should not have needed legislation to make the BBC face up to reality. The strike was a political action and the BBC was impartial in a way that materially helped the UWC.

At the Chequers meeting Gerry Fitt also raised the question of obtaining electricity supplies from Coolkeeragh power station, which enabled me to refer to the disagreements between the general manager of the Northern Ireland Electricity Service and John Hume. Conflicting advice, I pointed out, made decision taking more difficult but technical arguments must be paramount.

Oliver Napier talked about the next steps to be taken by the UWC, which would probably be into food distribution. He was gloomier about the future than he had been to me at the beginning of the strike. Brian, asked for his views on the loyalty of the RUC and UDR, thought that the RUC would remain loyal but that their instinct was always to avoid confrontation. He was confident of the UDR east of the Bann.

We then discussed fully the plan to take over fuel oil distribution. It would be an Executive matter and an order would have to be made under the proclamation I had issued. The army would secure the oil installations, escort the road tankers and protect the distribution points. Derry would be supplied by road with chemicals for gas production and oil would be supplied by small sea tankers.

I had told Harold beforehand that I wanted to implement the plan even though its results would be very limited, because without this action on our part the Executive would fall and the blame be put on us. In fact it was in far greater danger of falling for lack of Unionist support for Brian Faulkner, but that was an Ulster matter. In the discussion it was apparent that the Executive members were equally keen to act, and Harold agreed to the plan but pointed out that no commitment could be made until it had been put to our colleagues in Cabinet. We would be meeting that evening, when we would also discuss the broadcast that the Executive had asked the Prime Minister to make.

A statement was agreed and issued to the press, reaffirming that 'constitutional and political developments in the UK as a whole were, and would remain, the responsibility of the government and Parliament of the United Kingdom, and also so far as Northern Ireland was concerned, of the elected Assembly and the lawfully constituted Executive'. There would be no negotiations with the UWC, and power sharing remained 'the only basis for the peace, order and good government of Northern Ireland'. The government also welcomed the announcement of 22 May about the phasing of the Council of Ireland. No mention was of course made of the fuel oil plan but further steps were implied by the reference to a Cabinet meeting called for the evening, at which the Prime Minister and I would report on the situation in Northern Ireland and after which 'the Secretary of State will return to Belfast and will be in immediate touch with Mr Faulkner about the decisions taken by the Cabinet'.

Harold began his report of the Chequers meeting to the Cabinet by giving the background to the Executive's fuel oil proposal. He pointed out our lack of control on the ground and the attempt by extremists to establish an unacceptable 'neo-fascist' government – a description used by Gerry Fitt. The extremists would probably seek to avoid a confrontation with the troops but nevertheless, if some essential services were restored, there would no doubt be an attempt to disrupt others. I held strongly that if no action was taken of the sort now recommended, the Executive would collapse over the weekend, though I emphasised what I had told Harold, that this might happen whatever steps we took.

There was no question of asking the army to take over the province, which would anyway require unacceptable numbers of troops and could not succeed. What we were seeking was some action to show moderate opinion that the government and the Executive had the will to govern and were capable of influencing events, something to retain their credibility. The contingency plans for which the Executive sought agreement could be implemented quickly and did not commit us to subsequent action in the power stations. I was firmly against the latter. A few of the army technicians who were standing by might be needed as a last resort to help with the growing water drainage problem resulting from the lack of electrically driven pumping, but I neither wanted, nor sought, permission to use them to take over the power stations.

There had never been any disagreement with the army over this or over the numbers of men required for general security duties or the time of their arrival, despite later rumours to the contrary, and it was clear at the Cabinet meeting, as it had been earlier in Belfast, that the army was always concerned about the extent to which it was right to use troops for civilian tasks when life and limb were not directly threatened. The idea that the forces are always clamouring to take on industrial disputes, let alone take over the country, is a figment of the imagination of fringe left-wing elements and fringe right-wing soldiers too much influenced by events in the colonies.

Roy Mason explained that the fuel oil plan would need extra troops to drive tankers and protect them while in transit, and emphasised that we were seeking only to supply the same amount of petrol as now being distributed by the UWC. Any more would be too much of a task given the problem of driving tankers on routes not known to the drivers. It was on this limited basis that my Cabinet colleagues authorised the action.

In order to activate the plan, Roy was to instruct the GOC Northern Ireland. The handling was left to the Prime Minister and ministers concerned, who would take decisions 'within the limits of policy that we had discussed'. We were also instructed to look at the food situation in Catholic areas in case the need arose to take steps, though in fact these areas were not faring too badly – Derry was near the border and the UWC had made sure of petrol supplies to West Belfast.

In the wide-ranging discussion on the strike at the Cabinet meeting, I reported that the stranglehold of the strikers was affecting the telephone system and that many operators could not be trusted. I warned of similar problems in the reserve forces in some parts of the province. After the strike was over, an indication of this problem was that six members of the UDR were dismissed: they had worked with the UWC. There were rumours that some members of the RUC were also supporting the strike, though nothing was ever officially reported to me. It was, however, certain that the police and their reserves came out of the majority community which supported the stoppage. In any case the RUC was not structured or organised for movement around the province and it simply could not act quickly enough. Neither it nor anyone else had contingency plans for dealing with the sort of political/industrial stoppage that had been threatened many times since 1972.

There were other problems facing us, I told my colleagues, such as the distinct possibility that the flying control and safety staff at Aldergrove would walk out. The concern was not so much over civilian flights but how a walk-out would affect the RAF's role in flying extra men and supplies into the province. I had asked for steps to be taken to preserve this link with the outside world or, more accurately, with another part of the UK.

At the end of the meeting, we considered contingencies should the situation further deteriorate. The Chancellor of the Exchequer was to look into the worsening financial position of Harland and Wolff in the context of economic sanctions. This decision reflected the strong feelings in the Cabinet against the UWC and its supporters, who rejected Westminster but wanted its money. As far as I was concerned, sanctions could wait till another day – they could not possibly be imposed without causing repercussions that would far outweigh the original action. It was the oil plan that mattered.

I returned to Belfast and late that night telephoned Brian Faulkner to tell him that everything was agreed. On the Saturday morning I called one of the regular security meetings, at which the GOC Frank King, the Chief Constable, the Commander Land Forces, Stan Orme and Jack Donaldson reported to Frank Cooper and me on events in the province since we had been away. There had been a particularly nasty example of intimidation in Ballymena, where Catholics had been murdered – murders which were dismissed by loyalist paramilitaries as mistakes resulting from 'disobedience'. I was assured that every possible charge would be brought against the men responsible, who were being looked for in the Rathcoole area along the northern shore of Belfast Lough. The army reported that the Provisionals were presently keeping a low profile. I was surprised to hear that they had approached one army battalion in Belfast to suggest a ceasefire until the end of the UWC strike. Reports by the army and the police stated that there were few road blocks despite alarmist BBC broadcasts, although there were some felled-tree booby traps on roads in Armagh, Tyrone and Fermanagh. Intimidation against the power stations was worrying but it was felt that the petrol shortage would work to the government's advantage. It was the old story of alienation of the general public.

The carnival air in Belfast was described. There was no shortage of food and petrol on sale, although it was reported that the lack of rubbish collections could prove a problem and because of the difficulty in banking money, too much cash was being held in shops and offices, which made armed robbery even easier. The UWC had taken over fifty-six petrol stations, which had proved hard to counteract because it had been done with the agreement of the employers! After further discussion of fuel supplies, officials were instructed to look into the particular problem of supplying petrol to the small fishing ports in County Down.

I raised again the question of air control at the civil airport at Aldergrove and the GOC told me that the RAF was to provide air controllers, fire-tenders and personnel searchers. I also brought up the issue of providing information for the media, since Dick Francis had come to see me shortly before to discuss the need for us to provide the BBC with more government information. I was assured that the BBC was putting out government bulletins when they were received and had no intention of relaying the instructions of the UWC over the air or giving their telephone numbers to the public. We had our problems on information; perhaps the BBC had theirs about people not carrying out instructions from above.

Following the meeting, Stan, Frank Cooper and I discussed the fuel plan with the GOC and CLF, who had been notified of the Cabinet decision by phone the previous evening. The important issue was timing, and we were strongly advised to implement the plan on Sunday night/early Monday morning. One reason for making it then rather than that evening was that the UWC was expecting something to happen on Saturday night, when it was anyway planned to pick up loyalist paramilitaries in the Rathcoole area. Plans for this pick-up were not to be given to the RUC and the army would have to be concentrated in Rathcoole, where we had to allow for the possibility of the paramilitaries being prompted to take on the army.

I agreed that it was not absolutely necessary to act that evening and although the Prime Minister's broadcast was due then and would create an expectation of action in the media, it was decided without questioning to implement the fuel oil plan on Sunday evening, 26 May. It was implicit that the next morning we would reassess the actual methods to be used in the light of Harold's speech and the action in Rathcoole.

I informed Harold of our decision, with which he was in full agreement. He decided that he would proceed with his broadcast as scheduled, given the expectant mood in the province and the concern of the people in Britain at events in Northern Ireland. I saw an early draft of his speech on Saturday afternoon and showed it to Brian

Faulkner. Afterwards I telephoned Harold with some suggested alterations, most of which he accepted although the offending word 'spongers' remained. Understandably, this was badly received by all shades of Unionist opinion, from the business establishment to the working class. I suspect that the No 10 press advisers argued strongly for the word's inclusion, but it was certainly Harold that determined it. He had, after all, over the years been forthright about how offensive he found the word loyalist.

The constraints under which we were all working were very clearly brought out in a letter which I received from the GOC on the Sunday morning. This was written before the Chequers meeting where we had agreed to implement the fuel oil plan and it had therefore been overtaken by the Cabinet decision but it reinforced the advice, which we had received consistently from the Ministry of Defence, that any attempt to use the army to run essential services under the conditions then prevailing would almost certainly make the situation worse, given the general hostility of a substantial section of the population. It followed that the army should only be used when services had broken down completely, when they could be seen in a humane and rescuing role. As the GOC pointed out, the province was calm, and functioning by courtesy of the strikers; power was sufficient for vital services; petrol and oil, through army auspices, were reaching vital users; gas production had ceased in Derry but otherwise the nearness of the Republic made the city well placed.

I accepted his point as it applied to a general take-over. We had never been in any doubt that at the best of times the army simply did not have the capability, given the technologies concerned, to keep all the services going simultaneously, and to attempt to do so against the background of civil unrest of the kind we were then seeing was, frankly, unthinkable. The General need not have worried that he would be asked to do the impossible. From the beginning the purpose of our contingency planning was that set out in the Northern Ireland Office report on the strike at the end of May. This pointed out that, while the government had brought extra troops and technicians to Northern Ireland, it had not the intention, nor had it the means, to move in to the supply of essential services. Indeed, the report had gone further when it emphasised that all the papers consulted had shown that the government had realised that such intervention could lead to armed conflict with the strikers and to industrial sabotage of power stations and other installations. A grandiose scheme had never been on the cards.

Interesting though the General's letter was, it could not at this stage affect the decision made on the fuel oil scheme, but on the Sunday morning, before I finally authorised action, I talked to Frank King at the Castle. He wanted me to take into account that after the successful Rathcoole pick-up the night before, the local UDA and UVF units were raring to have a go at the army. I later learned that Craig had gone to persuade them not to over-react, for the politicians were convinced that the existing strike action was going to succeed, and soon. At the time, however, it seemed possible that the paramilitaries would act, if only to show what 'spongers' could do. Despite this and the generally gloomy situation that faced us in governing the province, I still wanted to proceed with the plan.

That morning the UWC had announced a new oil distribution plan for the province which was exactly the same as the one that John Hume and the Department of Commerce was ready to implement. It had been leaked by supporters of the UWC within the Department. This problem had been made equally clear the previous Wednesday, when the Northern Ireland Electricity Service had announced that if no supplies of hydrogen and propane gas were forthcoming, the Ballylumford power station would have to close – and at once the necessary supplies had been made available. Quite simply, the services for which the Department of Commerce was supposed to be responsible were now under UWC control. Indeed, that Sunday morning the UWC had decided that it would close all electricity power supplies if the fuel oil plan was implemented.

However, it was not any of this that convinced me that I should consult with the Prime Minister, but the news that Brian Faulkner was near the point of resignation. When I saw him after Harold's broadcast he was downcast and though his own broadcast to the province, to be made on Sunday evening, must have been on his mind, his mood was due to more than that. There had been further defections from his Party and the behaviour of some Executive members showed a disunited team. His mood reinforced my doubts that the Executive would last until Sunday evening. The position was very serious: it meant that the Executive was all but over and consequently also the strike.

Given the doubts about telephone security, a normal discussion by phone to the Scillies, where Harold was staying, was out of the question, and the special security link did not allow for a proper discussion. Hence I arranged to fly to Culdrose in Cornwall where Harold would helicopter in to meet me. I felt it important for my journey not be publicised and asked Frank King to accompany me in my helicopter as far as Aldergrove so that it would look at the Castle as if I was going back with him to Lisburn. However, when I arrived at Culdrose after a nostalgic flight over the valleys of South Wales where I was nurtured, it was to find that my trip had already been announced on BBC news! Was the leak from prying eyes at the Castle or from Aldergrove? Or was it from other sources?

There was no air of crisis when I briefed Harold on developments since our Friday meeting and particularly on the intention of the UWC regarding oil and power. I told him that the Executive was even more seriously at risk. Roy Bradford at least was ready to resign and some SDLP members were not firm, particularly Paddy Devlin, who had given me and then retracted a letter of resignation, though I was sure that Gerry Fitt would stand fast. The Executive would either break that day, before the fuel oil plan was carried out, or the day after.

I showed Harold Frank King's letter and he accepted its good sense. He pointed out, however, that its conclusions were based on the assumption that the existing system of government would continue. This he considered unrealistic and agreed with me that the Executive would break. We should be considering a return to direct rule.

Before we had time to discuss the implementation of the oil plan in detail, a long flash-telegram arrived from the Northern Ireland Office in Belfast. It advised that because of the UWC's pre-knowledge of the plan and the need that day to alert junior civil servants, which would lead to further leaks, the result of going ahead with the plan would be chaotic. We did not have enough soldiers to cover all eventualities, and we were heading for public humiliation. We should therefore announce that we were not going to interfere in the strike 'other than to save life or limb' and instead were going to step up our law and order measures. There was also a message from Stan Orme, who had discussed the telegram with Frank Cooper and, as the senior minister present in the province, insisted that his contrary view be brought to my notice. He firmly disagreed.

The advice had to be taken very seriously, I told Harold, but despite it and all the other developments, I still wanted to go ahead. Harold was of the same view. He commented that the Northern Ireland Office administrative view was no doubt correct but, as with the GOC's letter, there was a wider context to be considered. Whatever we did, the Executive would almost certainly fall, but it must not fall because of indecision on our part. The Cabinet had decided in favour of the fuel oil plan; it would require overwhelming arguments to go against it. There were none. The Cabinet decision would be carried out.

As we talked on the tarmac at Culdrose about to board our respective flights, Harold advised me to prepare for direct rule and questioned me on the necessary House of Commons procedure. I returned to Belfast and the fuel plan went into operation that night.

Early on Monday morning, Frank King reported that the plan had been successful in Belfast. It was now a question of waiting. I made a statement for the early radio news:

> I have this morning authorised British troops to take control of the distribution of petroleum products to essential users in the province. This action, which has now taken place, is in fulfilment of the Prime Minister's undertaking on behalf of the government to maintain essential services. It has become necessary in the face of continuing interference with the normal distribution arrangements, backed by violence and the threat of violence.
>
> No parliamentary democracy, accepting as it must the rule of law and order, can accept that a group of men self-appointed and answerable to no one should decide when and where and to whom the essentials of life shall be distributed within a part of that democracy. The troops will be withdrawn immediately on the resumption of normal services.
>
> The army, together with the RUC, will implement the direction of the lawfully constituted government on the bulk distribution of petroleum products and their allocation to essential users who at first will have to be strictly limited in number. Detailed arrangements will be made public separately by the Department of Commerce. I have also instructed the Chief Constable and the General Officer Commanding to take all measures they consider necessary to maintain law and order.

Gerry Fitt rang me very early to say that the Antrim Road had been full of vehicles from Girdwood Barracks since 5 am and that his people were buzzing at what was going on. I told him that the oil installations had been occupied without any trouble, though I refrained from mentioning that the oil companies had not been very helpful at this, any more than at any other, time during the strike.

The petrol stations – seven in Belfast, two in Derry and the rest scattered around the province – were to be open from 11 am to 3 pm. They had been quickly surrounded by barbed wire and protected by troops. The petrol and oil were to be issued by civilians of the Department of Commerce and six thousand essential users were the only people to be served. We had realised that this restricted distribution would cause trouble, particularly as many of those who had wanted action, including the CBI, were not aware of the limits of our capability.

I had appealed in my statement for those involved in the strike to consider carefully how they reacted to events. 'Pull back from the brink now. Let us all work together for the good of Northern Ireland and break away from the theme of Irish history – violence. Give peace a chance.' Some hope, was my real feeling: such words were outside the vocabulary of the UWC and their friends.

It was not long before we heard their public response – a call for an intensification of the strike. It would be only a short time before the power stations started their final run-down, and the problem of sewerage would grow steadily worse. The permanent secretaries of the Northern Ireland Departments asked to see Brian Faulkner and painted a sombre picture of the economic and social position. They were, I think, right to do so. I have never accepted the view of some SDLP politicians that their behaviour was somehow traitorous. The job of senior civil servants is to present the facts as they see them and to give advice. The job of the politician is then to make up his or her mind. There are times when this decision taking is extremely difficult, far harder than obtaining applause at a Party conference or making a brilliant speech in the House of Commons, and far harder than writing a newspaper editorial.

Any disloyalty at that time came from politicians themselves or from a few Northern Ireland civil servants further down the line. The major policy and security papers were always handled perfectly correctly and I was always served well. Nearly all those working directly under me were in any case not part of the Ulster scene, but the few from Northern Ireland were no exception in the trusted team.

One would not have thought from the newspaper reports on the events of Sunday 26 May that the only disagreement that there had been between me and my advisers was over the fuel oil plan. For example, Robert Fisk of *The Times* records in his book *The Point of No Return* that on the Sunday 'the army formally tells Rees they cannot operate power stations on their own'. There had not been a proposal to man the power stations, which I was firmly against anyway, but I do not believe that Robert Fisk made it up.

The talk about rows with the army over that weekend came from Lisburn, from those in the Army Information Service with press contacts, and not from the army staff who knew the facts. At a Cabinet meeting in London a few days after the strike ended, Denis Healey for one was very angry at the leaks and their source – as a former Secretary of State he knew what he was talking about.

At lunchtime on Monday the 27th Gerry Fitt spoke in an RTE radio interview in favour of the 'courageous' action of the British army and explained that, as much as he would have liked to see Sunningdale fully implemented from 1 January, he with the SDLP had to face up to the realities in the province, including the possibility of a holocaust. They were brave words, typical of Gerry, but he was wrong in believing that the power-sharing Executive was now far more secure than it had been the previous week.

Dr Paisley, on the same programme, said that the army had come in at the request of the SDLP – it was always Paisley's line to put the Catholic party in a unique position. More important than this usual posturing was his conclusion that if the Executive fell, the strikers would have won their point and there would be a return to direct rule. In this event I was confident that the politicians would jump off the strike bandwagon and there would be no need to tell the strikers to go back to work.

As an indication of what was happening amongst Brian Faulkner's Assembly followers, the words of a Mr Nelson Elder on the programme were significant. He said that he could no longer support the Executive, indeed he had already resigned from the Party, and he was calling for a special meeting of the Assembly group to put down a motion deploring the use of troops. Clearly, Brian had every reason to have been considering resignation for the last few days.

On Monday afternoon the Executive met and, presented with the facts of the deteriorating situation, Brian recommended that an independent arbitrator be brought in to find a way out of the impasse. In his memoirs, he wrote, 'It was generally agreed that some way should be found to communicate with the strikers but it was emphasised that care must be taken to ensure that the Executive did not seem to be weakening the position of the Secretary of State nor paving the way for the IRA to press successfully for talks with the Executive.' In fact no final decision was to be taken until the following day, for understandably the SDLP members present did not wish to be involved in the climb down.

Late that same afternoon Glen Barr announced the UWC plans in response to the fuel oil operation. On Tuesday Ballylumford power station was to close down and electricity, gas, milk, bread and animal feedstuff would become the responsibility of the British army. Also, undertakers – i.e. Protestant undertakers – would be asked not to bury the dead! He said that there would be no confrontation with British troops, although Jim Smyth complained that in Dundonald soldiers had called those blocking the streets 'bastards'.

In the evening Brian Faulkner came to see me. As I wrote in my diary, 'I knew that the Permanent Under-Secretaries had been to see him, that the industrialists were giving in – what a yellow-livered lot they are – and that the farmers were unwilling to continue. It had to be faced that the community were in favour of what the Ulster Workers' Council was doing. Ulster nationalism was growing.' He told me sadly that he was disappointed with some members of his Executive: Roy Bradford was over in England for the weekend; Paddy Devlin and Ivan Cooper of the SDLP had gone to Dublin, claiming that they had been prevented by a hostile crowd down near the border from returning to

Belfast – a point disputed by the RUC; and his own Assembly supporters were weakening in the face of local opinion. He was, he said, about to resign. I realised, as he did, that this was inevitable and even though I again rejected his proposal of a mediator – the Archbishop of Canterbury or Lord Grey – I asked him not to take the decision until the morning.

Afterwards I saw John Hume and, without saying anything about Brian, I asked him what was going on. He replied that Brian Faulkner was absolutely firm, which was clearly not the case. That evening I also had a report from some of my staff who had made contact with members of a deproscribed paramilitary organisation: the mood in the UWC was 'no surrender'.

The next morning, the 28th, the economic and social situation was reported as much worse. The DHSS, under the control of the Executive, was opening additional offices to pay the increasing numbers on social security! Electricity cuts were to be longer than ever before – up to eighteen hours in twenty-four. Throughout the day the front route into Stormont was blocked by a tractor demonstration by farmers, who were addressed by Glen Barr, John Taylor and Ian Paisley. 'Rees must talk with the UWC' was a favourite placard.

Brian Faulkner met his back-benchers and was told that their support for him would end unless a dialogue with the strikers was begun. Later in the morning the Executive met and the Unionists with the support of the Alliance Party, and against the wishes of Gerry Fitt, John Hume and Austin Currie, decided that I should be informed that negotiations should begin between the government and the UWC, through a mediator.

Brian asked for a formal meeting with me and reported the Executive's decision. He was not prepared, he informed me, to accept responsibility for seeing his beloved Northern Ireland gradually grinding to a halt. Support from his own people had fallen away. He again put the case for a mediator and said that unless I would accept this, he was going to resign and with him the other Unionists. The others could speak for themselves. He finally advised me to initiate negotiations amongst the parties to see if power sharing could be preserved on some other basis.

I could not accept this and I formally accepted his resignation. Brian said that he would make clear to his administration that they should take their own decisions, which was a curious way of putting it since with the Chief Executive gone the Executive was finished as far as I was concerned. I explained that I would not negotiate with the UWC because the point at issue was the whole future of the constitutional framework in Northern Ireland and particularly power sharing and Sunningdale.

In the circumstances I would first report to the Prime Minister and my Cabinet colleagues, and it would then be necessary to have consultations and discussions in the province under the provisions of the Constitution Act.

It was a very emotional occasion, coming at the end of a fortnight of great stress. Brian wanted me to know that he personally had no grudge against the British government and that I had been correct and honourable in all my dealings with him. In going he had no complaints of any kind. I willingly returned the sentiments. I told him that he had been extremely honourable throughout and that I admired his courage. British governments had expected too much of him: he had been obliged to go into a political no man's land with his troops left far behind.

Stan Orme, whom I had asked to come to this final meeting, expressed his deep personal and political sadness at the ending of the power-sharing experiment. He told Brian how moved he had been by the manner in which Brian had finally come to the conclusion that the odds against him were too great. I shared his feelings: as much as the writing had been on the wall from the veto of the loyalists, we had believed in the changes made since 1972.

Brian went back to Stormont to meet his colleagues. The SDLP and Alliance 'heads of departments' decided not to resign, but they were ignoring reality – as I told them when they came to see me. Gerry Fitt was playing a game that the SDLP was still in office, but the situation was too serious for pretence. I decided that the constitutional position needed to be clarified and at 2 pm that day I issued a statement that I had accepted the resignation of Brian Faulkner, Chief Executive Minister, together with the resignations of Unionist members in the Northern Ireland administration; that under the terms of the Constitution Act 1973 'there is now no statutory basis for the Northern Ireland Executive'; and that 'arrangements exist for the continued government of Northern Ireland in accordance with the Northern Ireland Constitution Act. In particular the Secretary of State remains responsible for the preservation of law and order.'

Brian Faulkner spoke from the steps of Stormont, giving the reasons for his resignation. Gerry Fitt issued a statement asserting the opposition of the SDLP to negotiations and asking his supporters to stay calm. Later, after a vote, the Assembly stood adjourned.

During the afternoon differing views came from members of the Ulster Workers' Council and their political collaborators. Paisley wanted a General Election: 'Keep the English out. Keep Dublin out.' Let Ulstermen meet 'face to face' to sort out the trouble. Harry West wanted a period of direct rule. William Craig was against a broader-based Executive. Glen Barr said that the strike would continue and a statement from the UWC headquarters asserted that it was still on because the strikers' demand for new Assembly elections had not been met. However, now that the Executive had broken, I was sure that the strike was going to end and that the coalition of workers and politicians would not last. The UWC had served the politicians' purpose and was now expendable.

The Irish Cabinet met and issued a dignified statement regretting the end of a 'great experiment in co-operation'. It put the blame on a sectarian backlash against the IRA, and there was some truth in that, for many loyalists in the North do not distinguish between the IRA and the Irish government.

The Provisional IRA joined in the rash of statements with one suggesting that the Irish government should resign because its policy of supporting the British had led to a 'fascist victory' – and this from people who had been against the power-sharing Executive! Another statement came from Africa, where President Idi Amin offered himself as a mediator!

That night celebrations were held in all parts of the province, and the traditional bonfires were lit in the Unionist streets of Belfast. It said something about the support for the UWC that the next morning when Stan walked up to the Castle – we were still camping out at Stormont – he found the door locked and was met shortly afterwards by the breathless and apologetic doorkeeper, who explained that he had overslept after being up all night at the 'victory celebrations'. It was one small sign that direct rule was not going to be too difficult from the Protestant side.

I went over to Britain where at Chequers, prior to a Cabinet meeting, I discussed the next urgent steps with Harold, including the recall of Parliament. They were important steps but they were overshadowed by a statement from UWC headquarters made in the presence of Craig, Paisley and West: 'In the understanding that the British government will respond to the will of the Ulster people, as demonstrated during the constitutional stoppage, the Council have recommended a phased return to work.'

The UWC's statement also still insisted on fresh Assembly elections and, under pressure from the paramilitaries bruised by the Rathcoole pick-up, on the release of the thirty-one loyalists held under interim custody orders and on the ending of detention without trial. Nevertheless, the phasing of the return to work was announced, and oil and petrol would be normal from the following week as long as British troops were withdrawn. We made an appropriate announcement about the ending of our fuel oil scheme, and the extra troops prepared to return to Great Britain. The stoppage was over.

The UWC had won a great victory. They had succeeded because of their control over electricity supplies and the massive support from the community. Whereas in 1972 the old Stormont system had been brought down by the violence of the Provisional IRA, by the SDLP and the minority community, in 1974 the power-sharing Executive was brought down by the UWC, the United Ulster Unionist Council and the majority community. As I told the Prime Minister in a minute of 31 May, there was a feeling of tit for tat: the republicans had toppled Stormont, the loyalists had now brought down the Executive. It was one victory each.

The chances of success for power sharing in the future seemed remote and fanciful against this background. In my diary, written late at night with the words of Paisley and Craig still ringing in my ears, I was very gloomy: 'I am absolutely convinced that power sharing cannot work.' I had it in better perspective in my minute to Harold when I pointed out that from the start of our taking office, and regrettable though it might be, the probability had always been that it was only a matter of time before the Executive fell. The strike had brought it all to a head. The Westminster Election had started the process and the effect on popular opinion of the IRA bombing campaign, particularly the big bombs in the cities, had fuelled it. Support for the Faulknerites had dwindled even further. This was not to say that power sharing was wrong in principle or that it would not work, but that it would not work against this background and given some elements of the Sunningdale agreement.

With the wisdom of hindsight, it may be that the Executive could have worked if it had been given the time. It was what I had hoped. Even so, many of its members did not behave sensibly: too many of Faulkner's men wasted time in tittle-tattle against their leader; and too many of the SDLP members spent too much time in Dublin, thus reinforcing the distrust of loyalists. The adverse reaction of loyalists to the Council of Ireland might have been overcome if the SDLP in general had acted with more flexibility, and if its elected members had recognised earlier that the concept could not be proceeded with until there had been another Assembly election. By the time it was realised and accepted, it looked like a victory for UWC pressure.

Looking back at the problems facing the politicians, the emotional strain of that time must have affected all the members of the Executive and I have often wondered how a British Cabinet would have behaved under similar circumstances. Government is, however, often difficult. To be elected is one thing; to sit in an office and take decisions is another. Crises do arise and without political cement in Cabinet, or

Executive, the collapse comes sooner rather than later. If there had been Cabinet government in Northern Ireland without a Northern Ireland Office and a United Kingdom Secretary of State, the Executive would have collapsed earlier than it did.

There was also the fact that the RUC was not organised in a way that would have enabled it to respond quickly in the first days of the strike. To many of its members, the stoppage was anyway not an industrial dispute but a political one, and one that in their hearts they supported. Throughout the strike, it was the army that had been my only firm base. Whatever my feelings about the information service at Lisburn, the army had performed well during a difficult period, and had in Frank King a wise soldier in command. It had been quite frightening to know that there were leaks, that not even the telephone was secure, and I was grateful for the reassuring presence of the army.

Overall, although there may have been marginal mistakes in the handling of the Ulster workers' strike, I feel strongly that there was, and is, no way of putting down an industrial/political dispute supported by a majority in the community. The counter-insurgency methods used by the army for dealing with the Provisional IRA and other paramilitaries were not appropriate to a political strike. Those who from far away advocated the use of detention to put down the strike did not consider the numbers involved and how many Long Keshes we would have had to build. It is one thing to fight the IRA and quite another to fight a whole community.

Sunningdale had been pushed down the throats of the loyalists. It had been a London/Dublin solution that had ignored the reality of the situation in the North of Ireland and especially the lack of support there for the Faulkner Unionists. It had enabled the UUUC to rally the loyalists at the February General Election with the poster cry, 'Dublin is only a Sunningdale away', a cry that had brought success to the Ulster Workers' Council strike.

Chapter 4

PICKING UP THE PIECES

Even in the darkest days of the strike I had been thinking of the future, and my thoughts had gone further than just a return to direct rule. If in May 1974 the Whitelaw policy road was coming to an end, I would have to find something more long-term to take its place. If Sunningdale had been too orientated to London and Dublin, I would have to bring policy back to Ulster, to try to involve all the politicians there in a search for a better way of sharing power in a devolved government. This was the real lesson of the Ulster workers' strike.

On security, I would have to build on the work begun in March to reassess the role of the army and the RUC. The police must lead, not follow, and I needed to reverse the decision taken in August 1969 to put the GOC in overall charge of security. We needed more policemen and less soldiers. Changes in security policy almost meant looking into the Emergency Provisions Act and the procedures for detention. However, much as security mattered, I could not allow either the Provisional IRA or the UDA to drive me into a laager mentality so that political change took a back seat. Politics and security had to move together.

In the aftermath of the strike I realised that the chances of success were not great in either field. My mood was strongly influenced by the evidence in the province of what I termed Ulster nationalism, a term that Ted Heath took me to task about in the House of Commons. 'Surely,' he asked, 'it would be Ulster nationalism only if there were a genuine desire by both communities or by a majority of the majority community to go it alone for independence. . . . I do not see clear evidence that this was a movement for Ulster nationalism as we understand "nationalism" in any common, modern form. It was action which always used to be termed the "Protestant backlash" . . . and the term "Ulster nationalism" is a misnomer, a dangerous one.'

Protestant backlash it was, but I still stick by my use of the phrase 'Ulster nationalism', for the feeling went deeper than a backlash. The cause of the UWC had been the cause of a large proportion of the majority population. Moreover, after the strike, politicians and others in the province were talking of 'independence'. Harry West, a loyalist if ever there was one, had referred in public to breaking the link and, in the House of Commons, to the UWC as 'a body of honourable men'. And Official Unionist Assemblyman John Taylor had gone so far as to advocate 'negotiated' independence.

I was not alone in noting the feeling. Neil Ascherson wrote in the *Observer* on 2 June: 'Among all the excited visions now bursting into speech, the idea of an independent Ulster nation is the most powerful.' He called in aid not only Harry West, Bill Craig and the leaders of the UWC but also 'some of the highest officers in the Orange Order itself'. He went on: 'A people has brought down a government by showing its will on the streets: the first such event in Europe since December 1970 in Poland. The flags are out in many places, but they are no longer Union Jacks: the banners in the little brick terraces of East Belfast are the red and white flags of Ulster with the Red Hand in their centre.'

Whether or not his analogy with Poland was relevant, there was no doubt that the cry for independence was reverberating round the province at the end of the strike. I was certainly bearing it in mind as I reassessed government policy, and I hoped that they were doing likewise in Dublin, though all I knew was that the government there found my use of the term Ulster nationalism unhelpful!

From my arrival in Northern Ireland in March, I had realised that one of the weaknesses of Sunningdale was the lack of involvement of all the loyalist politicians. It would have been revealing for ministers from the Irish Republic to have met Harry West and Ian Paisley, and equally valuable for loyalists to have met Jack Lynch and his Opposition spokesmen. Such a conference might well have collapsed but there might also have been less ambitious proposals, particularly for the Council of Ireland.

The strike had also confirmed my feeling that we ought to try to bring the loyalist working class into the political arena, especially when I saw how quickly the UWC and the UDA were dropped by the politicians once the strike was over. As Ken Gibson of the UVF said in a much later interview for the *Belfast Telegraph*: 'I wouldn't touch politics again. The people made the strike successful. Afterwards there was a lot of backstabbing among politicians taking the glory, even though they had little part in it.'

In reassessing policy I also had to take into account the mood in Great Britain. The demand to pull out and let them get on with it was coming from all quarters and was far stronger now than it had ever been after Provisional IRA bombings. After all, it was the loyalists, the people who claimed to want to stay in the UK, who had completely opposed the wishes of its parliament.

I put my thoughts on the constitutional future of Northern Ireland in my minute to Harold of 31 May. The theme that had emerged in the strike and was now gathering momentum was, I told him, 'Let Ulstermen try to work it out between themselves.' How was not yet clear but it would begin with an election for a Constituent or Consultative Assembly which would seek to agree on a form of government and a constitution for the province; its proposals would then be put forward to the British government. This Northern Irish government would have to be for the whole community, though what that would mean in terms of power sharing was not clear – it would not be power sharing as set down in the present Constitution Act which gave powers to the Secretary of State to decide on its meaning. The British government would take no part in the Assembly, though I pointed out that it might well be necessary for us to lay down certain criteria for it in advance, and there would have to be a time limit for discussions. A new Act of Parliament would be necessary for all this to happen.

Behind the suggestions was the growing feeling that the British could not solve the Irish problem and it would therefore be better to let the Northern Irish have a shot at it themselves. At the end of the day the North should deal directly with the South on all-Ireland matters and not through the British as intermediaries, and a new Ulster identity to include the republicans should be created rather than continuing to foster separate 'aspirations' in both Dublin and London. I warned Harold that it would be foolish to deny the risks of such an approach. The minority population would need a lot of persuasion that it was not a means of producing a Protestant state. But we should try.

Harold agreed to my general approach and this was the direction I then recommended to my Cabinet colleagues. They reacted favourably and I therefore made it the theme of my speech to the House of Commons in the major debate on Northern Ireland of 3 June. Much of the debate was concerned with the strike which had ended the Heath/Whitelaw policy and I reported on the background events to this:

> It was always clear that soldiers, sailors and airmen could maintain only to a limited degree the services necessary for the preservation of life, and that the extent to which this was possible was in certain areas dependent upon the co-operation of management. This was not forthcoming. . . . The timing of the operation [to supply fuel oil] was determined by the need for proper army preparation, by the situation on the ground, in the power, petroleum and other industries, which was changing from hour to hour, and also by a further security operation which was carried out on the Saturday night by the army.

I explained why I had not been prepared to negotiate with the unelected UWC: 'In the same way as I refused to be bombed to the conference table by the Provisionals, so I have been adamant that a sectarian strike by so-called loyalists and backed by paramilitary forces would not force me to such a conference table.' I had no doubt of almost complete support for this view at Westminster but I reminded the House that during the strike there had been those in Northern Ireland who had wished me to negotiate, including industrialists, churchmen and establishment organisations of a variety of kinds, and also the small Northern Ireland Labour Party.

I turned to the immediate future and because of the statements made by some politicians in the province since the fall of the Executive, I made it clear that I was not attempting to set up a new Executive and that in fact the day before the Queen had been advised that the Assembly should be prorogued. What was now needed was a short breathing space to enable me to point the way forward. As I had told Harold in my minute, there is a totally new situation and we should leave ourselves the maximum room for manoeuvre, while moving as quickly as possible. I did not think that the situation was without hope but that hope would dissipate rapidly if we were inactive.

I spoke out firmly to the House against the idea of pull-out and asked those who favoured withdrawal to make clear their disapproval of this extreme view, which was worrying in terms of security because of its effects on the paramilitary forces. I was surprised when Francis Pym for the Opposition suggested that in the Labour Party there was an 'orchestration of the demand to bring our soldiers home'. If I had recalled an *Observer* article of the day before, perhaps I would not have been so surprised. The headlines had read, 'Tories fear that Wilson is heading for pull-out', and it was written over a gossipy piece that showed the parliamentary lobby at its worst. It promised that concern about Harold Wilson's 'alleged personal inclination' for pull-out would be the 'dominant preoccupation of Tory leaders in the two-day debate'.

If this false gossip about a change in Labour policy was behind Pym's speech, then it was no way to discuss an important matter in the Commons, and I later voiced my concern to Cabinet colleagues, for I thought the speech an indication that the Conservative Party leadership would not stick by us in the future. I doubt, however, that Francis could have known that Reginald Maudling would say in the Commons debate shortly afterwards: 'It is a repugnant thought to consider the withdrawal of the protection of British forces seeking to maintain law and order within any part of the United Kingdom, but there comes a time when we must consider any possibility, however repugnant.' He was against the premature withdrawal of forces, which would lead to bloodshed, but interestingly he asked:

> Are we not perhaps drawn to this conclusion that the leaders of the two communities in Northern Ireland must sit down together and work out an Ulster solution between them? This must mean that those who wield the power effectively in Northern Ireland must be involved. It is no good men conferring about a solution if they cannot deliver the goods once they have agreed. But once this Ulster solution is reached, it will not be underpinned by the rest of the United Kingdom. If it is to be a solution on the responsibility of Northern Ireland, it must be maintained on the responsibility of Northern Ireland. Neither can it pray in aid the support and protection of Westminster. If both sides come together and reach a solution, then both sides must co-operate in making certain that it works.
>
> I suggest that we must be prepared to contemplate a total change in the constitutional relationship between Northern Ireland and the rest of the United Kingdom. I stress 'the rest of the United Kingdom'. Devolution of power in these circumstances would have to become real. What the new relationship would be in detail I cannot possibly adumbrate at this moment, but I submit that it is now that we must direct our minds to the possibility of a new framework in which greater devolution of power based on agreement between the communities is fitted into a proper United Kingdom framework.

I listened carefully to this, since a move towards a power-sharing government was still very much on my mind. It was, however, easier said than done; having just lived in the province through the Ulster workers' strike I was only too aware that power sharing was not on the horizon.

Another option I spoke firmly against was the integration of Northern Ireland with the rest of the United Kingdom. The mood for integration was anyway no longer strong in Northern Ireland, but there were some Tories and a few of our Party who were favourable to the idea, even though it flew in the face of the facts of Northern Ireland, just as did its obverse – unification.

The Prime Minister opened the second day of the debate and, talking of the strike, confirmed that the specific decisions about the use of troops to distribute fuel oil and to supply gas to Derry 'were taken on the Friday evening and the timing left to those who were in immediate control'. He was thus able to deny the allegation emanating from Paisley and taken up by the press that the SDLP had forced the use of troops. Harold went on to say that the commentators were equally wrong when they had stated 'categorically in a number of reports that there had been a reversal of a ministerial decision as a result of anxieties expressed by the armed forces'. He did not mention the difference of opinion with the army on the Sunday, and neither should he have done at that time. It did not affect the decision to move in on the Sunday evening and the media reports were anyway concerned with the operation of power stations, which had not been at issue.

The Prime Minister's controversial broadcast on the Saturday night was criticised on a number of occasions during the debate and Harold, referring to his use of the word 'sponger', turned on Paisley, who was wearing a symbolic piece of sponge in his lapel. 'All the spongers in the world are not capable of washing away the things for which he has been responsible in Ulster over these past weeks, or the actions and words on which a minister of a church that is based on the doctrine of reconciliation has deliberately sought to make reconciliation between the two communities impossible.' Harold justified his use of the word in the context of his appeal to citizens and taxpayers in Great Britain 'to continue to show patience' in the face of violence, and the need to find money for the results of violence and bring jobs to the province.

Harold had eventually agreed to my request for extra money for Harland and Wolff, after an initial dusty response, and he made it clear in his Commons speech that some money would be forthcoming. It enabled Stan Orme to promise that the extra funds for the yard would not be provided on the basis of the threat that if this or that is not done, the money would be withdrawn, although 'it will have to be done on a realistic basis, bearing in mind that ministers will have to come to this House to justify any expenditure'.

The debate showed that the Commons was troubled about Northern Ireland but blame for the downfall of the Executive was not put on the government. I knew that there were many Tories who were glad to see the back of Sunningdale and overall the Opposition was not clear about exactly what it wanted to do. However, what mattered was that Parliament had given general support to the direction I proposed to take. The detailed running of Northern Ireland was back on the plate of Westminster and the Northern Ireland Office.

We had decided that for a short period Stan Orme, Jack Donaldson and myself could cope with the extra responsibilities. Under the temporary constitutional arrangements, I would retain personal charge of law and order, security and financial matters. On 11 June Stan became head of the Departments of Commerce and Manpower and of the Office of Information Services, and the following day I announced that Jack Donaldson was to be head of the Departments of Health and Social Services. Later, on 25 June, he was also made responsible for the Departments of Agriculture and Community Relations.

It was soon clear that the workload was too much and that extra ministers were required. After discussion with Harold, I was joined on 27 June by Roland Moyle, a minister at the Department of Agriculture in Whitehall, who became head of the Department of Education and the Department for the Environment, and by Don Concannon from the Whips Office as Parliamentary Under-Secretary. Roland Moyle had practical experience of Northern Ireland in 1969–70 as PPS to Jim Callaghan and as adviser to the NILP at the Darlington Conference, and he soon found his way around. Don, whom I appointed to the Department of Finance and Housing, and of Local Government and Planning, was a former Coldstream guard and a miner. He had a direct approach and his bluntness went down well in the province, where people appreciated his plain speaking.

Our constitutional position, whereby junior ministers were sworn in as members of the Executive and consequently were responsible to the Assembly, was obviously anomalous and we needed to return to the system followed after direct rule in 1972, with UK ministers headed by the Northern Ireland Secretary responsible to the Westminster Parliament. The necessary legislation for this had already been put in hand after my meeting with Harold in Cornwall shortly before the end of the strike.

There was also a need to strengthen the civil service team in the Northern Ireland Office, and a further Deputy Secretary, Frank Armstrong, was appointed to work alongside Philip Woodfield. He settled in well but the strain of long hours and travelling soon led to his illness and return to London. He was replaced by Peter England, a man of wide experience at the Ministry of Defence, whose work over the next three years was to prove invaluable, though the physical stress of the job may have contributed to his tragically early death in 1978.

It was Peter who developed the organisation that we began to plan for in early June, which was to co-ordinate the work of the various departments, including the RUC and the army, to deal with civil emergencies. No preparations had been made for such eventualities since direct rule in 1972. The emergency committee of ministers that I had set up during the stoppage had been an ad hoc arrangement and it could not work efficiently without an administrative machine to carry out policy decisions. What we now aimed for was an organisation akin to the Civil Contingencies Unit in Whitehall, and Peter would run frequent exercises from a Stormont Castle 'operations room' set up on similar lines.

Information policy and co-ordination between government departments and security authorities were matters very much on my mind after the problems we had had in the strike. The chit-chat at Lisburn apart, it was not individuals but procedures that had been at fault, and it was to deal with this that Harold and his press adviser Joe Haines suggested Michael Cudlipp, a former deputy editor of *The Times* and chief editor of the London Broadcasting Company, for the post of Consultant on Public Relations. I met him, and liked him and his approach. He was appointed on a temporary basis on 15 July and brought a fresh, outside mind to the information scene which served us well.

Another problem I faced now that we were back to direct rule, the problem that had faced Willie in 1972, was that all Northern Ireland legislation had to proceed through Parliament at Westminster. I had been concerned about this while in Opposition and was equally concerned now. We certainly could not discuss on the floor of the Commons all the legislation that formerly went through the Stormont Parliament or Assembly, although major legislation would of course have to have the full treatment.

I discussed the problem with Ted Short, the Leader of the House, who was sympathetic to change. Since we were now approaching the end of the parliamentary session, we agreed to return to the difficult issue in the autumn. Correspondence passed between us, and Ted met with the official Opposition through the usual channels and discussed the possibilities with the Unionist MPs. Gerry Fitt, the lone republican, was not much interested in the matter.

There was never complete agreement but by January 1975 Ted Short was able to announce that there would be a standing committee where the Northern Ireland orders-in-council could be discussed and a Northern Ireland Committee consisting of Northern Irish MPs, topped up with interested British members, which could meet four or five times a session to discuss Northern Irish issues. Important as these amendments were, they did not change the basic fact that Northern Irish legislation did not receive the detailed questioning that it deserved.

After the Commons debate of 3 June, I was determined to issue a White Paper by early July which would explain the legislation required for direct rule and go on to detail the more complicated legislation to provide for a Northern Ireland Convention. As background to the White Paper, I instructed that the civil servants' paper on 'options' for Northern Ireland, set in train when I first arrived in the province, should be speeded up. There was not going to be a nice elegant solution lying around like a Sunday morning editorial but the discussion of all possible options, however unlikely, would be valuable to colleagues over in Britain and the recommendations of the paper would, I felt sure, buttress my case.

The officials moved quickly and by the second week of June their paper was on my desk. One merit was immediately obvious – the stark reality of some of the options put into perspective the over-simplified solutions that were being peddled at the time by people far away from the province. This was particularly true of the option of unilateral withdrawal: the paper bluntly concluded that its implementation would be followed by a catastrophic breakdown of control in Northern Ireland accompanied by major violence.

As for a gradual withdrawal, without some form of power sharing, the hand-over would be to a loyalist government which could expect no help from the government of the South against republican violence. An independent Ulster would be in an isolated position internationally, particularly at the United Nations, and the talk by some, including at one stage William Craig, of dominion status was a pipe-dream. Among other factors, it would still leave a UK government with some responsibility, and the Commonwealth in its modern form would anyway not give its support.

The other side of the coin was also considered – a complete hand-over to the South or to some sort of condominium. The officials' view on this was that the Protestants would fight, and that the Irish government would not contemplate such a deal in any case.

So much for the easy solutions: they were there only to show their unreality. Other options, such as integration, were analysed to show the difficulty of implementation. After outlining the various forms of integration – permanent direct rule, an arrangement similar to Scotland and Wales, or a county solution – it was plainly argued that any form would be resisted by Catholics in the North and by the Republic, that the degree of Protestant support for it was far from certain, and that it would not bring the Irish problem and violence to an end. Opinion in Great Britain would be divided. It was stressed that a policy of integration ignored the unique institutions in Northern Ireland, including the existence of a separate statute book. This was an important point not always understood in Great Britain. The province was different.

An inevitable corollary of integration with the United Kingdom would be a redrawing of the boundaries of the province. This was often put forward as a means of providing a loyalist province in the North, thus enabling a devolved government to work. It was an option on its own and was looked at also. Minor adjustments to the border would do little or nothing to affect the sectarian problem and any redrawing of the boundary with the aim of removing this conflict would, in practice, mean a transfer of population. As was clear from the map that had been prepared, only one-third of the Catholic population of Northern

Ireland lived in areas contiguous with the border, where Catholics and Protestants were often roughly equal in number; another third were in West Belfast and the remaining third were scattered throughout the rest of the province. In thes, as in everything else, Northern Ireland was complicated.

Any idea that the South was interested in a permanently established Protestant rump in the north-east of the island was also misconceived. I recalled that Gerry Fitt had often demolished the idea in the House of Commons: that Belfast Catholics would want to live in a smaller, more Protestant Northern Ireland was another typically English concept. Nor was it only the Catholics who would find it unacceptable. As one prominent loyalist had once told me, any redrawing of the boundary would have to be preceded by a referendum in Donegal and Monaghan where there were many of their kith and kin. A Southern government would never co-operate on that.

In the current circumstances, redrawing the borders was out, and so too was independence – there was no government to hand over to. The only way forward in Northern Ireland was to continue to work to bring the two sides together, and after all the analysis, it was not surprising that the option the paper favoured was some form of power sharing. Despite all the difficulties involved, the paper concluded that it should not be written off, even though it was most unlikely that it could be implemented on the basis laid down in the existing Constitution Act.

A new approach was required. The paper pointed out that since the first attempt at power sharing was largely due to the persuasion of British ministers, it was unlikely that a similar approach would now succeed. At this time it might be right to encourage the various political, and perhaps non-political, groupings in Northern Ireland to see whether they could devise models of power sharing themselves. This was of course the idea of the Convention already outlined in my minute to Harold and in the Commons, and was the policy that was being put in the White Paper.

I went to discuss the options paper with Harold and told him that I totally agreed with the conclusion apart from a suggestion that if the Convention took too long, UK ministers might have to play some part. I was determined that this should be solely an Ulster Convention. We decided to circulate the paper to the Cabinet sub-committee on Northern Ireland straight away; by the time we were due to meet on 12 June I also intended to provide a paper setting out the immediate steps I proposed to take.

In the latter paper I informed my colleagues that I had been consulting party leaders in the province. 'Consulting', I conceded, was a somewhat grand expression for the informal discussions we had had, but talking in small party groups helped overcome the politicians' feelings that they were being ignored and enabled me to clarify the pattern of events while sweetening for them the bitter pill of direct rule. I had assured them that there would be elections in the province and had discussed in a general fashion the timing of them. Whatever my earlier feeling had been in favour of speed, it was clear from the talks that time was needed to ease the situation in the province, where there was an air of political confusion after the strike. The Protestant leaders as a whole were firm that they would not operate under the 1973 Constitution Act but otherwise there was no clear agreement between them. Paisley in particular wanted no 'decision' by the government until there had been fresh elections, though in what type of body those elected would then work was not clear.

I emphasised to my colleagues that the Faulkner Unionist Party was very weak, for I wanted them to realise that, unlike Willie Whitelaw, I was dealing with a quite different set of Unionist politicians. I told them that the old Unionist Party might in time reform and bring together a different grouping of political interests; that the Alliance Party hoped to benefit from the disarray of the pro-Assembly Unionists; and that the SDLP would want a great deal of encouragement if they were to re-enter the arena in a constructive mood. I added that they were concerned about detention, that some were taking a more republican line and that relations with me were strained because I had not 'put down' the strike.

Overall, I emphasised that there was a widespread feeling that in some, as yet undefined, way, the people of Northern Ireland could, if left to themselves, resolve their own constitutional problems, including North/South relationships. Whatever reservations we might have about their prospects of success, it would be difficult to refuse to allow them to try. There was at least a possibility that they would reach some accommodation. In any event it would be seen as a constructive step forward in the existing political vacuum.

Finally, I spelt out the immediate legislative changes required for direct rule, which would provide for ministerial accountability to Parliament and for the Assembly's legislative responsibility to revert to Westminster. I proposed to use the existing electoral machinery for electing the Convention and to ask the Queen to appoint a Convention chairman in advance in order to avoid starting with arguments about this in the new assembly. I told my colleagues that, although it was always difficult to predict events in Northern Ireland, I thought that the main political parties would be prepared to participate in the Convention, but I would have to move quickly and intended to publish very shortly a White Paper in advance of the necessary legislation.

In the discussion that followed, my colleagues were broadly favourable to my proposals and I was ready for a full Cabinet meeting the following day. Here, there was some discussion as to whether a statement in the Commons might not be a better way of announcing policy than a White Paper, on the grounds that the policy parameters I was proposing might pre-empt the purpose of the Convention and so limit its freedom. Might not the Protestants refuse to co-operate? I promise to consider this, but my mind was in fact made up. The policy changes we had decided upon warranted a White Paper. A full explanation was necessary in a province whose leaders were likely to fill in gaps of a parliamentary statement in their own way. I was operating in Northern Ireland where constitutional matters were the stuff of politics.

Similarly, I believed that skimping on information to the House of Commons would lead to trouble. It is something that Mrs Thatcher ignored in December 1980 after her talks with Charles Haughey and as a result the talks were interpreted in a different way in the North and the South.

In his summing up to the Cabinet, Harold asked us not to reveal our discussions or conclusions outside; he had already advised me to tell the Opposition at an 'appropriate time'. He knew that even Cabinet ministers like to show off to the press, and somebody did indeed talk in the Commons on 'lobby terms'. The mention of independence in the document was subsequently taken by some of the media as the government's long-term aim, prompted by the Prime Minister. In most matters gossipy leaks from Cabinet do not matter much but when lives are at risk it is different and in Northern Ireland they were, and are.

Years later one of my Cabinet colleagues complained that there had never been the chance to discuss policy for Northern Ireland, but he must have conveniently forgotten the discussions at this time. Nobody disagreed with my basic policy then or at any time before or after. And it was on the basis of complete Cabinet support that I now prepared to return to Parliament with new constitutional proposals.

In the office we continued with our work on the White Paper and the following weekend was spent by Stan Orme, Frank Cooper, Philip Woodfield and I in editing and drafting. It was an exciting two days for we had to move fast. We could lean heavily on the work of the civil servants for the first five parts of the paper – the Problem; the Constitution Act of 1973; the Northern Ireland Executive January–May 1974; the Present Position; and Finance – but the last two sections, Law and Order, and the Next Steps, needed my imprint on behalf of the government.

The whole question of law and order cannot be separated from political and constitutional progress, and it formed a major part of the White Paper, but it is so important that I have dealt with it separately in the next chapter. One aspect of it, however, I shall mention here because it arose in a straight political context. The loyalist paramilitaries, stimulated by the UWC strike, were attracted by political action now that they had been deserted by the loyalist politicians. The feeling was not new and was the reason that I had earlier legalised the UVF, who now, on 23 June, announced that they were forming the Volunteer Political Party. The desire to act politically was there and I took the opportunity in the White Paper to address both loyalist and republican organisations of this kind: 'The Government welcomes the holding of discussions with various groups in the community which have extended towards establishing peace and withdrawal from violence.'

I went on to address the province's working class in general in the 'Next Steps' section of the Paper, which set out the idea of the Convention and the offer to the people of the province to shape their own future.

> It has become clear during recent discussions in Northern Ireland that many people will welcome an opportunity of this kind. This belief has been strengthened by a new awareness in the Protestant and Catholic working class of their real interests and by their wish to play a real part in political activity. Indeed, in recent months, various groups within the Northern Ireland community have shown an increased desire to participate in the political processes and a growing belief that they can best find for themselves political relationships which will be acceptable to them. The government believes it essential that participation in these processes should take place not only between like-minded groups but equally between groups which hold apparently strongly opposed views. Some time is required for political groupings to emerge and develop, to engage in discussion with other parties and interests and to clarify but not foreclose their positions.

Like the politicisation of the paramilitaries, that of the working class in general has not proceeded very far. Nevertheless both concepts, linked as they are by the fact that the paramilitaries on both sides come from this social grouping, had to be given a chance. It is ironic that fringe left-wing groups in Britain have shouted at me 'Arm the working class' to solve the problems of Ireland, when it is precisely the people in this category who are armed already.

The main message of the White Paper was, however, the Convention:

> The people of Northern Ireland must play a crucial part in determining their own future. No political structure can endure without their support and no just and stable society can be created without their full participation. Political structures should not be confused with political relationships. If the Northern Ireland community can reach a broad consensus of agreement, any one of a number of possible patterns of government might well be workable. If agreement is not reached, the troubles in Northern Ireland will not only remain but could intensify. No one will be able to turn this defeat into a victory. That is reality.

I spelt out what I regarded as the three basic factors that had to be taken into account by the Convention. First, there must be some form of power sharing 'because no political system will survive, or be supported, unless there is widespread acceptance of it within the community. There must be participation by the whole community.' Secondly, any pattern of government must be acceptable to the people of the United Kingdom as a whole and to Parliament at Westminster. And thirdly, the special relationship with the Republic of Ireland must be recognised: 'Northern Ireland, unlike the rest of the United Kingdom, shares a common land frontier. . . . There is an Irish dimension.'

We had discussed in the office whether we could build on the Whitelaw 1973 Constitution Act, which would save much time and new legislation. In the end I inserted a paragraph in the White Paper making it clear that the Act was still on the statute book and could be used if required, finishing, 'much of the content of that Act is not a matter for dispute. What is apparent is that there is little prospect of forming from the present Northern Ireland Assembly another Executive which meets the terms of the Act.' I realised the difficulties – the break-up of the Executive had been a symbol of loyalist victory – but at the back of my mind was the hope that the 1973 Act could still be a vehicle for 'devolution' in Northern Ireland.

Finally, there were the practical steps to be taken: the temporary arrangements for the government of Northern Ireland; the election of a consultative Northern Ireland Constitutional Convention, with an independent chairman and seventy-eight members elected by the single transferable vote procedure, 'to consider what provisions for the government of Northern Ireland would be likely to command the most widespread acceptance throughout the community'; and then the government's submittance to Parliament of the Convention's report and also the results of any referendum.

The date of the elections was still of pressing concern and now I had to take into account that there was also at least the possibility of a

General Election in the autumn of 1974 or spring of 1975. I therefore stated in the White Paper that the government would aim to give about four weeks notice of an election but that in the meantime we 'would hope that the process of discussion and consultation leading to an election to the Convention would develop on as wide a basis as possible'.

On 4 July the White Paper was published and I made a statement to the House of Commons in which I explained the major points in it and the need for legislation. Once again, with no political base in Northern Ireland it was vitally important that I had the support of the Commons. It was forthcoming from all sides, although Edward Heath wanted to debate the White Paper before the second reading of the actual Bill.

When he had come to see Harold and myself to receive an early copy of the White Paper, I had noted in my diary that he murmured something about it being difficult to maintain the bipartisan policy, which I put down to the fact that he had seen his Common Market and Industrial Relations policies in tatters and now his policy for Ireland seemed to be going the same way. I had spoken with Ian Gilmour in the previous couple of weeks but before his appointment in June as Opposition spokesman on Northern Ireland, Ted had left a gap. This may have led to poor communications between us, but his concern was understandable after all the hard work he and Willie had done to move Northern Ireland policy in the right direction. Bipartisanship would be alright for a while.

We had also kept the government of the South informed about the general direction of our policy. Frank Cooper had visited Dublin in early June; I had discussed the outline of the White Paper with Garret Fitzgerald on 14 June; and, more immediately, I had met the Irish ambassador in London to talk about it in the week before its publication. More detailed discussions were never considered, for we were not seeking agreement, and nor would the Irish government have wanted them. There were, however, some Irish press complaints about lack of consultation which, I learned later, came from the Information officials employed by the Irish government! We both had the same problem.

The almost universal support for the Convention proposal included a speech from Jim Molyneaux of the Official Unionists, who was fulsome in his praise of the Secretary of State 'not for having conceded various points to various people on various matters, but for his courage and realism. For a long time, while he was the Opposition spokesman on Northern Ireland affairs, we always felt that he was one of the very few Hon Members of the House who understood what it was all about.'

Gerry Fitt was more circumspect: he needed time to consult with his SDLP colleagues in Belfast. Philip Goodhard, one day to be a Northern

Ireland minister in the Thatcher government, praised the 'good sense' in my speech and in the White Paper, and Julian Critchley, Conservative MP for Aldershot, welcomed the new policy because of the 'reality' injected into a 'problem which has obstinately refused to yield to the politics of reason'. In a barbed remark to his own leader, Critchley made clear that he regarded Sunningdale as dead and he would 'refuse to wear mourning'.

I engaged in an altercation with Harry West, who alleged that there was political interference with the security forces. And this from a former Stormont minister! In contrast, Jack Mendelson, Tribunite MP for Penistone, backed up in a brilliant speech my opening remark that the White Paper was not the 'last chance'; too many people always argue after a crisis that the end of the road has come. From his and similar speeches, I was satisfied that my general policy was acceptable to Parliament and, judging by the feedback from about fifteen broadcasts that I did, it was acceptable to the country.

The legislation to implement the White Paper went quickly through its parliamentary hurdles and by then, mid-July, I was convinced that the Convention elections should not take place until 1975. The Unionist parties now wanted delay, and said so, as did the SDLP. And we in the government needed time in order to prepare the ground not only for elections but for the running of the Convention itself. There was always the chance, given a General Election looming within the year, that I was preparing the way for another Secretary of State.

In preparation for the debates in the Convention, I decided to publish a series of discussion documents to aid the Northern Irish politicians who would be involved. Since the problem of finance would be important to any future devolved administration – the storm clouds over public expenditure that I had witnessed in the last weeks of the old Executive were indicative of this – I turned first to the subject of finance and the economy; the paper was published in early September.

During the previous month it had become obvious that we were in the run-up to an autumn General Election. Harold Wilson and Bob Mellish, our Chief Whip, took up a dissenting speech by the Tory MP, William van Straubenzee, who had been a Heath minister in Northern Ireland, on efforts by some of his colleagues to give the Conservative Whip to Unionist MPs. Harold accused the Opposition of 'trying to wriggle out of the bipartisan policy . . . purely for political purposes to gain a few extra votes of doubtful antecedents in some future Conservative coalition government'. In the political situation of 1974 a few extra MPs made a lot of difference to which party would form the government.

These were only the opening shots in the campaign but by September all the talk was about the imminence of the General Election. At a Cabinet meeting Harold told us only that it was to be in October and I actually learned the date, 18 October, when I was down in Dublin. From this time I had to concern myself more with British matters. A minister was always on duty in Northern Ireland and I went over myself two or three days every week, particularly for the security review, but for day-to-day work I opened a mini-Northern Ireland Office in a civil service building in Leeds.

In Northern Ireland forty-three candidates representing eleven different political groupings were put up to contest the twelve Westminster seats. The Volunteer Political Party, the political wing of the UVF, put up one candidate. All the party manifestos were predictable. The SDLP was for power sharing; the loyalists were against. British political issues did not loom at all.

In the event Gerry Fitt increased his share of the vote in West Belfast but overall the SDLP vote was slightly down. In Fermanagh and South Tyrone a compromise republican candidate, Frank Maguire, defeated Harry West. The VPP candidate, Hugh Smythe, did badly but the combined Unionists – the United Ulster Unionist Council – won ten seats and their share of the poll went up from fifty-one per cent to fifty-eight per cent. Brian Faulkner's recently formed Unionist Party of Northern Ireland, outside the UUUC, made virtually no impact.

Other than personalities, which now included Enoch Powell for South Down, little had changed. The two communities had again delivered a vote based on the religious divide and the implication of the results for the future constitutional Convention was gloomy. The basic political attitudes in the province could not, however, be ignored; the reality of a loyalist majority in the province had to be accepted. My only hope for the future was that the 'Ulster nationalism' of the loyalists would grow into something capable of uniting a divided community.

Whatever the difficulties, the Convention was the only way to proceed. If the Northern Ireland politicians failed to find a way through, it would at least show the world, and give a message to the South of Ireland, that the blame did not all lie with the British. Meanwhile, there was much to do in preparation for the Convention. I could not sit back and wait for its success or failure, any more than I could sit back on the problem of law and order.

Chapter 5

PROBLEMS OF SECURITY

The Ulster workers' strike had revealed how much we depended on the army for basic security and the inability of the RUC to react quickly to events. It confirmed for me the need to reverse the decision taken in 1969 that the army and not the police should take the lead on security. While that position was maintained, there was no incentive for the latter to force the pace of change in tactics. The primacy of the police was my long-term aim and in my first major speech as Northern Ireland Secretary on 4 April, I had told the House of Commons that the cornerstone of my security policy was 'a progressive increase in the role of the civilian law enforcement agencies in Northern Ireland. So long as much of the burden is being borne by the army, it is altogether too tempting to many members of the community to undertake less than their share of responsibility and to feel that law and order is a matter for the United Kingdom government rather than for them. This is not a situation which can be allowed to continue indefinitely.'

Now that the strike was over, I wanted to translate words into action. I first looked carefully at the role of the Police Authority set up in 1969 as a result of pressure on the Northern Ireland government by Jim Callaghan. It was now too late to involve members of the Assembly in this but I could give the Authority more status and make greater use of it, as Jim had intended. This I began to do, in the hope of gaining more acceptability for the police in the community and of making the Authority more accountable.

I talked with Frank Cooper and with army leaders about getting the army out of a policing role and about ways of bringing the RUC to the forefront of the battle for law and order, with more expertise in crime detection and greater mobility. Our aim needed constant reiteration and discussion outside, as well as inside, the office, and we consequently made law and order a major section of the July White Paper. What we said then was important and, moreover, has stood the test of time.

We began with the Downing Street Declaration of 1969, on the basis of which troops had been sent to Belfast and Derry, and when the government had emphasised that troops would be withdrawn when law and order was restored. This simple view was no longer relevant: law and order could not be restored just like that and the 'temporary basis' had now continued for five years. As we stated in the White Paper:

> The burden upon the army is heavy. It has responded magnificently. The nature of the present conflict is, however, very different from 1969. The problem now is essentially that of dealing with relatively small numbers of ruthless and vicious killers and bombers who care nothing for human life or human rights. The army has in consequence had to respond and to change its tactics to deal with this threat. The army cannot, however, replace the police, nor should it be asked to be a substitute.
>
> The effectiveness of any police service stems from the fact that it lives within the community which it serves and draws its strength and support from that community. The community knows it and it knows the community. The people of Northern Ireland can make an essential contribution to ending violence, not by seeking to take the law into their own hands, but by showing their determination to create a just and stable society and by accepting the police service.
>
> Nothing would transform the security situation more quickly than a determination by the whole community to support the police service and co-operate with it. This is not happening. If it did take place, it would also have a fundamental effect on the need for Emergency Powers in Northern Ireland, including detention, the operation of which is currently being examined by the committee sitting under the chairmanship of Lord Gardiner. It would also enable the army to make a planned, orderly and progressive reduction in its present commitment and subsequently there would be no need for the army to become involved again in a policing role. This is the aim of the government and must be the wish of the overwhelming majority of the people in Northern Ireland and elsewhere.

I particularly wanted the terms on which withdrawal of the army could take place to be read by those in Ireland who called for the troops to go. After four months in my job, I had every reason to believe that, while the fringe Irish political groups in Britain took the word 'withdrawal' literally, the republican paramilitary groups in Ireland saw it slightly differently. They had learned the hard way from the Ulster workers' strike and the Provisionals at this stage in particular were aware that once the British troops were out, there would still be the loyalists.

The nature of the security situation had changed over the years and it would take time to achieve the primacy of the police. In the short run the only base from which to combat continued Provisional IRA violence was the army. The Provisionals had not altered their ways after direct rule in 1972, or when the Executive was set up; they were not likely to do so now, and neither would the other paramilitary groups. Violence had become a way of life. Moreover, since 1972 security had landed firmly on the plate of the UK government.

This meant that in the short term I had to renew the Emergency Provisions Act, as I had advised my Cabinet colleagues. While awaiting the report of the Gardiner committee, I had commissioned my civil servants to look at the Act to see if there were any minor changes I could make at this time. In particular, I was concerned about the section outlawing the wearing of paramilitary uniforms in public, which seemed in practice to be ineffective. However, because of the imminence of the Gardiner Report, I decided to drop the idea of making peripheral changes to the Act and asked Parliament to support the renewal of the law as it stood.

In my speech to the Commons I took the opportunity to refer to the major problem of detention, making the point that it could only be brought to an end when violence was 'checked'. I deliberately did not use the word 'ended': that was now a pipe-dream. However, I announced a small number of releases by executive action in order to show that releases other than those by the commissioners were possible. It was no more than that; my hopes were pinned on the Gardiner Report to provide a way of taking speedier action to end detention.

I also announced a variant of the welfare scheme which Stan Orme had been trying to get off the ground earlier in the year. An independent resettlement association was to be set up to help provide money and work for ex-detainees, which would, hopefully, prevent the drift back to violence. The press later described the scheme as a wet socialist idea, although in fact it emanated from the army. However, in the event this scheme also had to be abandoned, because the association became more a pressure group that concentrated on making representations about conditions in the Maze. The problem of reinvolvement in violence remained, and is with us yet.

The Commons renewed the Emergency Provisions Act for another year on 9 July, with only nineteen votes against. The Ulster workers' strike had come as a shock to some of those who normally voted against the emergency legislation and, given the emotion of the subject, the debate was reasonable and did not cause the problems anticipated from parts of the Labour Party. However, Gerry Fitt, who had seen his dreams of power sharing shattered and had put much of the blame on Stan Orme and myself, accused both of us of changing our minds on detention since the recent days in Opposition. This was not true and Kevin McNamara leapt to our defence, reminding the House of the views I had actually expressed in Opposition.

The episode led me to another late-night pessimistic musing on the role of the SDLP and its west of the Bann syndrome. Its leaders might have been on the Executive but it seemed to me to remain essentially a party of protest. It had potential but it was not yet a party of government. Late-night thoughts are not always the best and afterwards I had a better perspective. Northern Ireland is not Great Britain and in the cold light of day I appreciated that the SDLP faced special problems in the divided province. It could not, for example, come out in support of the RUC unless it was actually involved in government.

In a long memorandum of mid-June on the political situation in the province, I told my Cabinet colleagues that the SDLP would not lose ground in the forthcoming Convention elections: the Provisional IRA could not offer a political alternative and overall the SDLP 'would remain the voice of the bulk of Catholic opinion'. I referred to the Official and Provisional IRAs, and gloomily suggested that because of its coherent philosophy, the Official IRA represented the gravest long-term threat to Ireland, North and South. In retrospect that was foolishly expressed: all that I meant was that the Official IRA did have a political philosophy and consequently it would last longer than the Provisional IRA with its narrow paramilitary nationalist outlook. It is too early to tell whether this is true but since 1972 the Official Sinn Fein, the 'stickies' in Irish political talk, has been increasingly involved in community politics through the Republican Clubs, the Northern Ireland equivalent of the Workers' Party of the South.

The Official Sinn Fein's attitude had been made clear in a statement by its General Secretary: 'It must be the objective of Irish revolutionaries to win the support of the British working class for our struggle and not to incur their opposition and hatred by senseless bombing campaigns in Britain.' These sentiments were one of the reasons why, when I was pressed in the House of Commons, I refused to stop the 'Anti-Imperialist Festival' planned by the Official Sinn Fein to take place in Belfast in late July/early August. I felt that political meetings of this type were not my business.

When I sent my memorandum to Whitehall, I was in fact far more worried about the loyalists than the republicans. I told my colleagues that despite the good reception of the White Paper, we had to accept that loyalists 'resented imposition from London and resented in particular the Irish dimension', and that I was still concerned that some leading loyalist politicians were prepared to use violence in support of independence.

The security review that had arrived on my desk in early June had, however, quite rightly concentrated on the activities of the republican paramilitaries and I was now able to study its conclusions. When I had announced the setting up of the review on 4 April, I had given only a general indication of its brief. Its detailed remit had been to look ahead twelve months and, first, to re-examine the task facing the government and the security forces in restoring order and eliminating terrorism; second, to consider in detail the roles, deployment, concept of operations and tactics in order to meet that task; and, third, to present ministers with a range of possible measures for use according to how the situation developed. It was also laid down that the policy of co-operation with the Garda should continue, based on meetings of the Chief Constable of the RUC with the Chief of the Garda.

It was clear before the inquiry began that for the immediate future, the army would continue to be the prime force on the border and in the republican areas of Belfast and Derry. What I wanted from the review was a definition of the roles of the army, the UDR, and the RUC and RUC Reserve in all parts of the province, and also a reassessment of the role of the security forces in keeping public order on the streets.

On reading the review it was obvious that its preparation had been dominated by the army staff at Lisburn. They were accustomed to preparing reports of all kinds; the RUC were not. It was part of the syndrome that the army was not in the province to support the police but the other way round. The review, for example, recommended that the number of army battalions should be increased to sixteen, a recommendation that without any prompting from me was knocked on the head by the Minister of Defence. It was also recommended that no detainees should be released during the 'implementation of Sunningdale'. Sunningdale was of course over but by the time that I received the review I understood why the army felt as it did: they were in the front line. What I had to make clear was that my aim was not simply to end detention procedures but to replace them with better policing and a system of straight arrest followed by charges.

For the same reason I was against the recommendation to slacken the criteria on which a suspect could be served with an interim custody order. Behind this was the view that an interim custody order was valuable as a way of breaking up paramilitary groups, at least temporarily. Detention was not, however, brought in for that purpose. Another idea that jarred with me was that a Director of Information should be appointed not only to publicise the policy of the government but also to 'denigrate' the terrorists. I was not against such an appointment – and later for different reasons appointed Michael Cudlipp as Co-ordinator of Information Policy – but I was firmly against the idea of using 'black' propaganda. It is always counter-productive.

There were, however, many positive recommendations that needed acting on, particularly that for an increase in UDR, RUC and RUC Reserve numbers, and for the setting up of a civilian body to take over security duties in the Belfast shopping area. Both these recommendations would reduce the need for the army and I therefore authorised that they should be given priority, which meant an early approach to the Treasury. We also moved quickly to tighten the procedures in Northern Ireland for control of explosives and detonators, which had been recommended. We checked on the liaison with British authorities and I also took up the issue with the government in Dublin on my next visit there. Better co-operation was needed with the South, for many of the detonators and also the commercial explosive used in the North came from there.

One recommendation was to set up an auxiliary police force to carry out 'hullo hullo' policing and deal with ordinary criminality, which was not receiving proper attention. I did not know about the practicalities of this but I decided that it should be looked into, along with a recommendation for tighter controls on motor vehicles, too many of which were being used for car bombings after they had been stolen. I was also sympathetic to the idea that the Judges' Rules covering the interrogation of suspects in Great Britain should be extended to Northern Ireland. This was a matter for the Attorney General, and eventually the change was made.

The idea that it should be a criminal act to use 'unapproved' road crossings on the border was good in principle but it would have required too many soldiers to put into practice. Civilians used these roads in large numbers, as their families had for decades, and in several instances they had filled in the army-made craters intended to stop vehicles crossing. In any event the Southern authorities would not co-operate in closure. They wanted the roads open.

One concern the review body expressed was the need to provide secure accommodation for young offenders who were involved in violence, something which Frank King had already talked about to me privately. Because children were more difficult to detect, the Provisional IRA was using them as arms carriers and gunmen, and to set bombs. Such young people were often apprehended and charged but the existing law would not allow them to be sent to prison to await trial but only to remand homes, where security was poor. Since 1973, there had been a total of sixty-six escapes involving thirty-nine boys charged with terrorist or scheduled offences, three of whom had been charged with murder and two with attempted murder. Legislation was quickly prepared which would give me personally the power to commit to prisons young persons charged with scheduled offences and not released on bail. Parliament approved the Bill on 4 July, and meanwhile we had the hospital in the Crumlin Road prison prepared to house such young people. Jack Donaldson later arranged for all-Party groups to visit the remand homes and the prisons so that MPs could see for themselves the facilities provided.

Of all the recommendations of the security review, it was the increase in police numbers that mattered most. The police would need time to work out the full training implications of this but by August I hoped the work would be completed.

Such practical follow-up work does not proceed in an ivory tower: in Northern Ireland there is always a background of violence and tribal politics, with the constant possibility that one of the issues will be sparked into flame. An issue that did so in May and June 1974 was that of the Price sisters, which, although the direct responsibility of the Home Secretary Roy Jenkins, had a great effect in Northern Ireland and particularly in West Belfast where the sisters came from.

Marion and Dolours Price had been convicted in Britain in November 1973 on charges connected with two car bomb explosions in London on 8 March, when one person was killed and over two hundred were injured. They were sentenced to life imprisonment. After the trial the sisters were held in Brixton gaol where they began a hunger strike in support of a demand by the Provisional IRA that the two women and other Irish prisoners should be transferred to Northern Ireland. What the Provisionals wanted was their London-based team back home where its members could bask in political status. The SDLP joined the demand, responding to the outcry from the Catholic community, and so did the Roman Catholic Church led by the Primate of all Ireland.

As the hunger strike continued, doctors started to force-feed the sisters. Such a barbarous practice had long since ceased to be followed in Northern Ireland where, to put it bluntly, if a person chose to die, then so be it. Emotions now ran even higher. To British eyes, the saga was difficult to comprehend as the Price sisters' father appeared on television to plead for his 'wee children'. As I angrily said in my diary, they do not worry about the people they kill or injure; their ability for self-deception is very great. Comprehension became even more difficult when the Provisionals had the nerve to announce: 'The IRA make no threat. We simply state that as comrades of these girls we shall not rest until just retribution is exacted from Mr Wilson and his servants. No British government shall murder citizens of Ireland and expect to get away scot free.'

On 18 May the forced feeding was ended on medical advice and by 1 June Roy Jenkins could speak of the likelihood that the sisters 'may end their lives'. His long statement pointed out that the crime of these women was different in seriousness from those of other prisoners who had been transferred to Northern Ireland, none of whom had forced the issue by hunger strike, and that there were other Irish prisoners in British prisons. He was not prepared to agree to the demands of the Price sisters, nor to give a definite date for their transfer to Northern Ireland, although he used the important words: 'I believe it would be possible and reasonable for them to serve the bulk of their long sentences near their home in Northern Ireland.' This statement followed a discussion with me where I had made the basic point that, if these women were transferred, others would demand the same right and I therefore wanted a rational policy on transference, accompanied by stronger security arrangements at Armagh Women's Prison.

We would only know whether Roy's promise about the future would affect the sisters' attitude when the Provisional IRA had been able to consult with them. Meanwhile Roy was listening to Jock Stallard, MP for St Pancras North, Labour peer Fenner Brockway and Paddy Devlin, who were particularly interested in the Price case. According to Paddy, the Provisionals wanted clarification of Roy's words about future transfer. They were basically concerned about what would happen if the Labour Party lost an election later in the year. The SDLP had evidently been told by Edward Heath that he was on their side. I was sceptical about this and also about whether a future Tory government would be able to make the transfer without political trouble, but in any case I did not think that we should make any commitment to a transfer date.

Rumours circulated about the Provisional IRA's attitude but apparently the decision was that the sisters should not be allowed to die, and a long convoluted statement was issued by the prisoners on 8 June saying that they had decided to terminate their hunger strike. In the Republic, the Earl and Countess of Donoughmore, who had been kidnapped by the Provisional IRA on 4 June, were released. The kidnapping had presumably been intended to influence our policy on the Price sisters; it did not work.

Roy and I continued our discussions about the transfer and on 13 June he announced that the Price sisters might be transferred to a prison in Northern Ireland in the course of the year, 'subject to there being no great outbreak of violence or deterioration in the security situation'. In fact, they were moved in March 1975 to Armagh, where they received special category status. It reinforced the need to end this classification: why should these people be seen as political prisoners?

One sensible result of the whole affair was that Roy Jenkins later altered the policy on forced feeding in England and Wales to accord with Northern Ireland. Otherwise, the issue of the Price sisters faded from sight and the majority community, who had waited to see whether we would give in to the republicans, became increasingly caught up in their own issue, the 'third force'. This arose from the review body's proposals for an auxiliary police force, which by this time was under discussion by a relatively large number of people in the RUC and the civil service, and consequently became known to the media. Very quickly, the proposal was presented by a curious transmogrification as one for an armed, not an unarmed, force. Catholics saw it as a return to the B Specials or even the vigilante groups of the 1920s, while the loyalists saw it as a force that would be under their own control, not the RUC's. Emotions ran high and we were soon in trouble.

On 29 July I wrote to the Prime Minister and explained that since there was little prospect in the foreseeable future of attracting Catholics in any significant numbers into the RUC or its Reserve, or into the UDR, I was considering creating 'a new low-level Community Patrol Service' to enable the people in Northern Ireland to play a role in law and order without them having to align themselves directly with the existing security forces. In an accompanying note for the Cabinet sub-committee I emphasised that the force was to be unarmed and was largely to concern itself with the ordinary crime of its area and not with terrorism. Those arrested would be handed over to the RUC. I also stressed the need to ensure its accountability to the RUC, bearing in mind the possibility that a paramilitary group might try to take it over.

The problems involved were put forcibly to Frank Cooper by James Flanagan on 30 July. Such a force would degrade the RUC, the Chief Constable argued, and would be substandard policing. His objections were important and we were clearly not going to get far with the proposal. However, in case there was some variant of it that was practical, a working party of civil servants, senior RUC officers and members of the Police Federation was set up to look into it. The time for rational discussion of the real proposal had gone.

The public outcry about a third force had first surfaced in late June and the *Irish Times* of 26 June reported that at a meeting on the previous day West, Paisley and Craig had proposed to me that a third force or home guard should be set up. The notes of the meeting make no mention of this but it is not unusual in Northern Ireland for reports of meetings given to the press afterwards by politicians to be more subjective than objective.

On the same day as the meeting Liam Cosgrave had announced that his government was setting up a new volunteer force in the Republic to undertake local security duties in each city and town. Units of this force would be based on local Garda stations and would carry out patrols, report suspicious activities and pay special attention to unattended vehicles, which were, he said, the 'sneak artillery of the dealers in violence'. On 4 July Ian Paisley raised this in the Commons, reasoning that if the South had acted in this way, why not us?

On 12 July, the Orange Order anniversary, Unionist politician and former Stormont minister John Taylor told the crowd in Belfast that a new Ulster Home Guard would have to be formed. He said that it would be a force which London would learn to respect and which would be supported by loyalist politicians with or without London government legislation. The strike had shown the real strength of the loyalists and his message to London now was, 'We want to be involved in our defences and led by our own leaders and officers.' The same message was made to the crowd at Lisburn, where Knox Cunningham, a former Westminster MP and PPS to Harold Macmillan, stated: 'Trust no Westminster government, whether under Mr Wilson or Mr Heath. I ask you to press them for three things – an early election, fair representation at Westminster and a local force to combat terrorism.'

That this third force talk was coming not from paramilitaries but from the establishment made it less easy to dismiss. The spectre of an armed force set up by the Protestants haunted the province and touched raw nerves on both sides of the community. Allegations and counter-allegations from those 'in the know' were reported in the Northern Irish press, and by the time UK and foreign correspondents had put in their pennyworth, it seemed that we were moving towards civil war. It made no difference to the talk that in a statement on 24 July I made it clear that my aim was not to set up an armed force and that in any case a decision would not be made until I had finished discussions with all relevant authorities, including elected representatives. Neither was the absence of support from the UDA and other loyalist paramilitaries taken into account; their leaders did not want a third force of any kind. They considered themselves to be one already!

The consensus from all sides was that I was going to give in to the demand for a force of armed auxiliaries set up and run by loyalists. Paddy Devlin made another personal attack on me: apparently my statements, like those of all Labour ministers, were aimed at winning the next General Election. Would that it were so easy! The loyalists had got the bit between their teeth and Ernest Baird, deputy leader of the Vanguard Unionists, even announced in early August that enrolment for a loyalist home guard was going ahead well: a figure of 30,000 was mentioned.

My security people continued to pooh-pooh the whole business: it was one thing to set up a Provisional IRA or even an Ulster Volunteer Force, but third forces needed organisation of a greater kind. There was also lack of support for it from the loyalist paramilitaries, and this was confirmed when in early August I met representatives from the Ulster Workers' Council to discuss policing. They were blunt that they would not support a third force and afterwards Glen Barr, as the group's spokesman, told the press that they accepted that no armed force was envisaged by the Secretary of State.

Nevertheless the saga went on and on 15 August there was a mass rally of loyalists in Bangor where their own third force was supposedly to be set up. The television cameras were there and though the rally proved a flop, it helped increase the SDLP's concern for the minority community. There were attacks on me from Gerry Fitt as well as Paddy Devlin, and my resignation was called for. I asked them to come to see me but Gerry insisted that they were going to see Harold Wilson in London and even announced this in the press. Paddy wrote a letter to Harold which he showed to the Europa Hotel journalists and all 2,500 words of it were consequently published. The only reply he received was a curt private secretary letter, as happened on a number of other occasions when an attempt was made to bypass me and the Northern Ireland Office.

The SDLP leaders came to see me shortly afterwards to discuss policing and it was a particularly loud and fraught meeting, with people talking not so much about policing as army harassment. Gerry took the lead and expressed the SDLP's view that the army was playing a tough role in the province in order that people would ask for more policing. This was of course rubbish, and I wished that we were but half as clever as they thought.

It was all part of the SDLP's general attitude, for also at this time John Hume was raising publicly the issue of British 'pull out', which, he stated, was to be the government's policy in the forthcoming General Election campaign. Evidently, this was what lay behind the government's policy of an armed third force, and if the British did pull out, then the Irish Army would be involved. It was a quite remarkable statement, part of the phobia of recent weeks: there was no question whatsoever of the British leaving the Catholics to their fate.

I sent a minute to Harold, whom I knew was concerned about our poor relations with the SDLP, relating recent events. A Party delegation to London had met, without prior arrangement, Mr Heath on 19 August, and had talked with Jeremy Thorpe on the phone. I had briefed the latter and Ian Gilmour and Willie Whitelaw on our policy on a third force and when the SDLP had come to see me on 20 August I had referred them to all my statements about it. They now accepted that we were not going to set up an armed force of any kind but believed that the loyalists wanted to do so. They thought there was a possibility of another Ulster workers' strike and on behalf of the Catholic community they had to react. I also told Harold about the noisy meeting with the SDLP leaders when they had even said that Harold was clever enough to pull out for election purposes. All in all they simply did not trust us and looked back to the halcyon days of Ted Heath and Sunningdale.

Behind the SDLP's attitude was serious concern about how the Party would fare at the next General Election. This helped explain the attempt to get involved with other parties at Westminster and the vocal complaints about army harassment, which went down well in some Catholic quarters, where the role of the army was undoubtedly seen in this way. Now was not the time for rational discussion on the future of the province; we would have to wait until the Election was over.

The third force issue lingered on for some weeks afterwards but in a lower key. Northern Ireland, however, never does things by halves and in August 1974 there arose another security problem, in Newry on the border, which went largely unnoticed in Britain but which kept me and the Northern Ireland ministers tied to the province. I had visited Newry a few weeks earlier and had met the 45 Royal Marine Commando Unit and gone out on night patrol with the UDR. It gave me a knowledge of the town's layout and a general feel for the place which proved useful in the grave situation that now arose, involving the Commando Unit, the Newry and Mourne District Council and the local Provisional IRA. Marine patrols in the low-lying town centre were faced by shooting attacks from gunmen in the surrounding hillside housing estates and, when there was trouble, the army would switch off all the street lights from a master switch in the headquarters of the local UDR. The Provisional IRA gunmen, small in number in Newry but backed by a larger group in Dundalk in the Republic, demanded that the switch should be taken out of army control, and they backed their demand by threatening the workmen who maintained the electricity service. Indeed, they took the manager of the electricity showroom to a graveyard and threatened to kill him if repairs were continued, and in another incident an electricity workman was approached while on a repair job and told, 'Watch it son. You are for the jump.'

The situation was made even worse when one evening during a storm lightning struck a transformer in the Newry area and the town's electricity supply was cut off. I could not help thinking that God really was involved in this question of Ireland. The transformer was repaired but because of the intimidation the electricity supply service overall steadily deteriorated. Businesses could not operate, so people were laid off work, and hospitals, schools, old people's homes, were all affected. Despite the provision of mobile generators and a centralised social security payment system for Newry, away from the town, we were rapidly approaching a situation not unlike a miniature Ulster workers' strike. What concerned me most was that success for the Provisionals would lead them to try to control electricity distribution in other parts of the province – a tit for tat, to show the UWC electricity workers.

We had little help from the locals, not because they were on the side of the Provisionals but because they were not on ours. The local SDLP-controlled authority blamed everything on the military, and tension increased when the chairman of the Medical Liaison Committee announced that there was a problem of diseases spreading in the town – not, incidentally, the advice given to me at Stormont. The Provisionals meanwhile kept up the pressure, saying that they wanted the mobile generators to be switched off unless the electricity provided was for food and demanding that even factories outside the town should cease operating.

Stan Orme spent much time with Don Concannon on the necessary organisational work, while I kept in the background. However, on 3 September I called a deputation from the Newry and Mourne District Council to a meeting at Stormont. With me were the Permanent Secretaries of the various Northern Ireland Departments, the manager of the Northern Ireland Electricity Service and, to advise me on the military aspect, the Commander Land Forces. Thus, a local council attracted more top brass than all the local authorities in Great Britain put together could hope to do!

The council chairman opened the meeting by saying that the deputation represented a complete cross-section of the council and that they were unanimous that the war of words had gone on long enough. The Newry situation needed firm political action and if that meant giving in to the Provisional IRA, then the Council was convinced it should be done! I asked the councillors individually for their views and it was clear that the majority felt that the army had created the situation. It was alleged that the Marines switched off the lights whenever they went out on patrol, which was in total conflict with the policy of previous regiments, who had switched off only when incidents had occurred. Most of these anyway happened in daylight. When, however, the Council had made representations to the Commanding Officer following a series of fatal motor accidents at night, he had not had the courtesy to reply. The regiment's attitude was in general heavy-handed: they had, for instance, recently removed a tricolour flag from the Derryberg estate which had been flying for four years. The councillors suggested that the date of the regiment's departure should be brought forward.

They went on to allege that the people of Newry were suffering from grave hardship because of my 'fixation' with the safety of the army, which represented only one per cent of the population in Newry. The council was concerned for the other ninety-nine per cent, while I was showing a total lack of concern for all the people caught in the middle of my fight against the IRA! A further point was, however, that the Provisional IRA were responsible to no one and were fighting their game at the people's expense. As the Secretary of State, I had the responsibility to solve the situation.

Another of their concerns was that the economic effect of the blackout would be disastrous. While the Department of Commerce was doing a good job in supplying generators, small businesses were at grave risk. Business confidence was at an all-time low, and future investment in industry was in jeopardy. A further point, and one that certainly came as news to me, was that the RUC did not want the lights switched off. The council's final message was that control of all electricity supplies should be handed over to the Northern Ireland Electricity Service.

My response was short and firm. I could not put the lives of the security forces at risk. However, I was prepared to make a change: it was essential that the army retain control of the electricity supplies for the town's central area, but electricity for the remaining eighty-six per cent of Newry should be the total responsibility of the NIES. This was not acceptable to the councillors and the discussions went on for five and a half hours without us getting anywhere. The councillors simply wanted to give in and at one stage there seemed to be the possibility of a sit-in by them in my office. Eventually we all agreed to meet again the following day, but more long meetings then brought us no nearer a solution. It was complete deadlock.

That night in our cramped quarters in the Culloden Hotel, Frank Cooper, the CLF and I considered the situation. Out of the discussion came a possible solution: to relocate the main switch for the central part of Newry so that it was no longer in the UDR building but outside of it, and nearby, so that if a Marine patrol radioed that they were in trouble, the street lights could still be switched off in response, and quickly.

Before making any announcement I invited the Commanding Officer of the Marines and some of his officers to the Culloden to talk over the plan because I wanted to make absolutely sure that they did not feel soldiers' lives would be put at risk by it. They agreed to the new arrangement, although this did not prevent a low-level army statement to the press from Lisburn: 'The IRA has won in Newry now and will try the same tactic in other places. They will win these battles too.' The army, it was alleged, was 'disappointed at my decision'. This was as true as Dr Paisley's accusation at the same time that I was a 'fellow traveller with the IRA'!

On 4 September, as part of my general policy of bringing in as wide a group of people as possible, I put the plan to the full security meeting at the Castle, and in the evening Stan Orme and Don Concannon gave the Newry and Mourne Council the statement we had prepared for issue the following day. It made clear the two major principles on which I based my policy: that security must be maintained and under no circumstances was I prepared to place at risk the lives of members of the security forces; and that the industrial, commercial and social life of the Newry area must be preserved. It went on to state that the Northern Ireland Electricity Service would be responsible for the provision of all electric power in the area but if an incident should occur which endangered the security forces in carrying out their responsibilities, then they would take the requisite operational steps to protect themselves, including the reduction of street lighting, if necessary.

The councillors were, to use their own words, 'stunned', and issued their own statement unanimously accepting the two principles as 'reasonable and proper' and going on to state their belief that my action would 'go a considerable way towards achieving the elimination of terrorism from our midst' and made 'an important contribution towards creating harmony within the community and promoting genuine community effort for the rejection of violence. As representatives of the people of the area they demand the withdrawal of the threat against the workers of the Northern Ireland Electricity Service. It is essential that industry, commerce, schools and all the other areas of life in the community should now be allowed to return to normal. Those who try to prevent this are the real enemies of the people of our area.'

After the town had been without electricity for three weeks, the episode was over, and the Marines still operated electricity supplies in the area that mattered. As I told my Cabinet sub-committee colleagues on 6 September, the incident illustrated on the one hand the difficulty in getting the Catholic community to refrain from giving tacit support to the Provisionals and on the other hand the automatic reaction of almost all the Protestant leaders and their supporters to portray any settlement as capitulation to the IRA.

One decision over Newry which was significant to long-term detention policy was that I had told the army that I was not prepared to use the Emergency Provisions Act to detain members of the Provisional IRA who were the organisers of the campaign and who were popping backwards and forwards across the border. If there was a case for police arrest preparatory to a court case, then that would be a different matter. In practice, even if I had used the Emergency Provisions Act, it would not have been much use, since there would still have been reinforcements from Dundalk, and electricity workmen would still have felt too threatened to carry out repairs.

Despite the time-consuming problems of Newry and the third force, by the end of August new proposals for policing were emerging from the working party I had set up and from our office discussions. On 23 August I sent a minute to the Prime Minister giving him details of my proposals for a big expansion in the RUC and the RUC Reserve, including many more women, with some modifications to entry qualifications to widen the field; and also a recruiting drive to increase the size of the UDR. I also proposed an expansion of the small force of uniformed men and women with powers of search for illegal explosives, who had already relieved the army of duties in Belfast. The final proposal was to introduce local police posts. This was a new feature, which would involve setting up posts in rented premises, caravans, private homes or special police vehicles in locations where there was no police station. They would be manned jointly by the RUC and the Reserve, and their purpose would be to provide an acceptable focal point for maintaining local law and order. They would have contact with police stations, with fire, hospital and ambulance services, and with RUC mobile and foot patrols. The need for such posts was greatest in the country areas but they would be set up only where the local community expressed a desire to participate and originally this could only be in the loyalist areas.

As a result of the third force campaign in the province, the working party had for good reasons left alone the proposals for an auxiliary police force, but I still wondered whether there was not something that could be salvaged from the idea, and in my minute to the Prime Minister I told him that I was still investigating the possibility of a scheme which would involve local community wardens, working under the aegis of local government with support from the police, especially in areas of vandalism and social decline. The idea, I emphasised, needed further discussion and I was not proposing to proceed with it yet. It had to be kept quite distinct from the policing proposals because of the predisposition in Northern Ireland and the South to misunderstand our intentions. In the event I let the matter drop: it was a good English idea and no more.

I intended, I told Harold, to launch the whole policing scheme with full publicity on 2 September, and before then I would meet with the political parties and other leaders of opinion, and would provide appropriate information to Dublin. It mattered to talk with the RUC and accordingly I visited police stations in the province and also attended the cadets' passing out parade at Enniskillen and the annual conference of the Police Federation. I met church leaders, trade unionists and members of the CBI, as well as politicians from the Alliance Party and the SDLP, and Brian Faulkner and his Unionist colleagues.

I followed up the public announcement with a large number of television and radio broadcasts, and on 6 September I reported to the Cabinet sub-committee that the policing proposals stemming from the July White Paper had met with cautious acceptance from the Protestant community. The proposal that really mattered was of course the expansion of the RUC, which was the first vital step to achieving eventual police primacy.

An aspect of security that also concerned me at this time was RUC co-operation with the Garda, since republican paramilitaries from the North sheltered in and operated from the South. The poor relations engendered by the public attitude of the Southern government to the 'third force' made it unlikely that another meeting with government representatives would be productive, and this view was reinforced by obvious ministerial briefings to the Dublin press which supported the SDLP in its allegations about army harassment. The culmination was a letter of protest from the Taoiseach to Harold Wilson. That an independent government should support such allegations raised the hackles of some of my colleagues, even though it could be explained by Ireland's special historical circumstances. I was angry for my own reasons. The same kind of reasoning as the Dublin government's produced complaints about army softness from some loyalist quarters, and I commented bitterly about it in my diary: 'Everybody seems to be living off us, with the Southern government complaining about the British army but apparently not giving a thought to the deaths of British soldiers. Of course the army make mistakes, but this all-pervading carping is too much.'

Given my mood, it was surprising that a meeting between myself and Paddy Cooney, the Republic's Minister of Justice, ever materialised, particularly as there had been a further hiccup in relations in early September when an outline of the police proposals had been handed over to the Irish government at 4.30 pm one Friday and by 6.30 pm the details were in the hands of a British journalist in Dublin! Nevertheless, after the Taoiseach and Harold Wilson had met on 11 September, a meeting was arranged in Dublin for me on 18 September. That it proved possible at such short notice was probably due to the Irish government realising that the Labour Party might well win the forthcoming General Election.

I was accompanied by Jamie Flanagan and the day was spent discussing practical problems. There was of course no army representative there, which had the advantage of making Jamie the important man from our side and thus putting the police in the leading role on security. The meeting was a success and afterwards we were able to announce that we had reached substantial agreement on methods of improving cross-border security co-operation. We set up a number of standing committees on such matters as radio communication, which were to prove fruitful in the months and years ahead, and we agreed on the tightening of controls on explosives and detonators manufactured in the Republic. Legislation to implement the recommendations of the Common Law Enforcement Commission Report would go ahead in both our Parliaments.

We got nowhere, however, on cross-border co-operation between the Irish and British armies. Paddy Cooney had been adamant beforehand that no progress could be made on this, so we did not expect it. This did not, however, prevent counter-briefing yet again from Lisburn on 19 September, when it was announced that it was 'hoped' the meeting in Dublin would establish a four-way (British army, Irish army, RUC and Garda) radio communications link for the co-ordination of security, particularly in border areas. Such an outcome was never 'hoped' for, and the Lisburn statement was internal propaganda, the source of which could not be traced.

The sudden arrangements for a meeting may perhaps also have been because of vicious bombing attacks in the Republic. On top of the horrible casualties in Dublin in May resulting from car bombs planted by loyalist paramilitaries from the North, in June a 200lb car bomb had been planted in Clones, County Monaghan, by the 'Protestant Defence Brigade', which claimed 15,000 members organised in six county brigades, and as recently as 6 September the UDA had planted a bomb in Newton Cunningham in County Donegal. The attacks may also have provoked the meeting in Dublin on 5 October between the Taoiseach and representatives of the UDA. I was all in favour of this: the more the North and South talked with each other the better.

Overall, by the autumn of 1974 I began to feel that we were making progress on security, however slowly. The ending of detention was, however, more difficult. The Report of the Gardiner Committee to which I was looking for help was due in the New Year and I took the opportunity on 5 September, when I asked for evidence to be given to the Committee by any interested person or organisation, to say that the government recognised that detention 'even with the safeguards of the enquiries by independent judicial commissioners, raised grave issues of human rights and civil liberties'. I also reaffirmed the pledge to 'phase out detention consistent with the requirements of the security situation', and gave out statistics showing that a total of 321 detainees had been released between December 1973 and August 1974, 108 by order of the Secretary of State and 213 by the commissioners, while during the same period 238 interim custody orders had been signed, 43 of them for men previously detained. The purpose of publishing the figures and particularly the releases was to show that detention could be ended if there was a response from the paramilitaries.

Irish governments of whatever party were in an ambivalent position on detention because internment had been used intermittently in the South. Criticism could not be on principle but only on timing and method. Garret Fitzgerald, for example, in June 1974 criticised – correctly in my view – the way the Faulkner government had carried out internment, and went on to argue that there were about two hundred people that could be released from the Maze. Indeed, I thought, one could release the whole lot under certain circumstances but while the violence continued not all at once.

The detailed consideration of detention cases was taking up much of my time in the autumn of 1974 and not all those who criticised the procedures understood them – the initial signing of an interim custody order by me, the consideration of the cases by commissioners who had powers of release, and my releases by executive action. I did not accept all the applications for interim custody orders but I sometimes postponed executive releases when there had been a recent outbreak of bombings or killings. Other people had to be thought of: I was not willing to release men at a moment when their friends were blowing things up. The cry then was that I was being overruled by the army, or that I was holding detainees as political hostages. The press repeated the allegations and one of the quality papers went so far as to suggest that the GOC was not visiting the Castle because of bad relations over differences on detention. In fact Frank King more often came in the evening to the Culloden, where many decisions were taken, rather than to my room at Stormont.

Angry feelings about detention were inevitable and only the ending of the whole process could solve the problem. Then we would be able to close the detention compounds and also, once we had built new prison cells, the separate compounds provided for special category prisoners. Closing the latter would also diminish the importance of the paramilitary officers who presently commanded them; these officers negotiated with prison staff on regimes, etc., and decided whether prisoners would be accepted, after which a prisoner applied 'for residence' to the prison governor. The whole compound system had been a grave mistake that had not only made prison discipline impossible but had enabled the Maze to become a staff college for all the paramilitaries. It was not only detention that had to be ended but also special category status.

This aim was the subject of a memorandum to my Cabinet sub-committee colleagues on 6 September. I pointed out that it was not going to be easy, since I had inherited no plans for providing extra prison accommodation. A recommendation in the early 1970s for a new purpose-built prison to replace that in Crumlin Road had been shelved, and it would require about seven years to build a modern prison. Time was once again needed to deal with a problem that demanded immediate attention, as I had realised when I first looked into the question after the publication of the July White Paper. It was then, after a visit to the newer Magilligan Prison, that I expressed the hope that the Maze would be shut. Long Kesh had already become part of Northern Irish folklore.

Existing prison arrangements were without doubt poor, as the Gardiner Committee members confirmed when I met them in September. Prison building would take time, and they could not suggest any scheme that would deal with the problem quickly. Meanwhile, another short-term problem in the prisons arose with a threat of strike action by 1,900 prison officers in the province, whose responsibilities included the 1,500 prisoners with special category status. The prisons concerned were the Maze, Magilligan, Crumlin Road and Armagh Women's Prison. I was advised that the youth prison at Hydebank was unlikely to be involved.

No practical thought seems ever to have been given to what we would do if such a strike materialised, although the threat was apparently not new. For example, what role would we expect from the army? In a preliminary discussion it seemed that we might have to call in the reserve battalion from the UK in case we had to take over the Maze. From the Ministry of Defence, however, came the glum response that the army could not be involved inside the prison. As far as I was concerned, it was out of the question that, if the prison officers did strike, the army would guard the outside of the prison while the prisoners ran their own lives inside.

I sent a minute on the problem to the Prime Minister but before we had a reply, another problem arose. The date of the General Election, 10 October, had been announced when I was down in Dublin and it now appeared that the paramilitaries of all persuasions had decided to cause trouble in the prisons in order to influence the result in the province. The issue chosen was prison food, and in the first week of September both loyalist and republican prisoners began rejecting meals as 'inedible and insufficient'. Food was thrown over the compound fences and sanitation began to be a problem for the prison authorities. The issue was taken up by the paramilitaries outside, together with the fringe organisations which abound.

The prison food was in fact as good, if not better, than such food elsewhere, and on 9 September I authorised the stopping of food parcels, though not toilet requisites or cigarettes, into the Maze because it was easy to throw away prison food while there were other sources available. In response, during the following afternoon's rush-hour traffic in Belfast, hundreds of members of the UDA formed human chains and hijacked vehicles to block roads, as a protest against the quality of food served to prisoners in the Maze. The outcry continued and the following week both loyalists and republicans protested outside the prison. In the forlorn hope that facts mattered, I issued a statement on 11 September which itemised the food provided at the Maze and explained that special category prisoners were allowed food parcels and were able to purchase items from the prison shop, and that complaints could be made to the Board of Visitors. It was all to no avail. The street protests continued.

On 15 September I issued another statement on prison conditions – more sheets were to be made available, a new laundry would be built, food distribution would be speeded up – but it was rejected by a joint committee of the UDA, UVF, Provisional and Official IRAs! Andy Tyrie, the UDA leader, presented us with a thirty-six point improvement plan for the Maze, and the dispute spread to the Magilligan Prison.

By this time the press was full of the prison problem, and there was wide agreement from the vantage point of the Europa Hotel as to what the loyalists were going to do – we were again heading for an Ulster workers' strike. This was not our view in the office, not only because of a general belief that only a Sunningdale could bring a repeat of May 1974, but also because feed-back from within the loyalist paramilitary groups did not indicate it. Our sources were better than those of the media.

Given our view, and that the prisoners were hurting themselves more than us, it seemed logical enough to accept a loyalist statement of 22 September that their action was over. However, after three days, in true Irish style, it all started again, this time on the issue of compassionate home leave. Northern Ireland had developed its own distinctive and, indeed, liberal prison procedures, and one of the differences between it and Great Britain was that selected prisoners who had served a substantial period of their sentence could be awarded home leave in the summer and over the Christmas period. We were now accused of going back on this.

On the same day as the loyalist threats over parole, we learned from a smuggled out letter that the republican prisoners were planning to burn down the Maze and the Magilligan and Armagh prisons. We had a prologue to this on 1 October, when rioting broke out in the Maze, and on 2 October, when huts in the Maze car park were set on fire and some visitors got into the compounds.

Whether or not it was because by this time the army was available, and we had made this very apparent, the governor of the Maze on his own volition was able to negotiate a truce. Visiting and food parcels would resume, and the Provisional IRA announced that food and utensils would not be thrown over the fences. However, the loyalist trouble was not over and on 5 October, at the height of the General Election campaign, the UDA threatened an extension of their protest if we did not provide more liberal parole, improved laundry and recreational facilities, and increased allowances for spending in the prison shop. The prison issue was still rumbling on when polling day took place on 10 October.

Just as in Ulster the General Election campaign had proceeded as if British issues did not exist, in Great Britain, the Election had not been affected in general by the issue of Northern Ireland, nor in particular by the events in the prisons. In September there had also been the Provisional IRA murders in the province of Judge Rory Conaghan and Resident Magistrate Martin McBirney, and on 5 October there had been the bombings in Guildford in which five people were injured when bombs exploded without warning at two pubs. However, the issues that mattered were those that arose in Great Britain, principally the economy. It was a reflection of my own interest in Northern Ireland, not because it was an election issue, that I stated at my nomination meeting in Leeds in late September that to pull out of Ireland would lead to civil war. I also poked fun at Enoch Powell about free market forces and Harland and Wolff.

In my own constituency we had many good meetings and a good victory in the Election, with a majority of 15,000. The Liberals went back from second to third place. In the country as a whole, as I had predicted in my diary in September, there was a lower poll than at the last Election, with the Tories and Liberals doing less well than last time. The Labour Party gained eighteen seats and obtained an overall majority of three in the House of Commons. All talk of coalition was ended, and we were again in government, not because the electorate was turning to us but because the Liberals had taken votes mostly off the Tories. However, this time our majority was enough to govern for a period of years not months, for it totalled twenty-four over the Tories and the disparate minority parties were unlikely to combine together to assist Mr Heath. And I was still Secretary of State, but this time I had seven months of hard experience behind me to help buttress my aims of achieving the primacy of the police and involving all the elected politicians of the province in discussing its future devolved government.

Part III

SECOND PERIOD OF OFFICE

October 1974–September 1976

Chapter 6

REVIEW OF POLICY

The beginning of a new term of office is the time to look again at policies and now that the General Election results had given us a clearer mandate, it was possible to set longer sights on our policies for Northern Ireland. I had no second thoughts about the general direction in which I had recommended we should travel and at the Cabinet sub-committee meeting on 24 October, I presented a paper on future policy which dealt with all aspects of the Convention.

I stressed that our task now was to turn the attention of the Northern Irish political parties to the proposed Assembly. There was a danger that the leaders would demand mutually conflicting assurances from us and would take up positions from which it would be difficult to move them, but my job was to avoid this pitfall. Although it was idle to pretend that the Convention had a strong chance of succeeding – indeed there was a high likelihood of failure – this time the politicians could not blame the British for the outcome. The ball was in their court.

In the ensuing discussion, one of my colleagues proposed an early election to the Convention rather than waiting until March 1975, the date I was suggesting, because events in the intervening few months might become difficult to control. Another proposed that, since we believed the Convention would probably fail, it would be better to postpone it indefinitely and carry on with direct rule. It was even suggested that this would be supported by the Irish government and the SDLP, despite my considered view that the former only wanted reassurance that the Convention was not a device for us to pull out leaving a Congo situation, and the latter that it was not a means of handing over to the loyalists.

My heart sank in the face of such uncomprehending comments. Even if the Convention were a success, devolved government would still be a very long way off; nothing was going to happen quickly, and I knew that we had to involve the local politicians. The tone of the discussion irritated me. A few colleagues were casting doubts on policies on the basis of insufficient knowledge, and I realised afresh that the distance between Whitehall and Stormont can be measured in light years. However, it was all very much a minority view and the Prime Minister made some perceptive remarks, as did Denis Healey, who understood that we had to proceed on the basis of the Convention's success although, if it failed, we would not be able to shrug off responsibility for Northern Ireland.

Despite such powerful support I was still concerned about the ensuing full Cabinet meeting and on 28 October I wrote to the Prime Minister from Belfast, always a better place than London to see the reality of the situation. A discussion with local journalists the evening before had reinforced my feelings that we had to involve the Northern Irish politicians fully in the Convention. I told Harold that I was confident that we were right to press on with the Convention and that the election for it should not be until March 1975. I would shortly publish a discussion paper for the Ulster politicians on possible ways of running the Convention, with an introduction giving our aims, and I would also announce the name of the Convention chairman in due course.

Although there were dangers that the Convention would collapse, I told Harold that I nevertheless saw hope in our approach, for in the end a solution to Northern Ireland could only come from Northern Ireland itself, however long it took for the web to be untangled. If the Convention did break down, we had to be ready to develop a new political policy from the situation and although this was easier said than done, the parameters were clear: there could be neither a United Ireland on the one hand nor a move to integration on the other. Our aim would remain to move away from direct rule.

I turned finally to security. Should a breakdown of the Convention lead to another Ulster workers' strike, a number of contingency plans were being prepared, although the limits to what we could do had been shown in May. Meanwhile, our commitment was to tackle the problems of law and order. In the short term there was no security without the army but in the long run the role of the police would be crucial and it was encouraging that recruitment was improving and that at least some of the minority community were turning towards the police.

This reference to security reinforced the facts and figures I had given to my colleagues at the Cabinet sub-committee meeting, when I had told them that whatever we did on the Convention or any other political initiative, the violence would remain. Violence was endemic. This was borne out by the troubles in the prisons, which had begun on the evening of 15 October when convicted republican prisoners in the Maze attacked prison officers, ransacked the prison and set many of the buildings on fire. Eighteen of the twenty-one compounds were destroyed or seriously damaged, along with the prison hospital, the kitchen, the shop, the visitors' reception buildings and the internal towers. Prison officers repulsed an attempt to storm the main gate, and also managed to rescue from the cell block four prisoners who were in danger of being burnt to death.

Whatever the reluctance already expressed by the Ministry of Defence to involve soldiers within the prisons, there was now no choice but to use the army, for, as I had earlier made clear, I was not prepared to sit back in the event of a possible mass breakout. I approved the request of the Governor of the Maze for an army detachment to go into the prison and also gave approval to a limited use of CS gas by the army, and I authorised that the reserve battalion should be brought in from the UK. I visited the army operations room at Lisburn, which was very well organised, and I was impressed at the efficient way that soldiers could be deployed from all parts of the province. There was a lesson here for the police, for no police force could move as efficiently without a mobile reserve available and without pre-training for movement.

As I reported to the Commons once it reassembled on 30 October:

> Strong army reinforcements were sent to the area during the night and the outside perimeter was secured. As soon as it was light on the next day, the army moved into the prison in strength to restore order. Rather more than two hundred republican detainees who had remained in their compounds offered no resistance, but the remainder of the republican detainees, together with the republican prisoners, concentrated at the opposite end of the prison, armed with a variety of weapons including sharpened lengths of timber, steel piping, knives and iron bed-legs. When an attempt was made to disarm them, a vicious battle ensued with the army. CS gas and baton rounds had to be used before order could be restored.

Medical services were standing by from the start of the riot and despite alarmist rumours to the contrary, there were few casualties. Of over three hundred prisoners who claimed to be hurt, only nine were detained in hospital, three of whom had been discharged by the end of October when I reported to the Commons, and of the fourteen prison officers injured, the four admitted to hospital had all since been discharged. Twenty-three soldiers were injured but none of the sixteen sent to hospital was admitted as a patient.

Casualty details and reports of the prison situation were given by the Northern Ireland Office information services as they became available. Alarmist rumours were, however, an increasing problem and despite our intention to quash these, the more frequent the statements, the less chance they had of being completely accurate and the inaccuracies were seized upon to paint a grossly exaggerated picture.

I was concerned that the trouble did not spread to loyalist prisoners and detainees, who had not been involved in the Maze riot, and I therefore allowed Andy Tyrie, commander of the UDA, to visit 'his men' in the prison. As it was, the republican trouble spread to the three other main prisons in the province during Wednesday the 16th and road blocks were put up in Belfast, Derry and Newry. I later reported to the Commons:

> At Armagh Women's Prison the Governor and three female officers were seized as hostages when the prisoners heard rumours of death and serious injury to prisoners at the Maze. Fourteen hours later the prisoners released the hostages unharmed after two chaplains had persuaded them that these rumours were unfounded. There were no injuries.
>
> In Crumlin Road Prison, republicans on remand barricaded themselves on two floors during the afternoon; there was considerable damage but order was restored by troops in support of the prison staff with the aid of CS gas and baton rounds. There was considerable resistance and some 131 prisoners received injuries, mostly minor. Ten were taken to hospital for examination but all were returned.
>
> At Magilligan Prison some republican convicted prisoners burnt the kitchen, part of the hospital and a number of other huts. Order was restored by the prison officers. There were no injuries involving prisoners but three prison officers received minor injuries.

By 19 October I was able to announce that the prisons were quiet and repeated what I had said in many broadcasts: the riots would not influence my policy. The Gardiner Report would be the basis for any change on detention policy and on special category status. Meanwhile, immediate provisional measures had been taken to provide protective sheeting, field kitchens and mobile sanitary units at the Maze.

The whole episode had shown again our dependence on the army. Without it, as I had seen for myself on the night of the blaze, we could not have kept the peace or provided support for the prison officers, nor could we have supplied the civil equipment needed, such as temporary beds and bedding.

The prison violence aroused considerable emotion and affected public attitudes in Northern Ireland but it was taken as par for the course in the rest of the UK. Nevertheless, on 30 October, two days after my minute on long-term political policy to the Prime Minister, I was back to the hard facts of the short term with a report to the Commons on the prison riots. As well as the other aspects of the incident, there was the enormous cost: to repair the damage at the Maze was estimated at £1½ million and at Magilligan £200,000; Crumlin Road was considerably less. Restoration work had begun in the Maze and, in another report to the Commons a few weeks later, I was able to announce that the compounds destroyed in the rioting would be restored to their original condition by spring 1975, due to the work of three hundred Royal Engineers who had been flown into the province.

I wanted a full enquiry into the Maze destruction and I confirmed to the House that this had been set up under the Chief Inspector of Prisons at the Home Office. I mentioned that I had also arranged for a group of United Kingdom MPs to visit the Maze to see the conditions for themselves. Their reception by the prisoners was unlikely to be much different from that given to a group of Northern Irish politicians on 5 November, when Provisional IRA prisoners refused to talk with the SDLP members. It showed the problem faced by Catholic politicians in Northern Ireland and also illustrated the attitude of the paramilitary organisations to those who work through the ballot box.

That Northern Ireland is a world unto itself was shown again when David Morley, the 'IRA Commander' in the Maze, apologised publicly to Jim Craig, the 'UDA Commander'. He accepted full responsibility for camp damage and had, he said, made representations to the Northern Ireland Office to exonerate UDA members from the destruction!

When things go wrong in Ireland, they tend to go very wrong, and the problems in the Maze were no exception. On 1 November the prison authorities found a cache of imitation weapons, looted prison officer uniforms, plans of the prison and also drugs and medical equipment. Plans for a break-out were clearly afoot and, if nothing else, it was not surprising that in the early hours of 6 November, thirty-three republican prisoners escaped through a sixty-five-yard tunnel. The debris in the prison had made it difficult to detect the soil from tunnelling and, as the GOC revealed later in a television broadcast, even our aerial technical detection devices were not working.

Twenty-nine of the prisoners were recaptured a few hours later and three more that evening up in Andersonstown; one was shot dead by a sentry. There was some subsequent rioting in the prison and also an attempted escape by republican detainees from another compound. A hole in the ground was found outside the perimeter fence and led back to the compound where the huts had been burnt the previous month; once again the hiding of soil had been made easier by the debris that still littered the area.

I reported all these events to the House of Commons and Ian Gilmour responded by asking me to 'face the fact that the unrest in the prisons is made worse by the impression that the government at present in Northern Ireland are merely drifting'. He wanted an announcement about future policy and to know when the 'drifting' would stop. This was on all fours with the niggling in Cabinet and I reacted in the same fashion. I did not see that problems in Northern Ireland were going to be solved by an anodyne statement at Westminster from me about so-called political progress. If I had wanted to play the debating game, I could have asked him why his government had not done anything about the prison problem – prisons are not built overnight.

On 18 November I was ready to announce to the Commons our plans for a new prison at Maghaberry, County Antrim. Since the Cunningham Report in December 1971 to the then Northern Ireland government, a search had been going on to find a site for a new permanent high-security prison, and of sixteen sites examined, this was the most suitable. It would take four to five years to complete and would provide cell accommodation for four to five hundred male convicted prisoners. There would also be a separate new women's prison and a young offenders' centre for girls between sixteen and twenty-one.

I told the House that it was my aim to provide on the same site advance accommodation to which some of the convicted prisoners in the Maze could be redeployed as soon as possible. This new accommodation would be in cell form, with a capacity to hold seven hundred men, and was planned for occupation in early 1976. I also reminded the House that plans had already been made for the completion during 1975 of a new wing at Armagh Women's Prison. Closed borstal accommodation would be ready during 1976 at Millisle; and work had already started on a young offenders' centre for three hundred males at Hydebankwood.

After the statement, it became increasingly clear during our usual late-night office discussions that, despite the advice from the prison department, it was impossible to provide the advance accommodation at Maghaberry by 1976 because the necessary planning and legal procedures could not be gone through quickly enough. If I wanted new cell blocks by then, the short-term solution was to build them at the Maze. My feelings were strongly against this – I wanted especially to get away from Long Kesh/the Maze and all that was associated with it – but I had to face the practicalities. I could not wait. The new prison would go ahead but I would have to provide earlier extra accommodation elsewhere. After one of our late-night discussions and a swift decision by the GOC, we decided that army personnel would build one hundred single cells in four separate units at the Maze. On 5 February

1975, after Treasury approval, I was able to inform the House of Commons. The units were to be the famous H-blocks, copied from plans for a proposed new English prison, and they were vital to my policy of ending the use of compounds, and thus special category status and detention.

A report I had received from the International Red Cross on 22 November 1974 confirmed my need to act on detention. A delegation had visited prisons in Northern Ireland earlier in the year and though its report on the physical conditions in the compounds, on kitchens and educational facilities was generally favourable, it gave support to the complaints about detention procedures. In particular it mentioned the increasingly long delay before individual detainees were seen by detention and review boards. In some cases, it was alleged that detainees spent six months before appearing in front of the detention board, when the statutory maximum was twenty-eight days, and as much as eighteen months – twice the statutory length – before being seen by the review board.

The members of the Red Cross delegation said of detention:

> They feel that even more serious consideration than heretofore should be given as to whether the present system of detention answers the situation; whether the army is the appropriate instrument for searches; what are going to be the long-term psychological effects of detention to detainees, whose average age is around twenty. Whilst fully appreciating the difficulties and the problems which the authorities and the army are faced, the delegates feel very deeply that greater efforts should be made, if not to phase out or abolish detention, at least to avoid its being counter-productive, sterile and even destructive.

They were right. I had to end detention. But, as the Red Cross report concluded: 'As they become increasingly familiar with the situation in Northern Ireland and with the tensions resulting therefrom and as their understanding of the diametrically opposed points of view deepens, the delegates are increasingly discouraged by the intractable character of the problems involved.' They could say that again! However, I could not be 'discouraged'; I had to tackle the problems and to press on with political policies against a continuing background of violence.

I had told my Cabinet colleagues at the 24 October meeting that despite the prison troubles the overall security situation was much calmer than we might have expected. Our major problem, given the changed nature of violence since 1972 from street demonstrations and commercial site bombings to guerrilla fighting and individual killings, was intersectarian murders. Since the assassinations of Judge Conaghan and Magistrate McBirney in September 1974, there had, I told them, been an escalation of such murders. At the end of November I described the most recent outbreak to the House of Commons, in response to a question from Ian Paisley which reflected the concern in Ulster:

> At 1.15 pm on Friday, a car drove into the forecourt of the People's Garage, Springfield Road, and the occupants opened fire on the employees, wounding two persons, one of whom has since died. At 4.45 on the same afternoon, shots were fired from a Ford car into the Hole in the Wall club, Ballycarry Street: one man was shot dead and another injured.
>
> At twenty-one minutes past midnight the following night, the body of a man was found lying in a field off the Hightown Road, Glengormley, with wounds to the head and back. A taxi cab was found abandoned near the scene of the murder. At 11.48 on the Saturday night, a customer found the bodies of a man and a young woman in a store at the rear of the Edenderry Filling Station in the Crumlin Road. Both had been shot through the back of the head. The man was the manager of the filling station. On the same day, the owner of the Arkle Taxi Company in Clifton Street arrived at his premises and found his wife shot dead. A customer was lying dead in the waiting room.

The total figure, I reported, was thirty-eight murders since 16 September and although detection of such crimes was difficult, nine people had been charged with murder and more than forty had been held by the police for firearms offences.

Murder of this type was particularly upsetting for the community at large because it was easy to carry out and, once begun, difficult to stop: gun down any person walking on the 'wrong' – Catholic or Protestant – side of the road; respond to the news of such a murder by picking off, as happened, a child whose religion was known to belong to the 'other' side; and thus the retaliation continues. It was not easy to deal with and I was advised that on past patterns it would peter out but then start up again with no obvious immediate reason. No one group of paramilitaries was responsible.

The sectarian murders were horrible but the Birmingham bombings on 21 November, when 19 people were killed and 182 injured by explosions in two Birmingham pubs, were more than that. They showed the Provisional IRA's total lack of political understanding as well as their brutal and bloody methods. The carnage spawned revulsion even in parts of the world where Ulster was seen in classical colonial terms. David O'Connell, the Provisional's Chief of Staff, made the ghoulish statement, 'Our whole campaign has been geared to avoid civilian casualties', the falsity of which was evident in the whole story of violence in Northern Ireland. He even had the nerve to deny publicly that his organisation was involved in the Birmingham bombings. But it certainly was, and no amount of weasel words could cover the fact.

The denial was on the same level as a Provisional IRA statement following the discovery of a bomb on a civil aircraft in which the RUC Chief Constable and William Craig had been travelling from London to Belfast in July. The story then was that the bomb had been deliberately set not to work but to act as a warning. There was no doubt in my mind that the Provisionals had meant to kill on that aircraft, just as they had meant to kill, and were successful, in Birmingham. Killing is their business. They seriously believe that murder and maiming will bring them a united Ireland. The effect is the opposite: to reinforce every myth and prejudice in Northern Ireland. The gut reaction of Sammy Smythe of the UDA to the Birmingham killings showed the well of tribal feelings there to be tapped: 'When I heard of the bombings, my immediate instinct was to get bombs and go out and blow up every well-filled Catholic church in Northern Ireland.'

The climate of public opinion in Britain was transformed by the Birmingham slaughter. In the West Midlands itself, the lives of ordinary Irish men and women were made very difficult because of the anti-Irish feelings aroused, even though 123 Catholic priests publicly condemned the bombings. In my diary I wrote: 'The terrible sight of what was done on Thursday gravely affects all our views at the moment, and understandably so. I don't believe that one death is worth any movement in Irish history.'

I was concerned also about the funeral that was about to take place in Belfast of James McDade, a Provisional IRA lieutenant who had accidentally blown himself to bits in Coventry a few days before the Birmingham incident. An indication of feelings in the Midlands was that workers at Birmingham airport had refused to load the coffin, bound initially for Dublin, on to an aircraft on the day of the bombings. My concern about the funeral led me to fly to London to talk with the Prime Minister, for I was determined to be tough about the arrangements. Rarely can a funeral have had so much preplanning by top brass.

We discussed the security arrangements at Stormont, and it was planned for the funeral procession to come down in vehicles from the Ardoyne, through the Protestant areas and into the Lower Falls. I wanted no marching, no masks or rifle shots, as laid down under the Emergency Provisions Act, but because I was advised by the army that these instructions were too inflexible, I altered the wording so that circumstances could be taken into account.

In the event there was no problem. There had already been some reluctance to handle the coffin on its journey from Dublin to the border and there was some question whether the parish priests at St Paul's church in Belfast would give a Mass for the body. Very few people turned out for the burial and there was no trouble as McDade's body was almost unceremoniously put into the ground at Milltown Cemetery. The shame of Birmingham had spread even to Belfast.

On the same day as the bombings the Cabinet sub-committee had met to discuss an updated options paper prepared by the Northern Ireland Office, together with the so-called contingency plans asked for at the previous meetings. On the former the advice was again clear: although the chances of success were not high, the Convention road should be followed and plans for direct rule meanwhile prepared. My only comment was 'Hear, hear', and I emphasised once more that for the present there could be no move away from direct rule since, even if we wished to transfer government to Northern Ireland, it would be impossible since there was no one there in a position to take over.

A few of my colleagues asked in the light of the Birmingham bombings what the point was of trying to bring the sort of people who could act in this way towards political activity? Was it not a waste of time? Their questioning of policy was understandable but overwhelmingly the support was for the Convention.

The Cabinet sub-committee discussion of the contingency plans also went my way. On the key question of an all-out strike touching the raw nerve of political beliefs in the province, the report was absolutely clear: it would not be possible to maintain the commercial, industrial and essential way of life in Northern Ireland. This was of course right, as the Ulster workers' strike had proved, but it was Whitehall romance to suggest that in such a strike essential services would be maintained by agreement of the strikers.

I was certain that there would not be a strike over the Convention. Only a fear throughout the loyalist community that they would be joined to the South would provoke a repeat of May 1974. A strike from any other cause could be dealt with. Indeed, at the time of our discussion there had just been a strike in the Northern Ireland Electricity Service, along with disputes affecting road transport and water supplies. It was very definitely an industrial and not a sectarian strike, and middle management had been prepared to go into work, if necessary crossing the pickets in a private helicopter arranged by their trade union, which had asked for reassurances from me that their members would be able to continue work. Because I had been concerned to avoid any confusion with the UWC strike, I had met with the Deputy Chief Constable and the Commander Land Forces in order to stress that this was an industrial dispute, and that was how it had been dealt with.

My policy was endorsed by my colleagues yet again but this time for the new Parliament. Despite my Celtic gloom over the previous weeks, I had never been in any real doubt that it would be, for this was the policy which Parliament had approved in July and which had been endorsed by the electorate in October. I later put it to the Labour Party Conference on 30 November, when there was warm approval for a 'move forward towards fresh elections within Northern Ireland, a constitutional convention for the people of Northern Ireland, structured to allow proper discussion of the economic and social problems'.

The October General Election had led to our review of policy and it also meant that in this first parliamentary session I had to report to the Commons, which I did on 5 December. The report was particularly significant given the Birmingham bombings, which had caused the Home Secretary to announce on 25 November that the IRA was to be declared illegal in Great Britain and tougher anti-terrorist laws were to be introduced. Although the Convention was the main subject of my report, I first described the security situation in Northern Ireland, where there had been a significant overall reduction in violence since 1972. Bomb incidents had dropped from 115 a month in 1972 to 81 a month in 1973 and 57 a month up to November 1974; shooting incidents had similarly fallen, from over 10,000 in 1972 to 3,052 up to the end of November 1974.

This was, I reported, due to the right security in town centres, vehicle checkpoints, and control over explosives, which were all increasingly under the control of the RUC whose detection rate had greatly improved. 'The co-operation of the community is beginning to tell.'

The army's presence was still vital. 'Without it, there would be civil war. The only hope of avoiding a catastrophe in Northern Ireland, brought about by terrorist acts, is to retain an army capacity to prevent a bloody confrontation between the two communities.' If possible, there should of course be a reduction in the army, and a reduction from sixteen to thirteen battalions had been made in 1974. I added, with a wider audience in mind:

> It is not the wish of the British people that the army should continue indefinitely in Northern Ireland to fulfil a role that is properly that of the police. A planned, orderly and progressive reduction in the army presence can and will follow the ending of the present campaign of

violence, but it will not be withdrawn so long as it is needed to support the RUC in maintaining law and order.

After this I turned to the Convention. I wanted the political parties in Northern Ireland to begin preparations for this before the Christmas recess and I told the Commons that the one task of the Convention was 'to make recommendations about the future constitution of Northern Ireland'. I emphasised that any system of devolved government had to take into account financial and economic realities. With memories of the financial rows in the last week of the Executive, I pointed out that 'the very language of priorities means that hard choices have to be made'.

I reminded the House that I had published a discussion paper on finance and the economy in September, and that this had been followed up by a second discussion paper in November on constitutional procedures for the Convention. Ultimately these would be the concern of those elected to the Convention and it was important that they were considered now so that discussion in the Convention would take place smoothly and effectively.

Preparations for the Convention were already under way so that it would be ready to start work soon after the elections took place. The name of the chairman I would be announcing in due course.

On power sharing, or participation as it was now being called in the office, I promised to publish a third discussion paper in the New Year which would 'set out a wide range of methods by which devolved governments can achieve effective genuine participation and protection of human rights in societies which have split communities. . . . What is important is that the Convention should be seeking agreement among all parts of the community.' The paper, 'Government of Northern Ireland', was in fact published in February.

I concluded with the theme that I still think is the one that should underline all policy for Northern Ireland: 'It is only by Irishmen getting together, by discussion amongst themselves, that solutions can be found to the problems of their political future.' I hoped that Irish politicians would take note when I said, 'The Constitutional Convention offers an opportunity for all shades of opinion to participate in such discussion, and people throughout these islands will expect all those with strong views about that political future to seize this unique opportunity.'

As the final note I reaffirmed that there was an Irish dimension – 'a practical relationship ought to exist between two good neighbours with a common land boundary' – and I repeated the words of the Taoiseach in the Dail earlier in the year: 'I solemnly reaffirm that the factual position of Northern Ireland within the United Kingdom cannot be changed except by a decision of a majority of the people of Northern Ireland.' The Irish government could not be fairer than that, and, for what seemed the hundredth time, I asserted that no British government could, even if it wished, drive the North into the South.

In the debate that followed, there was general acceptance of my policy, although Ian Gilmour for the Tories again complained of a political vacuum. How this was to be filled he did not suggest, though he did notice that I had 'quite rightly' made much of the importance of the policing problems.

There was a flurry of concern about the use of computers by the security forces, based on an article in *The Times* which had alleged that a computer was being used to record personal information about nearly half the population of the province. I quickly responded that computers were only used for vehicle checks. The issue had in fact been recently discussed and I had not agreed to extend the use of computers; in my view there was already too much information being collected in Northern Ireland and I wanted more selectivity. Only the police were capable of judging this.

Jim Molyneaux, leader of the Official Unionist MPs, was optimistic that something worthwhile would emerge from the Convention, and Ian Paisley was obviously in favour since he had long argued for it. Gerry Fitt was understandably gloomy about it, which reinforced my feeling that it was going to be a hard job to involve the SDLP. I was left with the same view that I had expressed to my colleagues after the General Election results in the province: there was some hope for the Convention but nothing more. We had much preparatory work to do in the months ahead.

Given the strong feelings engendered in Great Britain by the Birmingham bombings, it was remarkable that on 11 December a motion to reintroduce the death penalty brought by Jill Knight, a Birmingham MP, was defeated by 369 votes to 217, with eight of the Unionist MPs voting for the reintroduction. Enoch Powell voted against: Northern Ireland or not, he stuck to his principles.

It was an emotional debate. My own feelings were strongly against: the death penalty is not only morally wrong but it is not a deterrent, and certainly not in the Irish scene, as the executions after the 1916 Easter Rising in Dublin conclusively showed. Moreover, when Keith Joseph said that he wanted the death penalty reintroduced in Great Britain but not in Northern Ireland, he was driving a coach and horses through the argument. Northern Ireland is the place where terrorism is a daily event, yet it was there that the death penalty would not apply.

Catholics that I afterwards spoke to in Belfast found it remarkable that in the face of bombings and killings there, MPs could vote not to reintroduce the death penalty. But I was not alone in my view in Northern Ireland. When I spoke to the army generals a few days before the debate, they were not in favour of capital punishment. As I recorded in my diary: 'Of course they aren't. The whole argument of Irish history is against it, and the reintroduction could only be thought up by someone who does not know that country. Which is not to refute that it is something that would be overwhelmingly supported by the electorate.'

Whatever the denials of the Provisional IRA over the Birmingham bombings, there were signs that the public revulsion over them was causing the Provisional leaders to back-pedal. There had already in November been talk of a change of mood in the Provisional IRA in Northern Ireland and, given this possibility, I had deliberately spoken on the question of detention in my report to the House on 5 December:

> Detainees are not held for their political views but because of their involvement in violence. It is sometimes argued that the British government is treating people held in detention as hostages. The truth is that the extremist organisations – and this means above all the Provisional IRA – are using these men as pawns since, by ending their campaign of violence, these organisations could transform this whole situation. Indeed, it would then become possible to consider further changes in the custodial system. A reduction in violence would create an entirely new situation.

Perhaps this was noted by some in the Provisional IRA and reinforced the effect of Birmingham, but in any event, on 20 December, following talks between Protestant churchmen and Provisional IRA and Sinn Fein members at Feakle in County Clare, the Provisional IRA unilaterally declared a temporary ceasefire. It was my opportunity to act not through legislation or the Convention but through unplanned events to bring about a fundamental change in the province – to make a move on detention. This was far more important in the short run than the Convention.

Chapter 7

THE CEASEFIRE

The talks at Feakle came out of the blue for us in the British government. Ever since 1969 when the army took over security responsibilities in Northern Ireland, there had been ad hoc street contacts between the army and paramilitaries on both sides of the divide, and from the time I had taken office in March 1974 I was being advised that, according to community workers, businessmen or journalists, the Provisional IRA were in a mood to move from violence. Nevertheless, I was always sceptical and remained so when in November I was told of some sort of approach being made by the Provisional IRA.

I could not, however, ignore it, particularly when I learned that Provisional IRA representatives – influenced no doubt by two General Elections and the Ulster workers' strike – were also talking discreetly with representatives of the loyalist paramilitaries. There was absolutely no question of us giving any consideration to discussions or negotiations but I authorised a member of staff to meet a member of the Provisional Sinn Fein, the body that I had earlier legalised along with the Ulster Volunteer Force, in order to find out what the approach might mean.

I was in the same mood of scepticism when also in November, at a dinner for educationalists at the Culloden Hotel, I learned that Mr Worrall, formerly headmaster of Methodist College and now Chairman of the New Ulster Movement, had mentioned during the meal that a number of churchmen were in touch with the Provisionals and also with loyalist paramilitaries. I had simply responded that we should leave matters alone; take note but not get involved.

It was against this background that I told my colleagues at the Cabinet sub-committee meeting on 21 November that when the Gardiner Report came out, I would consider further releases from detention given 'reasonable and reliable assurances from the Provisional IRA that they would maintain a ceasefire'. The aim was to end detention.

I returned to the same theme at a further meeting in early December when I reported on an early draft of the Gardiner Report. Using as a basis its view that the Secretary of State had the responsibility for ending detention, I would look for a way to lead to a ceasefire and thus create the circumstances by which I could end detention. I would report to Parliament on the Report in the New Year. How these circumstances were to be created, I had yet to see but there was at present, I informed my colleagues, a change of mood among the Provisionals which was making for new developments. These, as it turned out, were the Feakle talks, which took place on 10 December in a hotel at Feakle in County Clare.

According to the statement made afterwards by the churchmen who were present, the church delegation was composed of Dr Arthur Butler, Church of Ireland Bishop of Connor, the Rev A. J. Weir, Clerk of the Assembly of the Presbyterian Church in Ireland, the Rev Eric Gallagher, former President of the Methodist Church in Ireland, Ralph Baxter, Secretary of the Irish Council of Churches, and the Rev William Arlow, Deputy Secretary, the Rev Harry Morton, General Secretary of the British Council of Churches, the Rev Arthur MacArthur, Moderator of the General Assembly of the United Reform Church in England and Wales, and Mr Stanley Worrall of the New Ulster Movement.

The Provisional Sinn Fein delegation included Rory O'Brady, President, Maire Drumm, Vice-President, and Seamus Loughran, Belfast organiser. David O'Connell, reported to be the Chief of Staff of the Provisional IRA, was also present, accompanied by Seamus Twomey, Belfast Brigade Commander, and Kevin Mallon, in charge of the border units of the IRA. The last three left the discussion hastily after allegedly receiving a tip-off that the hotel would be raided by the Irish Special Branch, which accordingly did not find them when they went into the hotel.

The media of the world were soon reporting the event and shortly afterwards the group of churchmen asked to see me. We met in the Commons on 18 December, when they gave me a copy of the document they had presented at Feakle. It suggested that the Provisional IRA would consider its requirements for a permanent ceasefire met if the British government would issue a policy statement that included the following:

1 HM Government solemnly reaffirms that it has no political or territorial interests in Ireland beyond its obligations to the citizens of Northern Ireland.

2 The prime concern of HM Government is the achievement of peace

and the promotion of such understanding between the various sections in Northern Ireland as will guarantee to all its people a full participation in the life of the community, whatever be the relationship of the province to the EEC, the United Kingdom or the Republic of Ireland.
3 Contingent upon the maintenance of a declared ceasefire and upon effective policing, HM Government will relieve the army as quickly as possible of its internal security duties.
4 Until agreements about the future government of Northern Ireland have been freely negotiated, accepted and guaranteed, HM Government intends to retain the presence of the armed forces in Northern Ireland.
5 HM Government recognises the obligation and right of all those who have political aims to pursue them through the democratic processes.

The churchmen had received the reply from the Provisional Army Council a few hours before our meeting in the Commons. It had evidently emerged after eighteen hours of intensive discussion but was only a holding statement. It began by commenting on the churchmen's five points:

1 It is sovereignty rather than political or territorial interests which is the basic issue. Until HM Government clearly states it has no claim to sovereignty to any part of Ireland, the statement is meaningless. We accept that economic commitments must be honoured.
2 A noble wish with which we concur but we believe it can only be realised in the full community of the people of Ireland.
3 We feel you are referring to a truce. We see no difficulty in maintaining community peace if a bilateral truce is agreed between the British army and the Irish Republican Army. We would welcome discussions with loyalist groups to secure their co-operation in maintaining peace.
4 We accept that following a declaration of intent to withdraw, a limited British army presence will be maintained while a negotiated and agreed settlement is sought and implemented.
5 It is meaningless to talk about democratic processes while, among other things, 2,000 political prisoners are in jail.

The statement then went on to give the Provisionals' own set of proposals for forwarding to the British government.

1 The establishment of a constituent assembly elected by the people of Ireland through universal adult suffrage and proportional representation. The assembly to draft a new all-Ireland constitution which would provide for a provisional parliament for Ulster (nine counties) with

meaningful powers. The constitution to be submitted in national referendum within six months of the first meeting of the assembly, and its adoption to require two-thirds support of the total valid poll.
2 A public commitment by the British government to withdraw from Ireland within twelve months of the adoption of the new all-Ireland constitution. This commitment to entail an immediate end to all raids, arrests and harassment of the population and a withdrawal of troops to barracks.
3 Declaration of amnesty for all political prisoners in Britain and Ireland, and all persons on the wanted list. The amnesty to be given effect by immediate releases and to be completed not later than thirty days prior to the date of the general election for the constituent assembly.

On the acceptance of these terms, the Republican Movement would be prepared to order a total ceasefire. A number of matters would require further clarification and elaboration which would be discussed as soon as the ceasefire is established. The Republican Movement for its part would welcome tripartite talks with loyalist and British army forces to secure their co-operation in the implementation of the ceasefire and the maintenance of community peace.

Finally, the Provisionals stated that they found the churchmen's terms unacceptable but that they would declare 'a temporary cessation of activities' from 22 December 1974 to 2 January 1975, provided that 'British army raids, harassment and arrests cease for the same period; no show of provocation is carried out by the Crown forces; the reintroduction of the RUC into areas in which they are not acceptable is not attempted'. 'Any breach of these terms will be considered as a refusal to accept the eleven-day cessation and appropriate action will be taken to protect our people. We wish to have an indication of the British government's attitude before the 28 December 1974.'

From the comments of the churchmen at our meeting, it was clear that the Provisional IRA still wanted a thirty-two-county Ireland but the political wing realised that there was no possibility of a military victory and wished to participate in the Convention elections. My response, they suggested, need not be positive but nor should it be negative. They had made the strength of Protestant feeling in the North absolutely clear to the Provisionals and since the Feakle meeting, they had been reassured by the muted response from the loyalists that there would not be a backlash.

In reply I told them that I would consider their words carefully but I was not prepared to negotiate. If there were to be 'a genuine and sustained cessation of violence', it would create a new situation, but I made it clear that any possible ceasefire had to include Great Britain.

My response was deliberately ultra-cautious, for I did not want to give the slightest cause for misunderstanding in anything I said. News of the Feakle talks had already produced rumours throughout Belfast and the city seemed to be full of people claiming to be acting on my behalf; it earned them the ear of journalists and sometimes a pint. Dr Paisley had even accused me of being involved in the Feakle discussions and to have arranged the churchmen's visit, which had been confirmed, he said, by Stan Orme and Don Concannon!

Further, the group of clergy were good men but the Reverend Arlow in particular was a chatterbox and after our meeting he was going to Dublin, where Feakle had prompted other offers of intermediaries. That same day, Dr John Connell, the Labour Member of the Dail who had helped set up the talks between Harold Wilson and 'friends of the Provisional IRA' in 1972, approached the British Embassy in Dublin with new proposals to bring about peace. When I heard this, I told Harold's office to be wary. Belfast was bad enough without Dublin joining in.

Back in the Northern Ireland Office, we analysed closely the documents of the churchmen and the Provisionals. The latter's grandiose scheme for a unified Ireland showed the usual incomprehension of loyalist attitudes in the North and of their own lack of a political base, even in the Republic. Was there really a hope of translating this into action? Why had the Provisional IRA gone to Feakle? Perhaps its leadership believed that the churchmen had substantial backing from the Northern Protestant community or, far more likely, it wanted time to regroup and re-equip. I personally believed that the ignominy of Birmingham was a major reason but a combination of all these factors seemed the best conclusion to draw.

Whatever the Provisionals' motivation, on 20 December they announced 'a suspension of offensive military action in Britain and Ireland over the Christmas period'. The statement went on to say that after proposals for a ceasefire from church representatives at Feakle, the Provisionals had drafted counter-proposals embodying the three basic demands of the republican movement and these had been forwarded to the British government.

> This move has been prompted by the courageous and positive action of the church representatives whose approach, unlike that of others, was frank and constructive at all times.
>
> The truce is also designed to give the British government an opportunity to consider the proposals for a permanent ceasefire. The suspension of operations has been ordered on the clear understanding that a positive response will be forthcoming from the British government. We have

> noted a statement by Mr Rees to this effect and we expect a cessation of aggressive military action by Crown forces, an end to all raids, arrests and harassment and no reintroduction of the RUC, in uniform or plainclothes, into areas where they are not acceptable.
>
> We also trust that the British government will avail of this opportunity to bring to an end the evil of internment.
>
> The leadership of the movement await a reply from the British government to the proposals for a total ceasefire. If there is not a satisfactory reply by midnight, January 2nd, 1975, then the Irish Republican Army will have no option but to resume hostilities.

My brief response came quickly:

> The Provisional IRA have declared a unilateral temporary suspension of offensive military action beginning on 22 December. This is in response to the recent independent initiative by a group of churchmen. The churchmen came to see me in London on 18 December at their own request. Their purpose was to inform me of this initiative. I told them that if there were to be a genuine cessation of violence, there would be a new situation to which the government would naturally respond. This remains the government's position.

I was equally terse on the role of the army, stating that 'the actions of the security forces will be related to the level of any activity which may occur. No specific undertakings will be given.' I also endeavoured to dampen the rumours circulating about the ceasefire proposals:

> The government has received from the churchmen what it understands to be the Provisional IRA's proposals for a permanent ceasefire. I must make it clear that no proposals have been discussed or considered by the government. In these circumstances there is no question of the government giving any undertaking going beyond what I have already said. A genuine and sustained cessation of violence over a period would create a new situation.

However short this response, it had been considered at length in the office and discussed fully with the GOC and the Chief Constable, though the final decision was mine alone. I wanted to avoid any misunderstandings from lack of clarity in statements and it was for this reason that I also laid down the basis for meetings between staff and the Provisional Sinn Fein, which I now decided to put on a more formal basis than the sort of explanatory meeting I had already sanctioned.

The purpose of such meetings was to exchange views with the Provisional Sinn Fein, a legal body. There were to be no negotiations:

it was the Provisional IRA which had declared the ceasefire, unilaterally not bilaterally, and the government had stated publicly how it would respond and its future intentions. There was to be no deal on anyone's political future, and nothing was to be said that was at variance with my public statements and those made to the House of Commons. On this basis talks with representatives of the Provisional Sinn Fein took place from 22 December to 17 January.

Similar guidelines were laid down for any meetings with legal political wings of loyalist paramilitary organisations. At the same time I formulated the three basic points of all my statements in and out of the House of Commons: 'There had to be a genuine and sustained cessation of violence. The actions of the security forces would be related to the level of activity by the paramilitaries. Once violence ceased, the detainees would be progressively released.'

Meanwhile, I had received a final copy of the Gardiner Report. I took myself off to my Admiralty House flat for the day to study it in peace. The basic change it recommended was that detention should be put back firmly into the hands of the Secretary of State. It recognised that detention was a political issue and not a matter for the judiciary, though it recommended some sort of 'wise men' to look at my decisions. I suspected that the committee had started off with the idea of ending detention but had learned the hard way from its enquiries in Northern Ireland. One of the 'Faulkner' detainees, for example, had made it plain to them that if he were released, he would go back to killing. The Report consequently made no recommendation about ending detention. It was up to me.

I considered what use I should make of the Report and decided to make a statement to Parliament early in the New Year that if there was an enduring ceasefire, I would announce a phasing out of detention by the end of 1975 or mid-1976, together with a phased reduction in the role of the army and an increase in the role of the police. I would also announce the end of special category status, along with a new parole scheme. The parliamentary statement would include further references to the Convention, in which the Provisional Sinn Fein would be free to take part, and to the discussion paper on various forms of power sharing which I intended to issue.

These points were agreed by my colleagues at the Cabinet sub-committee meeting on 17 December, and the subsequent announcement of the ceasefire gave them added importance. I also brought up at the meeting the problem of contact with the Provisional Sinn Fein, for the people we were in touch with at a very low level were not political beings, which meant that we did not have the faintest idea what they were up to.

Ceasefire or not, I continued to act cautiously on security. I was not prepared to put lives at risk and would go only as far as to decide with the agreement of the GOC to reduce the size and frequency of army patrols, particularly in urban areas. I gave no instructions to the RUC: if the law was broken, the police would react; in republican areas there was anyway little or no RUC presence or information on criminals. Detainees continued to be released through the normal procedures with a handful being released by me using my executive powers. Between 22 December and 17 January, the total was fifty-two – there was a long journey ahead before Long Kesh was emptied. I did not, however, sign any interim custody orders during that period.

The response to the ceasefire in Great Britain was one of quiet relief; in Northern Ireland it was euphoric – to be able to go Christmas shopping without fear of death or maiming! One sensed the strong wish for peace in the community, and I tried to link this to the ceasefire in my message to the province on 24 December: 'It is my hope that the traditional Christmas spirit of peace and goodwill will endure not merely for a few days but will extend into the New Year and beyond. A cessation of violence in the weeks and months ahead will open up avenues of political advance. In the long run politics is more productive than the bomb and the bullet.'

It was all a matter of hope, particularly given the reactions to the ceasefire of the loyalist politicians. They saw the whole thing as a sell-out to murdering republicans – continuing the initial reaction of Ian Paisley, who kept up his wild allegations of a deal between myself and the IRA. We judged in the office, however, that the politicians were not for once speaking for their electors.

The SDLP leaders were worried too, for while as members of the Catholic community they wanted peace, they were concerned that the ceasefire would enhance the political role of the Provisional Sinn Fein. My own view was that as long as the Provisional IRA did not reject killing as its means of operation, protestations of political aims by the Provisional Sinn Fein sounded hollow and unconvincing. Another factor in the scene was that a new political party, the Irish Republican Socialist Party, had emerged in early December. It claimed, implausibly, to be devoted to non-violent policies, which certainly did not prove to be the case. However, as it was put to me, 'Like medieval pretenders to the papacy, the old and the new republicans have been hurling anathemas at each other.' The political pot of republicanism was clearly on the boil.

All our analyses of the situation in the Northern Ireland Office raised doubts about the future of the ceasefire, particularly given the instances – few as they were – of bomb plantings, but it was still operating at the end of the year and in my New Year message I spoke directly to those behind it. After emphasising yet again the need for 'a genuine and sustained cessation of violence' – the words could have been emblazoned in neon lights over Stormont Castle – I went on: 'I intend during January to set out more fully how the permanent cessation of violence would enable the army to make a planned, orderly and progressive reduction in its present commitment and how, once violence has ceased and is seen to have ceased, it would also become possible for those who are detained to be progressively released.'

I repeated my earlier words that the actions of the security forces would continue to be related to the level of any activity that might occur, but warned, 'I am not going to act precipitately before I am convinced that the opportunities are real and not illusory.' I was not prepared to barter the safety of the ordinary people of the province.

We did not know how the Provisional IRA would react in the weeks ahead but earlier signs had not been hopeful. In late December there had, for example, been small bombs planted in the homes of civil servants in Belfast and bigger bombs, including one at Ted Heath's home, in London. Office staff in contact with Provisional Sinn Fein members told them that if this was what was meant by 'ceasefire', my response would be in accordance.

The meaning of the ceasefire was the question we posed to each other in the Northern Ireland Office. We tried to understand the frame of mind of the Army Council which controlled the Provisional IRA from the South. The talks with the churchmen had shown a confused group of men but were they moved by the strength of the security forces or by reduced popular support? We concluded that the most we could hope for was a temporary prolongation of the ceasefire on 2 January, following a tussle between hawks and doves on the Army Council, which would face trouble in the Catholic community if the unilateral ceasefire was ended simply for the sake of it. What we wanted was a continuation to the point where the 'new situation' I frequently spoke of in public could be said to have come about. Only then could we respond.

The army staff in Northern Ireland understood that I had to work to this end, even if their own belief was that the Provisional IRA was simply gaining time for regrouping. They readily accepted that there had to be a low army profile and a small number of executive releases. The latter in fact amounted only to three – a Protestant man requested by a loyalist politician and a Catholic man and wife requested by the Cardinal – and, though an insignificant number in terms of the total detained, I was showing that I had the power to act on detention if I was given the chance.

I wanted to assess the situation for myself, not just sit in the Castle discussing it with officials, and as part of this Stan Orme and I met on 30 December the leaders of the Catholic Church and three main Protestant churches in Northern Ireland. All four men described the remarkable response which the peace campaign had evoked throughout Ireland but above all they emphasised their concern lest the opportunities now presented should be allowed to slip. Cardinal Conway estimated that some ninety-eight per cent of his community wanted Provisional IRA violence to stop and said that the current hopeful change of mood would evaporate if the ceasefire was not extended. If it was, further extensions would be easier to obtain. I should make a tangible response before 2 January in order to strengthen the doves on the Provisional Army Council.

When I asked him what this tangible response should be, he advised that as a gesture I should release a number of detainees, not enough to antagonise the loyalists but enough to help the moderates on the Army Council, and that I should stop 'army harassment' in the republican areas. Very fairly, he told me that, while it was not his own position, some Catholic bishops believed that a private message to the Provisional IRA, telling them the Feakle proposals were being seriously considered, would be better than a gesture on releases. This was also the general view of the Protestant leaders, who unanimously wanted me to leave any definite response until it was known whether the ceasefire was to be extended. They all, however, told me that the decision was mine: I was the politician!

The churchmen had also asked for a meeting with Harold Wilson in London. I told Harold that I thought this would show far more than any meeting with me that the government welcomed the involvement of the churchmen, and he promptly arranged for us all to meet at No 10 the following evening, 31 December. Frank Cooper was present on this occasion, and also Joe Haines.

We went over the same ground as in the previous meeting. The churchmen gave their views on the reason for the ceasefire, and agreed that the Birmingham bombings were the major cause though, to my surprise, it was argued that the United Kingdom Prevention of Terrorism Act introduced by Roy Jenkins after the bombings had played some part. Interestingly, Cardinal Conway thought that, important as Birmingham was, the Provisionals had been thinking of a ceasefire for some time.

The possibilities of a power-sharing government in the province were ranged over, from which it was clear that, whatever the views of the churchmen themselves, they could not guarantee that the loyalist community would support another effort in this direction. We also had a long discussion on the role of the army. I pointed out that while I could see that military action could be counter-productive, immediately we reduced numbers in republican areas we had protests from local Catholics. In particular I mentioned Ballymaccarret, where the Catholics felt beleaguered.

I was asked about using military police to replace ordinary soldiers in suitable areas; this, I told them, was our hope but we were short of army policemen. There were questions too about putting more soldiers on the border and having less on duty inside the province, which led to a discussion of the nature of the border and the loyalist belief that the Provisional IRA troubles came from the South, whereas in fact most Provisionals lived or came from within Northern Ireland. None of the churchmen wanted the British troops to leave and create a vacuum.

Another concern they voiced was over the role of the media. Could I not tell one editor, I was asked, that to say that my statement carried 'the stench of betrayal' was irresponsible? I suggested that they might like to meet newspaper editors in the province to see whether their influence was better than mine!

The meeting went on and on, with Harold being more generous on time than he ever was to the Cabinet. Afterwards, however, the press statement was brief, concentrating only on hope for the future and promising that we were all going to meet again.

Whether by cause and effect we will never know but the next day, 1 January 1975, the Provisional Sinn Fein issued a letter to me:

> ... There is in Ireland a great desire among all the people for lasting peace. Unfortunately, our country has not known true peace for many centuries. Instead we have had recurring cycles of war and truce, due to the colonialist policies of successive English monarchs and governments.
>
> We believe that a true and enduring peace must be based on justice. Where there is injustice, there cannot be peace. To establish a lasting peace in Ireland, the national rights of the Irish people must be respected and the basic cause of violence must be removed. This can only be achieved by a British commitment to disengage and withdraw from Ireland forever, and the establishment of a just social order and economic system which will give everyone a living in dignity and happiness.
>
> The present temporary cessation of hostilities by the republican forces provides your government with an opportunity to plan for peace by taking the steps necessary to make a phased and orderly withdrawal from Ireland. If British governments have relinquished sovereignty over other colonies in the recent past, why should the British government of today shirk the courageous decision to state publicly that the future of Ireland is

a matter for the people of all Ireland, and for them alone, to decide?

We ask you today to convey to your government this expression of the desire for peace with justice in Ireland. We ask also for the necessary response which will make possible the extension of the truce beyond 2 January. It must be a response which will be generous, substantial and courageous, and which will lead to the ultimate withdrawal of your government's forces and administration from Ireland.

Sinn Fein and the whole republican movement will not be found wanting in generosity either. There is no desire on our part to continue the struggle for one moment longer than is necessary to achieve the foundation of a lasting peace. Furthermore, we have published our proposals for a new Federal Ireland which would give all four provinces a considerable degree of autonomy and would thus guarantee the rights of all, irrespective of class or creed.

We wish you to bring these points to the attention of your government as a matter of extreme urgency, and we hope that the New Year which has just dawned will bring us a long way on the road to peace with justice and the creation of normal relations between the people of England, Scotland and Wales and the people of Ireland.

Again, we read this letter carefully in the office. It contained no surprises though at least the words 'ultimate withdrawal' showed that the Provisionals were aware of what would happen if the army left Northern Ireland at once. Contact between civil servants in the office and the Provisional Sinn Fein continued during this time on the basis of my public statements. On the following day, 2 January, the Provisional Army Council announced that the ceasefire would be renewed for a further fourteen days. In their statement, they said:

While recognising some minor developments as regards political prisoners and the role of the Crown forces, the response [of the British government] was not sufficient to warrant a permanent ceasefire. A satisfactory reply to the IRA proposals for a lasting peace was not received from the British government and it is elusory and deceptive on the part of that government to pretend that the root causes of the conflict can be ignored. A permanent peace will be established only when the causes of the war are courageously examined and eradicated. . . .

If substantial progress is not recorded by 16 January, the situation will be examined with a view to resuming offensive military action. The peace enjoyed for Christmas can be made permanent if the British government proves its sincerity by pursuing a reasonable and responsible policy. Peace with justice is the universal demand of all our people and the responsibility for granting same rests with the British government.

> The attitude of the Dublin government during the truce was most disquieting. There was no desire on their part for the truce and the harsh conditions imposed on political prisoners in Portlaoise was deliberate provocation. We call on the people to demand an end to the dangerous policy of the Dublin government.

This last part was a reference to a riot on 29 December by Provisional IRA prisoners in the Republic's top-security prison at Portlaoise, where troops had to be sent in to restore order after prison officers were taken hostage and serious damage caused to buildings. It was evidence to the world, should it have been needed, that the Provisional IRA and its allies had no strong political base in the South.

The fourteen-day extension gave me more time to consider my response to the Provisionals and also to Parliament, where I was due to make a statement on its return from the Christmas recess. It also enabled me to turn my attention to Dublin and Dr John Connell, who was again active as a self-appointed negotiator. On the same day that the Provisional Army Council announced the renewal of the ceasefire, he had taken a document based on discussions with the Provisional IRA to the British Embassy in Dublin.

In Dr Connell's view, the present ceasefire could only be extended if the British government came forward with positive political initiatives. The proposals he submitted were for the British Prime Minister to appoint a team of three mediators with full authority to talk with all sections in Northern Ireland in order to seek areas of common agreement, a permanent ceasefire and an end to internment and to prepare the ground for the proposed Northern Ireland Convention. The proposed members of this team were Sean McBride, Nobel prize-winner and UN Commissioner, who would be acceptable to the IRA, Desmond Boal, QC and former member of Stormont, who would have the confidence of the UDA and other paramilitary groups, and of such politicians as Paisley and West, and a British appointee such as Lord Gardiner, Lord Caradon, Lord Ritchie Calder, Joe Grimond or Philip Noel-Baker.

Once such political initiatives were seen to be taken, and they would have to come from Harold Wilson himself, the Provisional IRA would evidently be prepared to extend the ceasefire. A mediation period, John Connell informed the British diplomats, was vital to the success of the forthcoming Convention and would have wide support. It had, for example, been discussed with Sean McBride, who was optimistic of its chances. Cardinal Conway too had blessed the scheme and it had been explained to Mr Cosgrave and Mr Lynch. The latter had welcomed it and discussed it with his Fianna Fail front bench.

John Connell went on to argue that, because he was not suggesting a 'negotiation', the proposal would not be objectionable either to the SDLP or to the loyalist political parties in the North. Indeed, and to my surprise, he asserted that Desmond Boal was 'convinced' that this approach offered the 'only chance' of extending the ceasefire and that it would be welcome to politicians such as Paisley and Craig. As for the Provisionals, there was much talk in its ranks of a return to violence and without this initiative the ceasefire would break down. Connell, however, was confident of the Provisional IRA's consent to the plan because he had talked with its leaders, including the hard-liner Joe O'Hagan. He added that he had persuaded the Provisionals that a 'declaration of intent' to withdraw was not a practical objective.

What were we to make of all this? We were all sceptical, particularly about the response of the Northern politicians, and we felt sure that the long road ahead still had to begin with the Convention. However, I knew that the whole matter would not remain confidential for long so I authorised a prompt reply to Dr Connell.

I had made it known, I recalled, in the White Paper of July 1974 and again in my discussion paper on the Constitutional Convention in November that we would welcome discussions between those of like mind and of differing or conflicting opinions. Hence anything of this nature, which would assure Protestant paramilitary organisations of the genuineness of the intention of Catholic paramilitaries to eschew violence and vice versa, was welcome.

I concluded firmly, however, that there could be no question of the government negotiating with proscribed organisations, either directly or through persons authorised to act on their behalf. The essence of the government's proposals for the Constitutional Convention was that it was an opportunity for the people of Northern Ireland to take an initiative. It was in Northern Ireland that the problem arose and only there that it could begin to be dealt with.

What would happen next in Dublin we did not know, but meanwhile we continued to burn the midnight oil in the Northern Ireland Office, now at last moved to the renovated Speaker's House at Stormont which provided much better working and living conditions. From there, on 3 January, I submitted a series of memoranda to my colleagues on the Cabinet sub-committee. I reminded them that the position in the province had changed fundamentally since my paper in November and that, although everything we now said and did must take the ceasefire into account, there was no question of any negotiations with the Provisional IRA. I proposed to make my promised statement on the Gardiner Report to the Commons on 14 January. This would now make the Provisionals' attitude to the extension of the ceasefire and my views on the ending of detention particularly relevant.

At the subsequent Cabinet committee meeting, my colleagues readily agreed to my approach; even the British press was making approving noises about developments in Northern Ireland. I started a round of meetings with political parties and other groups in the province. After one with representatives of the Ulster Workers' Council, they publicly accepted that I was not negotiating with the Provisional IRA. This was important to me, and in marked contrast to the disbelieving views of the loyalist politicians, who were airing them through the ever-open doors of the television and radio stations.

The meeting with Ian Paisley on 7 January was unusually emotional, even given the nature of meetings in Northern Ireland. I had deliberately arranged it for mid-afternoon, knowing from experience that this would put a time limit on it because political visitors to Stormont always wanted to be back down-town by 5.45 to speak on television or radio. I opened the meeting by reading my New Year message of appeal for peace and co-operation, adding that I did not expect to see eye-to-eye with Dr Paisley on all matters, particularly on the future of detention.

At first, all went as would be expected. His reply matched his public statements: it was Democratic Unionist Party policy to accept the necessity of maintaining some sort of detention powers, although he would wish these to be in a form which would give maximum rights to the individuals concerned. On the current situation, he averred that all right-thinking men wanted peace 'but the precise definition of peace was crucial'. The people of Northern Ireland wanted peace through victory over the men of violence, so the choice lay between demanding unconditional surrender of the IRA or defeating them militarily.

He expressed anger at the compensation awards to participants in the Bloody Sunday riots, which he compared to the smaller awards to those who had died in the defence of Ulster. He had a point there. He was also angry because, 'unlike certain Catholic and ecumenical churchmen', loyalist MPs who represented the majority community in Northern Ireland did not have access to the Prime Minister, who had twice refused to see them. 'They would never ask again.' I tried to explain that Prime Ministers were busy people and that the churchmen were in a different category at that time. MPs had the House of Commons.

Then we got to Feakle. The story he wove around the original Feakle meeting and the later visit of the churchmen to me bore no relationship to the facts and was the usual conspiratorial Paisley analysis, on a par with his December revelations on Feakle. It was natural, he claimed, that the people of Northern Ireland, aware of the

Prime Minister's proposals for a united Ireland, would be perturbed. As an elected representative, he demanded to know what those proposals were and what messages had been conveyed from the government to the Provisional IRA.

Quietly, in contrast to his approach, I reiterated that I had discussed no proposals with the Feakle clergymen and that after meeting them I had stated only that if there were 'a genuine and sustained cessation of violence', which meant one that lasted, it would create new opportunities for progress. I told him that next week I would explain to the House of Commons in greater detail my views on the relationship between a permanent ceasefire and the possibilities for a phased reduction in the army presence and for a progressive reduction in the numbers in detention.

It was to no avail. At that point the meeting departed from the norms of civilised political dialogue as Dr Paisley insisted stridently on receiving an answer about the nature of the IRA's proposals and the British response. I repeated the facts already given, but was met with continuing disbelief. Finally, I lost my temper and told Paisley and his party to leave the Castle. I was not prepared to continue a meeting with anyone who in effect called a member of Her Majesty's Government a liar.

In the ensuing mêlée, members of the delegation, particularly the Rev Beattie, were heard to question my sanity and to wish me and the entire British government to leave the province. Various forms of verbal abuse were hurled, which my private secretary rated 'worthy of a third-rate prep school'. I cannot speak for prep schools but what went on was certainly puerile.

I and my officials walked out of the Cabinet room, leaving Dr Paisley and his group still there. My staff were clearly worried, not least because I had acted out of character, and there was concern about simply leaving Paisley's party in the Castle since we were flying to England immediately after the meeting. I told them as we went to the helicopter that Paisley would be on radio or television within the hour and, indeed, we heard his version of the meeting on the news that night as we drove from Northolt airport to Westminster.

News of the meeting brought me a flood of congratulatory letters and telegrams! Paddy Devlin had heard on the Belfast grapevine that when the Rev Beattie had squared up to me round the table, fists akimbo, I had told him 'Shut up, you fifth-rate politician', and Paddy wrote in protest – 'Fifth-rate, no, tenth-rate, yes!'.

It was probably the views expressed by Paisley after this meeting that prompted David O'Connell of Sinn Fein/Provisional IRA to make a statement on 12 January which condemned 'the politicians of violence in the North and South for doing their utmost to sabotage the ceasefire'. Again, it gave me hope that the Provisionals could see at least to some degree that it was the loyalists they had to face up to in the long run.

Two days later I delivered my Commons speech. The words had been gone over again and again, more than any budget speech, for this was not only an important statement to Parliament but a brief to officials who would be in contact with the Provisional Sinn Fein. I began with my first response to the ceasefire: that the actions of the security forces in Northern Ireland would be related to the level of any activities which might occur. Now I spelled this out:

> The security forces are still on their guard. Vehicle check points continue to be manned to prevent the movement of weapons and explosives, and those against whom there is evidence of involvement in criminal acts will continue to be arrested and brought before the courts. The watch on the border has not been relaxed.

On the other hand, I pointed out that the army had been able to reduce the size and frequency of patrols, particularly in urban areas, and had largely avoided the questioning of people and search of their homes. There had been no major incidents, and I had not signed any interim custody orders since 22 December. I repeated yet again that given 'a genuine and sustained cessation of violence', the army would 'make a planned, orderly and progressive reduction in its present commitment', but only if I was convinced that the price would not be lives lost and property destroyed and that the RUC was in a position to take over the major law and order role.

Given the events of recent years, these were brave words and would even prove foolish, but this was what I wanted to achieve and had set out earlier in the White Paper. It led me to the subject of detention and I once more put the legal position, which I knew would be made stronger because it was the basis of the Gardiner Report:

> The government have acted legitimately and consistently within the terms of the European Convention for the Protection of Human Rights and Fundamental Freedoms in restricting certain fundamental freedoms. The crucial point is that only the government can decide, in the light of the situation as a whole, when to start bringing detention progressively to an end.

My immediate plans were progressively to release detainees but I would not act precipitately. Any early releases would be judged in relation to whether there was a genuine and sustained cessation of violence. Only then would I act more quickly and until then I could give no undertakings.

The political side of my speech centred of course on the Convention which might, I reflected, appeal to the loyalist paramilitaries since they had whetted their political appetites in the UWC strike. I revealed publicly for the first time that individuals associated with organisations such as the Ulster Defence Association, the Ulster Volunteer Force and the Volunteer Political Party had already given their views to my officials. 'The same opportunities exist for the Provisional and Official Sinn Fein who, like the Ulster Volunteer Force, were deproscribed by me in May last year and are free to take part in genuine political activity within the law.'

I addressed my concluding remarks to all the paramilitaries:

> The questions being asked throughout the whole community is 'Can there be peace?' The people of Northern Ireland say 'Yes'. The government have responded positively and will continue to do so. We await a similar response from the Provisionals and the other paramilitary organisations.

The response in the Commons was encouraging. Ted Heath on behalf of the official Opposition was particularly helpful. He had visited Northern Ireland just before Christmas and from that could report that the security forces had clear instructions to arrest those against whom there was evidence of criminal involvement. It was an important point and in reply I stated that between 22 December and 13 January, forty-five people had been arrested for offences connected with firearms, murder and hijacking. I also confirmed that there were no negotiations with the Provisional IRA. The aim of our contact with Provisional Sinn Fein members was to ensure that our view reached the IRA and vice-versa; nothing else was involved.

Jim Molyneaux as leader of the Official Unionists at Westminster congratulated me on my handling of the delicate situation which, he said, 'had inspired and will continue to inspire confidence and trust throughout the whole Northern Ireland community'. This meant a lot to me personally, given the feelings expressed by other loyalist politicians. On the other hand, Gerry Fitt was obviously unhappy about the situation. He and the other SDLP leaders had consistently opposed the Provisional IRA and disliked any idea of their 'political' role. However, as always, he called for more releases from detention.

Alan Beith was co-operative for the Liberals, and I also had the help of Kevin McNamara on our back-benches. He had contacts with

Northern Irish 'republicans' and it was to them he referred when he asked if I was aware that no one would lightly forgive any person or organisation who broke this very fragile peace.

My base in the House of Commons was firm, and there was approval in the press. *The Times* leader on 15 January stated: 'Mr Rees is proceeding with a sensible combination of caution and firmness.' None of this, however, was enough to satisfy the Provisional IRA. On 16 January its leaders announced that the ceasefire would not be extended. A statement was issued to justify their decision, which first detailed their version of events up to now, including the fact that I had (quite properly) refused to give them an early copy of my Commons speech, and went on:

> The published text of [Mr Rees's] speech has been given detailed consideration by the leadership of the movement and the following facts have been carefully assessed.
>
> 1 There is nothing in Mr Rees's speech relating to the peace proposals submitted by us for a termination of the war.
>
> 2 The truce was not observed by the Crown forces, with the exception of the Christmas period. Increased enemy activity was noted in Ardoyne, Leeson Street, Falls Road, Turf Lodge and St James' areas of Belfast. Civilians were stopped, searched and photographed in Newry, Jonesborough Village was saturated by troops on two occasions and soldiers withdrawn from other areas were replaced by RUC and UDR. A Sinn Fein meeting in Derry last Saturday was surrounded by British troops and the pursuit of wanted republicans continued unabated.
>
> 3 Instead of releasing a substantial number of political prisoners, only three internees, two republican and one loyalist, were freed before Christmas. Last year when there was no truce, 65 internees were released. The number discharged since is an insult to every member of the Irish race. We wonder if the British government feels it is dealing with cattle rather than human beings. We had been assured that the British government would show its good faith by particularly releasing a substantial number of people who live in appalling conditions and many of whom are entering their fourth year in concentration camps.
>
> 4 Volunteer James Moyne died in Long Kesh after being repeatedly refused elementary medical treatment for his illness.
>
> 5 A concerted campaign of brutality against political prisoners in Portlaoise, Crumlin Road and English prisons became very apparent during the truce.
>
> 6 Compassionate parole, a normal procedure at Christmas time, was refused by the authorities in the prisons, North and South.
>
> 7 Staff-Captain James Greene, O/C North Armagh, was assassinated

in County Monaghan by a British execution squad. The funeral cortege on arrival in Portadown was harassed by the RUC.
8 The arrest of Kevin Mallon by the Dublin authorities was a severe blow because of the vital role he played in the whole peace initiative. The increased harassment by the Special Branch on both sides of the border has made it extremely difficult for republicans to promote the peace initiative along realistic lines.

In view of the above facts but principally due to a total lack of response by the British government, the Army Council cannot in conscience renew the order suspending offensive military action first issued on December 21st last, reaffirmed on January 2nd and due to expire at midnight tonight, January 16th.

. . . We reaffirm our willingness and sincerity to engage in worthwhile talks with the appropriate authorities to secure peace and justice in our land. . . .

The statement was full of bogus reasons for ending the ceasefire and further confused by blaming us for actions allegedly taken in the South. At the end it did, however, express a willingness for further talks. This was probably the price extracted by the doves on the Army Council and it left hope of another ceasefire, especially as reports were filtering back from Belfast that the Provisionals there had expected the ceasefire to go on longer.

Since my House of Commons speech had apparently not come across as other than tough and unyielding, I made a series of carefully prepared public statements which repeated all the points I had been making since 22 December. I tried to sound out the real reasons for the Provisional IRA's decision by talking to people in the province and on 17 January I again met with leaders of the church in Northern Ireland, who all acknowledged that I could not accept the Provisionals' reasons for ending the ceasefire, given my Commons statement and the positive steps I had taken. They thought that one reason for the lack of republican response was the poor reporting in the Northern Irish press.

Cardinal Conway, while acknowledging that the eight points of the Provisional IRA were 'a complete fabrication', wanted me nevertheless to help the doves in the Army Council and he urged me to establish and maintain a dialogue. The Catholic community, he warned me, had short memories and the army must not provoke antagonism. Overall, the churchmen thought that the Provisional IRA might return to a ceasefire.

The following day I flew up to Derry to talk to the Protestant clergy there. They told me that there was undoubtedly a desire in the

Provisional IRA to end violence and that the Catholic community as a whole wanted peace. While in Derry, I took the opportunity to go and talk also to Bishop Daly, who was always aware of what was going on in his Catholic flock, and I visited the army and the police. At Altnagelvin Hospital patients gave me their reading of the situation, and I also obtained the views of local councillors and Vanguard Assemblyman Glen Barr, leading light in the UWC strike.

All these meetings were useful and because I thought it would be particularly valuable, I talked again to the main group of churchmen on 24 January. I assured them that I would remain true to the policy announced to the House of Commons on 14 January and that although there would be no lowering of the security forces' guard, they would not over-react. From the tone of the meeting, which confirmed the will for peace in the Catholic community, I felt that there was at least a chance of a return to a ceasefire, though this was not being reported by my officials in contact with the Provisional Sinn Fein.

In the Northern Ireland Office we analysed the reasons why the talks had broken down. It was evident that despite all our efforts, the Provisional IRA had not understood what we were saying, and we were convinced that our basic problem lay with the Provisional Sinn Fein representatives in Belfast, who were inexperienced and not up to their task.

That they did not understand the nature of the role of the security forces or their relationship with me was brought out in a later report in the *Sunday Times* of 18 June 1978, which said that when the Provisional representatives wanted to send a courier to Dublin in time for a meeting of the Army Council, 'the Northern Ireland Office would not supply a safe conduct pass to see him through such British army checkpoints as he might meet'. Of course the Northern Ireland Office, whatever was meant by that here, had no status in security operations except in regard to overall policy; a piece of paper issued by the Office would, rightly, have been questioned by any soldier on duty.

Because of this kind of misunderstanding, I authorised that in future contact with the Provisional Sinn Fein should be at a higher level and away from Belfast and its incestuous gossip. One of the Sinn Fein representatives was to come from Dublin and since it was almost certain that the security authorities there would know, I authorised our ambassador in the South to tell the Irish government what was afoot. They probably knew anyway.

Another problem had meanwhile arisen from Dublin, where Dr John Connell had been persistently trying to get in touch with Harold Wilson via Tony Field, who had once worked in the Prime Minister's office. I asked our Dublin ambassador to point out to Dr Connell that

Field no longer worked for Harold, but he was not to be deterred. In the end he went to London and spoke to Joe Haines and Albert Murray, a former MP and now manager of the Prime Minister's political office. They told him that all they could do was pass on his messages to me for consideration. I had been kept informed of these various moves and when Harold spoke to me, he was firm that there was to be no freelancing. All talks would take place in Northern Ireland.

This was not the only freelancing effort. On 13 January a senior member of the Labour Party told me that he had been approached indirectly by the Provisional IRA through a member of the Dail, acting of his own volition and not as a Provisional representative or spokesman, to ask if he would assist with any discussions with the British government. He was strongly against the Convention, which he thought would be disastrous because the Unionists would gain the majority of the seats. What was needed to secure a permanent ceasefire was a declaration that British troops would start to be withdrawn from Northern Ireland in twelve months' time.

Again, on 16 January, when I was attending an all-day Cabinet at Chequers unconnected with Northern Ireland, a ministerial colleague phoned me from London to say that an English Catholic priest passing through London en route to Dublin was offering to mediate. He knew all the right people! I told my colleagues to leave well alone. 'Say nothing, or you may be adding to the long list of self-appointed intermediaries that abound in Dublin and Belfast, who would use a conversation with you to prove they mattered.' A half-cocked version of this story appeared in the press, which did little harm but helped stir the already muddy waters.

On 19 January, with no sign of a further ceasefire, I issued another statement:

> The government's policy was set out in the statement I made in the House of Commons on Tuesday, 14 January. I stand by that policy. There is no question of anyone being sold out and the government's concern is for the safety, welfare and future of all the people of Northern Ireland.
>
> I would ask everyone to take into account the desire to see violence brought to a lasting end. Many ill-founded rumours are circulating. There is much speculation. There is a real need to distinguish fact from fiction and those who report have a particular responsibility at this time to avoid turning speculation into expectation.
>
> The government sincerely wishes to see a situation come about where discussion and politics take the place of violence. It is working to that end

> within the framework of the policy I announced in the House of Commons. It will continue to do so.

Perhaps as a result of this, on 21 January we received in Northern Ireland from the Provisional Sinn Fein their idea of the steps to be taken which would enable them to maintain the ceasefire:

> Freedom of movement for all members of the republican movement.
> Cessation of all harassment of the civilian population.
> Cessation of all raids on lands/homes/other buildings.
> Cessation of arrests of members of the republican movement.
> End of screening/photographing/identity checking.
> The right to carry concealed short arms solely for self-defence.
> No provocative displays of force by either side.
> No reintroduction of RUC/UDR into designated areas.
> Agreement on an effective liaison system between British/Republican forces.
> Progressive withdrawal of troops to barracks to keep within the implication of the bilateral truce.
> Confirmation that discussions between representatives of the republican movement and HMG would continue towards securing a permanent ceasefire.

These proposals went beyond my approach of sticking firmly to finding a means to wind down violence and in particular of refusing to protect those who had committed criminal acts; nor would I engage in a 'bilateral truce'. I would certainly have made a positive general response, though making my position clear on these points, if a series of Provisional IRA activities at this time had not altered the picture. On 19 January a young boy had been killed in South Armagh, and on the following two days there had been a bombing campaign in Castlederg, Dungannon, Eniskillen, Strabane and Belfast. In the face of this, I told my officials to end all contact with the Provisional Sinn Fein while violence continued.

I reported all this to my colleagues on the Cabinet sub-committee on 23 January and informed them that the UDA and UVF had been contacted to reassure them that we were not negotiating with the IRA and making concessions. I warned them that, even if there was a new ceasefire, we might be faced with an outburst of violence from disaffected Provisional IRA members. We had reached stalemate in our contact with the Provisional Sinn Fein in Northern Ireland and the prospects of a ceasefire were uncertain.

There was still talk coming from Dublin that a ceasefire would happen and indeed a motorcycle messenger delivered to my Middlesex home a document which Dr Connell had delivered to Albert Murray at No 10. It was from an 'Irish Republic organisation' and after spelling out in detail what had happened in talks with the Provisional Sinn Fein in recent weeks, it informed the Prime Minister that it was prepared to stop activities in Great Britain and, under certain conditions, in Northern Ireland. Obviously, Dublin was trying to bypass me because I had stopped the contacts with the Provisional Sinn Fein in Belfast.

When Harold and I discussed this document, we at first considered making it public, rather than letting news of it seep into the press with the inevitable comments about Rees's lack of response, inertia, etc. However, on reflection we decided it would be better, since the document had come to Albert Murray, to send a 'civil servant reply' that the message had been passed on to me and that my responses would be gravely damaged if there was violence in any part of the province. Any talking had to be done through me and my staff.

This did not stop Dr Connell coming back to London again later, though it was a waste of his time. However, our reply to his message reached Northern Ireland on the ever-active Irish grapevine and talks with the Provisional Sinn Fein began again on the strict terms already laid down. There was no question of bypassing the due processes of the law and anything that was said had to relate to my words to the House of Commons. It was particularly vital to me to obtain the support of the Commons for I had no base in Northern Ireland, and I now needed to report to Parliament on events since the breakdown of the ceasefire. It was also an opportune time because in early February I was due to issue another discussion paper in preparation for the Convention and I wanted to present it to the House.

My speech to the Commons on 5 February was, I think, the most important I had ever made on Northern Ireland and I tried to raise the whole business of the ceasefire above the usual level of let us release fifty people and see what the response is. After referring to the discussion paper, which was concerned with possible structures of government in Northern Ireland, and again emphasising that the Convention was entirely a forum for the people of the province, I turned to the ceasefire.

> The policy I outlined [on 14 January] contained the elements which could bring an end to violence and set in motion a process of discussion. I sought to get away from the daily catalogue of violence and open the door to a new situation in which discussions and political activity could take place in a constructive and peaceful atmosphere. I also sought to bring about progressively a change in the role and commitments of the army

and said that if there were a genuine and sustained cessation of violence, I would gradually release all detainees.

I reported that there had been meetings with elected representatives both at Westminster and in Northern Ireland to discuss not only matters arising from my statement but also the economic and employment situation in the province. But there had also been meetings with the Provisional Sinn Fein:

> I wanted to ensure that the government's policy was clearly understood. Indeed, it would have been quite wrong if I had not arranged for the government's views to be fully explained and clarified. The future of Northern Ireland is a matter for the people of Northern Ireland. There is no question of bartering their future away. I should make it clear that I have received indications that the government's policy was not being understood and also that there was a continued interest in trying to bring under control what has now become worrying but sporadic violence.
>
> My officials have been under very clear instructions to explain the government's policy and to outline and clarify the arrangements that might be made to ensure that any ceasefire did not break down. Explanation has been the key to the meetings. The difficulties in communicating and explaining carefully and fully the government's policy, not only to the Provisional Sinn Fein but also to other organisations, are very considerable. These difficulties have not been made any the less by rumour and speculation, much of which has been both untrue and unhelpful.

Because it was important to make our security policy clear – misunderstanding on this had led to the breakdown of the ceasefire and my officials needed to be able to use my words – I repeated that the actions of the security forces would be related to the level of any activity that might occur. 'The security forces will do their utmost to bring criminals to justice before the courts and they are having very considerable success. In the past few days, thirty-four people have been charged with serious offences, five with murder and two with attempted murder. Nearly a quarter of a ton of explosive has been seized and about half the explosive devices placed have been neutralised by army technical officers.'

Because of the recent Provisional IRA bombings I had fired a warning shot over the heads of the hawks by signing some interim custody orders. This was despite my views on detention and I justified it to the Commons: 'I cannot accept a situation where lives are at risk through failure to deal with a resumption of violence and sectarian murders. I have therefore, in relation to acts of recent violence, signed seven interim custody orders during the past few days.'

I concluded:

> The situation in Northern Ireland is both more fluid and much less clear-cut than has been the case for a long time. There is a different attitude in all sections of the community. People want to see an end to violence but they want this to be a genuine, and not a temporary, change in the situation. My duty is clear. I must find out whether there can be a genuine and sustained cessation of violence from wherever it comes. I shall do both.

Ian Gilmour for the Opposition expressed understanding of the difficulties over the last six weeks but wondered whether, given the 'rumour and speculation', there was too much secrecy about the meetings that had taken place. Would it perhaps clear the air if further meetings – if there were to be any more – were more open? I suppressed my astonishment at this and replied that it would not be right to say whom my officials had met. 'There have been meetings with the Provisional Sinn Fein and others on the other side of the community but they have taken place in Northern Ireland.'

He went on to ask in what respects the Provisional Sinn Fein still misunderstood the government's policy and what further explanation was necessary, to which I replied:

> What does the phrase [genuine and sustained cessation of violence] mean practically? On these matters I am very much led by my security advisers. It is no good my pretending that four months' ceasefire in which arms and detonators are moved about, and in which there is regrouping, constitutes any genuine and sustained cessation of violence. The fact that there is no noise looks as though there is not violence, but violence might be being prepared. We all know that knee-capping has been going on in various areas. I want to cover the whole situation because I must not allow myself to be taken in by the phrase 'genuine and sustained cessation of violence'. There are practical reasons why these matters should be looked at, even though they may be passed on second-hand, because just to use the phrase is not enough.

When responding to a question from Jim Molyneaux, I referred also to the activities of splinter groups. This was a problem I wanted stressed in the discussions with Sinn Fein. 'It is sometimes not possible for me to be advised clearly on who is responsible for what. Even if we were to obtain a genuine cessation of violence, there might be more splinter groups because people who have been used to using the gun for four or five years find it difficult to break away from that kind of activity.'

A later question from the Tory benches gave me the opportunity to restate my policy on releases:

> Overall, the way to end detention is clear and simple. Let us stop violence in Northern Ireland. Let us stop the killing. There was the instance last week of the killing of the ATC boy of sixteen, whose father spoke so bravely after the death of his son and said he did not feel angry against anybody in the community. I could not have said that. Then there was the murder of the young boy down in Forkhill, who was blown up. In the face of that, for God's sake let us stop it, and then we can end detention. The killing of the RUC sergeant last week is an equally bad example.

The Commons response was generally favourable to the direction we were taking and back in Northern Ireland my officials returned to the talks able to emphasise that British government policy was as set out in Parliament. Practical arrangements for monitoring and preserving any ceasefire were the priority, after which, given the new situation of a genuine, sustained cessation of violence, further discussions would be needed.

In this situation there would, for example, be no need for proscription and those wishing to return home to live in peace would be free to do so. There would be no actions by the security forces which would be interpreted as harassment by the civilian population; they would concentrate on law-breakers. Interim custody orders would not be signed, with the aim of ending detention; the use of screening, photographing and identity checks would be ended. Individuals at risk of assassination would need protection but the law provided for this by making gun permits for self-defence available from the RUC. The army would gradually be reduced to peace-time levels and withdraw to barracks, and replacement policing would have to be achieved by the co-operation of the community – area by area – over a period of time.

At the same time as pointing all this out, my officials emphasised that such action depended on the Provisional IRA ending all offensive operations and hostilities, which included murders, woundings, knee-cappings, kangaroo courts and all forms of intimidation, plus armed robberies and hijackings, and the illegal purchase, manufacture and holding of arms, ammunition and explosives.

The talks resulted in an announcement on 9 February of an indefinite ceasefire by the Provisional IRA:

> In the light of discussions which have taken place between representatives of the Republican Movement and British officials on effective

> arrangements to ensure that there is no breakdown of a truce, the Army Council has renewed the order suspending offensive military action. Hostilities against the Crown forces will be suspended from 6 pm, Monday, 10 February 1975.

Once again I needed to report to the Commons, especially given the continued speculation about the nature of the talks with the Provisional Sinn Fein, which caused problems in loyalist, SDLP and Dublin circles by reinforcing the belief of a British sell-out. On 11 February, Robert Fisk in *The Times* referred to 'inspired leaks' from the Provisional IRA in Dublin that 'British civil servants had agreed to twelve points put to them by the Provisionals over the past fortnight'. The points allegedly included not only the release of internees, less activity by the army and the right of IRA men to carry personal weapons, but also provisions for discussions between Provisional IRA officers and British soldiers.

Although, as Mr Fisk said, 'the four meetings between civil servants and Sinn Fein representatives during the past six weeks had involved only the arrangements for a ceasefire and the steps necessary to ensure it does not break down', he felt that this did not exclude the existence of the leaked points. He reported that according to one 'usually reliable Provisional source' in Dublin, the British had rejected the request to carry guns and he went on to list the alleged points:

> 1 The release of perhaps 100 internees within the next two or three weeks. No definite figure, but the IRA expects more men to be freed than Mr Rees was prepared to release during the Christmas truce.
> 2 An effective if not total withdrawal of troops to barracks, meaning that the government could return perhaps 3,000 to 4,000 soldiers to Britain within six months.
> 3 The end of arrests by the army in Roman Catholic areas, the end of the military 'screening' (by which young men are questioned and photographed) and the end of big searches.
> 4 Provision for discussions between Provisional IRA battalion commanders in Belfast and the commanding officers of army battalions. The IRA says it has asked for this to ensure that no violation of the ceasefire leads to an end of the truce.
> 5 The end of military checkpoints and road blocks in Catholic areas.
> 6 No immediate attempt to reintroduce the Royal Ulster Constabulary or to introduce the part-time Ulster Defence Regiment into Catholic areas. The government, in fact, is committed to reintroducing the police into all parts of the province; if such a demand has been conceded it would have to be for only a short time.
> 7 The ceasefire agreement should be formalised by a document drawn

> up by the British. Some Provisionals in Dublin say that such a document exists and was shown to Mr Rory O'Brady, the President of Provisional Sinn Fein, in the presence of Sir Frank Cooper, Mr Rees's Permanent Secretary.
> 8 There should be talks soon between IRA leaders, as opposed to Sinn Fein leaders, and senior British civil servants. According to the Provisionals, the document they say was drawn up by the British refers to such meetings with the words 'talks with the leadership of the Republican movement'.

Comparing these with the points actually given by the Provisionals on 21 January, I concluded that facts had been sacrificed in order to show lukewarm Provisional IRA supporters of the ceasefire that the British were conceding important demands. *The Times* article appeared on the same day that I presented the facts about the ceasefire to the Commons and outlined the scheme to ensure that any future ceasefire did not break down. It had five main elements:

> First, a number of incident centres, manned by civil servants on a twenty-four-hour basis, will be established in various parts of Northern Ireland. These centres will be linked with my office in Belfast. Second, if developments occur which seem to threaten the ceasefire, these incident centres will act as a point of contact in either direction. Third, issues can be referred to my office in Belfast and clarified there. Fourth, cases referred up to the Northern Ireland Office will be considered, and a reply passed back to the incident centre for onward transmission. Fifth, if out of these exchanges general difficulties about the ceasefire arrangements emerge, then discussions will be arranged between my officials and representatives of legal organisations to clarify them.
>
> There will be full consultation by officials with the security forces on these arrangements, which will cover only incidents arising directly out of the ceasefire. . . .
>
> These practical arrangements can be only the first steps towards a permanent peace. There are many problems yet to overcome in a situation which is far from clear. There is no quick and easy solution and winding down from violence will not happen overnight.

I stated that the presence of the army would become progressively less obtrusive and that I would not sign any interim custody orders, though I reiterated that such actions were related to the level of any activity that occurred and anyone involved in violence would be prosecuted in the courts. 'If people go on below the surface acquiring explosives and arms and preparing for violence at some later date, then no one will expect me to regard the cessation of violence as genuine.'

There could be no illusions about the very difficult problems of securing a permanent peace and I said that the government would do all they could to help solve them. 'Patience, understanding and good will are needed, and a heavy responsibility here rests on the politicians and would-be politicians in Northern Ireland to seek out constructive solutions to deal with real problems that have persisted for more than fifty years. I hope now that a process of discussion and debate can replace violence.'

> My task now is to seek a permanent end to violence, which is the first requirement of any process of discussion in Northern Ireland. This was why I felt it right to take some first steps of a practical kind once I received indications that the Provisionals contemplated reinstating their ceasefire and that they accepted that practical arrangements were needed to ensure that it did not breakdown. That is what the talks have been about. There has been no question of bartering away the future of the people of Northern Ireland. . . .
>
> The situation is far from clear-cut. There is no ready-made or well-defined path ahead. I want to find a way forward, but there are many obstacles and many difficulties. It would be idle to pretend they do not exist. The fact that there is a ceasefire and practical arrangements for monitoring it are the first tentative and welcome steps.

It was helpful that John Biggs-Davison for the Conservatives asked me to confirm that 'no military or political price has been paid to the Provisionals'. There had been no sell-out: 'It would do no good if there were. One cannot sell out what one cannot control. What matters in Northern Ireland is that there are two communities. I have no wish to sell them out and I will never do so.'

I similarly assured Jim Molyneaux that the arrangements would 'in no way inhibit the police in enforcing the law' and I welcomed his condemnation of sectarian killings. Jim meant what he said: he never had any truck with murders. I used this opportunity to bring up the problem of those considering giving up paramilitary action. 'I am protected by machine guns and goodness knows what else. What about the people who want to go back to peace after having been involved in civil war? They are still afraid. We have to consider the wider issue of how we can get people back to a peace-time attitude. Sectarian murders do not help in that respect.'

Jeremy Thorpe asked about the incident centres and I told him that 'we shall site some of these buildings in rural areas. I am trying to be vague because I do not want them to be generally known, since it would be much better that they should not be known. There will be seven or eight in different parts of the province.' Jeremy also asked about a general amnesty for those holding arms, something which I knew others favoured but which I did not think was right at the moment.

> There is a great deal of fear, and people hold guns legally because they need them, particularly in rural areas. Those who hold guns illegally sometimes also feel that they need them for protection as well as for other purposes. . . .
>
> As long as there is a flow of weapons into Ireland as a whole from all parts of the world . . . as long as money is coming from all parts of the world to provide these guns, as long as explosives move across the border and through the ports, and as long as the detonators and timing mechanisms are available, there will always be explosions and killings. I am applying my mind to that problem because if I could stop these supplies at source an amnesty would have more relevance.

Prompted, I presumed, by Robert Fisk's reported 'leak', Julian Amery, the Tory MP for Brighton, asked me to assure the House that there was no truth in the 'reports from Dublin that there is an understanding between the government and the IRA that IRA personnel will be allowed to continue to carry side arms, and that the police and the UDA will not enter certain areas'. I referred to the report I had just given, in which nothing was hidden because I did not believe anything should be hidden from the House, and told him: 'There have been no signed documents. Nothing has been said about the police. With regard to them, the situation is clear. They have not been in certain areas for a very long time. What I wanted to say about the police, I have said in my statement.' I pointed out, as I had to Jeremy Thorpe, that many people in Northern Ireland were afraid and carried arms legally. Among them were people coming to see me at Stormont Castle, who left their arms at the door. That might sound surprising at Westminster but the law in the province gave the right to carry side arms and I would stick by the law.

Although the House of Commons again gave me its support, there was disquiet among the Northern Ireland members. John Carson, the Unionist MP for North Belfast, came to see me later to voice his concern over my contacts with the Provisional Sinn Fein and I tried to reassure him that I had not done a deal. Gerry Fitt had said in the debate that if there was any discussing to do on policing policy, then it ought to be with elected representatives. This was too much for Stan Orme, given the SDLP's reluctance, however understandable, to do precisely this and he exclaimed to me, 'Get up and tell him'. It was not my style, however, although Stan was right. He cared a lot about the SDLP in general and Gerry in particular but he was exasperated with this double talk. When a few days later, Gerry pressed us privately to make interim custody orders against loyalists, Stan turned on his heels: he was against detention for both sides.

The incident centres were also of particular concern to the Northern Ireland members, though I had explained in the House to Gerry:

> I think that we might find ourselves with splinter groups. Other organisations are being formed. I want to be sure that if something happens somewhere, my officials can find out whether those who claim that they are operating a ceasefire have been responsible for it. That may sound a little naive on the surface, but I am convinced that it will help the security forces in the way I have described. It will be the other way round as well – there will be a point of contact in either direction.

I also gave a positive assurance to Bill Craig that I would guard against the possibility of the incident centres developing into a collaboration with criminals and that any information received that would be of interest to the police would be passed on to them. A few days later, I gave a fuller answer to a written parliamentary question about the centres:

> They will be set up at North Belfast, Armagh, Dungannon, West Belfast, Londonderry and Newry. . . . If developments occur which seem to threaten the ceasefire, these incident centres will act as a point of contact in either direction with Provisional Sinn Fein. . . . This is their sole purpose. They will not take complaints from the public. They will not in any way interfere with the work of elected representatives or of the security forces organisations.

The situation in the province remained uneasy. The ceasefire existed but we were a long way from a genuine cessation of violence. I needed to keep my colleagues closely informed and on 18 February I submitted a paper on events since the Feakle talks to the Cabinet sub-committee. I reminded them of the strategy I had outlined in early December before the ceasefire. My aim was to do whatever was necessary to promote a ceasefire, short of conceding anything of substance to the Provisionals or of producing a loyalist backlash. A ceasefire could create the conditions in which the Provisionals' military organisation would be weakened and would find it more difficult to start a campaign again. There might even be an outside chance of them being sufficiently tired of violence to want to give it up and rely on political activities.

Although there were dangers in the ceasefire, not least that the Provisionals would use it to regroup and start a new round of violence, I was convinced that the policy I had advocated in December was the one to follow. I had to use the opportunities presented by the ceasefire and I obtained the agreement of my colleagues that in the coming weeks, provided the ceasefire continued, I would announce the release of eighty detainees and the withdrawal of one of the emergency battalions in the province; the battalion would return if the situation made it necessary.

The ceasefire was uppermost in our minds but our policy was to look to constitutional change as well as to security. The two were intertwined and though the catalogue of death and destruction in Northern Ireland diverted attention from constitutional developments, they had not been forgotten. I told my colleagues that plans for the Convention were proceeding so that we would be ready for elections to it and I obtained their approval for an early announcement of the appointment of the Lord Chief Justice as the Convention's chairman.

As I had said in December, our handling of the security situation and the Gardiner Report could have a major influence on the atmosphere in which debate on the approaching Convention took place. The Convention was important to political advance and it would now go ahead against the background of the ceasefire.

Chapter 8

THE CONVENTION

In the Whitelaw period of office I had often thought that a preliminary assembly of Ulster politicians might have been a useful precursor to a Darlington type of conference. It was, however, the Ulster workers' strike and the fall of the Executive that had directed my mind and eventually government policy towards the idea of an elected Convention where Ulster politicians would come together to discuss the future of the province. Since then and after the July 1974 White Paper we had been preparing the ground for it. Stan Orme had done his best to nudge the loyalist working-class paramilitaries towards political action, and the ceasefire gave a glimmer of hope that the republican paramilitaries might also move this way despite their belief in an all-Ireland solution. However, one never knew how events would work out in Northern Ireland and, as I had told my Cabinet colleagues in November, I was not seeking anything more than a short step forward.

The White Paper and the subsequent legislation and discussions in the House of Commons had brought the intended Convention to the attention of the people of Northern Ireland. When the discussion paper on the economy of Northern Ireland was published in September, it began the process of providing detailed background information for the Convention, and I geared my public statement in particular to the Northern Ireland politicians.

The paper described Northern Ireland's basic economic and demographic features, including its interdependence with Great Britain, and went on to look at the key problems of attracting new industry and providing employment, before finally describing the level and nature of public expenditure and the way it was financed. I regarded the paper as important, not only because it was the first time such a detailed description of the Northern Ireland economy had been published in one document but also because decisions on finance had been a source of trouble in the last days of the power-sharing Executive. A future devolved administration would have to think hard about expenditure priorities.

I had always found it particularly irksome, even before I went to Belfast as Secretary of State, that loyalist MPs at Westminster consistently supported the Conservative Party's policy of denationalisation and belief in free market forces but supported subsidies to state-owned industries and high public expenditure in Northern Ireland. I therefore deliberately asked in my September statement: 'Will the elected representatives want this type of intervention or should industry be left to fend for itself and be influenced purely by market forces? If market forces alone determine economic policy in Northern Ireland, the economic situation would be transformed for the worse. Certainly towns like Newry, Strabane, Londonderry, would be adversely affected. The continuation of Harland and Wolff itself in its present form or at all would be put at risk.'

Further discussion papers were in preparation but it was only after the October General Election had given us a stronger mandate and I had again obtained Cabinet approval for my policy that I could be certain that they would be needed. Accordingly, the second paper, 'Constitutional Convention Procedure', was published on 20 November and again I took the opportunity to point out the purpose of the Convention. Because of the underlying loyalist attitude that Westminster was of little consequence – to belong to the UK was one thing, to accept the decision of Parliament another – I stated: 'The Convention will take place under the authority of the Westminster Parliament. Northern Ireland is a part of the United Kingdom and it is for this reason that the report of the Convention will be transmitted to the Westminster Parliament which alone has the authority to decide what is to be done and which has the legislative power to make that decision effective.' In other words, the Convention would not be a law-making body and, sensing trouble ahead on this, I continued:

> If it seeks to proceed simply by majorities trying to coerce minorities or minorities being obstructive rather than constructive, then it will fail. If the Convention does not pursue the search for concessions, if it seeks solely to count heads rather than to reconcile differences, then it will fail. It will have failed not only to meet its statutory terms of reference but, even more seriously, it will have failed the people of Northern Ireland. The price of failure would be high. There is no ready-made alternative solution.

I repeated the terms of the Northern Ireland Act and the fact that there would be seventy-eight members elected for the twelve Westminster constituencies but by the single transferable vote. I reminded the politicians that the Convention Chairman would be appointed by the

Queen and would be an independent figure of high standing and impartiality, not drawn from the elected members and with no power to vote. He would preside over the Convention, be responsible for order and the proper conduct of business, and no doubt be the person through whom reports would be transmitted to the Secretary of State. It would not be the same job as a Speaker in the Houses of Parliament for while the Chairman had to be impartial, he also had to be ready to help the Convention as a whole to reach agreement and produce a report.

We had had long discussions in the Northern Ireland Office on how to give guidelines to the Convention on setting up committees, working parties or study groups, but all that we could do in the paper was suggest proceeding this way. The possibility was also mentioned of obtaining outside specialist advice and I expressed hope that the Convention would visit other countries to see how problems of a similar nature to Northern Ireland's had been resolved. To help here, we attached to the paper the proceedings of the 1946–47 Convention on the relationship between Newfoundland and Canada, and those of the 1972 Australian Convention on relations between the states. The details of the failed Irish Convention of 1917–18 – not the best of omens! – were also included.

I reminded the political parties that the record of proceedings would be 'absolutely privileged' and it was for them to decide whether all meetings were reported. The first meeting would, however, be at a time and place determined by me and I might give directions for regulating the Convention's procedure until it had agreed upon its own rules. Much more important than this was the outcome of the members' deliberations and I repeated that the final report had to be in tune with the Convention's terms of reference and provide for a government which would command the most widespread acceptance throughout the community. If necessary more than one report could be submitted to me.

The Commons was in session at the time when the discussion paper on the Convention's constitution was issued and I had been able to emphasise its main points to the House. I announced that the Clerk to the Assembly would discuss Convention arrangements with the Northern Ireland party leaders before the elections in order to avoid undue delay afterwards and that I would aim to give about a month's notice of the date of the elections, which would take place in early 1975.

My statement was received well, although the inward-looking Northern Ireland newspapers tried to find grounds to bolster either the Catholic or Protestant case in my introduction to the discussion paper. The Republic's press was the same: in the South they had not yet come to terms with the Ulster workers' strike and showed the usual lack of understanding of the Protestant working class in the North.

One rather curious reaction to the discussion paper came from Gerry Fitt, who asked me whether we could not now call the seventy-eight people in the old Assembly back again. I told him no, but reflected that it was at least a sign that the SDLP would participate in the elections, though it would need time before its leaders would say so publicly. The loyalists would also need time, particularly the working class, whose political hopes had been dashed by the politicians after the Ulster workers' strike. I therefore told my Cabinet colleagues that the elections would be in March or April.

A point which I had left open in the second discussion paper and in statements to Parliament was the name of the Convention Chairman, although I had almost decided on Sir Robert Lowry, the Lord Chief Justice of Northern Ireland. I recognised the difficulties which he might find in remaining in such an important judicial post after the Convention was over but, towards the end of the year after considering other candidates, I decided that he was the best man for the job. He was an Ulsterman and although of Unionist background, he would, I was sure, have the respect of all sides. Once I had obtained the approval of the Lord Chancellor, I would be able to reveal my hand at the appropriate time.

On 5 December, with the Cabinet discussions over but with Christmas looming and politics likely to be pushed into the background in Ulster, I had reported to the House of Commons that we were entering a new and important phase – the actual setting up of the Convention. I praised the previous Conservative government which had 'endeavoured in the Constitution Act 1973 to find a way in which devolved government could take place in Northern Ireland on the basis of consent. This followed upon long and widespread consultations with the political communities in Northern Ireland and with many individual citizens. I want to make clear my support for what the Conservative government did at that time.'

I meant what I said, and it is a mark of the attitude in the House of Commons to the problems of Northern Ireland that a government spokesman could speak in this way. I emphasised, as I had in the discussion paper, that the Whitelaw 1973 Act could be a way through in the months ahead: to use it as a base for future constitutional developments would save a great deal of time both in the Convention and in Parliament. The Convention's aim, I repeated, was to win 'support and respect throughout all parts of the community' and I also again referred to the Taoiseach's statement that unification could only come by consent. This was accepted at Westminster but was simply not believed in the North; perhaps, however, repetition would help.

In his reply for the Opposition, Ian Gilmour raised a valid point: 'If all the members of the Convention remained encrusted in the positions which they adopted at the election, it is obvious that there could be no widespread agreement and the Convention would fail. . . . The American Constitution would never have been constructed at Philadelphia if delegates had not been prepared to move some way from their original position.' It was a stirring analogy but Northern Ireland was very different from the thirteen British colonies of North America in the late eighteenth century.

He went on to suggest that 'to break the isolation of the Convention from the rest of the community', it would be valuable to have 'one or more consultative or advisory meetings' in session at the same time, for example, the 350 local government councillors in the province could meet in the Ulster Hall, Belfast, to discuss the proceedings in the Convention. I hardly dared imagine what would happen if we followed this idea; in any event neither the loyalist nor the SDLP politicians would have accepted it.

My reaction was similar to his further proposal that the community organisations and paramilitary bodies should 'come together in public places'. When Kevin McNamara queried if this should include the proscribed Official and Provisional IRA, Ian Gilmour floundered and said 'No, only the non-proscribed organisations'. This would of course have meant that the UDA could be present but not the Provisional IRA. Given that the Feakle talks were only a few days away, it was interesting that the official spokesman for the Opposition seemed prepared to involve paramilitary groups in talks.

Jim Molyneaux sensibly warned that while he was optimistic about the Convention, we should not expect too much from it: the UUUC would be standing on its General Election manifesto of no power sharing. He wanted me to set up in advance of the Convention a proper (i.e. as in Great Britain) local government structure in the province. This wish to give more power to local authorities was something the Unionists continued to ask for in the following years and it was even promised in the Thatcher government's manifesto of 1979. It has never been proceeded with because even a Tory government soon realised that a return to loyalist-controlled authorities would offend the minority and would retard any possibility of a devolved administration at Stormont.

Gerry Fitt wanted the government to spell out clearly the conclusions it would accept or reject from the Convention. This was precisely what I had done in the July White Paper, in my foreword to the discussion papers and in my parliamentary speech. Behind Gerry's question was his wish to return to power sharing, though he conceded that the 'Irish dimension' envisaged by the SDLP might not initially or in the short term approach the Council of Ireland of the Sunningdale agreement. Would that such an attitude have been taken in March 1974 when I arrived in the province: the UWC strike may have been prevented.

Strong support for the Convention came from Dr Paisley: 'It will be the first time that elected representatives of Northern Ireland have had the opportunity to discuss the future government of Northern Ireland. I advocated in the House before the Assembly was set up that there should first be an elected constituent assembly to discuss the future of Northern Ireland. That was never done.' He was right. But as much as the idea had crossed other minds, I reflected that to have had a power-sharing Executive for however brief a period had been advantageous.

Whether the Convention would be successful or not, our policy was once more approved by Parliament. It was not to remain the main subject of political discussion for long because shortly afterwards the Provisional IRA ceasefire captured the public interest both in Northern Ireland and beyond. However, preparations for the spring elections to the Convention went on behind the scenes and on 5 February the third discussion paper, 'The Government of Northern Ireland', was published. I made a statement to the Commons on the same day which, although primarily about the ceasefire talks and the general security situation, also explained the purpose of the paper.

The document was in three parts, the first of which discussed the means by which democratic countries developed institutions to suit their own needs. It described the pattern of institutions which had evolved in Britain – Cabinet government, collective responsibility, etc. – and explained why such a system had proved unsuited to the special needs of Northern Ireland. The second part outlined the existing constitution in the province which, despite the fall of the Executive, was based on the Northern Ireland Constitution Act of 1973. It covered the 'excepted' and 'reserved' powers for the UK government and the 'transferred' powers for the Executive in the province, and reminded the Convention members of the various sections which dealt with discrimination on the grounds of political or religious belief. This part also explained the nature of local government in the province, which had been restructured following the Macrory proposals of 1970 and consisted of twenty-six elected district councils, with appointed area boards for education, health, etc., plus such bodies as the Housing Executive and the Police Authority.

The third part looked to the future. After pointing out the general factors laid down in the Constitution Act which had to be borne in mind, in particular that a Northern Ireland government was concerned with regional government for the community, it examined various constitutional safeguards, such as a weighted majority and a blocking mechanism, which would enable a particular section of the community to prevent or delay legislation it considered against its vital interests. The methods used in Fiji, New Zealand and Mauritius to give special representation to minority groups were considered, as was the second chamber approach of Belgium and Switzerland, and the possibilities of separate communal councils, plebiscites and referenda.

Another possibility was government by executive committees – not to be confused with consultative or monitoring committees, which were already allowed for under the 1973 Constitution Act. Instead of a government department having a single individual as its political head, it would operate under the direction and control of a committee, and because we thought this method might be an answer to the Convention's difficulties, we added: 'A system of executive committees would have the effect of involving a wide section of public representatives in the day-to-day work of government. The more widespread such participation, the greater would be the possibility of softening those divisions which would otherwise exist between those who are exercising power and those who are not.'

The debate following my report to Parliament on 5 February confirmed the message from our informal chats with Northern Ireland politicians – the Unionists and the SDLP would participate in the Convention elections. It also confirmed my view that if we had moved earlier, they might not have been willing to do so: time matters in Northern Ireland. I did not, however, know whether the Provisional IRA would involve themselves politically.

By mid-February, preparations for the elections were well advanced. The time had come for me to announce the name of the Convention Chairman and after contacting Sir Robert Lowry, I did this on 21 February. He decided not to give any television or radio interviews but to hold a press conference at which he would answer questions. This was against the advice of my staff and I liked him for holding to his own line.

At the conference he stated: 'I shall not now or at any time comment on the prospects, progress or likely outcome of the Convention. To do so would be in my opinion quite inappropriate and would, moreover, derogate from the position of the members of the Convention whom, once they have been elected, I am resolved to serve to the best of my ability.' This all confirmed to me that the appointment was the right one, and it was widely welcomed in Northern Ireland and by William

Whitelaw, who was standing in for Mrs Thatcher as leader of the Opposition.

Ronald Blackburn, who had been Clerk to the Assembly, was officially appointed Clerk to the Convention at the end of February and Dr J. A. Oliver and Dr M. N. Hayes, both distinguished Northern Ireland public servants, were appointed to assist him with the preparations. They had all been involved in this work for some time and they now prepared a timetable of events up to and including the elections and the first full meeting of the Convention. I left to the Chairman and his staff the question of meetings with politicians, financial support and the preparation of research and background papers.

I was not yet willing to announce a date for the elections. As I had said in reply to questions in the Commons, it would be foolish to make an early announcement. I did not want to repeat the experience of William Whitelaw in 1972 and 1973 when he had given dates for elections only to find that events meanwhile blew him off course. By early February I was thinking of a date around the end of April, the beginning of May, but I wanted nothing firm because of inevitable leaks. The recommendation made to me in the office in early March was for 24 April, which I decided to move forward to 1 May. At the same time I decided on 28 March as the date to dissolve the Assembly elected in June 1973; this was necessary under the 1973 Constitution Act before the forthcoming elections took place.

My decision to move the polling date forward a week was influenced by another escalation of intersectarian killings. The election run-up had created an atmosphere of tension which seemed to encourage the murderous activities of the province's psychopaths and I wanted a slight delay in the hope that matters would calm down. The killings inevitably highlighted the subject of policing, which the Northern Ireland politicians discussed with me and which led me to state in the Commons on 12 March: 'It may be that the Constitutional Convention will have ideas to contribute to this very difficult question of policing. But it must be clear, as with the work of the Convention as a whole, that a final decision on this will be for the House to make.' Policing under democratic accountability would be important one day.

An aspect of the Convention that also concerned me was the status of its members. They were to be elected to find a constitution for the province and nothing more but I had agreed that they could make representations to ministers and departments on behalf of their electors. I had not wanted to go this far but, as I explained in a statement: 'There is little doubt that many people will naturally turn for advice to those whom they have chosen to represent them, albeit in a body of a special character' and consequently I intended 'to give enquiries on personal cases from members of the Convention the same kind of close attention as that currently given to approaches from other types of public representatives'. A point on which I was not willing to make any concessions was access to prisons for Convention members. There would be strong reactions to the politicians from the prisoners and it could only cause problems.

The Convention was not a parliament and had no legislative powers and I wanted to make sure that the people of Northern Ireland were aware of its purpose and nature. The information department prepared a leaflet to be delivered to every home which clearly set out the Convention's basis. It stated that the aim was to seek a political solution that would have widespread acceptance. No solution was ruled out but a majority would not have the right to impose its will in all circumstances and nor would a minority have the right of veto. It emphasised that the Convention's report would be put to Parliament at Westminster and that a referendum of the Northern Ireland electorate could be held on any questions connected with the report.

The leaflet went on to spell out 'realities' – the in-word in the office at the time – particularly the finances of the province: the taxes raised in Northern Ireland did not cover expenditure and the additional money which had to be provided from Westminster had increased from £125 million in 1971–72 to some £350 million in 1974–75. In pointing this out, we were trying to show up the weakness of the 'independence' lobby. We also included an appeal to the community to support the police, for which the army could not be a replacement.

As well as the pamphlets, the information office issued numerous briefing statements for the press, and I and my colleagues laced our speeches with references to the Convention. The media reported them but our British speeches and information leaflets did not come across to an electorate living in a province torn by murder and tragic injuries. As I wrote in my diary on 16 March after a meeting with CBI and union representatives, 'It is quite clear that we are failing to get people to see what the Convention is about. We have put out advertisements and I want to try once again this week. Perhaps it will need the actual election to concentrate minds, but we just can't make news.'

However, we kept on trying and in all my speeches I emphasised the Ulster nature of the Convention. So did Harold Wilson when he visited Northern Ireland on 25 March and publicly announced 1 May as polling day. 'The Convention will be elected', he told the province, 'by the people of Northern Ireland. It will meet under an Ulster chairman with Ulster members representing Ulster people. It offers a great chance for people here to work together to produce proposals which can be a major step on the road to a lasting peace.

Such an Ulster solution would be the best solution.'

By this time it was clear that the election was going to be fought between the main political parties of recent years. Our earlier tentative hopes that the loyalist paramilitaries would go into politics never materialised, and their anger against the politicians who had dropped them after May 1974 was shown when the UVF disrupted a UUUC meeting to demand a say in the selection of candidates for the Convention election. On the other side, although the Republican Clubs – i.e. the Official IRA – finally put up seventeen candidates, the Provisional Sinn Fein decided in the end not only not to stand but to boycott the elections altogether, on the grounds that this was the 'only way to make Britain and the loyalists see sense'. According to them, the Convention was part of a package of concessions made after the UWC strike and its only possible outcome was a loyalist take-over endorsed by the British. This curiously convoluted logic was far too clever. The political boycott was, as it nearly always is, a face-saver, particularly when combined with intimidation to keep voters at home.

Another republican group that decided not to stand was the recently formed Irish Republican Socialist Party, largely a break-away group from the Official Sinn Fein. Bernadette McAliskey, one of its leaders, had earlier claimed that the Party was 'in principle' prepared to fight the election, but a decision not to participate was taken by a small majority at the Party's first conference, on the grounds that 'there would be no political advantage to be gained from the Convention' since it was doomed to a short life, and because of the 'Official IRA's murder campaign against IRSP members'. The latter was the real reason.

When the party manifestos were published, they showed that the essential features of the parties' policies had changed little since the time of the General Election in October 1974, but that attitudes to the Convention had changed over the previous six months: parties were now putting forward their views in a positive and forthright manner. The UUUC manifesto stressed the link with the UK and advocated increased representation at Westminster and the reintroduction of a Governor-type figure, but its essence was: 'Government would be formed from the party with a majority in the Northern Ireland Parliament, although special opportunities should be provided for the minority community by powerful back-bench committees. Policing should be an internal matter.'

The manifesto of Brian Faulkner's Unionists – the Unionist Party of Northern Ireland – referred to Sunningdale but now rejected the Council of Ireland. They were against direct rule but supported minority involvement in government provided that the minority openly supported the 'majority's right to decide its own future' and the forces 'legally appointed to maintain law and order'. The Alliance Party supported power sharing in a devolved administration with a considerable measure of control over law and order, and it castigated the Republic for its continual constitutional claim over the North.

The SDLP argued for power sharing and an internationalised 'Irish dimension'. It saw the Convention as a conference table at which those elected might seek a solution through trust and agreement. 'The best security that can be provided is through a system of government which commands the loyalty of all. SDLP would not hesitate to pledge full support and loyalty to the police service of a fully agreed system of government.' Their manifesto stressed that policing arrangements should not be considered in isolation but as part of an overall political settlement.

The Northern Ireland Labour Party's aim was to reconcile all sections of the community but by a fundamentally different approach: through committees supervising all departments in a strength proportional to the number of seats held by the parties. It wanted a 100-member parliament elected on a list system. The Republican Clubs argued the case for a thirty-two-county solution and attacked the Provisionals' facile claim about the Convention.

None of the manifestos gave much hope of leading to an agreement in the Convention; the election speeches gave even less. For example, on 24 April, William Craig asserted the right of the Protestant majority to decide its own future: 'We will no longer tolerate a denial of British standards of democracy and justice.' John Hume attacked the UUUC for its connections with loyalist paramilitary organisations; Enoch Powell stated that Northern Ireland should be treated exactly like any other integral part of the United Kingdom; and Brian Faulkner, developing an unusual theme for him, said that some people would not accept permanent direct rule and that the repartitioning of Ireland was being widely discussed as an alternative if the Convention did not reach agreement.

At this stage the issue of election malpractices arose. The Alliance Party alleged that postal votes – intended as a means of diminishing intimidation – were being manipulated on a large scale by both the SDLP and the UUUC; that a 'postal vote factory' had been operating from a school and that attempts had been made to fill out postal vote applications in the names of people who had died. Austin Currie of the SDLP made similar allegations about malpractices in Fermanagh and South Tyrone. This was a matter for the Chief Electoral Registration Officer but there was little doubt, as Enoch Powell pointed out after the election, that unrestricted postal voting was a cause both of intimidation and of malpractice.

Whatever the merits or demerits of election forecasts, nearly everybody in Northern Ireland joined the guessing game. My staff turned their hand to it and in mid-April suggested that the UUUC might get as few as forty-two seats, with about twenty going to the SDLP and the other sixteen dividing between the UPNI, the Alliance Party and the NILP. A week later the suggestion was that the UUUC would get forty-six seats, to the detriment of the centre parties. The nearer to polling day, the more tribal loyalties would reassert themselves.

My diary of 20 April reflected my thoughts about the future: 'I am having a look at what will happen after the Convention, not just if it breaks down but if we have to have a period of time before the next form of government evolves. I have spoken to the GOC and the officials are looking at the security side.'

The immediate security situation was also concerning me and on 29 April I issued a statement:

> The people of Northern Ireland are about to go to the polls to choose those who will represent them at the constitutional Convention. The exercise of this democratic right to play a part in determining the shape of their own political institutions is rightly foremost in the minds of Ulstermen of all political persuasions. But none of us can afford to ignore the continuing horrifying level of violence in the community. If it persists unchecked, rational political debate could become difficult if not impossible.

Whatever our appeals, there was little doubt that the Convention election was going to be decided once more on the simple issue of tribal allegiance, with the exception of those people who voted for the Alliance Party and the group of middle-class Catholics who voted Unionist. However, just in case the results were unexpected, I asked my security people for an assessment of loyalist paramilitary reaction. In their view, much of the energies of the UDA and the UVF were being taken up in fighting each other. The leadership of the UVF had disintegrated and was in the hands of young thugs, while the UDA was continuing to try to build up its own grass roots political organisation but was finding it a very slow business. The resulting frustrations in both paramilitary forces might cause them to make a dangerous incursion into the political field if the election results were displeasing to them.

I conceded that this might be the outcome but, unlike in May 1974, they would not now have support in all parts of the community. As I had told my Cabinet colleagues once more, if there was a repeat of the Ulster workers' strike, there was little we could do but for other eventualities we were now prepared. We were much better organised in the Castle with our operations room and a good control system.

On election day a Westminster all-party delegation visited polling booths throughout the province and I invited Airey Neave, newly appointed as Opposition spokesman on Northern Ireland, to accompany me on visits in the wider Belfast area. There was a bit of trouble in the Creggan when a crowd of youths stoned the security forces, and there was a shooting incident in the Divis area of Belfast which was part of the Official IRA/Irish Republican Socialist Party feud and unconnected with the election. Otherwise all was quiet and I commented in my diary: 'We had put the police in charge of everything and I think it was noted. This may not be world-shattering but it illustrates what I would like to do, which is to make the police the important element in security in Northern Ireland.'

Once the polls were closed it took two days to carry out the complicated counting procedure under the single transferable vote system. It was, however, already clear from the way the transferred votes were being passed down the counting boards that Protestants had voted overwhelmingly for Protestants and Catholics for Catholics.

On 3 May, when the count was completed, I sent a telegram to Harold Wilson reporting that the elections had passed off calmly, with the RUC taking the lead in security, and that the sixty-six per cent turn-out was little lower than at the October General Election; in the 1973 Assembly election the turn-out had been seventy-two per cent. I then gave him the number of seats obtained by the various parties:

Official Unionist Party	19
Vanguard Unionist Party	14
Democratic Unionist Progressive Party	12
Independent UUUC	1
Independent Unionist	1
Unionist Party of Northern Ireland	5
Alliance	8
Social Democratic and Labour Party	17
Northern Ireland Labour Party	1
Republican Clubs	0

I pointed out that the UUUC with forty-seven seats (including the Independent Unionist) had an overall majority of sixteen. Its leaders had been elected easily on the first count, as had Gerry Fitt and Paddy Devlin of the SDLP, although Unionist Roy Bradford had been heavily defeated. The UPNI had fared badly, with Brian Faulkner elected only at the ninth stage and deputy leader Leslie Morrell defeated in

Londonderry. The Alliance had held up well, particularly in the middle-class areas, and indeed their chief whip, Basil Glass, had topped the poll in South Belfast. The NILP had made very little impact, with David Bleakley the only member elected, and the Republican Clubs had done very badly.

I told the Prime Minister that the party leaders were evidently meeting with the Convention Chairman on 5 May to discuss arrangements and after that I intended to call the first meeting of the Convention.

In the office we looked more closely at the results of the election. The most striking feature was the swing in the Protestant vote from the liberal Unionism represented by Brian Faulkner's UPNI to the radical extreme of Ian Paisley and William Craig. Twenty-one Unionist members had followed Mr Faulkner into the division lobbies of the defunct Assembly but in the constitutional Convention his new Unionist party would have only five members, which did not include such notable candidates as Leslie Morrell and Peter McLachlan who had also failed to get elected. Harry West's Official Unionist Party, which would have seemed to be the natural home for erstwhile Faulkner supporters, had only increased its seats from eleven to nineteen, while the Democratic Unionists had gained six and the Vanguard Unionists five seats.

The SDLP were downcast by the loss of two seats compared to the Assembly, although some loss of votes was inevitable. Even the more optimistic Catholic voters could hardly expect the Convention to produce constitutional proposals as favourable to their interests as the former power-sharing Executive, and others may have abstained because of the Provisional IRA's boycott, possibly fearing future intimidation rather than any actual intimidation on polling day. It was also worth noting that, although the Republican Clubs did not win a seat, nearly 15,000 people voted for them, or rather, the Official IRA.

The SDLP were particularly put out by an exhortation from Conor Cruise O'Brien in the Irish government to take a realistic view of the position. In a radio interview he pointed out that the loyalist majority in the Convention clearly excluded a power-sharing Executive and it was not in the power of Dublin or London to bring it into being. There was, he said, no possibility of an Irish dimension being put into institutional form and the only outcome would be continued direct rule from Westminster.

My own gloomy conclusion from the results was that they revealed what we had known when we first arrived in the province in 1974: the majority was against the whole concept underlying Sunningdale and Brian Faulkner's twenty-two seats in the old Assembly had not been a reality; Sunningdale was a British solution imposed from the outside. In the office we tried to look beyond the election results. Some felt that the UUUC would begin by devoting its time in the Convention to presenting a 'reasoned' case against both the Council of Ireland and power sharing. Others, more optimistically, thought there was the chance of a deal between the UUUC and the SDLP because whatever their differences they preferred each other to the British. A power-sharing Executive could emerge but we would play no part in helping it to do so. My role was not to be that of William Whitelaw.

The majority view about the loyalist paramilitaries was that any fears of action from them were groundless, although evidently one wing of the Provisional IRA in Dublin was apprehensive that the UDA and UVF would push the loyalist politicians to seize power. On the other hand, another wing of the Provisionals evidently thought that a squabbling Convention would lead to the sort of chaos in which 'one more push' would have the Brits out. These Provisional Army Council characters, I reflected, lived in their own little world but there was something in this last view. The Provisional IRA could never 'push out' the British but another UWC strike or similar loyalist action supported by the majority in Northern Ireland could transform the situation: the British dimension would be put at risk and indeed would probably be ended. It was the loyalists who had held and still held the key to the link with the United Kingdom.

Whatever the future, the Convention was now to begin. On 5 May I announced that its members were to receive £2,500 a year plus travelling expenses – Northern Ireland politicians may be easy to criticise but they certainly do not make money out of their political activities, which, moreover, put them in constant personal danger. The following day I reported to the Commons that the first meeting of the Convention was to be on 8 May in the Assembly Chamber at Stormont, after which it would be for the Convention itself to decide times and places of meetings, together with rules and procedures.

I told my Cabinet colleagues at this time that I thought the political parties in the Convention would treat it seriously but that it would be unrealistic to expect them to find a 'complete solution'. Our aim must be to guide them towards finding as large a measure of agreement as possible and, in other areas, setting down a clear statement of differing positions. If we achieved this limited objective, it would be something. As for anything more, Irish history had shown how events could quickly alter a situation and as these unfolded in the Convention and outside, they might lead to an agreed form of government – or to an abject failure.

The Convention opened in formality, with the Clerk reading my order under the 1974 Northern Ireland Act and then my letter of good wishes. The Chairman followed with his own well-chosen Ulster message: 'Truly, it can be said of Ulster that her children are gone into captivity, a terrible captivity involving their hearts and minds. Can we help to deliver those children?' He went on to remind the members that they were not a legislative but a deliberative body, which I hope came across from him with more effect than it had from me in the past few months.

Harry West responded for the UUUC on the lines that the majority in the Convention would not take advantage of the minority, and Gerry Fitt was similarly circumspect but did not view the outcome of the deliberations 'with any degree of optimism'. A committee was set up under the chairmanship of Dr Paisley to draft the rules of procedure, and its first report was presented when the Convention met again on 22 May. He pointed out that thirty-four of the decisions were unanimous, which was of itself encouraging, but nevertheless the SDLP remained concerned that, based on the proposed discussion procedures, the final report of the Convention would be heavily biased against the minority.

Press reports of this prompted the Irish government to take the matter up and I had a message from Dr Fitzgerald, who was in Lebanon at the time, that I ought to interfere under the Northern Ireland Act or else the Convention might break up. I replied that it would be a mistake to believe everything that appeared in the press about the rules committee, or about the Convention in general, and our policy continued to be to distance ourselves from the workings of the Convention. Parliament had decided that it was for the elected representatives of the people of Northern Ireland to take the lead in shaping their own future, and the UK government had no locus to impose rules of procedure on the Convention now that the opening meeting was over.

Rules of procedure were, after all, merely the means to enable the Convention to carry out its statutory duty, which was to provide a form of government acceptable to both communities, and that was what mattered. In any event, it would almost certainly be politically disastrous for me to intervene at this very early stage, or at any other time, in the Convention's work. All those concerned with the future welfare of Northern Ireland had to face the harsh fact that, if the Convention failed to reach agreement on its own rules of procedure, then the whole Convention would be called into question and would fail. Never believe the newspapers, especially from afar, was my thinking.

I preferred to follow the views of Sir Robert Lowry, who told the Convention that he did not consider the rules invalid. It took another eight sessions, up to 12 June, before the full draft rules were approved, a delay that I found more encouraging than not for it showed that the members did not want to hurry anything through. Robert Lowry proved himself a masterful chairman on more than procedural matters and held his own when tempers became frayed, as when Glen Barr walked out not to return, he said, until loyalist prisoners held in Scotland were returned to Ulster, and when cries of derision greeted a message from church leaders.

Many people had told me that all the politicians would do was heighten tension in the province, but in practice the opposite happened. By institutionalising political talk the worst sting was taken out of the arguments. Loyalist politicians continued to raise in the House of Commons the subject of intersectarian killings, which were not over with the election, and also the question of the ceasefire, but Stormont was now the focus of attention. Accordingly, at Westminster they failed to get much debating time on these subjects, and because I continued to make regular statements from the despatch box, there could be no complaint of lack of information.

The work of the Convention proceeded slowly. Four sessions between 17 and 24 June were spent on debating the motion: 'That this Convention commits itself to devising a system of government for Northern Ireland which will have the most widespread acceptance throughout the community; declares its abhorrence of violence from all sources and looks forward to open political negotiations within the Convention.' It was supported by all parties and approved without a division.

On 25 June a debate, largely involving the UUUC, was devoted to the motion: 'That this Convention assures the people of Northern Ireland that members will endeavour to discharge the responsibilities placed upon them by Parliament but emphasises that secret negotiations or agreements between HM Government and destructive elements in the community could prejudice the work of elected representatives in the Convention.' The whole purpose behind this was to 'discuss' the allegations of an agreement between the Provisional IRA and the British government.

The next day the Convention decided, by only one vote, against broadcasting their proceedings. The first three days of July were wholly given over to a motion from Gerry Fitt that the Convention devote its attentions 'to structures and systems of government designed to deal with the immediate human, social and economic problems of Northern Ireland'. All sides agreed to it and there was much talking, with the final day's debate finishing at midnight. The Convention then adjourned for six weeks but decided that during the recess private inter-party talks would be held: the three months of leisurely progress had clearly not been wasted.

The public exchange of insults between some members and remarks such as Mr Overend's, expressing pleasure at the police batonning Gerry Fitt in the past and a desire to squeeze Paddy Devlin's neck, had been, I was told, par for the Ulster course. More revealing were the debates on such important subjects as the aims of the Convention, in which Harry West, Gerry Fitt and Oliver Napier all spoke out firmly in favour of a devolved administration and against direct rule.

In Harry West's words, 'Our half-century of devolved government, wherein we had our own parliament and government, gave political and social expression to a self-consciousness that has been sadly lacking ever since this highly unsatisfactory system of direct rule was imposed upon us.' Oliver Napier talked of the possibility of erecting a common Ulster identity. 'Whether we believe it or not, we have far more in common with each other than any of us have with the Southern Irish, the English, the Scots or the Welsh. . . . I look forward to the day when we will all see clearly that our loyalty is to this province and its people. In that limited sense we could all be loyalists.'

Ian Paisley referred to the disillusionment with both London and Dublin, and John Hume, in an analysis of the loyalist tradition, made a speech that all sides regarded as impressive. Addressing the loyalists directly, he said, 'The real security your tradition has rests in your own strength and numbers and in nothing else. It does not rest in Acts of a British Parliament. The history of Anglo-Irish relations is littered with Acts of the British Parliament giving promises to the Irish Protestant population, every one of which has been broken.'

He went on to call for a partnership between loyalists and republicans, which would require a re-examination of attitudes both in the North and the South, where 'the government, the political parties and the people . . . have to ask themselves where their political dogma or political commandments have led them or led us in the North'. He then made the interesting comment that 'power sharing' and the 'Irish dimension' were both British phrases and admitted: 'We are under no illusion, and never have been, that power sharing is an unnatural system of government. But we are living in an extremely unnatural situation.'

Harry West took the opportunity to put the whole matter of independence into a loyalist perspective: 'A system of devolution has to be recognised as the most acceptable form of future government for Northern Ireland' but 'if it is totally rejected by Britain, or if the British government no longer accepts Northern Ireland within the United Kingdom and desires to break the Union, a negotiated independence would have to be examined.' The latter was not a policy that I could work for and would only arise if events took a wrong turn, but when Harry West could reach such a conclusion, it had to be taken into account. We could not ignore the possibility of independence being on the agenda, and neither could the Dublin government, however strongly they felt about it.

I was heartened by the views on policing expressed by two important Convention members, Austin Currie and William Craig. The former stated his belief that, given an agreed constitution, there would be no difficulty in setting up an acceptable police service in all areas, and Craig, a former Stormont Minister of Home Affairs, argued forcibly for the transfer of police functions to a Northern Ireland executive. It reinforced my feelings that control of the police by a devolved government was at the heart of any solution to the problem of security. Any move towards it would require a gradual reduction in the numbers and role of the army. Ulster politicians would never have responsibility for the British forces.

Craig's strong support for inter-party talks was also encouraging, and even Ian Paisley in a radio interview talked of the atmosphere of good will in the Convention which he did not believe was false optimism. Were the talks perhaps to prove the way through? It was in this optimistic spirit that the House of Commons approved a further extension of direct rule on 26 June.

I gave my own analysis of events to my colleagues on the Cabinet sub-committee on 3 July. I warned that there were undercurrents of tension beneath the harmonious surface of the Convention. Both the UUUC and the SDLP were looking to their backs, and the former in particular would be anxious not to suffer the same fate as Brian Faulkner who in loyalist folklore compromised with the republicans. I added to my memorandum suggestions about the possible steps open to us if the Convention ran into difficulties, for example, private discussions with the parties, public intervention by me to clarify a particular question, dissolution and later recall of the Convention. I also included a section on what we might do after the Convention – a referendum, a fact-finding enquiry, a conference of Northern Ireland parties to develop any agreement reached in the Convention, and a continuation of direct rule.

This was a paper exercise. If the Convention did fail, my own strong view was that the last option was the only one available to us, and I felt that this was the direction in which we were heading. Indeed, I concluded to my colleagues: 'Initial good will has been bought by avoiding the dividing issues. It remains to be seen whether the inter-party talks in the recess will enable the Convention to make progress on its task in the autumn.' I had been advised more optimistically that the seemingly slow progress in the Convention since April had welded its members and a kind of Ulster nationalism was manufacturing itself. I wondered, however, if the politicians could build on it. There had been too many false dawns.

Nevertheless, the inter-party talks began. I had no involvement with them: no British government representative could have been involved without them ending at once. They were talks for Ulstermen, not for outsiders, and all I knew was that they were principally about power sharing. I kept my distance but listened carefully to the public statements of the politicians. Remarkably, little was said privately by the participants but that all was not well seemed likely from a comment made by Harry West at the end of July when, out of the blue, he suggested that the Convention should turn itself into a legislative assembly to implement the proposals put forward by the UUUC. The plan was for a trial period of four years, following which the members would go to the electorate. It was promptly turned down by Bill Craig, who pointed out that the Convention had not been elected for that purpose.

A further indication of the problem facing the loyalist politicians was Enoch Powell's assertion, made at the same time, that the future government of Northern Ireland must be decided by the United Kingdom as a whole, not by the people of Northern Ireland; Ulster should be treated as an integral part of the United Kingdom, with the same representation in Parliament and the same forms of government as the rest of the United Kingdom. Here was a Westminster leader of the Official Unionists arguing for integration, while the Ulster leaders of the party clearly wanted the opposite, devolution.

Liaison between Mr Powell and his loyalist colleagues in the Convention was not good at this time and I was told that he felt let down by them over an agreement reached on devolution policy. As I noted in my diary of 28 July, his loyalty was to the Queen in Parliament, whereas the Ulster-based Unionists was more to a kind of Bob Jones Protestant Queen.

Private though the talks were, they were not taking place in a vacuum. It was a difficult time in the province: all sides were suspicious of the ceasefire, vicious sectarian murders were being carried out and there was again much loose talk of British government policy moving towards independence for Ulster. Ian Paisley averred on radio at the end of July that the loyalists would not seize power under any circumstances but that if the British government ended the union, they would have no option but to negotiate independence.

The independence issue had been inflamed by an unfortunate incident in early June. A new member of the Northern Ireland Office staff who had been seconded from the Foreign and Commonwealth Office to work in the community relations department was alleged to have mentioned independence at a private meeting with some loyalist figures and to have said that the British were getting fed up with Northern Ireland. These injudicious words were relayed back as evidence that we were moving towards a policy of independence for the province. They reached Enoch Powell, who wrote to me at the end of July raising the issue. I have always believed that this incident planted the seed in Enoch Powell's mind of a Foreign Office plot to break the link between Great Britain and Northern Ireland. He has clung to the notion ever since.

I can only speak for what I know, which is that I kept in close touch with Jim Callaghan and then Tony Crosland as the Foreign Secretaries and they left contacts with the South about Northern Ireland to me. The Foreign Office officials who worked for me in Northern Ireland followed the policy I was pursuing for the province and the one minor apparent exception that came Enoch Powell's way proves rather than disproves the point; it had already been decided that the man should return to London before Enoch's letter of protest arrived.

The talk of independence did not come from the government but from loyalist paramilitary sources and to counter it I issued a statement towards the end of August saying that, whatever the outcome of the Convention, Northern Ireland would continue to be governed with full accountability to the United Kingdom Parliament. There was no question of the government abdicating their responsibilities in Northern Ireland; we were seeking a long-term political solution to its problems.

The political atmosphere was not helped by a press conference statement from Ernie Baird of the Vanguard Unionist Party after a meeting between me and his deputation. He warned that if the report of the Convention was not accepted at Westminster, many leading public figures would have no alternative but to abandon the political scene and 'try to bring pressure to bear in some other way'. So much for his loyalty.

Even Oliver Napier was at it. He let it be known in a speech that he suspected that the British government did not believe the Convention could produce a solution and 'in that situation, the British government know what we all know in our bones, that the will for continuing direct rule is just not there'.

The inter-party talks continued but I was not surprised when in the third week of August it was announced that the resumption of the full Convention was to be postponed until 9 September to allow more time for them. Such news as had leaked out from discussions between the

UUUC, the SDLP and the Alliance indicated that some, although not much, progress was being made to reconcile the UUUC's and SDLP's basic position on minority representation in a regional government. The two sides were in something of an impasse, with neither able to tell their supporters that they had won acceptance for the position set out in their respective election manifestos, and neither party wishing to be held responsible for the breakdown of the Convention; each hoped to throw the odium on the other.

It was reported to me that William Craig – whose political antennae were in my view probably the most sensitive in the province – judged that the real confrontation was yet to happen and he was standing aside from the shadow-boxing. In these circumstances 'the traditional whipping boy is the British government' and, true to form, the loyalists were seeking to distract attention by allegations of British failure to control republican violence, and the SDLP by allegations of British failure to control Protestant violence.

I was of course the main target and, helped by gossip from two Tory backwoodsmen at Westminster where Parliament was in recess, the press story was that I was to resign or else bipartisanship would end. Harold Wilson promptly dismissed this, but it was true that bipartisanship was not what it was when we were in Opposition. Front-bench Tories were opposed to the ceasefire, the ending of detention and my policy on security, and bipartisanship depends on policy agreement not on some old-boy parliamentary affinity.

The breakdown of the talks seemed inevitable and I was awaiting news of it when a member of the Convention staff came to tell me that the parties seemed to have come to an agreement, and an interesting one: the UUUC were prepared to write into the constitution that there could be a coalition in a time of emergency, which could be for a period of four to five years and which would be set up purely for the sake of Northern Ireland. The analogy was the Churchill Coalition of 1940–45. Perhaps there was hope after all, but my response was to wait and see what would happen for there had been no previous sign of an agreement.

A day or two later I learned that a UUUC policy document was circulating among the Convention parties that gave the impression that in an emergency the UUUC could form a temporary and voluntary government with the SDLP. It proved, however, to be another false dawn. On 8 September the UUUC overwhelmingly repudiated any idea of a coalition, with only William Craig voting in favour of the idea. Their decision may have been influenced by some particularly nasty killings of loyalists in Armagh. It also seemed that Paisley may have played a part in the downfall of the coalition idea by what I described in my diary of the time as 'his double-crossing act', although he vehemently denied this later in the Convention. Enoch Powell also helped, with Jim Molyneaux, to kill the plan in internal UUUC meetings.

The situation was not improved by Gerry Fitt who happened to be at the Castle one morning to meet with a civil servant and afterwards walked straight into my room when I was in the middle of a meeting with hard-line loyalists. He beat a hasty retreat in his best merchant navy gait, but the loyalists deduced that the SDLP had the run of the office! On such silly incidents is the conspiracy theory of politics based.

After the UUUC rejection of the coalition on 8 September, William Craig came to see me on another matter and, with tears in his eyes, said that he was going to have to resign. I told him not to, and though he went back briefly to continue his fight, it was to no avail. The inter-party talks failed and the rejection of the coalition idea was later confirmed at a UUUC meeting on 18 September. William Craig poured his heart out publicly by declaring that the UUUC had devalued the Convention and had been less than wholehearted in its attempts to restore devolved government to Northern Ireland. He also said that the SDLP had deserved better treatment at the hands of his Unionist Coalition partners. Who would have expected words like that from Bill Craig two years previously? His actions cost him the loss of all support from his Unionist partners and a split in his Vanguard Unionist Progressive Party, with nine of its members leaving to form the United Ulster Unionist Movement under Ernest Baird.

Even after the coalition idea had been rejected by the politicians, one of my staff came to tell me in the second week of September that a local television personality was acting as an intermediary and wanted to know if the British government would move quickly if a coalition was proposed. I thought it a curious way of setting about matters since we had not been involved and everything we heard was at second hand. I replied that we would have to know what we were acting on before we could give any firm commitment. Nothing further came of this.

I warned my Cabinet colleagues that the Convention with its in-built UUUC majority would now vote in favour of its scheme for a return to majority rule with no power sharing. The discussions after the Convention recess went on for weeks but on 7 November this is what was endorsed, by 42 votes to 31, despite an attempt by the Alliance Party to reconsider the UUUC Report and extend the life of the Convention.

Back in Whitehall, the Cabinet Office advised Harold to have Northern Ireland policy looked at again: it was concerned that the end of the Convention would bring a repeat of the Ulster workers' strike. The situation was, however, simply not comparable. The Convention Report revealed a failure by Northern Ireland politicians to agree among themselves, whereas in May 1974 it was plans devised by Dublin and London which had been rejected by the loyalists; there was now no Council of Ireland to bring together the majority community of all classes. However, I thought that although it was overdoing the educative process, there was no harm in going through the list of options again.

Independence and integration were put forward only to be knocked down without further ado, and similarly the option of majority rule with 'special provision for the minority' and 'direct rule centred on Northern Ireland' – i.e. changes in local government and an elected or nominated council. It was an academic exercise and none of these policies was discussed as a possible alternative. They did, however, show my colleagues that direct rule with perhaps a return to the Convention was the only option, and the main point for me was that nobody was pressing for changes in this policy. I had full support.

On this basis I made a statement in the House of Commons on 10 November, two days after receiving the Convention's Report. I said that there was no quick and easy solution in Northern Ireland and the province would continue to be governed from London; Convention members would still be paid because I regarded it as essential that they were available for further consultations on constitutional matters, including of course their Report.

This had contained few surprises. It began by attacking the concept of two communities in Northern Ireland and the attitude of the Irish Republic to the North. The devolved government it recommended was a Northern Ireland parliament and government, with the Queen represented by a governor; Westminster representation should increase from twelve MPs to between twenty and twenty-four, and the office of Secretary of State for Northern Ireland should lapse, with those services that were not devolved being the concern of a Secretary of State 'for the devolved regions' or of a senior Cabinet minister. Here they were again running the whole of the United Kingdom!

The single transferable vote system should be used for the first election but thereafter the parliament of Northern Ireland should legislate on the franchise, elections and disqualifications for membership of the parliament, which should be unicameral with seventy-eight to a hundred members, all of them British citizens. The new devolved government should have powers broadly similar to those conferred by the Government of Ireland Act 1920, together with control of the police, prisons and the criminal law.

The Report was against any temporary arrangements for forming a government, and recommended that the formation and operation of the executive should conform to the practices of the UK parliament, with no compulsion to include any particular group or party, although it proposed that a committee system should be devised for each department of government to make parliament more effective. A Bill of Constitutional Rights to guarantee the stability and integrity of the Northern Ireland Constitution was proposed, together with a general Bill of Rights and Duties to protect the rights of individual citizens.

There was a section on social and economic priorities and to achieve these the Report recommended a provision for a divergence in approach to spending and taxation from the rest of the United Kingdom. Surprisingly, there was also a section on external relationships, which should be the responsibility of the Westminster government in consultation with the government of Northern Ireland. The Irish dimension was recognised but any imposed institutionalised association was rejected. There should be dual representation of Northern Ireland at Strasbourg, Brussels and New York!

Finally, power sharing or coalition was identified as the only barrier to substantial agreement. This section of the Report contained the interesting statement: 'Agreement does not need to be unanimous to be real.'

The proposals in this UUUC Report were very revealing, for they basically recommended a return to 1920. The same philosophy was shown in the clause of the accompanying draft Bill which reserved to the Prime Minister of Northern Ireland the sole right to request the armed forces of the Crown to assist in maintaining public order. The loyalists may not have wanted the 1920 Government of Ireland Act at the time but they certainly wanted it now.

One other, although essentially minor, aspect of the Report that revealed much about the outlook of loyalist members of the Convention was the reference in it to me denying members reasonable status, i.e. not treating them as MPs. The issue had festered since February, although after a meeting with Sir Robert Lowry and the Convention Chief Whip on 13 June, I had tried again to explain that the Convention was not a legislative assembly and its members had been elected for only one, obvious, purpose. Clearly, it had not stopped the rankling, which was linked with anger over personal expenses: these covered claims for travelling to and from the Convention but not for other travelling in the province. It seemed to have gone unrecognised that against Treasury advice I had increased the members' salaries.

The UUUC Report was clearly not going to win acceptance at Westminster, and equally clearly it was far from the views expressed in the minority reports. The SDLP held that 'no peaceful solution of the Northern Ireland problem is possible without power sharing in government and an institutionalised Irish dimension'. It wanted a partnership between the two traditions in Northern Ireland but accepted that the majority in the province wanted to remain part of the UK, asserting – with the UWC strike in mind – that membership of the UK implied 'accepting the will of Parliament and the equal rights of all citizens'. It also proposed a referendum in both parts of Ireland to allow the people to show their support for the new institutions to be set up.

The Alliance Party wanted devolved government within the UK; no change in this link without the consent of a majority of the people in the province; extra representation at Westminster; and a Bill of Rights. In the section of their report on the structure of government, it proposed a Chief Minister, elected by the Northern Ireland parliament, and a single transferable vote system within this to choose a Chairman of Committees. Their scheme for the allocation of portfolios was delightfully complicated but perhaps, I reflected, this was a way of making the system work.

The proposals by Brian Faulkner's Unionist Party of Northern Ireland deliberately excluded any in-depth analysis of the situation in the province and went straight to the point. Northern Ireland was part of the UK but there was a need for devolved government, as the experience of direct rule showed. Like the other loyalist parties, it wanted an elected legislature with the same powers as in the 1920 Constitution but with a nominated second chamber composed of members representing the trade unions, the employers and community groups. (Shades of the Weimar Republic here.)

The Northern Ireland Labour Party, who were advised by Adam Curle, the Professor of Peace Studies at Bradford University, supported strongly the concept of a voluntary coalition as a means of setting up a crisis government. If there were to be a return to direct rule, the Secretary of State should be advised by a Council of State made up of local people to keep him in touch with the province.

None of these minority reports was very surprising but in any event they would not be acceptable to Parliament, if only because they were not acceptable to the UUUC. The real stumbling block was power sharing and it was this fundamental issue that I had to pursue. There were still the difficult problems of finance and law and order, but the prime need was to form a developed government for Northern Ireland. Most of the politicians wanted to get a devolved government of some kind going again and I was determined to use this period after the dissolution of the Convention to talk with the political parties, before reporting to Parliament in the New Year.

At the Cabinet sub-committee meeting on 11 November we discussed a paper that I had submitted on the political situation. I reported again on the idea of a voluntary emergency coalition put forward by

William Craig. There was a story coming from 'political circles' in the province, I told my colleagues, that once we rejected the UUUC-slanted Report and reconvened the Convention for further study, the UUUC – having discharged their obligations under their manifestos – would be free to look again at the situation. This, it was argued, would mean that Craig's idea would prevail and the parties would reach agreement on some form of emergency coalition.

My own view, I said, was that this scenario was inherently implausible. Craig had been isolated in the UUUC, largely by the activities and dominance of Paisley, and, more important, the loyalist electorate would give the idea little support. They had already made their strength abundantly clear twice in 1974 and again in the Convention elections. Nor was it certain how the SDLP would react. While they liked Craig's emergency coalition idea, they had burned their fingers in the first Executive and this time they would be looking for firmer guarantees.

We needed to move carefully. If we reconvened the Convention with carte blanche to try again, we would be exposed to significant risks, and we would be no less exposed if we summarily dismissed its Report. To try to sidestep these difficulties, I proposed to maintain the momentum of discussions with the political parties outside the Convention and then perhaps to reconvene it with a specific remit. I warned my colleagues that we had to avoid all talk of crisis. There was no crisis in Northern Ireland and my job was not to provoke one. Our aim was to move forward, but with no time limit. I did not have an answer to the problem; continually to talk of solutions was, I asserted, an English disease.

I spoke so plainly because I was annoyed that on the agenda was yet another Cabinet Office options paper, this time produced in association with the Think Tank. As far as I was concerned, the latter had been valuable for making economic valuations to counter those of the Treasury, the City or financial journalists, but when it came to political judgments, no. Cynically, I asked my private secretary to invite them over to West Belfast for a month!

The paper was presented with the clarity I had grown to expect from civil servants and covered all the usual options. Repartition, as a demographic map made clear, would not solve the problem: a border change to exclude the predominantly Catholic population of South Armagh from the UK would arouse the fierce resentment of the majority community in Northern Ireland and the Catholics of the North would regard it as isolating them even more.

Independence was similarly rejected. I pointed out that there was no governmental structure to hand over to, except district councils with limited power. Although many loyalists hankered after the idea, it was not a policy we could work for, and it would be a mark of failure if events brought about such a situation. The paper also rejected majority rule, as it did the idea of a resident minister 'involving local politicians in a regional council with some executive responsibilities, leading to a "new form" of power sharing but with law and order still with the UK government'. This was simply majority rule under another name.

The preferred option was direct rule in a province 'distanced' from the UK, which would emphasise the importance of finding a solution within Northern Ireland itself and might lead to a new form of 'community participation' in government. Once more we had covered old ground and drawn the same conclusions.

As I told my colleagues when I opened the discussion, I regarded the paper as a dictionary of options but not a text for action. They agreed with me that for the present we should seek to contain the position in the province by continuing direct rule with good administration and effective police action. And we should persevere in trying to find common ground during the consultations on the Convention Report that I was now about to undertake. This meant in fact that we were moving towards a recall of the Convention for a limited period, the mechanics of which I had yet to decide.

My work was now to try again to bring the two sides together, using whatever chances the talks outside the Convention might give. In the background was the so-called ceasefire and the continuing horror of intersectarian murders. Certainly the Provisional IRA would not leave the politicians in peace if they showed any sign of agreement. Political change and security policy had, as always, to move hand in hand.

Chapter 9

THE LAW AND THE ENDING OF DETENTION

While preparations for the Convention were being made in early 1975, we were also preparing legislation to amend the Emergency Provisions Act introduced in August 1973 to give the security forces special powers to deal with terrorism in Northern Ireland. From the time of my appointment I had been wanting to make changes in these special powers and the first step towards this had been to set up the committee under Lord Gardiner to make an independent investigation of the measures used to deal with terrorism in the province.

The analysis and conclusions of a respected outside body would carry more weight than a government investigation and I hoped that the Gardiner Report would lead to informed public discussions before we proceeded to legislation to amend the Act. As I had told my Cabinet colleagues in November 1974, overall I was looking to the Report as a means of moving towards the ending of detention, and I continued to see it in this light even when the Provisional IRA ceasefire brought the opportunity to move more quickly.

In its recommendations, the committee needed to strike a balance between protecting the lives of the security forces and the general public and protecting civil liberties and human rights. Its members, some of whom were from Northern Ireland, spent long periods in the province, visiting the prisons, the police and the army, and taking evidence from individuals and groups representing all sides of the community. The resulting Report, which I had received in December 1974 and which was published the following month, was thorough, intelligent and clear, and it is a tribute to its relevance that it has stood the test of time.

It began with the general point that there was a need to work out a solution in political terms 'to promote social justice between classes and communities'. This was of course undoubted, given that it was accepted that no solution could be worked out overnight. Then, on the main issue, the Emergency Provisions Act, it stated forthrightly: 'The British government has acted legitimately and consistently within the terms of the European Convention for the Protection of Human Rights and Fundamental Freedoms in restricting certain fundamental liberties in Northern Ireland.' In its basic approach, the Gardiner Committee was thus clearly in line with the government; it was the details of the Report that called for attention.

It considered that the emergency powers should be limited both in duration and scope. For example, trial by jury should be restored as soon as possible, even though its investigations had shown that the new system of non-jury trials was working fairly and well, that the right to a fair trial was being maintained and the administration of justice had not suffered. Similarly, although it could not recommend the ending of detention, it felt sure that this could not remain a long-term policy. The 'grave decision' to end it could only be made by the government in the light of the prevailing situation. I had told my Cabinet colleagues in December that this was the committee's opinion, and it was particularly helpful in giving me a basis for my policy on releases.

The Report criticised the existing law on detention procedures and recommended that the sole responsibility for the detention of individuals should lie with the Secretary of the State but acting on the advice of a 'Detention Advisory Board' consisting of three British judges who would examine each case within twenty-eight days, after which a provisional custody order could be made. Detainees would have the right to appear before the Board but not to be legally represented or to be present when other witnesses were being questioned.

The existing release procedures were also criticised and a similar recommendation made that the Secretary of State should have sole responsibility for the release of detainees after advice from a 'Release Advisory Committee'. This was something that we would have to look at carefully, together with the recommendation to establish a small pre-release centre where detainees could be given assistance with the immediate problems of resettlement.

The Report recognised the need for the Royal Ulster Constabulary to be accepted throughout the whole of Northern Ireland and expressed the hope that the minority community as a whole would support normal policing in their areas and recruitment to the RUC. I could not quarrel with this pious hope: I had been expressing the same one since March 1974. The committee went on to say that the existing procedures for complaints against the police – and no government could have said this without provoking cries of disbelief – were already more thorough than those in existence anywhere else in the United Kingdom, with all complaints being fully investigated. It nevertheless recommended the introduction of an independent means of investigating complaints as an important step towards restoring universal confidence in the RUC.

My hopes of constructive criticism about prisons in the province were realised when the committee condemned the extensive use of compounds rather than cells and urged the government to find suitable sites on which to start immediately building temporary and permanent cellular prisons. We were doing this and I was pleased to have confirmation of our approach. I felt, however, that the Report was too ambitious in suggesting that detainees should be housed in a completely separate prison from convicted prisoners and if a suitable army camp or other large building could not be converted quickly, a new temporary prison for detainees should be constructed by the fastest possible means. Security problems alone would prevent this happening quickly and I thought it would be better to tackle the problem by ending the system of detention itself.

The Report was equally helpful when it bluntly stated that the introduction of special category status had been a serious mistake and recommended that steps should be taken to end it at the earliest practicable opportunity. It also recommended that no amnesty should be given to special category prisoners, all of which gave support to my own views.

Time was needed for the implications of the Gardiner Report to be considered by those most directly affected, which apart from the Northern Ireland Office included the police and the army, the Home Office and the Lord Chancellor and Attorney General. However, by the end of January I had obtained approval for the proposal that the Secretary of State should be responsible for releases and agreement that I should reject the proposal for a three-judge tribunal to advise me on this. It had to be my job alone to consider the security information and make a judgment: to involve others would cause delays and increase the number of lives at risk in the province. I also emphasised again to my Cabinet colleagues that in order to end special category status, I needed time to provide alternative prison accommodation and to work out an appropriate scheme of parole.

I briefly referred to the publication of the Gardiner Report in the House of Commons on 30 January in response to a written parliamentary question, stating that it gave support to the legitimacy of government policy. Before I could report on all its recommendations in detail and proceed with draft legislation, I needed further discussions with colleagues and also with the Northern Ireland political parties.

The initial response to the Report in the province was predictable. The UUUC was not going to offend the loyalist paramilitaries by speaking out against special category status which, in the words of a

UVF spokesman, 'the special category prisoner has fought hard and long to obtain. They are people who have taken up the gun and the bomb to defend this country. They are political prisoners.' The UPNI, having no paramilitary connection, had no such qualms and Brian Faulkner in particular was pleased that the Report had criticised detention procedures. They were, he said, 'diversions that successive Secretaries of State had introduced to try and make it look like a judicial process. It was not a judicial process.'

The Alliance Party was statesmanship itself, praising me for taking time to study the Report, and welcoming the recommendations for a Bill of Rights and fair employment legislation. The SDLP kept their heads down. They were understandably disappointed that the Report contained no firm recommendation to end detention but they courageously placed the blame for its continuation on the Provisional IRA, one of whose Sinn Fein spokesmen threatened mass hunger strikes and worse if special category status were to be ended.

We were obviously going to have trouble ending special category status but we would anyway have to move slowly on it until the new prison cells were available. However, I could continue releasing detainees and, with the aid of events, move more quickly to end detention.

Discussions on the issues raised by the Gardiner Report continued through February and March. The work of drafting an amended Emergency Provisions Act was far from easy and it became clear that it would not be ready before early July, by which time the existing Act would have expired. I therefore obtained the approval of the House of Commons to renew the old Act, which would lapse as soon as the amended Bill went on the statute book. In the event I was able to go to the Commons for a second reading of the new Bill on 27 June.

The key point of my speech was that the situation in Northern Ireland required security forces able to act against violence. Emergency powers were therefore still needed, including the power to detain, for if the ceasefire did not hold and terrorism and intimidation returned, my aim of ending detention would also founder. I then told the House that I intended to leave the question of a Bill of Rights, recommended by the Gardiner Report, to Vic Feather and his Standing Advisory Commission on Human Rights and also perhaps to the Convention. In fact my support for such a Bill had weakened the more I learned of the paramilitaries' attitudes. It was indicative that the many changes introduced by the previous government to buttress civil liberties seemed to have left those who used guns quite unmoved.

After announcing the details of changes in the Bill – written statements, bail, legal aid, clarification of search and arrest powers – I turned to the Report's recommendation that a general offence of terrorism should be created. I told the House that we were against this because it was preferable for the law to deal with specific rather than general offences. The new Bill would, for example, make it illegal to recruit to a proscribed organisation or to teach without authorisation the theory of making bombs or using weapons. It would also be an offence to collect information about the armed forces, the police, persons holding official office, court officers and prison officers, or information likely to be useful in planning or executing an act of violence. This last point was a reminder of the Provisional IRA documents found in May 1974 that were a plan to take over large areas of Belfast. The Bill also made it an offence to wear hoods or masks on the streets – something which I had found objectionable since my arrival in the province.

Then I turned to the changes in detention arrangements, explaining that there would be only one person to advise the Secretary of State on detention, rather than Gardiner's recommendation of three advisory judges, which was not practicable because it would be too slow, as well as increasing the security risk. I also did not accept the Gardiner proposal of a pre-release scheme to help detainees to return to ordinary life. As had become apparent early in 1974, ideas like this, however good in principle, did not work in practice. The paramilitary leaders were against them and once detainees knew that they were to be released, they refused to co-operate. I was, however, willing to fund an independent advice bureau in Belfast to co-ordinate the work of voluntary organisations in giving help to those released detainees who wanted it.

I also referred briefly to special category status, and simply stated that the combined opposition of republican and loyalist paramilitaries to ending it made any change in the law impracticable until we had new prison cell accommodation to house the detainees concerned.

One change that I did make was to shorten the period for renewing the Emergency Provisions Act from a year to six months; if there were to be special powers, then there must be special procedures. The shorter period before the Act would again have to be approved by Parliament meant that we would be able to react more quickly to any changes in the security situation.

The new Emergency Provisions Act went through Parliament without any trouble, for the House of Commons and the country in general accepted that the special circumstances of terrorism needed special laws. When the Bill had completed all its stages in August 1975, I felt a satisfaction that was rare in my job. The promise that I had made in Opposition and on my appointment as Secretary of State to

Northern Ireland – to investigate the emergency laws and introduce new legislation – had been fulfilled.

No such satisfaction had accompanied the passing of the Criminal Jurisdiction Bill which I brought to the Commons for second reading on 19 June. It stemmed from the April 1974 report of the joint British/Irish Law Commission, set up under the Sunningdale agreement to report on measures to ensure that persons committing crimes of violence, however motivated, in any part of Ireland might be brought to trial irrespective of the part of Ireland in which they were located. The Commission's proposal for an 'extra-territorial' extradition method, by which fugitive offenders accused of serious crimes of violence could be brought to trial on whichever side of the border they were arrested, was, as the Commission was aware, a compromise measure of doubtful effectiveness – although after my time it was put to good use in the Twite case – and I had little enthusiasm for the Bill that translated it into legislation. This was not published until January 1975, principally because the reciprocal legislation was not introduced into the Dail until November 1974. In the Commons debate on the second reading of the Bill, I gave the background to the problem:

> Since the troubles started in Northern Ireland, no person accused of a terrorist offence in Northern Ireland has been returned from the Republic to face trial. Twelve persons wanted for 'terrorist' offences committed in Northern Ireland have now been set free by courts in the Republic on the grounds that their offences were political or connected with a political offence. A further seven are contesting their return to Northern Ireland before the courts. Some of those concerned have been accused of murder or attempted murder. There have been instances where a fugitive has returned to Northern Ireland to resume his activities.

The judges in the Republic were not being perverse in not allowing extradition; they were simply carrying out the law. To explain why that law is not changed means an understanding of the force of history which prevents a people who do not condone violence by republican killers from accepting that by treating them as politically motivated, any real contact between North and South, let alone unification, is made impossible.

In the discussion that followed my speech, members showed that they did not see the mixed court method as the best solution but agreed that there was little point in taking the matter further. Harold McCusker, the MP for Armagh, rightly called the solution 'second-best', and I agreed with him publicly; I was not prepared to say one thing in the office and another outside. However, one piece of

Sunningdale had been implemented even if it did not work as intended.

By June 1975 when the Criminal Jurisdiction Bill went through Parliament, the unilateral ceasefire announced by the Provisional IRA in February was still in operation, although there were regular reports that it was on the verge of breakdown. Contact between my officials and representatives of Provisional Sinn Fein had continued, based strictly on my public statements and the guidelines I had laid down. Consequently, the discussions were mainly concerned with the means of monitoring the ceasefire, particularly by avoiding misunderstandings about the role of the security forces, although occasionally they ventured into general political issues such as the Convention elections, the EEC referendum and the economic problems of Northern Ireland. I approved of such general discussions as a way of encouraging political thought but any move towards discussing a public or private declaration of withdrawal from the province was always firmly rejected.

What we kept stressing was the need for a genuine cessation of violence. The Provisional Sinn Fein representatives were questioned about the continuing outrages, which included the murder of policemen and soldiers, and bombings in London, Belfast and elsewhere. My officials warned that the meetings could not be held against a background of violence and indeed the talks were suspended several times for this reason. In early March during one of these crises, I had been sure that the ceasefire was going to end. I talked it over for hours with Frank Cooper one Sunday afternoon, and told him that I felt something must be done about the situation. In particular I needed to make a statement to the Commons, not only in order to keep Parliament informed but also to provide more material for the Provisional Sinn Fein to consider.

Following my informal talk with Frank, I had more formal discussions with my security advisers, and especially the GOC and the Chief Constable, about a Commons statement. I was due to make one on 12 March about a new policy for the treatment of young offenders and I now decided to extend it to cover the ceasefire, making reference in particular to the incident centres which had been set up to prevent a breakdown. Although I had explained in the Commons in early February how these functioned, the rumours about them had persisted and the subject had continued to rouse strong feelings amongst the politicians on both sides of the community.

Gerry Fitt, expressing the concern of the SDLP and the Irish government, had asked me in the Commons: 'Does he realise that spokesmen for the Provisional Sinn Fein movement have been taking every opportunity to try to indicate to the people in Northern Ireland that they have been given a responsibility for the policing of the areas in which the centres have been set up?' It was true that the Provisional Sinn Fein had opened their own so-called centre in West Belfast and were acting as if it had been given governmental status, but I told Gerry: 'There is no question of policing being passed on to anyone else. The army has not withdrawn from the areas in which it is involved and the police have not withdrawn from other areas . . . I cannot be responsible for statements that are made by anyone else.'

Unionist MP John Carson came to see me privately about his concern that 'we had done a deal with the IRA' and also about the assertions being made by Seamus Loughran of the Provisional Sinn Fein that there was going to be in effect a return to no-go areas. I tried to reassure him and afterwards authorised the Information Department to issue another statement:

> It should be clearly understood that the incident centres which have been set up in various places in Northern Ireland have the sole purpose of acting as points of contact by telephone to help ensure that a ceasefire should not break down. They will be linked up to the Northern Ireland Office in Stormont Castle. The staff manning the centres will not negotiate with anyone; they will pass on all messages received only to officials at the Northern Ireland Office.

It was not enough. The press conjecture and Belfast gossip continued, and the issue was raised again by representatives of the various political parties in the province when they came to see me to discuss the Convention. I issued further explanatory statements, but to no avail. The concern over the incident centres was all part of the rumours about the nature of the talks with the Provisional Sinn Fein. When the Official Unionists brought this matter up, I told them that there was no 'deal' by which law-breakers would be allowed to remain at liberty because of a ceasefire. I pointed out that in the previous week there had been twenty-six arrests on very serious charges and stressed that where there was evidence of an offence, every effort would be made to bring the culprit to justice.

In a written answer to a parliamentary question about the centres from John Biggs-Davison for the Conservatives, I said that 'some two hundred reports have been made to government incident centres by Provisional Sinn Fein and by security forces. In a number of cases the use of the centres has made it possible to remove misunderstandings which otherwise might have endangered the ceasefire.'

None of this was enough to quieten the general concern expressed by both sides of the community and by government spokesmen in the South. There was talk of vigilantes in the Catholic areas, which particularly worried the loyalist politicians, and I saw Harry West and Jim Molyneaux to quash such talk and ask them to play matters down. Nevertheless, it was clear that the loyalist paramilitaries were put out by the talk of vigilantes and I arranged a meeting with them in which I assured them that there was nothing to this talk. I told them that I understood their feelings and the history behind them, and I talked about the part that they might play in the Convention, to which they seemed to respond favourably, although as it turned out this was not to be.

The subject of vigilantes may have been put to rest but not the incident centres. The reference to them that I had decided to make in my Commons statement of 12 March was short but positive and by opening my speech with it I hoped to help settle the matter.

> Since the ceasefire resumed on 10 February, there have been no major incidents between the security forces and the Provisional IRA. The government incident centres set up to communicate about possible misunderstandings which might threaten the ceasefire have been of practical value.

I went on to say that there had been a considerable reduction in the size and frequency of army patrols and in the scale of searching and questioning. I then gave the latest information on detention and announced a programme for the release of detainees which, depending on the security situation, I hoped to complete by Easter. I had signed no interim custody orders since the ceasefire resumed and, if all went well, the present total of 122 detainees released since the original ceasefire on 22 December 1974 should increase to 160 by Easter. After that I intended to carry out a further release programme, again related to the security situation.

This brought me to the subject of policing and again I put forward my policy:

> There can only be one police service. The government want to achieve a situation where the RUC, accepted and sustained by a law-abiding community, becomes the major organisation for law and order. This is not a role for the army. . . . It is not going to be achieved overnight. It does not involve trying to flood the difficult areas with policemen. The plain fact is that the army will have to carry out some ordinary policing functions in some places for some time to come.

I added that I intended in due course to introduce an independent element into the police complaints procedure in Northern Ireland, as was also intended in Great Britain. This, I hoped, might influence the worrying attitude of the republicans to policing. The attitude of the loyalist politicians was of no less concern, particularly given that they seemed to want to control the police in a future devolved government, and I therefore said on the subject of police control:

> There is a delicate balance of functions to be achieved between government – the Home Secretary and Secretary of State for Scotland in Great Britain and myself in Northern Ireland – and local government in the shape of a Police Authority and the Chief Constable, who is operationally autonomous. The achievement and maintenance of this relationship is of fundamental importance to the liberty of the citizen.
>
> On this basis it may be that the constitutional Convention will have ideas to contribute to this very difficult question of policing. But it must be made clear, as with the work of the Convention as a whole, that a final decision on this will be for this House to make.

My statement was of course being made with the Provisional IRA ceasefire always in the background and I repeated what I had said in the House on 14 January: 'The government seek a lasting peace. . . . A permanent cessation of violence would enable the army to make a planned, orderly and progressive reduction in its present commitments.' I said that this was still my aim and that if the security situation permitted, further reductions would be made in army force levels. I also looked forward to further relaxations in security so that people could move about more easily.

I then raised obliquely the problem of getting the paramilitaries to back away from their violent activities and return to a normal life. I had talked about this more specifically in my February statement to the Commons and I wanted my officials to continue to discuss the question in their contact with the Provisional Sinn Fein. It was with this in mind that I said: 'I am convinced that now is the time to look at some of the wider implications of the problems that six years of violence have created in Northern Ireland. These problems are a tangled skein; I want to make a start on unravelling them. The ceasefire has highlighted the need for action.'

The ending of special category status was linked up with this and one way of smoothing the way towards it was to have a parole scheme similar to that in Great Britain. This was easier said than done, for it would involve considerable paper-work and visits to prisoners and their families, and one could imagine only too well the position of probation officers in Ulster, who played a major role in parole decisions. All I therefore said to the Commons at this time was that I hoped soon to submit a parole scheme for convicted prisoners along the lines of the British one.

I concluded my speech with a general statement of my own philosophy on the province: 'It is my strong personal view that it is wrong to look at the many problems in Northern Ireland as if there were some ready-made textbook solution. What the government will do is to respond positively to a developing situation.' I appealed to those who would be elected to the Convention to respond in a similarly positive manner.

The questioning that followed showed the subjects that were causing concern to the Opposition parties. Airey Neave for the Conservatives turned to the hardy annual of support for the police by political leaders, by which he meant the SDLP. I could only reply from hard experience:

> I do not believe that I can do anything to get support from leaders for the police. It is something that emerges and evolves. It is interesting that in the ceasefire the subject of the police and support for the police as a whole becomes a subject of discussion, and I hope that in the Convention we shall see it come to fruition.

The debate enabled me to talk of the Police Authority and police accountability, a subject equally relevant in Great Britain today.

> There are those in Northern Ireland who believe that the Police Authority runs the police. People in this country know that that is not the case, but it is important to get the relationship right. I do not believe that we have got it right with regard to the Police Authority, but I have no immediate plans for dealing with that.

Local liaison committees were being suggested as a means of making bridges between elected representatives and the police, and I said that if anybody in Northern Ireland had any ideas about this, I knew that the Chief Constable would be prepared to listen.

Again I brought up my aim of reversing the roles of the army and the police so that the latter would take the lead in the fight against terrorism. I mentioned the effort and success of the RUC in dealing with the recent outbreak of violence:

> There have been feuds between various groups such as the Irish Republican Socialist Party and the Official IRA. There have been inter- and intra-sectarian killings and woundings. The number of deaths since 10 February has been 14, and 124 people have been injured. None has been a member of the security forces. . . . In the same period, 16 people

> have been charged with murder and attempted murder, and another 53 charged with other serious security-type offences.

I had earlier been a witness to the feud between the Official IRA and its breakaway group, the Irish Republican Socialist Party whose military wing was the Irish National Liberation Army. The break had originally been on ideological grounds but the arms that the defectors took with them soon became the point at issue and each side accused the other of gangsterism, kidnapping, torture and assassinations. We knew that at least the last allegation was true from an incident in late February when I had visited the Divis Flats in Belfast. As I stepped from an armoured car, a shot rang out and an official IRA man lay dead, victim of the IRSP. The press report made me sound brave to have been there, but my wife Colleen had walked round the flats the week before with only an army officer as escort.

Attempts had been made to find a peaceful solution to this dispute and on 14 March, two days after my Commons statement, the two sides suggested a truce. However, less than a week later the chairman of the IRSP, Seamus Costello, who was afterwards killed in the Republic, claimed that the truce had been broken on six occasions and consequently 'the Belfast members and supporters of the IRSP are now left with no option but to defend themselves whenever the need arises'. The internecine fight went on, and later there also arose the fight on the loyalist side between the UVF and the UDA.

My 12 March statement and the questioning afterwards formed a further brief for the talks with the Provisional Sinn Fein, but I wondered what effect they would have, for there was nothing there to meet the aims of the Provisional IRA. As my diary of 16 March showed, the ceasefire and the talks with the Provisional Sinn Fein representatives were balanced on the edge of breakdown. 'The general complaint is that the rate of releases is too slow. Their people on the ground want swifter results. Counter to this is the view from my people that by spreading releases over the long term, the Provisionals up in the Maze do not want the ceasefire ended. I think there is much sense in this view.' In any event, while the ceasefire with all its weaknesses lasted, I would be able to continue making releases from the Maze, and the Provisional IRA would find it difficult to justify to the minority community a return to the old scale of violence.

Despite the decline in army activities, another complaint that arose in the talks concerned an incident between soldiers and the Provisional IRA in which it was alleged that a couple of republicans in Belfast had been shot. As usual it was difficult initially to get the facts of the matter: the army claimed that they heard shooting and responded. What was clear, however, was that the Provisional IRA were having problems with their men on the ground. My officials were instructed to use the incident to show the merits of a return to proper policing.

This subject was of concern to the Provisional Sinn Fein, who were complaining that I was continually coming out with talk of policing, which was making their position very difficult. But policing was what I believed in, and from the beginning I was under no illusions that more policing in republican areas was going to be easy or come quickly. I was made particularly aware of the practical difficulties after discussing the matter with police chiefs, and as I said in my diary of 16 March: 'If only I was in a position to assure the Provisional IRA, not that anyone who has committed a crime would not be chased, but that those who had never done anything would not be chased.' As long as the Provisional IRA was on so-called active service, it would be extremely hard to persuade its members to take a peacetime attitude. As my diary entry concluded: 'As much as I want policing back, how on earth we do it in a way that will satisfy the Catholic community, let alone the Provisional Sinn Fein, I just don't know.'

A few days later, on 20 March, the distrust of the loyalist politicians about the ceasefire was in evidence when the Commons debated the order to raise substantially the licence fees to hold guns in Northern Ireland. This order, which was aimed at improving the control of firearms in the province, had actually come into force at the end of November 1974 but that did not prevent allegations that it had been prompted by an agreement made with the Provisional IRA after the ceasefire. It was reported to the Commons that in the view of loyalist politician Frank Millar, the guns order was 'a carefully planned exercise aimed at weakening still further the Protestant population'.

By 30 March I was reporting in my diary that talks between my officials and the Provisional Sinn Fein were not proceeding well and we had heard second-hand that David O'Connell in Dublin wanted to contact the Prime Minister direct in London. He asked about the possible reaction to two letters that he intended to submit. They concerned the role of the troops on the ground and the need for a 'declaration of intent' by the British government to leave Northern Ireland, although one great change was that the Provisional IRA would seemingly settle for an 'independent' Northern Ireland; their one concern was to have the Brits out and thus end the British influence.

I was sceptical about the independence point but in any event, if the O'Connell letters ever arrived, we would simply respond by saying that Northern Ireland was part of the United Kingdom and there could be no declaration of intent. There would be no negotiations, no deals. We would carry on responding to a genuine cessation of violence. I told my

Cabinet sub-committee colleagues that my short-term aim was the same as it had been from the start of the ceasefire: to create the conditions in which the Provisional IRA's military organisation might be weakened. The longer the ceasefire lasted, the more difficult it would be for them to start a campaign again from scratch, and in this period of peace I hoped political action would be given a chance. Eight hundred years of history were not going to be undone overnight and all that we could do was to help the situation unfold.

I heard no more of the direct approach from Dublin but the Provisional Sinn Fein publicly aired its views at the traditional meetings commemorating the Easter Rising. Seamus Twomey of the Provisional IRA Council addressed a crowd of four thousand at the Belfast Milltown Cemetery and repeated the old demands: a declaration of intent by the British government to leave Northern Ireland; an amnesty for all political prisoners and the withdrawal of troops to barracks. There could be no permanent ceasefire, he warned, until these demands were met. David O'Connell was on the same theme at Carrickmore, County Tyrone, when he said that English rule must be ended, even if that required five more years of hard fighting. The Army Council's Easter message from Dublin stated that the Provisional IRA would settle for no permanent agreement that did not include a programme of planned and orderly withdrawal of the English establishment from Ireland and that there was a limit to the Council's patience over the present ceasefire.

In early April when the ceasefire had lasted, with a break, for three and a half months, we analysed the situation in the office. Numerous incidents in South Armagh suggested that Provisional IRA 'volunteers' there were not entirely under control, though a bomb in Belfast on 2 April – announced as a 'warning' to the government – was probably authorised. These were relatively small activities and given the obvious lack of movement towards British withdrawal from the province, the pressure from the rank and file to resume full-scale violence was increasing. Countering this was the feeling for peace in the Catholic community, which was as strong as ever. Would the Provisional IRA or the community win?

A few weeks later we learned that the Provisionals had decided, after a discussion in the South, to maintain the ceasefire policy. It enabled me to continue emptying the detention compounds and I told my Cabinet colleagues that some two hundred of those who had been in detention when the ceasefire began had now been released. I also told them that it had been possible to lower the army profile while not lowering its guard, which had had some success in reinforcing the taste for peace in the republican areas.

One question that arose as the numbers in the compounds dwindled was the reinvolvement of the released paramilitaries in violence. Arguments about it were bandied about in the media and some commentators put forward figures from 25 per cent upwards for those who returned to violence. My security advisers thought such figures suspect; violence had anyway rocketed when internment had been introduced in 1971 and the existence of detention was a good recruiting cry for the paramilitaries. Detainees were not prisoners of war to be locked up until the end of hostilities. The main benefit of detention from the army point of view was to put paramilitaries out of circulation for short periods and in 1975 this was increasingly being achieved through more effective police action in arresting terrorists and bringing evidence to the courts.

Before I made any releases, there were discussions with the army and the RUC, either directly or through the various committees, after which I looked at the names on the list and discussed them with individual policemen or soldiers. The decision at the end of the day was mine; there was nobody else to decide. By mid-April, the numbers in detention were down to about 350. I released at this time all but three of those interned during Brian Faulkner's government, and all the women detainees. In my diary I said: 'The Provisional IRA, I feel sure, is not going to go back to violence on 1 May [the Convention election]. They would be absolutely stupid to do that. We still have to answer the question of what happens in the long run, but we are unwinding detention now.'

The GOC, Frank King, never advised me to stop the releases but he regularly discussed with me the rate at which I carried them out and gave me his professional judgment on the immediate effect of my policy. We agreed that a problem would arise if as a result of the releases there was a return to the previous scale of violence or if the response from the Provisional IRA was muted. I made it clear in our discussions that detention had been a political decision and as far as I was concerned it had been a failure. This would have been so even if a few people – 'the correct ones' as it was put to me – had been detained in 1971. Detention of any sort was counter-productive.

Frank King was normally the wisest of men but he made a speech in April that caused a political ruction. He had been addressing a St John Ambulance Brigade conference in Nottingham at the request of an old friend and had ended his talk, on urban guerrilla warfare, by saying that it was a pity in a way that the ceasefire came last year when we were beating the Provisionals and that there would be a problem at the end of the day. It was an unofficial speech and I could just see the General standing there talking in his philosophical way, but there was no doubt that he had slipped up and a row in the Commons was inevitable.

Jim Wellbeloved, then a Labour MP, put down a private notice question about it on 14 April. I pointed out that the conference was not specifically related to Northern Ireland and was not organised by the government or a political party. 'There was no question of the GOC making an official speech, of giving a press hand out, or of any press briefing. Indeed, I understand from the GOC that he spoke from notes and did not believe that any members of the press were present or that any of his remarks would be reported, let alone reported out of context. He was concerned solely with some of the practical problems that result from urban violence and he had no intention whatsoever of criticising government policy.'

I did not duck the political embarrassment that the speech had caused the government but told the House that I had accepted the GOC's personal regrets made to me at Stormont Castle and indeed I had agreed that his tour of duty should be extended by six months. Frank King was a first-class soldier and I emphasised that 'there is no question, and never has been, of political responsibility for security policy in Northern Ireland resting other than with me. This has never been changed, nor is it at issue now.'

I took the opportunity to restate government policy, relating it to my original statements on 14 January. This policy was 'formed after full consultation with the security forces and with the Secretary of State for Defence'. The role of the forces would be related to the violence of the Provisional IRA and it was of the 'utmost importance that everything possible should continue to be done to bring those involved to justice before the courts, and this is happening with considerable success.' I repeated my previous words on detention: 'The crucial point is that only the government can decide, in the light of the situation as a whole, when to start to bring detention progressively to an end. . . . I do not propose to act precipitately, and any early release must, and will be, carefully judged in relation to whether the cessation of violence is genuine and sustained.'

An awkward period of questioning followed from both sides of the House. Among my own party, the GOC's remarks had fuelled the belief, fostered by the criticisms of one or two retired Generals, that the army was a right-wing group and pro-Conservative. On this same day a former chief army information officer attacked the policy of phasing out detention in a BBC interview. His words were reported in *The Times* on 15 April: 'I think that Sir Frank [King] and most soldiers in Northern Ireland are desperately concerned that what has been called a political gamble may end up with the IRA, when they have got enough of their men back in the ranks, starting up with their offensive again. If that happens, I think Mr Rees will bear a very heavy responsibility for soldiers' lives being lost.' These chatterings angered me and I complained to Frank King about this one. His common-sense view was that the very source of the words, from a retired information officer, was enough to put them in perspective. To Labour members, such army talk could only add to their distrust and in my reply to Jim Wellbeloved, I reiterated that detention was entirely a matter for me and, as proof of government policy being carried out, I announced that four hundred detainees had been released since the previous autumn.

The concern of the Conservatives was that I was still making releases although there was violence in the province. I told Airey Neave: 'There has been some violence from the Provisional IRA in recent weeks but very little – which is not to say that it could not happen again. Almost all the violence in Northern Ireland is internecine between the UDA and UVF. The ceasefire on the part of the Provisional IRA should not be mixed up with other sorts of violence unconnected with the Provisional IRA. They are distinct.'

I then proceeded to cap Frank's slip-up with one of my own. Enoch Powell asked me to confirm that releases could not be the subject of a 'bargain, whether implied or explicit, between Her Majesty's Government and any other person or persons', which I of course did, saying again that releases were my sole responsibility. But instead of stopping there, I went on to say that in May of last year an assassination squad had been assigned to kill me and that I had signed an interim custody order on a loyalist concerned, whom I had released some weeks ago. It was foolish of me to have revealed this incident, which caused my London home to be besieged by journalists and photographers, much to the discomfort of my wife and family. My only justification was that I was trying to show that I realised from a personal point of view the dangers inherent in releases. Like Frank, I had acted out of character and I was particularly unhappy about it because I disliked any personalisation of my part in the dangerous life of Northern Ireland.

Overall, and despite my mistake, the Commons questioning after the GOC's remarks passed off quite easily. The main reason was that Frank's speech did not show any fundamental disagreement with me on detention, and as I commented in my diary, 'There are fringe problems with the army but I am absolutely convinced that overall there is no real problem.' By far the worst interpretation of his words was made in the Republic where the press had a field day with such lines as 'British army out of control' and 'It showed the army determining policy, as at the time of the Ulster strike'. As ever, this was rubbish.

I was not deflected from continuing releases, though I was constantly quizzed in the Commons on my policy. On 17 April, for example, John

Biggs-Davison asked: 'Is the Secretary of State aware that Lieutenant-General Sir Frank King is by no means alone in his anxiety lest the hard terrorist core be prematurely released? Will he consider whether it might not be better to lay down that a stated number of months of tranquillity should elapse before further releases take place?' I replied with the Provisional IRA in mind:

> There is anxiety about the reinvolvement of anyone who has been detained. When I have detained persons – like other Secretaries of State – it was only on the evidence of involvement or suspicion of involvement in violence and not for political reasons. Of course there is anxiety. However, I am not prepared to deal with the ending of detention in this block way. I must deal with it on an individual basis and on the same individual basis as I deal with each case in the first instance. Nevertheless the speed with which it happens must be related to the amount of violence that occurs and to any evidence I may have – which I cannot reveal – about the movement of arms, the restocking and the training that goes on. I have to take account of that factor in judging whether a ceasefire is genuine and sustained.

When Airey Neave brought up the question of releasing hard-core detainees, I explained:

> When it comes to making a judgment of who is hard-core, what does the word mean? It may mean those who are on the brigade staff and who are not involved in violence. That may be a matter of judgment. They may be more important than the man who, the records tell me, may have been involved in ten bombings, six killings and so on. It may be that the staff arrangements are far more important. To the soldiers on the street, however, the man who fires the gun is more important than the brigadier. I cannot make a hard-core list and say 'Below that there is no problem'. Everyone is a problem and I have to make the judgment.

I pointed out to Tam Dalyell, who had spoken out in my support on releases, that I could have wished that 'those four hundred released since July 1974 had been measured against far more peace in the province over that period'. Violence had not ended with the ceasefire but it was a different kind of violence and detention was inappropriate to it.

I was particularly concerned at this time over sectarian and intersectarian violence. With the Convention election on 1 May about to take place, loyalist violence against republicans escalated. The RUC's intelligence in the loyalist community had always been reasonable but with the increasing efficiency of the police it was now impressive. For example, after Jamie Flanagan came to see me and told me about the killings, I noted in my diary: 'They were done by a small group of Prods, some of whom were in the Ulster Defence Regiment. The necessary screening on entry had failed to weed them out. The RUC found three or four guns which have done about nineteen murders.'

The whole community of Northern Ireland was affected by this nasty and bloody violence. Apart from the straight battle between the UVF and the Provisional IRA, there were the internal feuds between the UDA and UVF, the Provisional and Official IRAs, and the Official IRA and INLA. Worst of all was the killing of innocent Catholics and Protestants simply because of their religious labels. Nor was it even that simple. Many years later a Belfast woman recognised me on a London bus and spoke to me about her son who had been shot in West Belfast in the mid-1970s. 'It is a difficult area close to the "other side",' I said. 'No', she replied, fingering the crucifix at her neck, 'he was killed by my side!'

Sometimes it all seemed to me like Chicago gangland. At one point the UWC and the Ulster Loyalist Central Co-ordinating Committee attempted to mediate in the loyalist paramilitary feuding, but to no avail. The internecine fight went on and finally waned for no obvious reason. After one particular incident at the end of April when two UDA men were killed, we brought UDA and Provisional Sinn Fein representatives together to explain that the murders had been carried out by the UVF. We wanted no misunderstandings that could cause the feud to escalate. We were an interventionist government!

Because I wanted to draw attention to the nature of the killings in the province, I prompted a parliamentary question about them, explaining in my reply:

> Sectarian assassination is a much abused term in Northern Ireland. It should be restricted to cases where there is knowledge – not just suspicion – that a member of one community is killed by a member of the other community for purely sectarian reasons. . . .
>
> 'Inter-factional' is the term applied to murders within one or other community for reasons connected with the security situation. In practice this means that until a case has been cleared, it is impossible to be certain whether the murder was carried out by a member of the other community. A murder which may appear to be sectarian could turn out in fact to be a 'disciplinary' killing. Again, the motive of the murder may have been basically criminal – for example, to pay off old debts under the cloak of sectarian strife.

I drew attention to the successful efforts of the police to deal with such crime and concluded with my constant theme: 'Conviction before the courts is the best way to stamp out these murders and punish those who have committed them.'

This was also the best method to deal with violence in general, which as I told my Cabinet sub-committee colleagues on 16 May was changing in nature. The scenes once familiar on television screens of large crowds throwing stones at a beleaguered police force or helmeted soldiers with riot shields had given way to indiscriminate and then selective bombings and shootings. Now, with the ceasefire, Provisional IRA attacks on commercial and prestige targets had almost ceased and there had been a dramatic fall in incidents involving the security forces.

I was advised, I told my colleagues, that the Provisional IRA leadership intended to maintain the ceasefire for strategic rather than temporary tactical gains. Their declared objective was still a declaration of intent from the British government to withdraw from the province but they now seemed to think that the 'natural evolution' of events would bring their objective nearer, although they still believed in 'evolution by violence'. I reflected that one needed a degree in philosophy to make sense of it. My own thoughts were more practical: the Provisional IRA had learned the strength of the loyalist paramilitaries in 1974 and realised that it was not only the British they had to take into account. Moreover, the minority community, sickened by years of violence, now badly wanted peace.

Whatever the reasoning behind it, the ceasefire still existed and I told my colleagues that I was presently considering with my security advisers the number of troops that would be needed in the coming months and the nature of the task that they would be called upon to fulfil. I warned that it would be a long slow job to win the co-operation of the Catholic community for any form of policing in the republican areas and only political advance would forward the timing.

I tried evaluating the consequences of the ceasefire, reasoning that if it was maintained for long enough, the Provisionals' power to dictate events might begin to weaken. The situation had changed for them as well as for us, with the government in the Republic now making serious attempts to track them down, perhaps spurred by a fear that the ceasefire could be about a deal between the British and the Provisionals. If the Provisionals were to return to a campaign of violence, we would lose the limited room for manoeuvre we now had, but for the meantime I proposed to continue seeking to maintain the ceasefire on the basis of my Commons statement of 14 January. In particular, I intended to continue with the steady release of detainees. My colleagues agreed.

The paper on the changing nature of violence that I had submitted to the Cabinet sub-committee on 16 May was one of the regular series of papers I sent to my colleagues evaluating the security and political situation in the province. The papers were the result of much discussion, easily arranged among the small staff all living and working in our Stormont quarters, and were usually written by my advisers but with my imprint on those dealing with subjects such as the ceasefire and detention. Their preparation was more than a duty; it was the means of keeping my Cabinet colleagues informed of developments in Northern Ireland. Without them they would have been dependent on the media, whose occasional 'revelations' about the talks with the Provisional Sinn Fein muddied the political waters.

One reported at this time was from the Rev Arlow, a member of the group of churchmen at the Feakle talks, who alleged that 'he had reason to believe that the British government had given a firm commitment to the Provisional IRA that the army would be withdrawn from Northern Ireland if the Convention failed to produce a structure of government'. My blunt denial of this had no effect. The politicians joined in, with Dr Paisley calling on Ulstermen to set up an independent state and Glen Barr announcing that the Ulster Loyalist Central Co-ordinating Committee, of which he was chairman, had drawn up plans for a provisional Ulster government in the event of a British withdrawal. Harry West for the Official Unionists asked the Prime Minister for clarification of the British government's contact with the Provisional Sinn Fein, and the SDLP leaders told both Harold Wilson and me that they also believed the British government had decided to pull out 'after the Convention'.

I commented in my diary of 29 May: 'It was as if withdrawal was going to happen the following day.' There was no doubt, however, that the Rev Arlow was tapping a strong feeling in the province, which meant that my denials of the allegation and my House of Commons statements on the ceasefire fell on disbelieving ears – if they were heard at all. I was angry, as I said in my diary, that the Rev Arlow – who claimed contact with a Cabinet minister – could romance in this way on a serious matter in which people's lives were at stake. Nor was it the end of his activities, for in July he claimed in an interview for the Alliance Party newspaper that the British government had been 'unofficially contacted' before Feakle and repeated his allegation that since then the Provisional IRA had received a firm commitment that troops would be withdrawn from Northern Ireland.

On 3 July I reported to the Cabinet sub-committee that the Provisional IRA in Dublin evidently wanted if possible to maintain the ceasefire until they saw whether the tide of events would bring about the British disengagement which their campaign of violence had not achieved. The lack of any move towards British withdrawal was, however, causing problems with the rank and file members and was one reason for the sporadic outbreaks of violence. The Convention had disappointed the expectations of the Provisional IRA by not collapsing in acrimony early on, thus denying them the easy option of resuming their role as self-appointed defenders of the Catholic community against Protestant oppression. They would either have to resume violence without the support of the Catholic community or continue to wait for the end of the Convention. I repeated my view that the Provisionals were learning that they had to face the loyalists rather than the British in Ulster; the UWC strike was the first lesson, now it was the Convention.

A week later I informed my colleagues about the arrest in Dublin of David O'Connell on a charge of membership of the IRA. There had been much press speculation that the arrest of the man who had undoubtedly been the leading Provisional at large, and therefore presumably the man who masterminded the ceasefire, would bring the hard-line military men to power in the Provisional Army Council. The ceasefire might thus come to an early end. No one could be sure, however, for no one knew enough about the factions on the Army Council to assess the likely effect. Whatever that was, it would probably take some time to work itself through.

Meanwhile Provisional IRA incidents, though still few, were on the increase. On 9 July, for example, a number of bombs were exploded in government offices in Derry, in protest at alleged army harassment. McGuinness, the Provisional leader there, subsequently made it clear that the Londonderry battalion intended to maintain a 'low profile' but would continue to react to what it regarded as 'harassment'. More serious for us was the problem in South Armagh where the Provisionals acted independently of Belfast and Dublin alike. On 17 July four soldiers were murdered and one seriously injured in an ambush near the border village of Forkhill; the Crossmaglen Provisional IRA claimed responsibility. So much for Provisional claims of reacting only to army harassment, and so much too for the so-called ceasefire.

When I reported this incident to the Commons, informing them that a man had been arrested and had appeared in court charged with murder, the Tory front-bench spokesman rightly questioned me about the ceasefire but then asked for a return to the use of detention in South Armagh. Apart from other reasons, this made no practical sense. Many of the ringleaders in the area operated from Dundalk across the border and experience had shown that the detention of one leader simply meant that another appeared a few days later. Detention had not stopped violence there and as far as I was concerned what mattered was to arrest the perpetrators as quickly as possible and use the courts to convict them. Again I repeated to the Commons that the security strength was related to the level of violence.

At the next Cabinet sub-committee meeting I reported that the Provisional leaders in Belfast were under pressure over the ceasefire. They had been unable to tighten their grip on the population of the Catholic areas and their own followers resented their impotence to react to the continued presence of the army. This had led to propaganda about alleged army harassment in republican areas of Belfast, which had been seized on by the media as evidence of an imminent end to the ceasefire. The line the press was following had emanated from the reports of a meeting of the Provisional Army Council on 20 July and the carefully worded statement put out in the name of the Belfast Brigade the following day. This was to the effect that the ceasefire had not been called to lower the British army's profile but to provide the opportunity to negotiate the three basic republican demands: a declaration of intent by the British government to withdraw from Ireland; an amnesty for all republican prisoners; and self-determination for all the Irish people.

Clearly our talks with the Provisional Sinn Fein, which were in fact becoming very infrequent, were not affecting their basic aims but, as I told my colleagues, my advice was that the ceasefire would be maintained, probably till the autumn, despite the arrest of David O'Connell. At the end of the meeting I put my immediate policy to my colleagues, which was to continue on course, always seeking to deprive the Provisional IRA of any excuse to return to a campaign of violence on grounds likely to appeal to the Catholics. Above all I proposed to continue releasing detainees at a rate which might lead to the emptying of the compounds by Christmas.

The decision to go ahead as firmly as this had followed one of my chats with officials. Two reasons lay behind it. One was that I could move more quickly now that the number of cases coming before the courts was increasing and the other was that my officials could point out to the Provisional Sinn Fein that while my aim was clear, its implementation was up to them. If they allowed violence to erupt, then executive releases would have to end, with adverse effects in the Catholic community.

My colleagues agreed with my decision and I made it public on 24 July in a supplementary answer to Jim Molyneaux in the Commons:

> I hope that the situation will progress sufficiently to enable all the detainees to be out by Christmas. Policy on detention will continue to be

> related to the level and nature of violence prevailing but under the terms of the law I have to make the judgment on each individual case in the light of the right of the community to be protected as well as the need to consider the right of the individual to his freedom.

Jim and others thought I might not have thought through this reply since I was speaking off the cuff but I afterwards disabused them: to empty Long Kesh by Christmas was my firm aim.

We still faced security incidents, not the least of which were retaliatory moves by the loyalist paramilitaries. A UVF representative had even claimed that the killing of Provisional IRA activists and the elimination of Marxist-Leninist revolutionaries 'was in keeping with the principles of a just war'. One of the nastiest murders occurred in the early hours of 31 July when, as reported to me:

> The Miami Showband, whose members were returning to Dublin from an engagement in Northern Ireland, were ambushed by a group of men wearing military-style uniforms and were ordered out of their van at gun point. It appeared that while two of the ambushers were placing a bomb in the van, the bomb exploded, killing them both. Other ambushers then opened fire on the five members of the band, killing three and seriously injuring another.
>
> The UVF subsequently admitted that they had been involved, something which they could hardly deny after an arm with the letters 'UVF' tattooed on it had been found in the wreckage – and alleged that UVF members patrolling the area had been fired on. This unconvincing explanation has not been believed in Northern Ireland, least of all by loyalist politicians, whose leaders have condemned the attack. Feeling also ran high in the Irish Republic and our ambassador there was summoned to be told of the Irish government's concern.

When I discussed the matter with the Chief Constable, I was encouraged by the information he was able to give about the men he thought were involved. There were to be no quick results for the investigation took years of effort and it was not until 1981 that a man was sentenced for his part in the murders. It was a particularly brutal crime and in the following weeks there was increased Provisional IRA violence in the country areas near the border, to which the UVF responded as part of a so-called counter-offensive. I was told that this loyalist group had been responsible for the deaths of twelve people and the injuring of forty others.

August also brought us other problems. A minor irritation was that we were back to the leaks about the points allegedly agreed with the

Provisional IRA and which Robert Fisk this time brought up in an article in the *New Statesman*:

> The Dublin government has now reached the stage of simply refusing to believe some of Mr Rees's statements. Civil servants in the Republic still possess a list of twelve concessions which they claim the British made to the IRA in return for the ceasefire. One of these concessions is believed to have been permission for certain Provisional officers to carry arms in the North. Mr Rees's office denies that there is any truth in this; but if the concession was never made, how was a Provisional able to control traffic in the Falls with impunity two weeks ago while brazenly holding a machine pistol in his hand?

Of course there was no truth in the so-called concession; one only had to consider the many occasions before the ceasefire when members of the Provisional IRA appeared with guns in various parts of the province. However, it helped play into the hands of the loyalist politicians and paramilitaries, who ever since the army had arrived in the province in 1969 had complained about the lack of policing in the Belfast and Derry republican areas. Since the ceasefire and the contacts with the Provisional Sinn Fein, and the election of the Convention, the whole question of policing was raised and especially the lack of it in West Belfast and the Bogside. The cry from the UDA and UVF was that the police only bothered about them and not the Provisional IRA or, more recently, the Irish National Liberation Army.

Against this background there arose one of those incidents that led to argument and counter-argument and seemed as if it would never stop. It began with a letter to me from William Craig alleging that Seamus Twomey had been arrested by the army but then released because of a 'ceasefire deal'. I told him that I was about to give a full reply to a priority written question about this in the Commons but would point out straightaway that there was no question of an army patrol having arrested a suspect who was, or was believed to be, Seamus Twomey.

The parliamentary question, from Jim Molyneaux on 7 August, asked what considerations had led to the decision not to apprehend the so-called Chief of Staff of the Provisional IRA when he was in Belfast in July and whether any assurances of immunity from arrest for such persons had ever been given. Before commenting, I read out the Brigade's report of the relevant incident on 28 July:

> A foot patrol was in the busy shopping area near the Whiterock crossroads with the Springfield Road. They saw a man who looked not

> unlike Seamus Twomey enter a shop. The patrol reported what had happened and was asked to get a positive identification. This it was unable to do because there were only four men at the spot and a crowd started to gather in the area. Two other foot patrols in the general area arrived to give support to the first patrol. An army vehicle was sent from Springfield Road RUC Station with RUC men in it to assist, but by the time they arrived the man had been seen to get into a taxi and drive away. Road blocks were set up but the taxi did not pass through them. The man was not positively identified and no one was arrested. There was no question of any decision not to apprehend.

I then made the point that a criminal prosecution needed evidence and not rumour. I said that I was unaware of the sources from which these inaccurate allegations came. If the Hon Member had any evidence that would lead to a criminal prosecution in Northern Ireland, I hoped that he would make all information in his possession available forthwith to the RUC. My information came from the security forces.

The crucial part of the question was, however, about immunity and I repeated what I said in the House on 14 January: 'Those against whom there is evidence of involvement in criminal acts will continue to be arrested and brought before the courts. . . . There is no immunity for those who are wanted for criminal offences.' I emphasised that the police, assisted by other security forces, were responsible for the enforcement of the law and that the Director of Public Prosecutions was completely independent of government in deciding whether proceedings were taken in the courts, something which many Northern Ireland politicians, schooled in different traditions, seemed to ignore. I also gave the statistics of charges for terrorist offences since the beginning of the year, which totalled an impressive 682, a substantial proportion of them involving members of the INLA and UVF or small associated groups who had been responsible for much of the recent violence.

These figures showed the increasing success of the security forces in bringing criminals to justice during the ceasefire period and I wanted them as widely known as possible. I asked the information staff to get them into newspapers throughout the United Kingdom and in the Republic, where all sorts of rumours were bubbling. Our ambassador in Dublin was sent my written parliamentary answer together with more background briefing, which included a reminder that Twomey had addressed a crowd at Belfast's Milltown Cemetery on Easter Sunday and had undoubtedly been in Northern Ireland since from time to time. The simple fact was that there were no criminal charges outstanding against Twomey in Ulster, though it now seemed that the Garda in Dublin had indicated that he was wanted on charges there. If the occasion arose, the RUC would therefore legally be able to hold him while they notified the Garda, which could then apply for extradition.

The ambassador's briefing also explained, for his information only, the rules for the arrest of prominent members of the Provisional IRA now that there were no detention procedures. If picked up by the army at a vehicle checkpoint, for example, they would be handed over to the RUC, who alone would decide whether to bring charges. My role as Secretary of State was simply to be informed by the army of an arrest after it had been made.

The story about Twomey and ceasefire deals was nonsense but there was more to it than mere misunderstanding or maliciousness, as became clear when we looked into it further. Earlier in the year a briefing compiled by a junior army officer had been issued which said, quite correctly, that 'Seamus Twomey, Chief of Staff of the Provisional IRA, aware that he is no longer a wanted man, was seen this week at his house in 12 Trostan Way [Belfast]. He has been relatively open in his movements.' This document or part of it had come into the hands of Ian Paisley.

The matter was not going to rest there and I had asked the army to issue a statement explaining that the phrase 'no longer a wanted man' was a loose reference to the fact that the list of persons wanted in connection with interim custody orders, which included Twomey, had been discontinued with the suspension of such orders. The man was no longer an army target for detention and neither was anyone else. As the statement went on to point out, 'The position on arrests by the security forces remains as has been stated by Mr Merlyn Rees that those against whom there is evidence of involvement in criminal acts will continue to be arrested and brought before the courts. There is no immunity for those who are wanted for criminal offences.'

The RUC had also issued a statement that Twomey was not on any police wanted list but if he was found by them he would be arrested on sight because there was a warrant for his arrest in the Irish Republic – Twomey had escaped from Mountjoy Jail, Dublin, in 1973. If found, he would be picked up and sent over the border to the Garda. He would have the right of appeal in a Northern Ireland court against extradition but he could waive this right.

Given that this had been known, what now concerned me was why Twomey had not been handed over in the first place to the RUC and eventually the Republic. I asked for an explanation and it became clear that in the early days after the ceasefire when I had ordered the end of the use of detention, there was poor liaison between the army and the police. The army was used to arrest leading to an interim custody order and not to the collection of evidence leading to charges by the police.

An army instruction had been circulated to battalions on 16 March clarifying the arrest procedures 'for persons wanted on a criminal charge' but it had obviously not had the desired effect. What was for sure was that neither ministers nor civil servants had been involved.

Paisley was still in on the act and on 29 August he accused me of misleading the House of Commons in my answer to Jim Molyneaux. I issued yet another rebuttal, but that did not stop John Biggs-Davison raising in *The Guardian* the issue of a 'scandal' that had been revealed. I wrote to him personally, referring yet again to my statement of 14 January that those people against whom there was evidence of criminal involvement would continue to be arrested and brought before the courts. I told him that 'this is a matter strictly for the Chief Constable and I have not attempted, and would not attempt, to influence him in the discharge of his duty'. I cited the 730 charges made so far in 1975 for terrorist-type offences, testifying to the successful activities of the RUC, and pointed out that I had made a basic change in not signing interim custody orders. Assuming that a leading politician would not have made the allegation of a scandal without evidence, I asked him to send the information to the police, reiterating that criminal charges were a matter for them and the Director of Public Prosecutions, not for me.

Another Tory front-bench spokesman, George Younger, joined in with a statement and I reflected that Westminster was getting more like Belfast every day – issue a statement, do not check the facts, just get your name in the papers. However, the issue quietened down at the London end after Harold Wilson and I met the Opposition leaders at Westminster on 10 September. In Northern Ireland the allegations went on for some months, with Paisley still making noises about the affair as late as December.

The Twomey allegation had never been a personal problem because there was no question of a general government or individual involvement in a deal. It had been a nuisance by reinforcing rumours but the row had at least enabled me to distinguish publicly between administrative detention by me and arrest through the courts, a distinction that was understood by those that mattered in London and Belfast. More difficult to deal with were the allegations about the twelve points supposedly agreed with the Provisional IRA, which came up again on 22 September with an article in the *Daily Telegraph*.

The article, by the paper's Dublin correspondent Kenneth Clarke, was prompted, it was claimed, by information 'revealed' when David O'Connell had been arrested earlier in the year. Under the headline '"IRA Peace Plan" Found in Eire Raid', it read:

> The allegation that Mr Rees, Ulster Secretary, has done a peace deal

> with the Provisional IRA is being strongly revived, I understand, on the basis of a document which is now in the hands of the Eire Special Branch. This document is said to contain a list of twelve points on which the Provisionals have agreed to negotiate a permanent Ulster ceasefire. It was found when David O'Connell, the Provisionals' leader, was arrested in Dublin in July and its existence was admitted at his trial by a senior Special Branch officer.
>
> What is acutely embarrassing to Mr Rees, however, is the suggestion now circulating that the points were agreed at a meeting early this year and that Sir Frank Cooper, Permanent Under-Secretary in the Northern Ireland Office, met Rory O'Brady, President of Provisional Sinn Fein, near Londonderry, to add the finishing touches.

It went on to say, correctly, that in the speech I had made in Cardiff the week before I had again denied that there was any deal and had stressed that the ceasefire was the Provisionals' and not the British government's. There then followed the serious allegation 'from sources who should be well informed' that 'Mr Rees has given the commitments demanded by the Provisionals and that he finally agreed to do so when they threatened to bomb the London Underground system'. I assumed that this was the Rev Arlow again, and once again it was not true.

The points allegedly in the document were given as:

> The eventual withdrawal of British troops to barracks, with the removal to Britain of 3,000 to 4,000 inside six months.
> An end to arrests, screening and persistent searching of houses in Catholic areas of Northern Ireland.
> Immunity from arrest for certain named people.
> The issuing of gun licences to certain people.
> The establishment of incident centres.
> The release of 100 detainees within weeks.
> An end to detention by a specific date.
> Discussions at local level between the army and the Provisionals.
> No permanent road blocks and check points round Catholic areas.
> The Royal Ulster Constabulary not be introduced immediately into Catholic zones.
> The Provisional IRA to be able to talk direct to government representatives.
> The British government to draw up a ceasefire agreement.

A further comment in the article was that the 'twelve points' had been the subject of discussions between Harold Wilson and Liam Cosgrave at a meeting in Helsinki. This was also palpable nonsense and, as the report related, it had been denied by the Dublin government; if it had not, we would have done so. The Dublin source of the report was made particularly clear with the claim that followed: 'Relations between Dublin and Westminster are strained and senior officials speaking in private in Dublin plainly state they are suspicious of Mr Rees's handling of the Ulster crisis and what they regard as his soft approach to the Provisionals'. The chit-chat with 'senior officials' and my 'soft approach' I thought rich given the Irish government's policy on extradition and the freedom accorded to the Provisional IRA in the Republic. If officials had acted in this way in London, they would have been sacked.

The Irish government had already denied the story that a document listing twelve points of a 'peace deal' with the Provisionals had been found in Dublin and was in the hands of the authorities. When Garret Fitzgerald telephoned me about the *Daily Telegraph* article, he said that he had never thought that I had concluded an agreement with the Provisional IRA – and hence the government's categorical denial of the story. I had always believed that Irish Intelligence knew a great deal about the Provisionals! I told him that I would be issuing a denial and that Jack Donaldson would speak about it in the Lords where, because the Commons was in recess, the matter would be dealt with. Garret was surprised at this: their Senate system was more sensible, for ministers in the Dail could speak in the upper House. However, I preferred to handle the matter this way and when I was contacted to ask whether I would make a personal statement in response to the Opposition lords, I gave a rude reply. As far as I was concerned the truth was clear from everything that I had said before.

In his speech to the Lords, Jack Donaldson first referred to the Irish government's statement that the story about the document was 'completely false and utterly without foundation', and went on:

> The existence of various documents purporting to belong to the Provisionals has been public knowledge since early this year. For example, one alleged document was extensively covered in a report in *The Times* on 11th February 1975.
>
> The government have been fully aware since before the renewed IRA ceasefire of the existence of twelve points and indeed of other points made by individuals and organisations claiming to represent the views of the Provisional IRA. The government's attitude towards such points has been fully covered by statements made by the Secretary of State in the House of Commons from 14th January onwards.
>
> In particular it has been made clear that the future of Northern Ireland

is a matter for the people of Northern Ireland and there is no question of bartering it away; that the action of the security forces will be related to the level of activity that might occur; that a cessation of violence would bring its own results; that if there is a genuine, sustained cessation of violence there will then be a progressive reduction of army numbers, an end to detention . . . and to screening, photographing and identity checks; but that anyone involved in acts of violence will be prosecuted in the courts.

There is no immunity from arrest for anyone against whom there is evidence of involvement in criminal activities and who can be brought before the courts. It is an offence in Northern Ireland to carry a gun unless a licence has been issued by the RUC. There has never been any deal to release one hundred or any other number of detainees. The position about incident centres was fully set out in the House of Commons on 11th February 1975. The government have at no time contributed financially to those centres run by Provisional Sinn Fein.

The government's policy has been fully set out in the House of Commons. This will continue to be the case. It has not been, and will not be, influenced by threats, distortions or lies.

As far as I was concerned, there was no more to be said on the subject, although I later repeatedly stated in the Commons that there was no basis for the allegation about Frank Cooper's role. However, another allegation about the talks in circulation at this time proved to be longer lasting. It concerned housing rehabilitation work in West Belfast which, it was claimed, had been contracted to certain firms as part of a deliberate policy of assisting released detainees and, further, this policy had been formulated by government as part of a deal with the Provisional IRA to secure their ceasefire in December 1974; hence action to end the fraud was inhibited by the political desirability of preserving the ceasefire.

The allegation, originally brought up by MP Jill Knight, was nonsense. I refuted it in the Commons and, on the advice of the Attorney General, referred papers about it to the Director of Public Prosecutions, who did not take the matter up. Don Concannon had handled the administrative work for me and I trusted him completely; there would have been no condoning of anything underhand by him. An investigatory commission into this and other matters was set up by Roy Mason when he later became Secretary of State for Northern Ireland but until it reported, the allegation ran through the political alleyways of the province and indeed the South. In July 1977, for example, Dr Paisley claimed that 'the housing rehabilitation schemes had been agreed by the IRA and the Northern Ireland Office as part of their truce arrangements', and in September of that year Jill Knight claimed a 'cover up'. In January 1978 the *Irish Times* ran a headline: 'Belfast's Watergate may be in housing'. When the commission finally reported in July 1979, its conclusion was categorical: 'We find no truth in this allegation either as regards a deal or connivance in a fraud.'

Allegations and leaks were all par for the course in Northern Ireland. They were of little consequence to me personally, as long as they did not put lives at risk, but they took up time and energy that could have been used to better effect. They also strengthened the feelings in some quarters in Ulster, and indeed the South, that dark deals were being done on a British pull-out; the design was to hand over the province to the Provisional IRA. In fact by the autumn of 1975 the talks with the Provisional Sinn Fein had almost petered out, although the ceasefire remained in being.

There was also a further escalation of UVF violence in the autumn and I decided that legal action against it was necessary. The UVF had no political wing that could alone be encouraged, which is why I had deproscribed the whole organisation in early 1974 when there was hope of it acting politically. It was now only a question of deciding the date to reproscribe it. I discussed the matter with the GOC and the Chief Constable in late September. They both had information that could lead to arrests and I did not want to drive the UVF suspects underground too soon.

On 3 October I was advised that the time had come to act and I called in a number of leading journalists for a briefing. I remember in particular talking to Derek Brown of *The Guardian* about the UVF and the pros and cons of reproscription, and was just about to tell him that I would be announcing the reproscription of the UVF that afternoon when a note from the GOC arrived asking me to keep the decision quiet and not make the announcement until midnight. Derek wrote a piece for *The Guardian* that I was not going to reproscribe the UVF yet and the paper went on to the streets as the radio was announcing my change of policy!

The actual reproscription order passed through the Commons' procedures on 4 November. In the years since, the UVF have continued their murderous activities and in 1977, for example, twenty-six UVF men were given a total of seven hundred years imprisonment, including eight life sentences, as a result of fifty-five charges, four of them for murder; and nine Scottish members of the UVF were also awarded long prison sentences for offences that included murder.

The Provisional IRA also continued their sporadic activities in the autumn of 1975, with South Armagh as ever a special problem. By this time the incident centres were being used less and less as the police, the law and the courts became of growing significance. The Provisional Sinn Fein had rarely used the centres in the way envisaged and although in June we had decided that they still had a value, we now decided to close Newry, which was particularly little used.

Shortly afterwards, on 12 October, Enoch Powell in a colourful speech at Bannbridge stirred the ceasefire pot by calling for the immediate closure of the other centres, while accusing the civil servants involved of 'near treasonable activities' and of remaining in 'diligent communication with thugs and murderers'. The life of the incident centres was almost over and on 4 November I warned publicly about their diminishing usefulness. On 10 November the Provisionals closed their Londonderry centre and the following day I closed all the rest. From the lack of reaction by the Provisional IRA I assumed that they had obtained their pennyworth of propaganda from the centres and did not care any more. In any case they did not use the occasion to announce the end of the ceasefire.

I went on with my policy of releases and as the list of detainees became shorter, it was obvious that my decisions to release were arbitrary. One example I recalled in my diary: 'On Saturday I was book-browsing in Belfast, carefully guarded by the police in and out of Queen's University bookshop, which had been bombed in the past. I thought it to be empty of shoppers but a small West Belfast voice from way down below asked if I was "Mervyn" Rees. I nodded. A little boy told me that his brother was "in the Kesh" and asked me when I was going to release him. He was a "good brother", he added. I took his name and when on Sunday I looked through the list, I noted that the brother was due for release in a fortnight. I released him in the Monday group.' Another arbitrary decision! In fact the whole system of detention, from my signature of interim custody orders to my signature for releases, was arbitrary. That is why it was wrong and counter-productive.

By late November I was almost down to the last group of detainees and twenty more releases were arranged for the last Saturday of the month. Then just before, on 27 November, Ross McWhirter, editor of the *Guinness Book of Records*, was murdered in London after his campaign to raise reward money for the arrest of IRA bombers in Britain. The Home Secretary, Roy Jenkins, was given a rough ride in the Commons about it, including a request from Hugh Fraser to speak to me about my releases in Northern Ireland.

As I commented in my diary: 'The idea that if I release men in Northern Ireland they all dash over here to kill is wrong. In Great Britain they do not understand the nature of detention. Of course I had detained people who had shot and killed, but on evidence that would not stand up in any court, and some had been detained for involvement in the Provisional IRA; the aim was to break up active service units. The best way to deal with these offences is to get criminals through the courts. In Northern Ireland they understand almost completely, maybe not amongst the soldiery but amongst the officers and certainly amongst the police. I won a battle there over the year: people can see that detention ought to end, that it is a sore, that to end it is the only way to get the Catholic community on their side.'

I flew back to England the evening before the twenty releases were due to be made and arrived home to receive a phone call from a senior official in the Northern Ireland Office with a message from his opposite number in the Home Office. Apparently Roy Jenkins, who had just left for Israel, had asked me not to make any more releases until he had talked to me.

I was put out. I could understand his attitude after the difficult time he had had in the Commons, and in the past I had often delayed releases when there had been some violent outrage. However, any problem for Roy was in Britain and his intervention was going to cause me difficulties in Northern Ireland. Both the UUUC and the SDLP wanted the end of detention and I had recently told the party leaders that I was going to do it quickly. If I delayed releasing until mid-week, it would be nearly a fortnight since I had obliquely told the politicians what I was about and they would start saying, 'Ah, somebody killed in Great Britain and you stop doing it.' And they would be right. As far as Roy's problem was concerned, if some of the ex-detainees did try to enter Britain, they would be checked when they came in and, quite simply, they would not be allowed entry.

I decided to telephone Harold on the Sunday and told him that I needed to release quickly. Northern Ireland and Great Britain were two different ball games. I understood Roy's problem but my aim was to get everybody in detention out and that is what I proposed to do. There was no great divide between me and Roy; it was only a matter of timing. Harold took the point and told me to go ahead in the way I had planned, leaving a message for Roy through the Home Office official explaining that I had to act fast.

The twenty releases were made, which left only the last group of detainees to deal with. On his return from abroad, Roy asked me to delay on these because it could colour the capital punishment debate to take place on the following Thursday. He was worried that MPs would think that my releases would lead to more deaths in Britain.

He brought the subject up in Cabinet, which I was annoyed about. There was, however, no querying of my policy at all. Everyone was agreed: end detention. The only question left to me was whether I released all the group on Friday or half then and half after the capital punishment debate. If the meeting had gone against me, I would have resigned. I was fed up with what I felt were parliamentary games. Why consider altering policy with all the problems that would ensue because of misinformed pressure in the House of Commons? It was characteristic of Roy that at the end of the year he came up to me to say that he had been wrong about this issue. Later, when I became Home Secretary, I had to insist to Home Office officials that although violence of course overspilled from Northern Ireland, the link was not as direct as they thought.

On 4 December I told the Commons in answer to a question that 'seventy-three people were currently held in detention, of whom twenty-six are serving prison sentences', and pointed out in justification of my policy that since detention was introduced, the level of violence had been consistently higher than before. 'Last year I personally detained a large number of men under interim custody orders . . . not because I believed that detention would end the violence but because it undoubtedly dampens down any great escalation of violence. We might have to return to it again. This year more than 1,260 people have gone through the courts. I believe that that is the method that we should use rather than detention.'

I repeated my view that detention did not solve the security problem, at which point the Tory MP Winston Churchill angrily interrupted. I told him that if I took his advice, I should need six, or even eight, camps. His actual words were not recorded in Hansard but they had included 'traitor' and I was told that afterwards ex-Guardsman Don Concannon, all six foot six of him, took Churchill aside, lifted him by his coat lapels and told him in blunt Nottinghamshire language what he thought of him.

On the same occasion in the Commons, the security problem in South Armagh was raised by six MPs who had recently visited the province. I gave a report on the situation:

> Violence in South Armagh has continued unabated, and the Provisional IRA ceasefire has not been observed there. The security forces have responded to the violence and have received good co-operation from the security forces of the Republic, but the task is made difficult by the terrain, the proximity of the border and the limited assistance given by the local people.
>
> The police, supported by the army, are meeting with success in bringing before the courts the people thought to be responsible for this violence. As the Minister of State said in the House on 24th November, thirty people have been charged with terrorist-type offences in South

> Armagh since 1st August, including two people charged with murder, six with attempted murder, fourteen with firearms offences and eight with explosive offences. In addition, about three hundred persons have been charged under the ordinary law, for various offences.

Given the difficulties of the area, the security forces were doing remarkably well. The army's responses had not been inhibited by the ceasefire; the bandit country was simply hard to deal with. Almost all the people were against us and the nearby border gave the terrorists an enormous tactical advantage. I had often mused on the possibility of transferring the area to the South – not that they were likely to want it either! – but it raised too many other issues to be practicable.

As I went on to answer more questions that afternoon, I was pondering on how to deal with the final ending of detention. It would have to come within the next couple of weeks, probably days. That night when I got back to Stormont, I called a meeting of my advisers, where I learned that when I was down to the last twenty detainees, the Provisionals were going to stage a large attack to prevent me releasing them; they would be symbolic and I would be put in a difficult position. I decided to act quickly. The Commons had given their general acceptance to the imminent ending of detention and I had of course previously obtained the approval of my Cabinet colleagues. On 5 December I therefore issued the following statement:

> I have today signed release orders in respect of seventy-three people held in detention at HM Prison Maze. Forty-six have now been released from detention and the remainder will continue to serve sentences of imprisonment imposed by the courts for criminal offences. As from today, no one is held under a detention order.
>
> The rule of the law will be imposed impartially and firmly through the courts. Those who are guilty of crimes against the community will be arrested, charged and brought before the courts. If they are found guilty they will serve the sentences appropriate to their crimes. This is not merely right but infinitely better than relying on a system which has to be reviewed every year.
>
> There is no immunity for anyone who breaks the law. They will be hunted, caught and sentenced. None of us can live in peace unless this is so.
>
> No society can survive without the rule of law. So far this year, 1,136 people have been charged. The prison population has gone up by thirty-nine per cent. This is what matters – not a temporary system of detention.
>
> I do not want to go back to detention. The real responsibility rests with

> the people of Northern Ireland – above all with the minority community – and not with me. Detention has been a real and continuing cause of discontent. It has now gone. Many people on both sides of the community have pressed for it to go. It is their responsibility to see that it does not return.

There was some questioning in the Commons a few days later about why I had announced the ending of detention in a press statement and not in Parliament. It was not possible to explain fully, given that it was on advice about possible action by the Provisionals, but most members understood the type of wicket I was batting on. For me the emptying of the compounds was a big day and my own party was clearly very satisfied with this outcome of eighteen months in government. The Tory front-bench were, however, less than happy about it, even if those who had served in the province were on my side; so much for bipartisanship.

David Steel welcomed my policy as 'one step on the long road to the return of law and order' but went on to say that some members 'find it difficult to understand why there has been a dragging of feet on this question'. 'Ye gods!' I muttered to myself. As I commented in my diary, 'The Liberals would find life very difficult if they ever had to take an actual decision. Government is not a series of pamphlets.'

The press in Great Britain treated my announcement calmly and with understanding; in Ulster it divided on predictable lines. The Northern Irish politicians were not so predictable. Gerry Fitt, with the courage he had increasingly shown on security policy, told me that 'the overwhelming majority of both communities in Northern Ireland now want to co-operate fully with the government to eradicate the men of violence from their midst'. His colleagues, however, found praise more difficult and instead raised other issues, criticising the Unionist demand for a return to greater responsibilities for local authorities and questioning the government's social and economic policy. Hugh Logue claimed that while the province may have been more unfairly administered in the past, it had never been so poorly or inadequately governed as now. I commented in my diary: 'In Ireland you answer the question and the question is changed.'

The one certainty was that I had stopped the use of detention procedures earlier in the year and there were now no more detainees. The powers to detain were still on the statute book but to remove them could wait until a legislative opportunity occurred. Since that time there has never been real pressure in favour of using detention again. Occasionally people have argued that if small groups of dedicated leaders were put away, the Provisional IRA would be fundamentally weakened. I simply do not believe it – and neither have my successors.

As I repeated to Airey Neave in the Commons in December, the best way to move against these men is through the courts. Indeed, I was pressing strongly in the office that those who had self-classified themselves in prison as members of the Provisional IRA, INLA or UVF – all illegal organisations – should be prosecuted for membership on their release. There had been the recent example of a released detainee revealing himself on television at the gates of the Maze as a member of the Provisional IRA by virtue of the prison compound he had been in – yet no action was taken. In the following months I extended the argument about prosecution to include those coming out from the special category compounds but I was advised that the status accorded them by Willie Whitelaw left us with no basis for action that would stand up in court.

By the end of 1975 the talks with the Provisional Sinn Fein had stopped altogether and as far as I was concerned the Provisional IRA ceasefire was over. Although it had given me an opportunity to end detention, it had never brought the genuine sustained cessation of violence that I had asked for when it first began. Since, however, the Provisional IRA had called the ceasefire, they could also end it. This was not just a personal view but one based on much discussion with my security advisers who were unanimous that a unilateral ceasefire should only be ended unilaterally. If the Provisional IRA chose to end it, it would be their job to justify the decision to an angry Catholic community and to a world where my action on detention had weakened their propaganda on 'internment without trial'. The Tory front-bench spokesmen did not see it this way and, despite my efforts to explain my decision, kept chasing me to call to an end to the 'so-called ceasefire'. Again, so much for bipartisanship.

The Provisional IRA never in fact made an announcement that the ceasefire was ended, not even when I made a statement that special category status would not be accorded after 1 March 1976. Given the outcry about this when the Gardiner Report had been published, the lack of immediate reaction was surprising; the response was to come later.

At the beginning of the ceasefire I had thought there was at least a chance of the Provisional IRA getting itself involved in the politics of the Convention but the reports to me of the talks with the Provisional Sinn Fein had soon shown that real politics were outside its ken. There were, however, the elected political parties of Northern Ireland and I had been considering my next political steps since receiving the Convention's Report in November. The ending of detention had softened the mood in the province, particularly amongst the Catholic minority, and it reinforced my view that I had to bring the Convention politicians together once more at Stormont. There was always a chance of success.

Chapter 10

THE CONVENTION RECONVENED

In early November 1975, after considering the Convention's Report, I began preparing for talks with the Northern Irish political parties with the aim of reconvening the Convention. My Cabinet colleagues had approved my general policy of consulting with the politicians to try to find common ground between them, and in informal discussions with ministerial colleagues and officials at Stormont Castle, we had all agreed that it was good sense for the Convention to be recalled for a short period in which its members could reconsider the specific issues of power sharing, finance, and law and order.

The statement that I would have to make to the Commons on the Convention Report was also on my mind and I wondered in my diary about what I would say: 'The reality is that the Convention has not come up with a solution. It is idle to pretend that a solution could have been obtained when we had not found one in the last four or five years. However, the politicians in the province have learned a great deal from one another, though it is a heavy price to pay for the learning process.'

I proposed to tell a reconvened Convention that they had as a basis the 1973 Constitution Act, which is much the same as the one now emerging for Scotland. I would ask the politicians if they were prepared to use it; if so, there would be elections to a fresh assembly. I would play no part in bringing the Convention parties together, although to help a coalition work, I might alter the Act to provide for fewer ministers. The large number in the power-sharing Executive had made government too unwieldy; only senior party members should be in a Cabinet or Executive.

I also mused in my diary on the idea of having a Chief Executive who was not of the political parties, which might make it easier to get agreement to a new committee system that would make for a legislative process on the lines of the House of Commons. 'We would have an emergency government for say three or four years and during that time, with the experience gained, we could continue to look at possible changes in the 1973 Act.'

These ideas were foremost in my mind as we prepared for the talks with Northern Irish politicians, which we expected would go on until late December or early January 1976. I emphasised to the ministers and officials who would participate in them that there should be no attempt on our part to negotiate new or common ground; that could only come from talks between the parties themselves, and they must firmly be made aware of this from the beginning. Two issues that I particularly wished to be discussed were finance and policing which, as well as the major issue of power sharing, the Convention Report had ignored. The nature of power brings its own problems and if there was to be agreement on power sharing, voluntary or otherwise, the political parties would need to be educated about the problems of finance and policing that would arise when they actually had to govern.

The views which the politicians expressed at the subsequent meetings are very revealing about the basic problems of the province, for nothing has changed over the years. On 17 November, Stan Orme, Frank Cooper and I met with UUUC representatives Harry West, Ian Paisley, Martin Smyth, Austin Ardill and William Beattie, a meeting which also showed that we were going to have difficulties in sticking to the agenda laid down, for they began straightaway by turning to the role of the Convention members in the period before its dissolution. They were welcome to meet ministers, I told them, but not civil servants in the departments. I did not like the Northern Irish tradition of members meeting directly with civil servants with no minister present; the old Stormont had been politically incestuous.

We eventually turned to policy and they insisted that if there was to be a devolved government, they wanted to 'control' the police, as the Minister of Home Affairs had done in the old days. This was no recipe for success in a divided province; nothing seemed to have been learned. They were crystal clear on the question of parliamentary sovereignty, asserting that they did not accept the control of the UK Parliament. The ending of the Stormont Parliament in 1972 by a Tory government had shattered them – as Martin Smyth put it, 'Fifty years of promises were swept away in nineteen hours' – and they were not going to see it happen again. They wanted a return to the 1920 Constitution and, unlike Enoch Powell, they were not countenancing the idea of integration.

On the following day we met the SDLP – Gerry Fitt, Paddy Devlin, Austin Currie and John Hume – and once again a significant part of the wide-ranging discussion was devoted to 'control' of the police. They did not want a return to the pre-1972 situation, when the Minister of Home Affairs appeared to be giving operational orders, but they were equally against the situation shown in 1974 when the police seemed to take no action against the Ulster workers' strike. They also said that, according to their information, the power workers would be 'neutral in any political strike in the future', a statement which showed that they had been talking with some disillusioned members of the UWC. On power sharing, they were sure that some Unionists would amend the Report when discussions were resumed and overall they had hopes from a recalled Convention.

The 18th was a long day, for we went on to meet other political representatives. Bill Craig and William Trimble of the Vanguard Unionist Progressive Party emphasised that an agreement on a future constitution could not be imposed from outside – it had to be left to Ulstermen – but an agreement could be made with the SDLP for a devolved government within the UK. Bill Craig said that he wanted a division of responsibility on security: the Police Authority should be responsible for ordinary crime and the Executive responsible for dealing with 'guerrilla warfare'. This was all too simple for me. Were there to be two types of policemen on the model of some European countries? It did reveal, however, that Craig, like the SDLP, realised that Ulstermen would have to face the gunmen with a united front in order to succeed. He was absolutely right that only Ulstermen could succeed in winning the security battle.

I asked Bill Craig's advice about my Commons speech in response to the Convention's Report: I was concerned about how it would sound in Northern Ireland. He told me that it was important that the government should not be seen waving a big stick to recall the Convention. We should say that we saw merit in the Report but, in the absence of agreement 'across the board', the recommendations did not help us to formulate a devolutionary package. However, we had noticed during the inter-party talks that there was a glimmer of hope that agreement could be reached, so we were asking the parties to take the Report back and once more explore the possibility of an agreement. He further advised that the guidance offered by the government should not be too precise, or it would sound like a dictation of terms and would call forth the wrong sort of response, although at the same time the reconsidered Report could not be too open-ended. Tact was important, for he felt sure that there were people in the UUUC who wished to get off their 'self-imposed hooks', particularly as the only alternative to agreement was indefinite direct rule, which no one in Northern Ireland really favoured.

Bill Craig did not see relations with the Irish Republic as an especially difficult problem. The UUUC had indeed considered a Benelux-type arrangement, and although much depended on the South's attitude, he was hopeful that Dublin would do its best to encourage the Northern parties to reach agreement and he expected a helpful statement from Liam Cosgrave in the near future. However, he said that the VUPP was strongly opposed in principle to the 1973 Constitution Act as the basis for forming a future Executive because it involved appointing the Executive by the 'diktat' of the Secretary of State and not according to the wishes of the people of Northern Ireland. I pointed out the amount of parliamentary time that would be required for yet another Constitution Bill – even if based on agreement in Northern Ireland – and after further questioning and my persistence, Craig and Trimble came round to thinking that an amended version of the Act might be acceptable as a corner-cutting device. This was encouraging, for it was precisely what I had in mind should that light at the end of the tunnel ever become the full light of day.

After this, we met the UPNI and the Alliance Party representatives. The former group, consisting of Brian Faulkner, John Brooke and Robert Hall-Thompson, were businesslike and turned immediately to finance. Brian, the spokesman, knew of course a great deal about it; he was against the idea of a block grant from Whitehall and preferred the pre-1972 position. On the question of a coalition, they thought there was a need for a guarantee that the SDLP would not at some time bring down the whole structure: to them, Gerry Fitt and John Hume had been the cause of the fall of Stormont.

Oliver Napier and Robert Cooper for the Alliance Party wanted more power over the police. English attitudes about this, they told me, showed the usual misunderstanding of Ireland. In the discussion that followed, I accepted that a republican government in the South could control the police without a Police Authority and could have special powers including internment, and that they had in the past executed members of the IRA. Let the English do any of this and there would be trouble. I also accepted that the North and the South had much in common because they had both lived through the recent civil war.

I asked them whether the 1973 Act, possibly amended to take out the Secretary of State's Executive-selecting powers, could be used as the basis for a new, perhaps interim, agreement. Oliver Napier replied that the Alliance Party was prepared to use the Act, with a return to ordinary majority rule after a five-year period, for they believed that by that time the whole face of Northern Irish politics would have changed out of all recognition. I put forward the possibility of me recalling the Convention and asking its members to consider operating, temporarily, the 1973 Act; if they agreed, there would be an election to an Assembly, an administration would be formed and meanwhile a Committee of the Assembly would consider changes in the Act with a view to putting proposals for a long-term solution to the Secretary of State. Oliver

Napier was again prepared to accept such an initiative, provided I was confident from soundings taken in advance that there would be agreement. He thought a sticking point for the UUUC was their categorical statement that there would be no SDLP members in the Cabinet. A way round this would be for the new agreement not to involve Cabinet government. The most important point, he counselled me, was to lay down at the beginning that there was only one need in any agreement – joint participation. Any more parameters would be counter-productive. He made the same point as Bill Craig: all the parties wanted devolved government and that was the carrot.

The next day we met Professor Lindsay, an ex-Vanguard Unionist who had launched the Dominion Party in the Convention. His idea was that in the short run there should be integration and in the long run dominion status. We did not have to give much time to that. Afterwards, we talked with Hugh Smyth, the so-called Independent Unionist representative, in reality a representative of the UVF. He told me to forget the Report; what I should do was bring back the Convention and see if its members could share power! He was far more interesting on other points. He told me that I should end detention – I could not tell him that it was in fact nearly over – and he spent some time raising the question of conditions in the Maze. He had spoken with Provisional IRA members there and they were interested in the idea of 'independence'. The UVF was only interested in this if 'Britain ended the knot'; his people in the Shankill were more concerned with economic matters. He wanted the 'welfare wing of the UVF', which was not involved in violence, to be recognised – in effect he was talking about a political wing of the UVF on the lines of the IRA's Sinn Fein. Altogether, it was a useful meeting: as the Secretary of State for Northern Ireland I needed to know what the paramilitaries were thinking.

On some occasions I met with the politicians informally, and over a meal with Official Unionist representatives I again raised the possibility of using the 1973 Act. It was quite clear that this was going to be very difficult but they saw that using it would be a quick way of moving. I thought that if they were not so afraid of having an election, they would have done a deal with the SDLP. It was interesting to have their view of the role in the UUUC of Enoch Powell, who went against the majority in not wanting devolution. They told me that Jim Molyneaux could soon crack the whip on him, which I thought showed an odd lack of understanding of the Westminster scene, and they also reckoned that Enoch would not get the nomination in South Down next time round.

I reflected in my diary of 24 November that although the talks had not solved any problems, they had given me a feel for the way I should respond to the Convention Report in my Commons statement. I was now certain that I was going to recall the Convention but I had yet to decide on timing. 'I am going to see the politicians again this week and I have to make up my mind when to give the reply to the Convention. Enoch very much wants it in the New Year. When I spoke to the UUUC representatives the other day, Paisley asked me about it and I told him either before or after Christmas. He gravely asked, "Will you be making it or the Prime Minister?" I told him it would be me and he immediately issued a statement revealing this!'

The Opposition at Westminster picked this up and, as I went on to comment in my diary, 'Mrs Thatcher in her speech at the beginning of the session said that it was indefensible that I was delaying; there would be a political gap. And this after I had explained to her in my room my problem on timing and she had then explained it to Airey Neave when he joined us! The point I had made was that there was no use in replying until we had something to say.'

On 25 November I again met officially with UUUC representatives, this time without Ian Paisley, who was delayed in London. I informed them that the White Paper on devolution for Scotland and Wales was due out next week and this affected the timing of my Commons response. Ah, they observed, they did not want to be caught up with the 'lesser schemes' across the water. They turned immediately to the subject of power sharing and the Rev Beattie, Paisley's deputy, said that he thought the SDLP was depending on the government to twist the UUUC's arm and the sooner the SDLP were brought to the 'point of reality' the better. After all, they were being offered something of great benefit to their community by the UUUC! Ernie Baird repeated his view that the SDLP's attitude was the fault of the government – i.e. me – in emphasising power sharing so much. The SDLP would have to face the fact that the UUUC had won the election in the province, so no power-sharing scheme would have widespread support. Harry West thought that the SDLP would press to get back into government but in the end would accept the best they could get out of majority rule.

Once again they showed that they had not thought out their approach to finance. All they wanted, they explained, was to get away from what they saw as Treasury domination of the detail of expenditure. 'Who doesn't?' I observed to my officials afterwards. I tried to move on to policing and security arrangements in a possible future constitution but they wanted to discuss the current situation instead. They simply would not accept that I personally did not instruct the army on which roads to block, nor my assurance that I did not hold the army back in Armagh. They claimed that a disproportionately high number of Protestants had been charged with offences compared with Catholics in the previous eight weeks, to which I could only observe that loyalist gunmen had been more active recently. In response to their question about talks between politicians and army officers, I told them that Unit Commanders could talk about local army work but policy above that had to be discussed with ministers.

On the same day I had a meeting with the VUPP, whose views about my reply to the Convention Report again interested me. Bill Craig was brief: reply quickly and the inter-party talks would begin – they were the only reason for a recall of the Convention. There was an added bonus from the meeting, for Glen Barr of the UDA as well as the VUPP was present and he told me that the paramilitaries had spoken to Paisley and reminded him of the need for a settlement. Paisley would not take kindly to that, we thought in the office, nor would he act on it.

The 25th was another long day, for we went on to meet the SDLP. Although we discussed finance and security, it was their advice on the possible recall of the Convention that was of more importance to me at this stage. Paddy Devlin wanted the inter-party talks before the Convention met, which confirmed my view that it was the talks that mattered most. I was also glad to hear that the Conservative Party had told them that the Convention Report was not acceptable in its present form. We were not going to have the 'orange card' played at Westminster, as I had feared at first.

By 7 December I had decided on the timing of my response in the Commons and I noted in my diary: 'In the course of this week I began preparing the memoranda [for the Cabinet sub-committee] in readiness for a debate on 12 January 1976. Basically the recommendation is to go back to the Convention to reconsider the committee system, etc. The loyalists have said that they will not come back, so we could be in an extremely difficult position.'

I continued to have further talks with the politicians and on 15 December met with the UUUC. It was a revealing meeting, not so much for what it showed about their views on policing and finance – though on the latter they emphasised that they wanted the power to vary UK taxation as it bore on Northern Ireland – but for the way in which it showed how the conspiracy theory dominates Irish politics. They first complained of a Dublin newspaper report that claimed the British government had told the Irish government that the UUUC Report would be rejected. I had in fact spoken with the Irish government about this, and I supposed the press report to be a garbled version: I certainly had not talked in the blunt way reported. They then raised the matter of a meeting between one of my junior ministers and local government representatives in Northern Ireland where they had discussed the return of wider powers to local authorities. It was untrue that such a discussion had taken place but they still made the point that this was a subject for the Convention parties and not for local councillors.

Finally Dr Paisley complained that I had misrepresented him on television when I claimed that he did not accept the sovereignty of the Queen in Parliament. He had, he said, always accepted this but if Her Majesty's Government attempted to put Northern Ireland out of the UK either 'directly or piecemeal', then the loyalists would resist as their forefathers had done!

Paisley was of course a past master of the conspiracy game. Before my time he had alleged that the IRA was putting poisoned pellets in the chicken runs in Northern Ireland in order to bring fowl pest! And in the autumn of 1975 he had claimed, as I noted in my diary, that 'bearded and hooded men had come to the Castle to see me and had flown off by helicopter'. This story stemmed from the fact that a specialist team regularly came in a van to make clearance checks of my room and their equipment was taken away by helicopter; whether the men were bearded I have no idea, but they certainly would not be hooded. Paisley seemed to have been given a tip-off by the security man at the gate who told him that he had been ordered not to stop the van. Paisley thereupon drove up to the Castle, knocked on the van and asked whether it was for sale. In my diary I described the reply as 'No. It belongs to the Northern Ireland Office', though the response included much more earthy 'friendly advice'! Paisley the detective had drawn the wrong conclusions.

Much more serious was his allegation at this time that I had set up a 'unit of psychological warfare to discredit and undermine the loyalist leadership in the province', which he linked to the number and role of Foreign Office officials in the Northern Ireland Office. He also claimed that for this purpose we possessed a list of second-rank loyalist politicians, though he had nothing to claim as a basis for this. It was all nonsense but it was a serious enough allegation to reach the floor of the House of Commons in February 1976; the 'debate' then went off like a damp squib even when Paisley claimed that his life was at risk. However, the story had been bandied about in the media in the weeks before and soured feelings in the province at the time when the Convention was being recalled.

After all the conspiracy talk at the UUUC meeting, we did not get very far on the subject we were supposed to be discussing, but in preparation for the January debate at Westminster they agreed to give me their written views to clarify some of their proposals, particularly on finance.

When I met the SDLP leaders later that day, I turned the discussion once more to the government's response to the Convention Report.

They thought that there was a fair chance of a recalled Convention reaching agreement, given the right parameters for discussion, since although Paisley and Powell realised that the Report was unacceptable and thought that would be the end of the Convention, other Unionists did not want direct rule. All that was needed, they said, was a month. Their own particular concern was that a failed Convention would drive the Catholics into the arms of the Provisional IRA. We then had a valuable discussion about security problems in general and special category status in particular. I had recently made the announcement that this would come to an end on 1 March 1976 and the discussion confirmed my view that we would run into trouble when that time came.

The following day I asked the Alliance leaders for their views on a return of the Convention. They told me that it would 'flush out the crypto-integrationalists' at Westminster who were at odds with the UUUC at home. They thought one month was too short a recall period and that two months would be better. I also met with Brian Faulkner and the UPNI representatives, who advised me to recall the Convention for a clearly specified purpose. Brian recommended that I play down the significance of Powell at Westminster – the focus of Northern Ireland politicians was Stormont and Powell was not a major figure in the province. We touched on the subject of finance, which they thought there was little point in discussing until the fundamental inter-party issues were settled, and we also talked about security policy. When the subject came up of the relationship between a Northern Ireland government responsible for the police and the UK government responsible for the army, Brian suggested I referred to papers sent to him in February 1972 by the UK government. Because of political conventions I could not do this but my officials advised me that the papers would not now be relevant; the discussions four years earlier had anyway not resolved the question of control of the army by local politicians.

In the meeting with the VUPP, also on the 16th, I told Bill Craig during our discussion of law and order that the RUC would never again allow political interference as in the pre-1972 days. We moved on to the key question of the recall of the Convention, on which Bill advised me to list issues that required further explanation, which would give the Convention something to do. The real work would be done in the inter-party talks, for he felt sure that there was a lot of support for a voluntary coalition amongst Official Unionists in the constituencies. The meeting also gave a sidelight on Northern Ireland politics when Glen Barr brought up a complaint from Andy Tyrie, leader of the UDA, about the Christmas parole scheme!

By this time the recommendations to my Cabinet colleagues were ready. Nothing in the latest round of talks had led me to alter my decision about recalling the Convention and on 17 December the Cabinet sub-committee met to discuss my proposals. I told them that the Convention Report, while in no sense the result of debate or argument, had provided the opportunity for Northern Ireland politicians to range freely over issues in the province without any interference by the UK government. It was now my judgment, based on the Convention's Report, my talks with the political parties and the feeling in the province generally, that in early January we should reconvene the Convention for a limited period to agree on a structure of government that would 'involve' both communities.

I told them that only the UUUC was opposed to this course and although a difficult situation would arise if they persisted in their opposition before a united wish at Westminster, I thought it very unlikely that they would carry their opposition to the point of industrial action because there was little popular support for their attitude. The UUUC would decide whether to attend the reconvened Convention when the announcement about it was made in the Commons in the New Year and the Convention's Report was debated. I proposed to publish a letter to the Chairman after this announcement was made, in which I would emphasise that the Convention's proposal for a scheme of government must command the support of both communities in the province and that there must also be general acceptance by all parties of the status of the police force. I would be having further meetings with the political parties in the New Year and meanwhile my officials would continue the discussions on the basis of papers prepared on such subjects as finance and the role of the UDR.

I also raised the issue of security, where the scene was continuing to change and we needed to reassess how to deal with it. I was therefore going to set up a review of security policy in the context of the ending of detention and special category status.

In the discussion that followed, my colleagues endorsed my proposals. One of them pointed out that the recall of the Convention would not be seen by the British public as a significant step forward. Of course it was not but this view ignored the deep-rooted nature of the Irish problem which prevented, and prevents, any possibility of a solution 'at a stroke'. What we needed to do was keep the temperature of political debate as low as possible. The Foreign Secretary thought that international opinion would be positive, which was encouraging, although I was much more concerned with the reaction of Northern Ireland.

There, the talks that now went on between officials and the politicians were reported to me as constructive, although in the discussions of policing the politicians were talking about police accountability when they in fact meant 'control'. When I returned to Belfast I resumed the talks personally and on 5 January I met the UUUC representatives. Harry West opened with a prepared general policy statement and a long criticism of the minority parties. The message was that there was no point in recalling the Convention if they had to discuss power sharing with republicans or consider an institutionalised Irish dimension. They remembered the 'disruptive tactics' of the SDLP in the Northern Ireland Parliament; all that the SDLP ever obtained at elections was twenty-five per cent of the total vote. They were sure that if there was a referendum following a voluntary coalition, the electorate would turn it down.

Ernest Baird threatened to boycott the reconvened Convention, and Ian Paisley told me that if I rejected the Convention Report I would clash with the Ulster people. I reminded him that he had said in the House of Commons that the Westminster Parliament was the place for taking decisions, but it was wasted words. He operated in two separate markets.

I asked them why the minority community had never supported the Stormont system. 'Ah,' said Reginald Empey, 'there had been unenthusiastic acquiescence.' The Rev Smyth said that it was all due to the 'all-Ireland mythology' peddled by the Dublin government. In that case, I responded, why should the minority accept it now? They came back undaunted: there were now new proposals; all the SDLP really wanted was 'fairness' – they had said so – and the Catholics would support the proposals when the present wave of terrorism passed.

When I concluded by telling them that the main need was to overcome the deep divisions in the community, Empey told me that the situation in the community had deteriorated only because of the intervention of the UK government. We went back over the reforms initiated by Harold Wilson's government in 1969, mentioning particularly the disbandment of the B Specials and the use of proportional representation in elections. No effect. It was Her Majesty's Government who had proved that violence paid. All I had to do was tell the SDLP to accept the UUUC proposals and the violence would be over.

I told the group that the government's policy was clear: we would not opt out of the province and nor could its people be forced into the Irish Republic. However, it followed from this that Northern Ireland was part of the UK and decisions were a matter for the UK majority. Empey, undeterred, asserted that the traditional 'Westminster spirit of fair play' was no use: there were two irreconcilables in Northern Ireland. The SDLP had been sergeants and now they would not be corporals. One member of the group said that it was the SDLP who had started all the trouble – they were undercover IRA! I denied this, pointing out that if the SDLP leaders went away, a large slice of their vote would go to Sinn Fein. Nothing I said was to any avail and as I afterwards commented in my diary: 'The level of discussion was remarkably low; it was all a pathetic performance. Perhaps Enoch is right – what they need is a good county council government.'

The meetings I had with the representatives of the other parties were much better in content, but I learned nothing new from them. On 8 January, the SDLP told me that they wanted power sharing; nothing else would do. The next day Bill Craig's group told me that the UUUC would come back to the Convention; a voluntary coalition was required and this was better than an emergency coalition. Brian Faulkner advised me to bring back the Convention briefly and tell the politicians 'No agreement, no devolution'.

By this stage I felt that I was becoming more Irish than the Irish. We were talking for the sake of talking, and the time had come to stop. The meetings had served their purpose. They had confirmed that most of the parties desperately wanted a return to devolved government, and they had also provided a means of avoiding an abrupt or crisis ending to the Convention.

It was in fact more positive than this for I now felt sure that, despite the number of Paisley/Baird rallies and pamphlets threatening a repeat of May 1974, all the parties would be back at Stormont. The final confirmation of this was a meeting that I had called with representatives of the UDA and other loyalist paramilitaries, on which I commented in my diary of 11 January: 'I do not think that there will be an Ulster workers' strike. Glen Barr made clear that Baird could not speak for the Ulster Loyalist Central Co-ordinating Committee. [The ULCCC had been set up after the strike by the various loyalist paramilitary organisations in the province.] This does not mean that we will not have problems when my response to the Convention is revealed but how these develop will depend on the way I respond in my speech.'

Events rarely go as planned in Northern Ireland and my carefully prepared speech for the Commons was no exception. The week before I was due to make it, there was an especially vicious outbreak of sectarian murders in the continuing trouble spot of South Armagh. The province was deeply affected and there was serious danger of a backlash. In Britain the murders, coming on top of the current talk of independence in Northern Ireland, brought public demands for withdrawal, voiced particularly in the press. On 12 January, only an hour before my own speech on the Convention Report, the Prime Minister made an announcement about the South Armagh murders, and I recast my opening statement to respond to the strong feelings aroused by the events there.

On 4 January, five Catholics had been killed in two separate incidents near Whitecross and the following day, allegedly in retaliation, ten Protestant workers were shot dead. The report given to me described how twelve men from a local textile mill had been flagged down in their van and between ten and twelve terrorists had ordered them at gunpoint to get out. At first the workers thought that they were loyalist gunmen and one of the Protestants nudged his Catholic workmate to stay quiet. In fact it was the Catholic whom the gunmen pulled out while the other eleven men were cold-bloodedly shot; ten of them were killed and the other seriously injured.

Stan Orme, himself a former factory engineer, had gone down to the mill the next day and spoken to the workmates of the murdered men, members of the Transport Workers' Union. When he returned, he could not at first speak for emotion. His feelings were shared throughout the province. The Feakle churchmen, who had been endeavouring to mediate between the murdering groups, refused to renew negotiations until the groups had 'restrained their own members'. The dangerous position of loyalists in South Armagh was highlighted and once more local farming families and their representatives demanded action. Although less was said about it, the fears of the Catholics in the area were no less justified; both sides were dying.

We had to take conspicuous action and, as Harold announced in the Commons on 12 January, we had sent over the reserve battalion and extra SAS soldiers. There were to be more home searches and more checkpoints for vehicles and people, with extra use of personal identity checks under the Protection of Terrorism Act. Surveillance of the border would be increased, since the gunmen often made their escape across it, and Harold also announced that 'a new information system, based on automatic data processing, is to be introduced by the army to handle existing records so that information can be processed and acted upon more quickly.' A number of other measures to increase control of vehicle movement were also being studied urgently.

Although we later reassessed security policy on the border and discussed it in the Cabinet sub-committee, none of the suggestions – and they were no more than that – for neutral zones and a mini Berlin wall were of practical value. The only sensible outcome of the ghastly murders was the increase in the numbers of the SAS: small paramilitary groups are best dealt with by small groups of soldiers. Better co-operation with the Irish army on the border would have helped but this was not at this time forthcoming.

The response in the province to the steps we were taking was predictable. The loyalists were in favour; the SDLP not: Gerry Fitt compared the SAS to the CIA, Seamus Mallon implied that the steps constituted 'punitive action against ordinary people', and Paddy Devlin thought the whole exercise 'cosmetic' since the SAS had always been in South Armagh. Equally predictably, O'Brady of Provisional Sinn Fein announced that the Provisional IRA found the presence of the SAS provocative.

The GOC also reacted strongly. He flew over from Lisburn to see me on hearing of the steps Harold had announced. He disagreed with some of them and said that he was in general fed up with the press and with all the arguments that the Rees' policy was wrong. It was his policy and he was not going to be driven from it by the press, which he thought was what was happening.

I told him that there was no other way for us to act. I knew as well as he did that there were only about twenty active Provisionals in South Armagh, who moved backwards and forwards across the border aided by units in Dundalk and parts of Louth and Monaghan, but Parliament and the press had decided that there should be extra troops. We had to respond to Parliament and, whether we liked it or not, to the press and public opinion. To explain the real position on the number of Provisionals would have made the situation worse, even though I accepted his argument that the response announced at Westminster – except for the SAS – was in fact too great.

If anyone should have been cross, I should. There was a 'white feather' gibe at me in the *Sunday Express* and an uninformed outcry led by the Opposition in the Commons. It was to be expected. Bipartisanship had not been much in evidence from the Conservative front- or back-benches recently.

When I came to make my speech on the Convention Report in the Commons, the atmosphere was charged from the earlier debate. Withdrawal was the issue on everybody's minds and I therefore had to deal with this issue first, and head on.

> The continuing and appalling violence in Northern Ireland has undoubtedly added to the groundswell of opinion in Great Britain that we should withdraw from Northern Ireland, cut Northern Ireland adrift and let the Northern Irish, whether Catholic or Protestant, fend for themselves. The government are in no doubt that this would be a grave mistake. It would solve nothing. I have no doubt that withdrawal and abandonment of our responsibilities would precipitate violence on an even greater scale than we have seen so far. And we must not assume that violence could be confined to Northern Ireland. It would spread to Great Britain and also to the Republic of Ireland. Withdrawal would be a short-sighted policy, but above all it would be an irresponsible policy.

I still regard that statement as giving powerful reasons for resisting demands for withdrawal, and I believe equally strongly about talk of an 'early solution' to the conflict. Because the two outlooks are closely linked, I went on in my Commons speech:

> Far too many of the solutions of the past have come to nothing. Anglo-Irish history is littered with the handiwork of those who have failed, although they thought that they had the solution. There is no easy way out of the enmeshed and intricate problems of Northern Ireland, and those who think that they have a solution should reflect upon eight hundred years of troubled history. The solution to six years of violence and a community divided by the facts of history must be worked out slowly and surely within Northern Ireland and have a firm base in the support of the people of Northern Ireland. It would certainly be a mistake now to think that a final solution will come immediately. It would be a mistake also to think that we could impose or enforce a constitutional system and expect it to work.

I concluded by reminding the House that Mr Heath's constitutional proposals at Sunningdale simply had not had a sufficiently firm base in Northern Ireland.

After this, I turned the focus of attention back to the Convention Report. I told the Commons that although the Report was in effect the UUUC's submission, it displayed a 'considerable measure of agreement amongst all the parties'. This did not mean that support from both sides of the community was at present forthcoming for the total system proposed in the Report, but it did lead me to believe that further progress could be made. On this basis the Convention would, I said, be reconvened from 3 February to consider specific matters that would be laid down by me. Once more my speech on behalf of the government to the Commons was to be an agenda for further discussions in the province.

I stated that I accepted in principle that the transferred powers in the 1973 Act would be returned to a unicameral assembly, and because we recognised that the committee system proposed in the Report represented an attempt to involve opposition parties more closely in government, we wanted the members of the Convention to look at it again to see if they could go further towards 'widespread acceptance'. This phrase of course meant a wider element of power sharing than the Unionists had been prepared to concede.

On the matter of finance I promised that the government would give a future administration 'as wide a discretion as would be consistent with maintaining the unity of the United Kingdom economy' but

Whitehall would retain the powers necessary to manage the economy as a whole, including the share of total expenditure to be allocated to the province. I warned that hard decisions would then have to be taken in Northern Ireland to determine 'priorities among the various transferred services'. Socialism, I had always been taught, had to speak the 'language of priorities' – it was a language the unionists and republicans would have to learn, together with the realisation that all talk of independence ignored the special social problems and lack of resources in the province.

I commented on the Report's law and order recommendation by saying that I accepted in principle that a future Northern Ireland administration would have responsibility for the police, but the transfer would be gradual. The army was, however, different. It could be responsible only to the government in London, which would also have responsibility for emergency legislation, as it would for judicial appointments and the courts.

The 'British dimension' referred to in the Report was about the proposal to increase the number of Westminster seats, which I was particularly against if the province was to have its own devolved government, and I simply responded that the government did not feel able to recommend a re-examination of this question 'in advance of an agreement on a system of government commanding the most widespread acceptance'. My remarks on the 'Irish dimension' were stronger, for I was greatly influenced by how this issue had been overplayed at Sunningdale and afterwards, and I told the House that there was no need for an institutional framework such as a Council of Ireland. Co-operation should 'evolve positively and naturally', as the need arose.

I concluded by emphasising the main point – the need in Northern Ireland for 'some form of partnership and co-operation' – and reminding the Convention that it had to make this the cornerstone of their fresh deliberations if it wanted the House of Commons to translate any agreement into constitutional and legislative form. I pointed out that the more major the legislation, the longer it would require consideration, and I expressed the hope that the Convention members would make progress on the matters laid down within a period of four weeks, though I thought to myself that we would have to see what happened. The specific matters for discussion would, I stated, be spelt out in more detail in a letter to the Chairman of the Convention, which I would publish as a White Paper.

The Commons as a whole accepted the main points of my statement, although some of the Official Unionists were rather sceptical in their approach. They could not say too much since their fellow politicians in the province wanted the Convention to meet again. More significant were the differing views expressed by the Ulster Members on the possibility of a voluntary coalition. Bill Craig of course thought that this was the only way through the impasse, but Jim Molyneaux wanted a general election to provide a mandate for it first. Stan and I turned to each other on hearing this and agreed that it would be a sure recipe for disaster; only time would show that power sharing could work. Gerry Fitt took the opportunity to stir troubled waters by claiming that Dr Paisley had gone along with the discussions on a possible voluntary coalition and then reneged! Gerry was scoring points, but nevertheless he was pointing to the dangers ahead and he was right that the doctor could scupper it all.

My letter to the Convention Chairman was published on 16 January. It began by ranging over the recent talks with the parties and emphasising that Northern Ireland was a divided community, different in many respects to the rest of the United Kingdom for reasons of history, geography and tradition. Then came the request to the Convention to 'consider and report' on the following three matters:

1 How best agreement can be reached on a system of government built on the principles on which there is already widespread agreement, and providing for a form of partnership and participation, and which will command the most widespread acceptance throughout the whole of the community in Northern Ireland and in both parts of that community.
2 Whether a committee system might be of value as part of a wider and acceptable constitutional framework.
3 Whether progress could best be made on the basis of setting up a system of government which, though temporary, is capable of evolving over a period of time into permanent and agreed constitutional arrangements.

I expressed the hope that the Convention would be able to build on the principles to which there was already a wide measure of agreement and, in an attempt to keep the Convention from moving away from its purpose, said: 'The government is asking the Convention to examine only the matters specified in this letter in the light of the government's conclusions.' I was worried about that four-week period.

I reminded the Chairman that I had power to hold a referendum on any proposals the Convention came up with and said that 'any recommendations in this respect will receive careful consideration'. I meant this but I was, and still am, sceptical of referenda in Northern Ireland or anywhere else. I concluded with the hope that further discussion would lead to agreement which would enable Parliament to 'provide Northern Ireland with its own system of government again'.

I had to be hopeful but it was not easy given the political history of only the previous two years. Nor was there much sign that the UUUC was going to change its views. As I reported to my Cabinet colleagues on 27 January, although I saw the recall of the Convention as a device to get the UUUC to move from their stated position, Enoch Powell had called it 'blackmail', and Paisley and Baird were opposed to it completely. With them in the background, the UUUC would not compromise on the key issues of republicans in the Cabinet and the Irish dimension, and it looked unlikely that anything would deflect the hard-liners sufficiently to bring about a compromise. I told them that overall the prospects of significant movement within the Convention were not good, despite a growing understanding of the general mood at Westminster and of British public opinion.

On my return to Stormont after the Cabinet meeting, I was advised that the politicians had agreed to meet formally in the Convention and then proceed to another series of inter-party talks. Although this was hopeful, I still needed to consider what to do if the talks broke down, which seemed very likely, and on 30 January I therefore submitted another report to my Cabinet sub-committee colleagues. I told them that the strategy of the Convention Chairman and his staff would be to get the parties to consider new ways of breaking the log-jam on the central question of Cabinet membership; the talks would be arranged so that those between the UUUC and the SDLP were left until last. I thought that the trouble would come to a head about two weeks after the talks restarted, and the Chairman would then adjourn the Convention and report to me.

At that stage, after discussions with ministerial colleagues and officials in the province, the right course might be for me to see the Convention Chairman in Belfast and then return to London, where I would invite the Ulster party leaders, plus one or two supporters at most, to meet me. I mentioned the limitation on numbers because of the tendency of the parties to hunt in packs, which made effective discussion almost impossible. I would have separate meetings with each party to clarify their positions, and I pointed out to my colleagues that it would be better for these meetings to take place in London, not only because the party leaders would be 'playing away from home', but also because I should not run the risk of taking over from the Convention Chairman in Belfast. The dialogue would subsequently need to be broadened and we should have to consider whether the Northern Irish leaders should be seen collectively by the Prime Minister on the following day.

The overall question was what would be said to the politicians and I told my colleagues that I could not be precise at this early stage but I would remain in very close touch with Sir Robert Lowry, the Convention Chairman, who had sat through all the past debates and knew his Ulster. There were two possibilities. The first was a blunt warning that if the Convention did not succeed in reaching some sort of agreement, as Parliament and the other fifty-three million people in the UK wished them to do, it was the end of any early prospect of a system of government in Northern Ireland. The second was a warning in a lower key, accompanied by a few constructive suggestions for the parties to go away and consider in the Convention. Both possibilities had their dangers. The first was unlikely to bring an agreement and the Convention would almost certainly end. The government would also be open to the accusation of making threats. These objections applied less to the second course, but left the risk of the government being put in a position where we appeared to be negotiating.

I raised with my colleagues the question of at what stage, if at all, the government should intervene directly, something which had long concerned us. The strongest argument was not to intervene at all before the breakdown since the whole point of the Convention was that it was a Northern Ireland affair and we should not risk being accused of contributing to its failure. However, we should plan on the basis that we might have to intervene because in the new situation of the reconvened Convention, the government had to be seen to be doing all it could to bring about agreement.

I offered some preliminary thoughts on what I would discuss with the Northern Ireland parties in the event of a breakdown, concentrating on various forms of emergency governments for a limited period. One possibility was a two-tier system with a majority Cabinet but above it a government council which would include representatives of all the parties, who would have certain entrenched rights. Another was a much more developed committee system to take the politicians away from the 'yahoo' of the Stormont chamber. My own view was that the failure of the Convention to reach agreement would mean a definite end to it, at least for a while, but in case we did have to intervene, we should keep closely in touch with Sir Robert and he certainly should be present 'in a cross-bench position' at any meetings with the politicians. Only Ulstermen could find and make agreements and, who knew, they might surprise us.

This element of hope, however slender, was still with me when the Convention met on 3 February, for the members agreed to continue their work through inter-party talks chaired by Sir Robert himself. There was a tiny chance that they would find a way forward. 'In open forum it would be impossible,' I reflected in my diary.

The talks held between 3 and 23 February were formal in that they were authorised by the Convention and attended by the Chairman himself, and a Hansard service was made available should the parties require it. This was not always used and some parties asked only for their main statements and questions to be recorded, not the discussions that followed. Sir Robert made it clear from the start that he would not be recorded at all and in the published reports his speeches are marked by asterisks, which sometimes makes the reports hard to comprehend. At the time I was not sure that Sir Robert's decision was right but in retrospect I think it was. He was going to return to the bench and his questioning could have been misunderstood later.

The reports make interesting reading and the views and attitudes shown in them are still as relevant today. In one of the first talks, between the UUUC and the Alliance Party, Oliver Napier bluntly stated that an agreement between these two parties alone would not meet my criteria for an across-the-divide, power-sharing government. The SDLP could not be bypassed. David Bleakley of the NILP told the UUUC the same thing: 'The only viable government that I can see is a government based on broad community acceptance. Quite frankly, I do not think the UUUC or any other party could run this country unless it had effective support throughout the community.' That I believe is still the case.

Although David Bleakley had no power base in the province, he made a valuable contribution to an understanding of the problems facing us. He told the UUUC that he wanted an evolution of agreed institutions; the job of reconstructing the government would be a long one. I totally concurred with this: it had been easy to end Stormont at a stroke – for a Tory government – but a new form of government could not be reconstructed by the same stroke of a pen, which is why the idea of an emergency coalition under the 1973 Act was a sensible way forward, for it would allow time for changes that experience showed to be necessary. David also made clear his acceptance of the sovereignty of the Westminster Parliament, which Harry West for the UUUC could not accept; the party's acceptance of sovereignty had always been qualified and the talks made this obvious.

When Harry West went on to say that Unionists could not co-operate with people of incompatible views, David responded: 'This is a case of the pot calling the kettle black. Inside the Unionist ranks there are people with extraordinary views which we are going to have to "thole". To me they are no more difficult to contend with than some of the views with which I disagree held by some members of the SDLP.' He was referring to those Unionists who believed in independence and to those who associated with men of violence, some of whom were at the meeting. He had again spoken bluntly and said things that needed saying.

Brian Faulkner showed his usual clarity and professionalism in the UPNI talks with the UUUC. Faced by Harry West's opening question – 'I should like to ask Mr Faulkner if we are here as free agents to discuss this thing openly within the terms that have been set out in the resolution [of the Convention]. In other words, has he any understanding with any other party that is opposed to the Convention proposals?' – Brian simply replied, 'I am sorry but I do not understand what you are saying.' Harry West became less woolly, to which Brian told him straight: 'No. We have no arrangement with any other party on anything, but we do oppose the proposals made in the majority Report of the Convention.'

He then, in contrast to the waffle from West, pointed out that there was nothing for discussion during this one-month period of the Convention other than the three issues laid out in the White Paper, which meant 'some means of finding partnership government'. He stated that he was in favour of a voluntary coalition rather than a statutory one, and on being asked about the involvement of the SDLP in a power-sharing Executive, said: 'We are not necessarily adamant that the SDLP should be in a future Cabinet. We are saying that any Cabinet of Northern Ireland should include within its ranks representatives of all sections of the Ulster community who are prepared to accept and work within the constitutional position of Northern Ireland within the United Kingdom.' He was certain that the SDLP met 'that test at this stage' but if they departed from it in the future, then the UPNI would be 'quick to break off'. He was also satisfied that the SDLP would back the security forces. Given that the question about this came from Harry West in the presence of others who had been involved with the paramilitaries during the Ulster workers' strike, I thought it cheek, to say the least.

The crunch meeting between the UUUC and the SDLP was on 12 February, with West, Paisley, Smyth, Baird, Beattie and Ardill leading from one side and Fitt, Home, Currie and Devlin from the other. After Harry West's long opening speech about Sunningdale, the Convention Report and a possible committee system, John Hume explained why the SDLP had chosen the inter-party talks instead of the open Convention as the way forward; they believed that the only way to create circumstances in which the whole community could support a Northern Ireland government was 'for both sections of the community through their elected representatives to work together for the betterment of all the people'.

Back over the subject of the Convention they all went, and on to the nature of British Cabinet government, until Gerry Fitt interjected to ask the crucial question: 'Is it right to say that the UUUC, either in government or in opposition, would never co-operate with the SDLP?' There was no clear answer. John Hume tried again: 'Are we to understand Mr West as saying that there are no circumstances in which the UUUC would serve in Cabinet with the SDLP?' This time Harry replied, 'That is right.' It was all over.

There was in fact a short adjournment, demanded by Paddy Devlin, but it was only for the SDLP to agree on what John Hume should say on their return to the chamber: the talks were not getting to grips with the issues the Secretary of State had asked the parties to consider and the meeting should be terminated. John Hume expressed the Party's regret but 'we remain willing to negotiate with all the parties in the Convention on the basis of paragraph 24 [the three points]. We will be here at any stage if anybody wants to talk to us about it.'

It was not only the UUUC/SDLP talks that were over but effectively the whole series, despite further UUUC/Alliance talks on a three-part system of government – a cabinet, committees and a privy council of state – devised by the latter party. When I went to see Harold before the Cabinet sub-committee meeting on 18 February, I told him that Robert Lowry still thought that there was a chance of an agreement on the Alliance proposal of a three-tier government, but that I was sceptical. As far as I was concerned, the Convention was over and it might well be a waste of time to talk to the Convention members at all. The question was how to end the Convention in our own best interests.

Harold again brought up the possibility of a Lancaster House conference for Westminster and Northern Irish politicians, but I told him that I was firmly against this: it would not work unless we had something constructive to put forward, and in the light of the Convention we obviously had not. Harold asked me to think about it very carefully because he sensed that the House of Commons was increasingly bored and intolerant of the Northern Ireland question and we should not assume that there would be an easy 'lurch' from the failure of the Convention back to direct rule. The conference would be designed to keep the ball in play, although its real purpose would be to impress the Westminster parties of the 'insufferability' of the Northern Irish politicians and to stop the Ulster Unionists making common cause with the Tories. He thought that there was a risk of losing parliamentary support for direct rule if nothing 'glamorous' like a Lancaster House conference was produced. We left the matter there.

Frank Cooper referred to the possibility, given the events of May 1974, of a severe reaction from the Unionist paramilitaries aided by the loyalist politicians when the Convention ended. I again told Harold that I did not think that there was much danger of this; there would be far less popular support for it than the UWC strike, but we must of course be ready if it did happen.

Afterwards I commented in my diary: 'I put my view to the Prime Minister that we have to play the situation carefully in the weeks and months ahead. I must stand up in the House and say, "There it is – direct rule". He is a little concerned, no more than that. He wanted to know whether I felt that the House would stomach it and I said that they were not going to be asked to stomach it as a long-term policy but as a period in which, as the Cardinal of Ireland put it to me the other day, we "set no more exams for a time". What I have said to the Irish government and everybody I have talked to is please let us not try another solution to the Irish question.'

At the Cabinet meeting I reported to my colleagues that the Convention was all but over despite the Alliance proposal and that we had to be careful not to be blamed for its ending: the politicians there were adept at blaming everyone but themselves. We also had to watch that the Provisional IRA could not boast responsibility for bringing the Convention to an end and that we did not arouse the loyalist paramilitaries. We had, I pointed out, already discussed the possibilities should there be a chance to intervene constructively, however sceptical I might feel about this. If there was an irrevocable breakdown, I would report it to Parliament at the earliest opportunity, making it clear that the Convention would now be dissolved and that direct rule would continue but changes in its form would be proposed before the existing rules expired on 24 July.

I also mentioned the possibility of a London conference, even though I still thought that it would be fatal to parade the continuing story of Northern Ireland in the middle of London. However, it was the Prime Minister's suggestion, so I told my colleagues that 'perhaps' during the week after the parliamentary statement the parties at Westminster and in Northern Ireland should be invited to discussions at Lancaster House. I gave them the reasons that Harold had given me: to avoid a political vacuum and to give the Opposition parties the chance to witness the intransigence and unconstructiveness of Northern Ireland politicians, which would help ensure that bipartisan support for government policy in the province continued.

Because some of my right-wing colleagues seemed to think that there was an analogy between Northern Ireland and a colony moving towards independence, I reminded the meeting that as a result of the introduction of direct rule in 1972 there were now few Northern Ireland politicians capable of running the province. The old politicians of the past were irrelevant and the new breed of politicians, with a few exceptions, had not been schooled for government.

Two days after this meeting, I minuted my Cabinet colleagues that there was clearly now no alternative to direct rule. When I met Robert Lowry on 23 February, he confirmed that the Convention members felt that the assembly had run its course. The Alliance Party had continued to do its best to avert the collapse and its leaders had pressed for a meeting of the business committee. However, when this met it concerned itself only with procedure and decided that there should be a debate in the full Convention the following week on a UUUC motion calling for the acceptance of the Convention proposals. Obviously nothing was going to come out of this: what was there to debate? The motion before it constituted neither a report nor an answer to my letter of 14 January.

I informed Harold of this development and on 25 February sent him a minute for my Cabinet colleagues in which I stated: 'I am sure that no useful purpose would be served by any form of government intervention; it would be wholly unproductive.' Once the Convention ended, it would be necessary to make a low-key statement to the Commons saying that we contemplated no new action in the immediate future. This statement would avoid a crisis in the week following the end of the Convention; it was also a reflection of the view I had consistently put to colleagues: we should not stir up false hopes by pretending that there were other steps we could take to bring a return to devolved government.

There was growing pressure in the province for a referendum, I told Harold, particularly from Faulkner, Craig and the Alliance. There were also signs that the South was attracted to the idea and the Taoiseach might well want to discuss it with him next week. It was a possibility, too, that the loyalist paramilitaries would come out in favour of it, although this was very much tied up with the present power struggle between Craig and Paisley. A referendum obviously posed us with considerable difficulties, not least because of the implications for Scotland and Wales, but I had no doubt that in the Northern Ireland context alone it would be a mistake to commit ourselves one way or another at this stage.

On 26 February I reported further to my Cabinet colleagues. I proposed to make the Commons statement on Friday, 5 March; a debate would follow later. I told them that I had had a meeting in Dublin with the Irish government, whose concern was less the prospect of direct rule than that we might pull out. I had reassured Dr Fitzgerald on that score. My colleagues agreed with the approach I had outlined in my minute to Harold the day before. We should not be rushed into taking new decisions on future policy which, along with the suggestion of a conference of party leaders, would require consideration at a later meeting. They too felt that the referendum was not an attractive idea.

The Convention was about to end, and so also were any further admissions to special category status for convicted prisoners. The announcement that I had made in the Commons in November 1975 and again when I brought the necessary legislation to the House on 16 February had, to our surprise, brought no immediate response from the paramilitaries. Now, on 29 February, the day before the legislation went into effect, the first signs of protest began, temporarily overshadowing events in the Convention.

The issue of special category status had been high on our agenda since first taking office and it was not for lack of consideration that I had not ended it earlier. The office papers on the matter begin on 22 March 1974 and continue through to 5 March 1976 with a minute from Don Concannon reporting on arrangements for the treatment of prisoners convicted of offences after 1 March. We were simply unable to act without having prison cell accommodation and it was only when I decided to take the short cut of building the H-blocks at the Maze that we could begin to plan the ending of special category status in earnest. The new Maghaberry prison planned for 1984 did not enter into my short-term considerations.

Most of the office papers were concerned not with prison accommodation, which I dealt with myself outside committee, but with plans for a parole system which would reduce the prison population through earlier release. This would not only be for ODCs – ordinary decent criminals – but also for the special category prisoners. For months, Jack Donaldson and his staff considered a scheme on the lines of that used in Great Britain, with possible release after serving a third of a sentence and a full investigation of each individual case. This would in fact never have worked in Northern Ireland because the probation staff could not have carried out the investigations without risking their lives, and I should have ended the discussions early on.

However, it was only in early 1975, with the Gardiner Report's recommendation in support of the ending of special category status, that a reduction in the size of the prison population became of obvious importance. We considered a scheme which would have enabled us to use parole for ODCs only, but this was not legally practicable. A modification of the scheme, whereby ODCs would go before a parole board and other prisoners would be released according to my personal decision as Secretary of State, was also put forward. My experience of executive releases from detention made me dislike the idea, and my Cabinet colleagues felt similarly about it.

As I continued with the releases of detainees during 1975, the numbers in the special category compounds became more apparent. I was wondering what we could do when in May a new idea was put forward from the office. I wish I could acknowledge which of the ministers or civil servants came up with it – I suspect it was Jack Donaldson. The idea was simply to introduce, for Northern Ireland only, a scheme by which prisoners other than those sentenced for life, who had special release arrangements, would be conditionally released after serving half their sentence. If during the term of the remaining sentence, the released prisoner was convicted of a further prisonable offence, he would be liable to serve the balance of his sentence.

I was enthusiastic about the idea, but the Home Office officials were concerned because they did not want it for Great Britain. I argued that it was strictly applicable only to Northern Ireland and that all my advisers, who had specialist knowledge of violence in the province, were in favour. When I discussed the scheme with Roy Jenkins, he agreed to it and also to further proposals for improvements in the arrangements for the treatment of offenders, which were on lines already familiar in the rest of the UK: provision for community service orders, deferred sentences and hostel accommodation. The result, I told my Cabinet colleagues, would be that when the first order came into effect, about 350 prisoners would become eligible for release, of whom just over half would be special category prisoners. To avoid any feeling in Northern Ireland that I was granting an amnesty, I proposed to phase the releases over a month or two, although I might have to delay if there was a possibility of riots inside or outside the prisons.

My colleagues had agreed to my approach and I had outlined the parole scheme to the Commons on 5 November, announcing at the same time that two hundred cells would be available that month at the Maze prison. On this basis I would end special category status for those sentenced for crimes committed after 1 March 1976. I wished that I might have gone further and ended it for those already sentenced – seventy per cent of those in prison – had been convicted of serious crimes of violence – but, quite apart from the lack of prison cells, there were legal difficulties which appeared to rule out removing the concessions from existing prisoners because of the way the original Whitelaw decision had been reached in 1972.

The rioting on 29 February was only a foretaste of the problems that would arise over the ending of admissions to special category status. The major response was not to come until September 1976, after I had left the province, when republican prisoners in the H-blocks, beginning with Kieron Nugent, a nineteen-year-old Provisional sentenced for his part in a bombing mission, put themselves 'on the blanket': they refused to wear prison uniforms and covered themselves with a blanket. The protests intensified from 1978 onwards, with prisoners fouling the cells with excrement and smashing the furniture.

Despite all of this, I have no doubt that it was right to have ended special category status, which was confirmed by the judgment of the European Commission on Human Rights in December 1980. When the riots took place at the end of February 1976, the vicious murders in South Armagh in January were still fresh in my mind as an example of the true nature of paramilitary killings. To treat the perpetrators of such crimes as special, politically motivated people was morally and legally wrong; they were plain murderers. When the H-block hunger strikes of 1981 became a *cause célèbre*, I wished that the members of the media who were fêting the strikers could have witnessed the bloody crimes behind it all.

However, this was in the future. At the end of February 1976 the protest took the form of riots in which two people died and eleven were injured. Protestant demonstrators took to the streets of East Belfast and the brother of the Crumlin Road Prison Governor was kidnapped – probably the work of the Ulster Freedom Fighters – but he was, as we had expected, later set free.

The riots meant that I had to speak to the Commons on 1 March, only days before my Commons statement on the Convention. I reported: 'There was a great deal of hooliganism directed at deliberate disruption of life and wanton damage. Traffic was disrupted and roads blocked by hijacked vehicles. . . . There were over 150 bomb scares of which the great majority were deliberate hoaxes. . . . Government offices, schools and commercial premises were damaged by fire and churches were damaged by explosions.' The security forces had, I told the House, reacted promptly and decisively. Roads had quickly been reopened, order had been restored and nineteen arrests had already been made.

There was a danger that the feeling sparked off by the riots could merge with any feelings about the ending of the Convention, although I was advised that, despite the threats from Baird, there would be no repeat of the UWC strike. However, just in case we were about to run into difficulties, I had a word with all the parties in the House of Commons. I warned Mrs Thatcher and Airey Neave about loyalist protests and told them of my intention to make a low-key statement about the end of the Convention on 5 March when I would emphasise the problems of the economy. When I told Enoch Powell that the Convention would be ending, he said 'Thank God!', and was no less relieved to hear that the Stormont buildings themselves would be shut. He came with me to see the Prime Minister and agreed that our low-key approach was absolutely right. I told them both that there was little point in talking with the local politicians about the form of direct rule since they wanted the 'full panoply of government for Northern Ireland' and in some cases a government separate from the UK.

I concluded in my diary: 'I have to be very careful in the next few weeks. If I am to be moved shortly, I want to leave in such a way that the ends can be picked and darned together or rewoven so that something positive can develop. But it won't come in my time in Northern Ireland.'

The final Convention debate – though that is hardly the word for what went on – took place on 3 March. The idea of a voluntary coalition was put by William Craig, supported by fellow Vanguard member Glen Barr, and by the Alliance and the UPNI. David Bleakley at his sensible best reminded the members that it could be the last time 'for many a long day that this Chamber is a venue for elected representatives'. The loyalists dismissed the coalition proposal out of hand and Bill Craig was constantly interrupted with what he called 'crudity and coarseness' by a Miss Coulter and a Mr Hutchinson – both well-known loyalist 'politicians'. Glen Barr was also constantly interrupted, responding with 'I need big ears to hear big speeches from big mouths' and telling Mrs Paisley, 'Mind your own business, Eileen'.

Ian Paisley, in one of his interventions, told a story that was a new one on us in the office:

> A well known member of Vanguard, and a lecturer in law at Queen's University, was toying with his personal side-arm in a young lady's home. After seemingly unloading it, he pulled the trigger and surprise, surprise, it went off and the bullet embedded itself in a wall behind the girl, missing her head by a mere inch. Our man from Vanguard very quickly filled in the bullet hole, with Polyfilla. One wonders how good Polyfilla is for holes in the head.
>
> Mr Chairman, that might be an apocryphal story, but tonight the Hon Gentleman was certainly toying with a situation with which he was not prepared to come clean and out into the open.

Ernie Baird put his own gloss on history when he said that he found the proceedings hypocritical, for before 1972 there had been 'fifty years of progress, fifty years of peace and prosperity . . . the minority here were fairly treated'. His curious and illogical view was that 'loyal unionists' were not prepared to be governed indirectly from Westminster and he promised that if the Report was not implemented, 'We will face further conflict, confrontation and escalation.' The reasoning of his next point defeated me – 'Direct rule, or indirect rule, will lead inevitably to a united Ireland' – but I understood his conclusion that a united Ireland would not be accepted by the unionist and loyalist people and that he foresaw bloodshed and refugees.

Much of the debate continued in this spirit. Mrs Paisley called John Hume a 'twister, a political Jesuit twister'. Mrs Conn, another loyalist 'politician', was appalled by 'all the murderous acts that occur in this province' but was 'glad' when some people blew themselves up and were 'removed from the face of the earth'. Colonel Brush of the Down Orange Welfare justified his paramilitary organisation on the grounds that he and his friends were not allowed to join the reserve force, and I felt as Anne Dickson of UPNI did when she described herself as 'amazed at the content of this speech by an officer of the British army'. She could have added that he had been a Deputy Lieutenant of County Down! What he wanted, she alleged, was confrontation.

I was, however, reassured by the speech of Hugh Smyth of the UVF who, referring to the role of the politicians during the UWC strike, said that they could not jump on the paramilitary bandwagon twice. It was confirmation for me that the politicians no longer spoke for the paramilitaries, except when they opposed the ending of special category status. Ernie Baird, for example, was in favour of 'political status' for those 'misguided or otherwise who were doing their best at every level to bring normality back to this country' but was against it for 'rebels and gangsters'. When was a gangster not a gangster? It depended on which side of the divide he was born.

The usual conspiracy theory was in evidence when the Rev Beattie alleged that it was my hope that the 'Provisional IRA would be able to take over by force of arms before the loyalist population are in a position to resist them'. He also claimed that I had sent the RUC chasing after him in 'two places at the same time'. I did not know what he was on about but it reminded me of an alleged remark made by Paisley that John Hume recalled: 'I would rather trust the devil himself than the RUC.'

In Paisley's own speech in the Convention, he defended his role in the UUUC discussions of Bill Craig's document on a voluntary coalition and finished by saying: 'The British government now has a duty to tell us what the future of this province is to be.' On this he was absolutely right. The Convention was effectively over and I now had to take the next steps.

The next day, 4 March, I wrote to Sir Robert Lowry reminding him of my letter of 14 January in which I had decided that a four-week recall 'should be sufficient for the Convention to make progress on the matters referred to it'. I had now concluded: 'The report of the inter-party talks and of the debates which have taken place have made it plain that no progress has been made, or is likely to be made, in the Convention on reaching agreement on proposals which would command sufficiently widespread acceptance throughout the community in Northern Ireland to provide stable and effective government.' I told him that I had therefore advised the Queen to dissolve the Convention under the Northern Ireland Act 1974; an Order in Council would dissolve it on 6 March. I thanked him for the impartiality and independence of his chairmanship. He and his staff had indeed performed their roles impeccably, unlike most of the Convention members.

All that the Convention had done was to show yet again the basic divisions in the province and the paucity of political ability there. I was relieved that it was at an end, particularly given the rowdy scenes of the final meeting, and was sure that there would be no regrets or problems over it in the province. For the foreseeable future we were back to direct rule. I had discussed the situation with my junior ministers now that there were to be 'no more political talks and no initiatives'. They had done a marvellous job, as was evident alone from the long list of legislation that they had handled at Westminster on topics from agriculture and transport to education. They would now have to show themselves even more as fit for the 'positive' government which I was talking about, and I reminded them, 'We do not arise from Northern Ireland. We are not local people and anything we say or do must take that into account.'

My discussions with the junior ministers were part of the preparation for my statement to Parliament on 5 March. Earlier that day the Taoiseach visited Harold Wilson in London and at our meeting he confirmed the view I had earlier gained in Dublin: the Irish government wanted unification but accepted that there was no alternative to direct rule at this point. Harold, in one of the asides at which he was a master, indicated to the Republic's ministers – and thus to me – that I was to stay in Northern Ireland. I was pleased: I had no desire to return to Whitehall.

I began my Commons statement by announcing that the Convention was dissolved as of midnight that day. The role of the Convention members was over and Stormont would be closed. The people of Northern Ireland would now have to work only through their elected representatives at Westminster who 'will be the normal channel of communications with ministers'. Again I said that there was no instant solution to the problems of Northern Ireland:

> It would be a grave mistake to pretend that there was one, let alone to rush forward with some new devices. It is clearly not possible at this time to make progress towards a devolved system of government for Northern Ireland. This still remains the government's aim, but it does not

> contemplate any major new initiative for some time to come, though we shall always be ready to entertain constructive and responsible ideas from those in Northern Ireland who are prepared to work together for Northern Ireland.

I said that we now had to concentrate on the direct rule that had been with us since the Ulster workers' strike and the twin aims of government policy were to work to restore law and order by bringing criminals to justice in the courts and to improve the economic and employment situation in the province. In order to tackle these twin problems there was an 'immediate need for a period of constitutional stability'.

The discussion afterwards was muted. Airey Neave wanted me to set up an advisory body of some kind to prevent a political vacuum, but I told him that I was firmly against this – it was an English idea and there were plenty of advisory bodies in the province already – although I would be prepared to meet anybody who had constructive advice to offer.

Not surprisingly Jim Molyneaux supported direct rule but warned that the people of the province 'wanted the same degree of protection and security as is enjoyed by all other citizens of the UK'. Gerry Fitt identified the 'wreckers' and the 'man personally responsible for the downfall of the Convention' – the Hon Member for Antrim North – who 'did everything possible to ensure the defeat of the Convention'.

Bill Craig referred to his voluntary coalition idea, which he believed could have been agreed had there been a 'little more skill in the leadership of both sides'. He asked me to encourage further exchanges because he thought there was a real possibility of reaching agreement one day. I agreed with him that his concept, which did not require 'fancy franchises or devices, and which could have arisen from the community on a normal constitution', seemed worth discussing, but it 'needed wisdom, and the wisdom was not forthcoming'. However, I said that anything I and the government could do to encourage inter-party talks in the months and years ahead would be done. I could not in fact see much hope in this; it was direct rule that I needed to concentrate on.

One point that I wished to get across was that representations to my office must come from the Westminster MPs, and in my reply to Airey Neave I said that 'we must break away from the constant nonsense which takes place in Northern Ireland of demanding meetings with ministers, with the television cameras outside the door ready to play it up'. I was thinking particularly of a recent incident when Roland Moyle was on duty and thirty-five Convention members, including Paisley, had come down to the Castle demanding to see me. They were not allowed in because they had not made an appointment; I was anyway not there. However, when someone came out of the main entrance, they forced their way in and there was a scuffle in which a policeman had his arm broken. One of the members also managed to break a table when he sat on it! And these were elected representatives! The demands to see the Secretary of State had, as I said to Airey Neave, been accompanied by the suggestion that unless I conceded, 'my political career will be ruined'. I told the Commons that 'the "battle of the broken arm" is Paisley's last stand' and that I would continue to follow the 'procedures of the United Kingdom'.

My statement to the Commons produced no air of tension, as in 1972, since everyone had expected a continuation of direct rule. There was the same acceptance in the country in general and in Northern Ireland in particular, where the end of the Convention was a non-event. It seemed that the politicians' chagrin at the indefinite postponement of a devolved government was not shared by the population at large, and certainly there was no tension in the loyalist areas.

I did not consider the failure of the Convention a defeat. The world at large had at least been shown the falseness of the argument that Ulstermen could succeed where the English had failed, and once again that the problem of Northern Ireland was not capable of a nice easy solution. Within the province the politicians had learned too that if they wanted a devolved government, they would have to come to agreement amongst themselves. It was not, as they had come to believe since 1972, a matter of leaving it to the Secretary of State.

Although I had not written off a return to 'initiatives' at some future date, my job now was to make direct rule effective and in particular to pursue my policy of the primacy of the police.

Chapter 11

CONTINUING DIRECT RULE

In the weeks before the Convention ended, we had all agreed in the Stormont office that our future actions in the province would be based on two main principles. First, we would provide good government, concentrating on practical issues rather than constitutional aspirations or, as a later paper to my Cabinet colleagues put it, 'hobgoblins'. And second, we would not hesitate to legislate for the good of Northern Ireland simply because the measures might seem more appropriate for a local assembly; at the same time we would avoid making changes in institutions and procedures which could prejudice the possibility of reintroducing a devolved government or which could give direct rule an appearance of permanence or a move towards integration.

To show our commitment, we agreed to go out and about in the province as much as possible, talking to people and, more important, being seen to do so. A typical diary entry of mine from March 1976 reads: 'Went on Friday morning to the Antrim coast and visited the Coleraine Institution. The purpose was to talk about the 11-plus in the curious grammar school set-up in Northern Ireland. Then went down to Bushmills, the whiskey distillery, and on to a fisheries unit of the Department of Agriculture. Back to Belfast where I spent the evening with corporals of the Kings Own Scottish Borderers. On Saturday morning, the Lord Mayor's Show, on view to people right in the middle of Belfast. Addressed the Junior Chamber of Commerce in the evening, while Colleen had a group of social workers to dinner up at Stormont.'

I always learned something on these occasions, for example, the soldiers I invited for a meal one evening told me about their practical experience of work on the border and of co-operation with the police. There was still plenty of security work to do, although since the ending of detention security matters took up much less of my time, partly because I was no longer directly involved in them through the signing of interim custody orders and partly because of the growing importance of the RUC. This meant that I was now in a position to turn more attention to Westminster but I decided that I wished to concentrate my energies on the province. Despite this, within two weeks of the announcement of continuing direct rule I found myself involved, at least temporarily, in Westminster affairs.

I had known from Jim Callaghan that Harold Wilson was intending to resign but I was not expecting it to happen as soon as it did. Jim told me, as I reported in my diary of 13 March, that 'Harold had had a word with him some six months' ago, indicating that he would be going during this parliament; his aim was not to fight another election. I am sure that Jim was never given any idea of timing. Then, a week before the resignation, Harold indicated to him that he would be going "relatively" soon.' The announcement was in fact made on 16 March. I had never been close to Harold but I had great admiration for him and I saw his going as the end of an era. In my diary I commented: 'It is a Fleet Street way of putting it to say that he led the left "by the nose" but he did understand the Labour Party and all it stood for from his Lib/Lab Yorkshire background, through his father and uncle. I had a very high regard for him. Those who criticise him for lack of clarity misunderstand that the clear points in politics are often puffballs. His words "A week is a long time in politics" show his comprehension of the nature of party politics. He understood that policies develop.'

I had promised to be Jim's campaign manager in the election for the next Party leader and Prime Minister. He was the right man for the job and I thought it very important that he should get it. I decided that he should be kept out of the limelight during the campaign, and I agreed with Stan Orme, who was Michael Foot's campaign manager, that we should insist to our supporters on having no personal attacks. I knew that the electorate were rightly not enamoured of Westminster's childish point-scoring tactics.

There were about hundred members who might vote for Jim but in the first ballot the number was eighty-four, although ninety-two or -three had promised their vote. Stan and I compared notes on our 'promises', which explained the discrepancy in Jim's vote since some members had made double promises. Roy Jenkins pulled out of the contest at this stage and as I commented in my diary: 'I don't know what is going to happen to Roy. My regard for him has always been high, although he has never bothered to get out into the constituencies; this is his weakness.' The other candidates, Tony Crosland and Denis Healey, were, I thought, 'foolish to have entered the contest but I suppose that they felt they had to put markers down for the future'. In the final ballot, Jim was ahead of Michael Foot, as we had known all along from the arithmetic would be the case.

The speeches made on the announcement were of the highest

calibre, whether from Harold, Jim, the other candidates or from Cledwyn Hughes, the Chairman of the Parliamentary Labour Party. In Jim's acceptance speech he appealed beyond the narrow range of Labour Party support and showed his characteristic approach of never talking down to people. It was an occasion which showed the essential quality of Parliament. Afterwards when I went to his room, Jim told me how proud he was to be Prime Minister of the 'greatest country in the world'. Besides the personal pleasure I took in his victory, I was more than ever convinced of his rightness for the job.

Once he had seen the Queen on 6 April, Jim had to decide on ministerial changes. There was no question of a move for myself; I had told Jim in a short discussion we had immediately after his election that I wanted to go back to Northern Ireland. I was, however, marginally and briefly involved in the backroom manoeuvres about appointments. Stan Orme and I of course enjoyed a special confidence and he had told me the night before the result was declared, when we all knew what it would be, that Michael was going to speak to Jim about the 'top jobs'. The 'left' evidently did not want Roy Jenkins as Foreign Secretary and Michael was going to press for the promotion of Stan and of Albert Booth. When I told Jim this, he tersely enjoined, 'They will have to learn that I decide these things.' Like most Prime Ministers, he regarded the whole business as an unpleasant necessity.

I commented in my diary on 26 April: 'Jim told me early on that he was not going to offer Roy the Foreign Office. Whether it was a question of his going to Europe I do not know, but I do know that it was not because of Michael Foot but because he wanted to give the job to Tony Crosland.' Inevitably, the appointments caused ruffled feathers, and when two Cabinet colleagues went to Jim to object that they had not been moved to more senior jobs, he told them that they must decide whether to accept the present offers because there was nothing else; one of them was given twelve hours to consider. Both of course accepted. Stan Orme told me that he had taken the job of Minister of Social Security on the understanding that he would be offered something else later in the year, but there was no acrimony from him: he realised that the Cabinet was, quite simply, full.

There were difficulties too over some of the junior ministerial appointments. For example, Roy Jenkins wanted Alex Lyon to be moved from the Home Office – it was common gossip that they had rarely spoken in the Department for the past two years, with Alex regarding Roy as a 'drawing-room Liberal'. Alex went, but Jim replaced him with Brynmor John, whom Roy also did not want. When Jim overruled his objections, Roy told him that he had never been spoken to like that by Harold in all the time he had been Prime

Minister, to which Jim retorted, 'Harold is no longer Prime Minister'. Brynmor John was still at the Home Office when I later became Home Secretary and he proved a first-rate administrator as well as a sympathetic minister on immigration and race relations, with a far better understanding of the issues than many of those who talk a lot about them.

Jim had another chat with me about my own position but my mood had not changed except in being even further from the idea of a move. I commented in my diary of 26 April: 'What I would like to do is stick with this job, until July anyway, and I would not then object to going to the back-benches. I am finding that I am not particularly ambitious. I enjoy the Irish job but I have had enough of being away from Colleen and the children. Many people say that they are not in politics for the promotion or the glamour; I can only say that I enjoy being Secretary of State for Northern Ireland but I do not really want to move elsewhere.' The truth was that I was hooked on Northern Ireland and I wanted to get back there to carry on the work of direct rule.

I was sorely going to miss Stan Orme and also Jack Donaldson, who was moving to London as Minister of the Arts. I discussed the changes needed in the Northern Ireland team with the Prime Minister and agreed that Roland Moyle should stay on as Minister of State, responsible for the Departments of Commerce, Manpower Services and Education. He would be assisted by a new junior minister, Ray Carter, from Birmingham, who was to have special responsibility for education. Don Concannon was also to stay on, promoted to Minister of State, and responsible for the Departments of Environment, Health and Social Services, and Agriculture. A second new junior minister, Jimmy Dunn from Liverpool, was to assist him, with special responsibility for agriculture. For the time being we decided not to have a replacement for Jack Donaldson in the House of Lords. I issued a statement detailing the new appointments, with the Secretary of State retaining 'personal oversight of constitutional issues, security and law and order'. I also had 'direct responsibility for the Department of Finance', and was overall responsible for all the departments.

Gerry Fitt expressed his disappointment publicly with the ministerial appointments. He had vested his political future in the setting up of the Executive and power sharing, and was taking the return to direct rule particularly badly. He was also suspicious of Jim Callaghan's earlier support for the Northern Ireland Labour Party and of so-called deals with the Unionists at Westminster. He told me on 7 May that although Don and I were alright, the new appointments were part of a 'Protestant plot', a deliberate change of policy by Jim Callaghan. I tried my best to get across that this was a load of rubbish;

Jimmy Dunn was anyway a Catholic! I thought that a brief meeting with the Prime Minister would help cool the situation but it did not prove the best of occasions, as I noted in my diary. 'There was amazement on the Private Secretaries' faces as Gerry talked about "community groups" in West Belfast and indeed everything under the sun other than the immediate issue. They simply did not know how to translate it all into Private Secretaries' notes. But eventually Gerry turned to changes of policy and a rumour that we had done a deal with Enoch.' He was given his reassurance that this was not true.

Such meetings did not mean that Gerry was in our pockets. There were never any deals with him, or with anyone else, and Gerry was always his own man. So too was Enoch and at about the same time I arranged for Jim to meet him so that Enoch could express his views about local government and representation at Westminster.

It was not only ministers who changed at this time but also Frank Cooper, who returned to Whitehall to be Parliamentary Secretary at the Ministry of Defence, where he had served so long in the past. I was very sorry to see him go, and also his wife Peggy, and I wished that I could have said so publicly, just as I wished there was some effect in my denying the again-repeated allegation that Frank had been talking with the Provisionals during the ceasefire. Frank's replacement was Brian Cubbon, whom I had known at the Home Office and who had once been Private Secretary to Jim, who spoke highly of him. I realised that he was bound to have a different way of dealing with things from Frank but he was an able man and I thought that a changed approach at this time might well be good for Northern Ireland.

In his first few days in the office, we talked about Northern Ireland's economy. This was a deep-seated problem on which Stan Orme had spent much time over the past two years and now we had the opportunity to concentrate on it far more. It was a way of showing our long-term commitment to the province. As I later told my Cabinet colleagues, the economic situation in Northern Ireland had worsened; the factors favouring investment from abroad were disappearing and labour costs, like those for fuel, were no longer advantageous. There was an average unemployment figure of ten per cent but even more of a disgrace was the figure of thirty per cent for the west of the province.

At the time when the Convention ended, Stan Orme had prompted me to set up a review team to report on economic and industrial strategy for Northern Ireland, to establish a Northern Ireland Development Agency on the lines of those in Wales and Scotland, and to examine the structure of the Economic Council where government employers and trade unions came together. I had announced this in the Commons on 26 March, when Stan Orme also spoke of the particular problem of the Harland and Wolff shipyard, in which he had been closely involved since March 1974.

The world recession and the collapse in the demand for tankers had put the yard into serious trouble and Stan had worked constantly to help it and to persuade my Cabinet colleagues of the need to provide still more money. It was Stan who with much effort had worked out a scheme for workers' participation; that it has never come into operation is due to the attitude of the workforce. In 1974 we had brought the yard into public ownership, not for any doctrinal reason but to save it: whatever the role of its workers in the UWC strike of May 1974, the closure of the yard would have made thirty-six per cent of the engineering labour force in the province unemployed. If the later demand of the trade unions and workers there to be made part of the nationalised British Shipbuilders had been met, the yard would have closed long ago, as it would if we had followed a philosophy of free market forces, so beloved of Ulster politicians at Westminster. The real Ulster view was shown when the economic review – the Quigley Report – was published in September 1976. It recommended more money for infrastructure and technological investment, with subsidies to reduce energy costs.

The Report was a legacy of Stan's work, as was the Fair Employment Act of 1976 which was based on the recommendations of a working party set up in the days of Willie Whitelaw and chaired by the then Minister of State for Northern Ireland, William Van Straubenzee. Its work was to consider the problem of job discrimination on religious and political grounds. Stan had talked to me often about discrimination in engineering and he had quickly come to the conclusion that Catholics could not be given skilled jobs for which they had not been properly trained. The long-term answer was to improve training and apprenticeship facilities, which is the policy he had fostered and which we now developed under direct rule. The Fair Employment Agency set up under the 1976 Act met with scepticism from the Unionists but I believe that it has helped to ease the problem of job discrimination, which undoubtedly existed in the province.

Stan had also developed close relationships with the Northern Ireland Committee of the Irish Confederation of Trade Unions, which looked both to London and to Dublin. Its General Secretary, Billy Blease – later Lord Blease, worked hard on behalf of the Northern Ireland workforce but he and its other leaders faced the problem of representing members who had different political aspirations. There was always an undercurrent of opinion amongst the membership in favour of an Ulster-based trade union organisation, which surfaced whenever there was a particularly strong mood of 'Ulster nationalism'.

In Northern Ireland a trade unionist is first and last a loyalist/unionist, which is one reason why a Labour Party in the province could not succeed and why 'contracting in' and not 'contracting out' was the law there, unlike in Great Britain. Understanding this basic difference between trade unions in Northern Ireland and Britain was essential in looking at the province's economic problems.

When I met my Cabinet colleagues in early May, I asked them and particularly the Chancellor to consider the economic needs of Northern Ireland when making policy. By the time of this meeting, we had given careful thought in our new Northern Ireland Office team to effecting fair government for the province and I had submitted papers on our thoughts to the Cabinet committee. I told my colleagues that I was still firmly against the Tory suggestions made at the ending of the Convention for a restructuring of local government and the setting up of an advisory body at Stormont. The former would only favour the loyalists, and the latter was ignoring the lessons of history.

I recommended no change in the legislative arrangements at Westminster. Northern Ireland already did well for attention in the House of Commons, with a forty-five minute question time every four weeks, general debates, four meetings a year of the Northern Ireland Committee and a separate examination of Northern Ireland legislation. I was definitely opposed to the idea of a Northern Ireland Select Committee, mainly because of problems with security, but thought that the existing Expenditure Committee might also look at particular issues such as education and agriculture. To try to reduce the number of Orders in Council, British bills would be extended to the province wherever policy needs were identical but I would continue to protect the special nature of the Northern Irish statute book. I warned of the dangers of laws on homosexuality and abortion, where Catholic and Protestant alike were firmly against change.

I would be discussing these procedures, I told my colleagues, with the Northern Irish parties at Westminster before July when the direct rule legislation was due for renewal. There would, however, be few problems about it. Gerry Fitt was not interested in the mechanics of government and the Unionists would settle for more attention for Northern Ireland on the floor of the House.

One problem that did arise was over people in Northern Ireland not necessarily turning to the MP of their own constituency. I had reminded all the Northern Ireland ministers of my statement of 5 March that direct rule meant that the principal channel of communication with us should now be through the elected Westminster representatives. The difficulty of this 'English' approach was shown in early June, when

Enoch Powell complained to me that other Northern Ireland MPs were interfering in his constituency.

I knew of old that Catholics wrote to Gerry Fitt from all over the province, which is what Enoch's complaint was in effect about. We could not stop the practice but we tried to find a compromise by always having a copy of any correspondence sent to the relevant Westminster MP, with an explanatory note to the constituent. Gerry told me, however, that Catholics did not want this; they were afraid when they saw that a copy of a letter concerning them had gone to a loyalist MP. He gave the example of a woman in Belfast who had been 'burnt out' three times. He had written to Don Concannon about her and a copy of the letter had been sent to the appropriate loyalist MP. As a result she had received a telephone call warning her, 'You have been burnt out three times and we'll get you again.' As Gerry said, 'We are not in Great Britain.' Northern Ireland was different, and I directed that in future letters should only be sent on with the approval of the constituent.

In the province itself, there was little problem and certainly little opposition to direct rule. Public opinion polls showed that it was acceptable, if for negative reasons, to both sides of the divide: the Catholics preferred government from London to a loyalist government at Stormont, and the loyalists preferred it to a Stormont government shared with the republicans.

These views were not of course shared by the politicians, who still wanted devolved government – on their own terms. Some of them went to extremes. Ernest Baird, for example, claimed that direct rule 'with its nominated boards, its biased housing programmes and its encouragement of Southern involvement in our commerce and industry' would take jobs from loyalists which they had won by 'hard work and industry over fifty years'. He further alleged that the British government was 'deliberately creating a situation where a million Protestants would become refugees' and that Britain was ruling 'illegally' in Ireland.

Jointly with Ian Paisley, he promised that on 24 May firm action would be taken 'within hours' to prevent the destruction of their province. This was linked to a deteriorating security situation on the border and on 25 May the Ulster Service Corps, a loyalist vigilante group, intimated that they would begin covert and overt patrols of roads in mid-Ulster to try to curb increasingly frequent Provisional IRA attacks. There was nothing new in such threats and they all fell flat, despite flamboyant talk from John McKeague, a loyalist paramilitary, about taking a 'percentage of the minority with us in a new loyalty to Northern Ireland and to Belfast, perhaps with a new flag and a new national anthem'. What mattered was that there was no action from the UDA. Indeed its Commander, Andy Tyrie, left ostentatiously on a visit to Canada; he was not going to mobilise his men for the benefit of the politicians.

The response of Bill Craig was more meaningful. He damned the resurgence of independence talk as 'complete nonsense' and appealed for a round-table conference of all Unionists who wanted a strong devolved government within the UK. He claimed that the attitudes of the SDLP and the Irish government were 'encouraging changes in the political situation' and he was supported by John Hume, who believed that a new devolved administration was the only way to deal with the economic and social problems facing the province.

We wondered in the office if this meant talks were going on between the SDLP and some Unionists, but we thought this unlikely. In fact, representatives of the UUUC had five meetings with the SDLP between March and June, as we learned on 4 June, when the information was leaked by, it was alleged, Dr Paisley. The Official Unionists accused him of a breach of confidence, while Baird accused the SDLP of engineering a plot to split the UUUC, to which Martin Smyth counter-charged that he had acted in accordance with a mandate given him at the ending of the Convention. However, at a UUUC meeting on 7 June, a motion was carried – by no means unanimously – forbidding further discussion until all the relevant documents had been scrutinised. The feeling among Official Unionists and Bill Craig and the VUPP that the talks could succeed was, not surprisingly, shared by the Alliance Party and the NILP, and the talks were in fact renewed on 14 June.

A UUUC resolution passed on 28 June tried to set the record straight: 'The present talks involving the SDLP are with the Official Unionists only, and while recognising and accepting that the Rev Martin Smyth had understood that he had a mandate for the talks from the UUUC, the Official Unionists now confirm that two of the component parties – the DUP and UUUM – are not now, nor have they been, involved in these talks and that there was no formal mandate from the UUUC.' On the same day, the eighth meeting took place between the OUP and SDLP but little progress was made and in the *Irish Times* of 29 June, Harry West intimated that the talks would end within two weeks unless something positive emerged from them. He subsequently denied that he had intended to convey such a negative impression, saying that there was no deadline for the talks, which would continue for as long as there was anything to discuss, but that the OUP would be considering very carefully after about two weeks whether this was indeed the case.

With the agreement of the SDLP, no meetings were held during the two weeks leading up to 12 July, the day of the Orange marches, but much to my surprise there were hints in the speeches made then of a possible recall of the Convention. The next meeting was on 20 July and was followed on 23 July by two statements. The first, issued jointly by the OUP and SDLP representatives, was to the effect that wide areas of agreement had been reached on the need for a devolved administration in Northern Ireland with powers greater than those of the Assembly, but that a deep difference of view remained on the method of forming the Executive. The second statement was from OUP officials and paid tribute to the efforts of the Rev Smyth and Captain Ardill; it undertook to report areas of both agreement and disagreement to other parties in the UUUC and to HMG 'at the highest level'.

I was sceptical, asking in my diary: 'What agreements have they made? What are we supposed to be talking about? It is all an example of the never-never world some of the politicians live in when they talk of an agreement being reached and there is no sign of it.' The politicians were ignoring the realities of Northern Ireland politics. Direct rule remained the only policy for the foreseeable future and it was indicative that after the July meeting, Martin Smyth went off to the United States, not to return until the end of August.

Throughout the months since the ending of the Convention, there had continued to be security incidents involving the Provisional IRA and also the loyalist paramilitaries, particularly the UVF, but they were not comparable with the years before 1975. Even the ending of special category status after 1 March had not brought any announcement from the Provisionals of the ending of their ceasefire, although the last contact with them had been early in the year. Our view was still that they did not want to alienate the Catholic community and we were not going to give them any excuse to claim that we had ended the ceasefire. They had called it; they must end it.

This did not prevent the Tory front-bench from pursuing us in the Commons about the so-called talks. In reply I constantly emphasised that the security forces responded to the level of violence; the number of Provisionals arrested and convicted was improving all the time. I parried the questions about the talks in this way on firm security advice that we should not yet announce their ending. I was put into some difficulty on 28 April when questioned about a public condemnation of the talks by the Irish Minister of Justice but, as always, I emphasised that there were no negotiations.

The question of the talks was raised again in the Commons on 27 May, after a newspaper report that the President of Sinn Fein had said that he had found them valuable. Once again I explained that my staff had only talked to individuals belonging to legal organisations and added, 'The exchanges with Sinn Fein have not been anything like as frequent as many people appear to think, but there was great advantage in them about a year ago.'

Nevertheless, there was still questioning and on 1 July Ian Gow, then PPS to Margaret Thatcher, asked if I would make a statement about the discussions held by my 'department' with the Provisional Sinn Fein. I made my usual noises about no negotiations, but he came back to ask me if I did not think that the talks were damaging to the morale of the forces in Northern Ireland! I vented my feelings in the office afterwards about this naive opposition – do they really think that the contacts were a whim of politicians following a chat in the smoke-room and that the security chiefs did not know all about them? At the time, however, I restrained myself sufficiently to reply: 'I thought I was right eighteen months ago to take advantage of the opportunity to break the log-jam that had built up over the previous seven years. I would have been wrong not to attempt something then. If that is again necessary in the future, I shall do it.'

On the same occasion Airey Neave asked me to give the date of the last occasion on which the talks had taken place, which I told him that I was not prepared to do. However, by the end of the month I was advised that the considerations which had previously kept me silenced were no longer as important, and when the subject came up in the Commons, I said that 'there have been no talks since the early part of this year, and no talks are in prospect'. I added that nobody associated with me was involved in any talks currently being mentioned. 'Whether other people outside the government machine are involved, on their own initiative, in talking to the Provisional Sinn Fein is not a matter for me.'

This was a reference to a recent incident at an Oxford conference of the British/Irish Association when, as I told the Commons, 'I was approached by someone who claimed to carry a personal message from David O'Connell, threatening increased violence in Ireland if there were not an early political agreement between the parties. I did not seek that meeting; I did not know the man from Adam. I hope that because I received a message in that way, no one will say that I am arranging talks.' I had cut the man short, telling him that he had better speak to his own Foreign Minister, and I had had a word with Garret Fitzgerald, who was at the conference. The man was a journalist and I did not want an exaggerated account of the incident to appear in the media.

Early in August, the Provisional Sinn Fein's President, Rory O'Brady, confirmed at a press conference my announcement about the ending of the talks and claimed that the government had 'changed its attitude and is now bent more on a military solution' in Northern Ireland. He went on to say that it would be difficult for Sinn Fein to speak to people who had treated their President as he had been treated, like a common criminal. This was a reference to me excluding him individually from Northern Ireland in July under the Prevention of Terrorism Act.

The Provisional IRA ceasefire had never of course lived up to its name but it and the talks had helped me to make changes in security policy that would otherwise have been difficult to attain. In 1975 and 1976 the police increasingly took the lead in security matters, with more criminals going through the courts, and the policy of primacy of the police was increasingly accepted in Great Britain by Parliament. It helped in making it more widely understood in Northern Ireland that Enoch Powell, in a debate on 25 March, noted the increasing numbers in the RUC and its reserves and said of security policy: 'The whole operation has to be seen less as a military operation than as a police operation, and increasingly the UDR and the army must be part of a strategy which is a police strategy.' He went on to comment perceptively:

> Too often people who discuss operations in Northern Ireland seem to think that they are talking about a battle between armoured formations in the North German plain; and sometimes the army itself finds it difficult to distinguish the realities of Northern Ireland from the different strategic and tactical backgrounds in which its members have been trained and brought up. . . .
>
> There is not yet sufficient understanding on the part of the army of the mentality of the people and the environment in which they are operating. For that reason also I say that the army, as well as the UDR, has to be fitted into a pattern which will be under the primacy of the police.

His remarks complemented all that I was saying publicly and in the Northern Ireland Office about the role of the police. It was through them and the use of the law that terrorists should be arrested and convicted. Tory front-bench spokesmen were alleging at the time that terrorist leaders were not being picked up because of a lack of will on my part; since they have been in power, they have come to see things differently. What mattered was to have evidence that would stand up in court. Although it was frustrating that we could not charge those who came out of the Provisional IRA and UVF special category compounds with membership of an illegal organisation, I stressed in the Commons during the debate on 25 March:

> If I were to believe the stories, the rumours perhaps, of people in Northern Ireland who are members of proscribed organisations and if I were to put them in a list, the list would be very long. But rumour and innuendo are not enough. At the time of the Ulster workers' strike, there

> were those who said that certain well-known people were members of proscribed organisations or at least of paramilitary organisations. I do not know, and it is not enough to believe rumours. The fact has to be proved in the courts. Otherwise one is failing in arguing to people that the rule of the law is what matters.

I was certainly not prepared to use the methods of the South on membership, where the word of a Chief Superintendent would suffice for conviction. Sam Silkin, the Attorney General, made it clear when he said: 'I understand why this provision can be used in the Republic, but to translate it to Northern Ireland, where there is a divided community, would not be acceptable and it would set back the acceptability of the police throughout the community which, above all, is important in pursuing terrorism.'

The RUC's success in doing this was already showing in the increased figures for terrorist convictions, and co-operation with the security authorities in the Republic was also improving. It would have been even better if it had been possible to have a full extradition agreement to deal with known criminals at liberty in the South and also if more was done about the Provisional IRA's 'active service units' operating near the border. Relationships between our governments were, however, temporarily soured in early May by a border incident.

Members of the SAS had gone out to a covert observation post on the border, had missed their way and ended up three hundred yards over the border where, as luck would have it, the Garda had picked them up. They were in civilian clothes but had shown their identity cards. The Irish army had evidently been in favour of simply returning them, but not the Garda. A request for their unit to be informed, via the Garda's Dundalk line with the RUC in Newry, was not met. Meanwhile other SAS men had driven out to look for their missing colleagues and they too had been picked up! By 2 am, two men in uniform and six in civilian clothes were in Dundalk on charges.

We had previously been assured by the Irish government that any accidental border crossing by our soldiers would not cause problems but that morning, after contact between our respective Chief Constables, we learned that there was apparently a new ruling from the Republic's Director of Public Prosecutions. The men would continue to be held. I instructed the Ambassador in Dublin to see Garret Fitzgerald and tell him very firmly that this would do great harm to public opinion in Britain and that we were supposed to be operating together against a common enemy. Garret, however, was at a meeting and the Ambassador was unable to see him until later.

The incident was widely reported in the press and I brought it up at the Cabinet sub-committee meeting on 6 May. I thought that if the men were not released quickly, there would be considerable controversy and cross-border co-operation could be damaged. Jim, as promised, afterwards phoned the Taoiseach but by this time it was too late to drop the charges. The Ambassador arranged for a defence lawyer and the men were sent back on bail, at a cost of £5,000 each.

I issued a press statement in which I congratulated the army on its work and pointed out that many people were crossing the border in South Armagh, some of whom were murderous thugs, including the killers of the ten Protestant workers in early January. I cited the fact that over the years forty soldiers had been killed near the border, and in recent months members of the UDR had been killed there and seventeen soldiers had been wounded from shootings. I wanted to show the world that the security forces in South Armagh were not playing at soldiers, and to boost the army morale.

When the SAS soldiers came up in court in Dublin, they were acquitted on the charge of being in possession of arms with intent to end life and found guilty, with a fine of £100, for possessing unlicensed arms! Despite my inclination to refer tartly to Garret Fitzgerald's sarcastic public comment about the SAS's ability to map-read, I went out of my way to praise security co-operation with the South. The incident had shown that relations with the Republic were not easy and that with all the committees on earth, cross-border arrangements could still go wrong. I wondered whether perhaps it also showed that the Almighty was not at least partly on our side – imagine what could have happened when the men were picked up!

I was glad that I had curbed my ill-temper with the South over the incident. Such feelings are never a sensible guide to action and afterwards in Dublin I had a long and constructive discussion with Irish ministers and the Opposition leader Jack Lynch, in which they came up with valuable ideas for improving day-to-day co-operation on border security.

The co-operation between the RUC and the Garda was indeed good and was partly a reflection of the improved organisation of the RUC. We were still working steadily towards achieving the primacy of the police and by this time were nearing completion of the investigation into security policy which I had announced to the Commons on 12 January: 'With ministerial colleagues from other departments I shall examine the action and resources required for the next few years to maintain law and order in Northern Ireland. This will include how best to achieve the primacy of the police, the size and the role of locally recruited forces, and the progressive reduction of the army as soon as is safely practicable.' As I had also told the Commons, the Convention parties would be invited to give me their views in writing, which they had subsequently done.

I had laid it down at the start that there would be no change in the responsibility of the police to the law, nor in the responsibility of the army to ministers, who in turn were responsible to the UK Parliament. As work on our committee developed, we broke down our remit into various headings: the threat to law and order; the concept of securing police acceptance and effectiveness; the measures and forces required; the time-scale of change; changes in the law; public relations; community effort; and financial implications. The last posed little problem for within reason Treasury funds were available.

The work was considerable and time-consuming and on 14 June I told the Commons that I made no apologies for not yet revealing the results of our labours. 'The committee would not be much use if it had produced a quick report in a couple of months. Irish history is full of examples of quick responses and superficial proposals that have set off policy in disastrously wrong directions. My ministerial colleagues and I have been determined to avoid this kind of mistake and to take a long, hard look at what is involved in achieving the rule of law in the long term.' However, I was able, in advance of the full report, to announce to the Commons that the new Chief Constable 'has already set in hand a significant reorganisation both in RUC headquarters and in the field. The immediate purpose of this reorganisation is to enable all the available resources of the force to be focused towards the paramount objective of the detection of criminals, particularly terrorists, and the obtaining of evidence which can be used in the courts to bring those responsible to justice.'

I went on to announce three aspects of policy that were now being implemented. The first was the creation of three regional crime squads, which would be closely co-ordinated with the army and cover the whole province, corresponding to the North, South and Belfast areas and equating broadly with the existing army brigade organisation. They were based on relative British experience and would use the latest vehicles and communications equipment, adding technical strength and muscle to the human resources of the RUC.

The second aspect was the development of units at central headquarters and in the three regional crime squads to collate resources and intelligence in order to gain convictions. My experience of signing detention orders had made me particularly aware of the need for evidence and, as I told the Commons, I regarded this second aspect as one of the most important developments being undertaken by the Chief Constable. The third aspect, linked with this, was the development of specialised units dealing with forensic and similar technical work.

These changes, especially the centralised criminal intelligence scheme at Castlereagh, were to prove the main reasons for the increase in the number of arrests and successes in the courts over future years.

After discussions with my Cabinet colleagues, I was ready to report the results of the security enquiry to the Commons on 2 July. I began with a general explanation of police primacy:

> By securing police effectiveness is meant the integration and acceptance of the police in the community to enable them to administer law and order effectively. It does not mean a return to the past. This is a particularly difficult and challenging task because of the legacy of Irish history. There is a traditional sensitivity and antipathy to the police. This stems from the history of the island over the last seven centuries, and particularly from the enactments of the eighteenth century. We have to recognise that the police are not acceptable in all areas of Northern Ireland today. The police will consequently have to overcome the legacy of the past as well as of the experience of the last seven years.

I then announced the measures that we had concluded should be taken. First of all there would be an increase in the size of the RUC. Further specialist investigation teams, such as murder and fraud squads, would continue to be introduced, which might mean recruiting for and training in new skills or expanding the present specialist capacity. Arrangements were to be improved for collecting and collating criminal intelligence, so that relevant information could be presented quickly and accurately, and resources were to be expanded in each RUC division and used with more flexibility in order to concentrate on serious crime and preventive policing; these divisional specialist forces would together constitute a mobile force for deployment outside the divisions.

A special effort was required to make the RUC more representative of the minority community; the percentage of Catholics had declined in recent years, although there had been an improvement over the previous six months. This would, however, depend to some extent on political factors and on leaders in the minority community speaking up more frequently for the RUC. Expanded training arrangements were also needed, making use of the universities where appropriate.

The scheme for local police centres, which I had approved in September 1974, would be further developed. The purpose of these centres was to provide a police presence, offering advice and guidance for the public, and with immediate access to police resources, in areas where a full-time police station was not justifiable. The aim was also to encourage the minority community to support the police in their own areas.

Greater use would be made of the RUC Reserve where appropriate to relieve the regular police of extra work and to reduce the involvement of the army. The latter's strength and role in the future had been considered but I told the Commons that changes would depend on the success of the police and the amount of violence. The role of the UDR, on the other hand, would remain that of relieving the army of its task at vehicle checkpoints; the UDR's full-time sections would be increased for this purpose.

I felt that my report to the Commons, based on the work of the Northern Ireland Office and the RUC, spelt out the security aim that I had been working towards from first taking office. As I said in my diary of 10 July, 'I had told Jim that I wanted to stay in Northern Ireland because I still had work to do. I wanted to point security policy in the direction of the primacy of the police, and now it is there.'

I knew at this time that my period of office in Northern Ireland would soon be over and in the same diary entry of 10 July, I said: 'Whether it is policy for security, direct rule or procedure in the Commons, I want to get it cleared up in the next few months. When Jim was here on Monday he told me that Roy Jenkins is going and asked me if I would prefer to go to the Home Office or to the Defence Department. I told him the Home Office. I would not mind going to Defence: I could return there quite easily and would enjoy the international aspects of the work, but Home Secretary is one of the top jobs and I think it would be the right one for me to do. I am not consumed by a burning passion to get to the top but for the first time I have looked at jobs in a personal way. The whole question of race relations at the Home Office – where someone has to stand up and be counted but where someone also has to understand working-class attitudes in the face of the transformation of areas they have grown up in and been part of – I think that I could play a role in that.'

In our conversation Jim talked of other possible ministerial changes and asked my views about Fred Mulley for Defence Minister and Roy Mason for Northern Ireland. Jim makes up his own mind – as I had come to know only too well over the years – but I agreed with him about Fred Mulley: he had a distinguished war record and had been at Defence in the sixties; he had also written an excellent book on European defence. Jim reminded me that Roy Mason had held senior Cabinet posts and I added that he was not only able but had plenty of guts. My reservation was whether he would play the 'Irish game' with the local politicians, which could mean them coming to understandings at the end of meetings which did not last five minutes, not because of perfidy but because the political language spoken there is different to that spoken at Westminster. I knew what Jim felt about this from the way he had brushed off silly questions from a local journalist during his visit, and I was not surprised when he answered me with 'There will come a day when we will need someone who will look at it all from the outside.' 'So be it,' I told myself.

There was nothing definite in Jim's asking me about the Home Office. I did not expect any preferment because of my long friendship with him, and I was simply going to wait and see. Two weeks later, on 21 July, the conversation was pushed completely out of my mind when news arrived of a bomb explosion in Dublin which had wrecked the British Ambassador's car, killing the Ambassador, Christopher Ewart-Biggs, and Judith Cook, a Private Secretary in the Northern Ireland Office. Brian Cubbon was with them and he and the local driver of the car, Brian O'Driscoll, were both seriously injured.

I was in a Cabinet meeting when the first report of the explosion came through on the morning of the 21st and it was then thought that the dead woman was the Ambassador's wife and that Brian Cubbon had also been killed. Jim told me to stay out of the meeting and I brought Douglas Janes, the new Deputy Under-Secretary, and my Private Secretary over from the Northern Ireland Office to No 10, where we ran a mini-operations room. Further versions of the incident came in and it took about an hour to ascertain the facts.

I had known that Brian was going down to Dublin; he wanted to find his way around the government departments and make himself known to them; his predecessor had similarly made visits to the Republic. Judith, who was his Private Secretary, had gone with him. The story after that was related by Brian's driver, who had driven them from Belfast to Dublin. Brian and Judith were staying at the Ambassador's residence and had accepted Christopher Ewart-Biggs' offer of a lift in his car into Dublin, leaving their own car to be driven on behind them. They had not gone far down the road before Brian's driver saw the Ambassador's car ahead of him blown about thirty feet into the air. It was obviously a culvert bomb. The car was on its side when Brian's driver ran up to it; I cannot repeat his description of the scene inside it.

I was shattered. Christopher Ewart-Biggs had only recently been appointed but already I had come to appreciate his worth. Judith, whom I of course knew from the Office, was someone we had all marked out for higher things. She was young and exceptionally bright; I had often talked to her in the office and pulled her leg. We had the awful task of informing her parents, and afterwards Colleen and Peggy Cooper went to see them. Colleen later came with me to Northolt to receive the bodies being returned from Dublin. Nothing could cover up the grief I felt.

It was no comfort to know that if Mrs Thatcher had not decided there would be no compromise on pairing arrangements at Westminster, I would have been in Dublin and by normal arrangements would have been travelling in the Ambassador's car. The original intention was that I should fly down to Dublin accompanied by the usual civil servants and by Don Concannon and possibly other ministers. There had always been an understanding that the Northern Ireland team should be considered outside the usual House of Commons' games but now, following some parliamentary incident or other and with the government's small majority, the Tory Opposition was refusing to cover us in the voting lobbies. I had had an angry altercation about it with Humphrey Atkins, the Opposition Chief Whip, and used words that I later apologised for, though not for the meaning behind them. Whatever the House of Commons' reasoning, the government's Northern Ireland ministers should not have been affected.

It was about this time that Don Concannon had had to be flown all the way from Belfast to Northolt by helicopter – nothing else could be arranged at short notice – and then given a police escort to drive him to Westminster. The vote was on as he strode into the chamber, still in his coat, and threw his bag on to the table between the benches. The words he flung at the grinning Tories were unprintable. Most of them would have no idea of the situation in Northern Ireland and the need for a minister to be there, nor of the waste of money. Bipartisanship was a thing of the past.

It was, however, the reason why I was in London and not Dublin on 21 July. The very fact of the bombing suggested that the Provisional IRA had known that a visit to the Ambassador's residence was planned and it seems likely that they had known of my impending visit but had missed out on the changed arrangements. Certainly Tim Pat Coogan said in the 1980 edition of his book, *The IRA*, that Merlyn Rees was 'another supposed passenger in the car'. The bombing made it perfectly clear that the Provisional IRA were murderers. It is true of all their killings and when they affect people you know personally, the stupidity of their actions is brought home even more clearly. That they do not represent the people of Southern Ireland was shown by the shocked response there to the murders.

We could have been far more publicly critical of the Irish government for their lack of security control in Dublin, particularly given their own public criticism of us in South Armagh. I sympathised, however, with their difficulties. The murders showed the problem that the Irish government faced from the Provisional IRA and also, by this time, from the Irish National Liberation Army. The clouds of the past hung over their country too.

We were not without our own security problems in the summer of 1976. Despite my encouraging words on the publication of the security report, relations between the army and the police were now deteriorating. The army had been sent in to maintain law and order in Northern Ireland in 1969 because the situation demanded it and in the difficult years of the early 1970s it had been necessary for them to be in the lead. Now circumstances were changing and while the army agreed in principle with police primacy, it was difficult for them to accept it in practice, particularly given the determination of the new Chief Constable, Ken Newman, that the police were to be the prime force. Personalities mattered.

The more robust attitude of the police chiefs also accounted for the bad relations at this time between my office at Stormont and the army headquarters at Lisburn, which resulted in the press being told of their disagreement over a speech of mine on the rule of law. I asked for an end to be put to this, but when there were more 'unattributable' briefings, I blew my top. Both the Ministry of Defence and No 10 became involved, and Jim Callaghan was not amused. He expressed himself forcefully when he spoke to the GOC in my room at Stormont. There might have been a misunderstanding with journalists behind the press reports – even 'off the record' criticism would get out – but I was sure that there had been serious army criticism of my office and the RUC. I suspect that similar liaison problems in the early days of the Thatcher government led to the appointment of Sir Maurice Oldfield as security co-ordinator. That was, I think, a mistake. It must ultimately be the job of the Secretary of State to put such problems right.

The more I looked into the matter, the more I saw the need for better personal relationships between the army and Northern Ireland Office staffs. Losing the services of Brian Cubbon within a few months of his arrival had not helped. I discussed with my staff and with the GOC the arrangements for consultation that they should make. The GOC had no disagreements with me and in particular he accepted that the RUC was going to be the prime security force in the province, with the army in support of the civil power. Our liaison difficulties disappeared after that, at least during my time in the province.

Other security questions arose, however, in the summer, two of them connected with the republican rallies held on 8 August, the anniversary eve of the introduction of internment. The fact that I had ended detention did not affect the demonstrations, now concerned with the ending of special category status, any more than it had stopped the Provisional IRA's activities. Only a few days before there had been a series of explosions at Portrush in County Antrim for which the Provisional IRA had claimed responsibility.

In Belfast on 8 August Provisional Sinn Fein's Vice-President, Mrs Maire Drumm, addressed the open-air rally. Members of the press were around her as she gave her speech and they took down her words, which were published the following day:

> When the first boy or girl is sentenced and does not get political status, will you march after us till we pull this town down? If they do not maintain political status, by God, it will come down stone by stone. Long Kesh was burned once and the girls in Armagh took the Governor hostage and wrecked the jail. If it is necessary it will be done again. Long Kesh will be burned and we will destroy this town, and that goes for Britain as well.

There was, naturally, a rumpus. I was very angry and wanted to know why no action had been taken against Mrs Drumm; her words were surely incitement to violence. However, no member of the security forces had been in a position to hear her exact words because of helicopter noise and a straight newspaper report would not suffice for legal action. The police had been unable to obtain copies of the speech from any Provisionals and had been round to all the journalists, who would not help. As I recorded in my diary: 'The *Daily Telegraph* reporter had visited Mrs Drumm and was on the platform when she spoke, but he would not give evidence. He would not have to show himself in court – he could be behind a screen and have all the other protection procedures. For the press to stand on some sort of privilege on this is terrible when soldiers are dying in the province.'

I telephoned the *Telegraph*'s editor Bill Deedes to ask that his reporter should come forward. He seemed willing to help but when he phoned back later in the day, it was quite clear that he had been told by the proprietor to forget it. As I angrily exclaimed in my diary: 'This is from a newspaper which criticises my security policy and then one of its people acts in this way with the aid of the proprietor. It is indefensible.'

I had issued a statement likening Maire Drumm to Madame Defarge knitting at the guillotine and it had been broadcast all day on television and radio. As I commented in my diary, 'I had hoped that the law would enable us to get this woman, and also a solicitor living up at Cookstown who had spoken with approval of "soldiers going home in their coffins".' My anger was intensified by the death of three soldiers at this time who had been going out to try to prevent sectarian murders.

I was not going to leave the matter there and I spoke to John Whale of the *Sunday Times*, a first-class journalist who knew more than most about Northern Ireland. He, however, responded with talk about the 'ethical' problem involved. He later, on 29 August, wrote an editorial on the Drumm affair:

> The journalists were in this instance right to refuse. The chance of reprisals aside, if journalists give information in court against people who have allowed them to collect the information in their capacity as journalists, then they may well be denied similar information next time. And no bad thing, say the government: news about a parcel of dissidents is merely propaganda. Yet if newspapermen accept that, they are allowing the government to decide whom they report and whom not (and at a time when the minds of Provisional IRA sympathisers are as much in need of elucidation as ever, and when the BBC and ITV are under recurrent criticism for not being able to supply it). The whole history of war reporting shows that journalists have never served the country worse than when they have allowed their loyalty as citizens to restrict their catholicity as reporters.

I just could not agree. Of course there is an ethical problem for journalists and the media must be separate from government, opposition, the lot – but all I wanted was for one journalist to stand up and say that what he had reported was true. Where were the ethics? Everybody knew who had made the speech: it was made in a park, not in the lobby of the House of Commons.

In fact Mrs Drumm had been arrested on 9 August on a minor charge connected with contravening the Public Order Act by taking part in an unnotified public procession. Gerry Adams, later elected Sinn Fein MP for West Belfast, was amongst others also arrested for the same offence. However, the Solicitor General ruled that the charges be dropped because although a loudspeaker announcement had pointed out that the march was illegal before it began, Maire Drumm would be able to say that she had not heard it. She and the others were therefore released. I had meetings all day with my officials to consider other possibilities but I was hoisted with my own petard – it was evidence that was needed. I had to accept the force of my own words.

The problem about Maire Drumm was not the only one we faced on 9 August; there was also an incident involving Gerry Fitt and his family. Gerry had told me earlier of his concern about the republican rallies. He had never hesitated to speak out against the Provisional IRA and he feared for the safety of his home from some of the republican demonstrators. I asked my security people to note this and on the night of the rally, when Gerry rang me about it, I told him that I would check that the necessary arrangements had been made. The Chief Constable and the CLF were with me at Stormont – everyone was on the alert, making sure that our preparations for the rally were going as planned – and I spoke to them about the Fitts' Belfast home.

I later retired to bed, to be woken in the early hours by Gerry on the phone, saying, 'I will never trust you again.' He told me that his house had just been broken into and fifty demonstrators had come up the stairs threatening him and his wife Anne and one of their daughters, Geraldine, who was at home. Gerry had a gun and he had succeeded in driving the intruders off, but it was a very frightening incident and Anne, who suffered from asthma, had gone into an asthmatic spasm. Gerry had phoned for an ambulance, which arrived very quickly, but he complained that the police had not come until twenty-five minutes after he had reported the attack.

Gerry told his story many times that day – who could blame him? – and showed his customary sense of humour: he had, he said, kept asking himself as he stood on the stairs, 'Is this the way you are going to die, Gerry?' When he came to see me that morning, he said he had had another thought too – 'Gerry, you haven't been to confession for six weeks.' But the incident was no laughing matter. The media coverage was understandably enormous and we were in trouble. Why had the Fitts' home not been protected?

I was informed that an inspector had gone to see Gerry at 11.30 pm on the 8th to offer him more protection, but Gerry wanted people only to be 'nearby'. It was too dangerous to have security men waiting outside – static soldiers or police in a republican area get shot – but a security van was patrolling the area and it had gone past the house at a minute to four in the morning. The moment it was round the corner, a number of demonstrators appeared, who proceeded to knock down the door of the house. At two minutes past four a police patrol car went by and, seeing the numbers involved – fifty in Gerry's estimation, and certainly a crowd – radioed for the army. They turned up, which is why the crowd went, although Gerry had already driven them down the stairs, and at nine minutes past four it was all over.

I differ only on the timing from Gerry's version of the events, which, besides showing the bravery of Gerry and his family, pointed up the problems faced by the police and security forces. The republican crowd could only have been dealt with by having soldiers or police inside the Fitts' house. The lack of protection was certainly not for lack of will, as the accusation was made of me.

Gerry and Anne were and are our friends and Colleen went to visit Anne the night of the incident and stayed over a brew of tea – the police had asked me not to go because the presence of the Secretary of State in West Belfast would soon become known and would cause trouble. Our concern was not, however, shared by others and we received letters – from 'loyalists' – expressing 'pleasure' that the Fitts' home had been attacked.

Although such incidents showed the problems that we faced in the province, and despite the killings that were still taking place, the security situation by the late summer was comparatively quiet. There was an undoubted mood for peace in the community, which inspired a women's peace movement that caught the imagination of the world. It was prompted by the Maguire family tragedy on 10 August, when the three children of Mrs Maguire were run down and killed by a gunman's getaway car in the republican Anderstonstown area of Belfast. The carnage was witnessed by a local housewife, Mrs Betty Williams, and she and Mrs Maguire's sister, Mairead Corrigan, set up the 'Peace People' organisation with Ciaran McKeown, a journalist and pacifist who had been involved in the Civil Rights movement.

Peace rallies were held in all parts of the province and on 28 August some 20,000 people attended a rally in Belfast, which was preceded by a march up the Shankill Road. There were emotional scenes as Catholics walked through the heartland of loyalism for the first time in many years. I recall my wife Colleen preparing to go to the rally with friends and her reluctantly agreeing not to because her support would have been taken as mine and the government could not be seen to be involved. She felt no obligations to hold back once I had left the province, and when an Ulsterman slighted Brian Faulkner at a dinner of professional men which I had addressed as Home Secretary, she told him firmly that he was a typical middle-class Unionist 'sitting on his hands and letting others bear the burden'.

The main church leaders spoke out in favour of the peace movement and a large rally was held in Dublin in early September, supported by the World Methodist Convention, which was meeting there. The Northern Irish politicians were ambivalent. Gerry Fitt and Harry West gave their support to the new cause, but most were critical of these 'inexperienced' women. Dr Paisley was typical. He wanted 'peace through victory', which he supported with the text 'I come not to send peace but a sword'. The Provisional IRA reacted to the Belfast rally by bombing a pub in Glengormley which injured twenty-six people, and set off an explosion near a peace rally in Newry. Its counter to the peace slogan 'Aren't seven years enough?' was 'Aren't seven hundred years too much?'.

The Peace People were symptomatic of a mood. That the movement was not able to translate its feeling into practical action was due not to it but to a geological fault in the body politic of Northern Ireland. It was a fault made clear in early September when the Official Unionists and the SDLP met again on the return of Martin Smyth from the States.

At the meeting the Rev Smyth evidently showed little enthusiasm, and on 6 September the OUP, without previously communicating their decision to the SDLP, announced that the talks would be discontinued.

The explanation given was that the executive had decided there was no point in continuing 'unless there was a shift of ground by the SDLP or a response from the British government or other parties'.

The SDLP reacted with a statement in the *Irish Times* of 9 September, which expressed regret at the breaking off of the talks and revealed their proposals for changes in the 1973 Constitution Act, which we assumed had been under discussion. The points included: a greater measure of devolution, especially in policing; the power for a local parliament or assembly to request further extensive devolution, provided that a specified majority which was representative of both sections of the community agreed; a power-sharing Cabinet reflecting the proportional strength of those Assembly parties willing to form a government (an important qualification which would avoid the veto of Paisley and the OUP); a review of the working of the new constitution after two parliamentary sessions; the transfer of the functions of the Secretary of State under the Act to a Lord President; and a 'positive and freely negotiated' agreement between North and South on matters of common concern.

On this publication of the SDLP case, the OUP decided to reveal their position. Their proposals, published in the *Irish Times* of 14 September, were that: the basic principles of the Convention Report should be accepted; representation in the proposed European Parliament should be on a par with Scotland, with at least three members; representation at Westminster should be increased; a Cabinet should be formed on the normal British pattern; and there should be a twofold check on the Executive – a back-bench committee and a Council of State.

The nature of this Council of State had first been revealed by John Hume in an article in the *Irish Times* of 21 June when he had talked of it as exercising some kind of restraint or veto on the Executive. The OUP developed the idea in their September statement, explaining that the Council would have the status of a privy council and would be appointed by the 'Governor' on the nomination, by proportional representation, of Parliament. It would have a 'monitoring function' on public business, with power to delay legislation for a year, and would have executive responsibility in the field of human rights and related security matters. This could have been a way through the thorny question of power sharing, but without more public commitment it was merely papering over a deep crack and the SDLP could not accept it and neither, with Paisley in the background, could the Unionists.

The talks had ended. A devolved administration was the only way forward that I could see for the divided province but I had to accept that the Unionists, despite their inclination, were not able to compromise given the feeling of their electorate. Nor could I ignore the fact that the

Provisional IRA and other paramilitaries could not have operated unless they tapped a thick vein of support. We had to press on with direct rule and with combatting terrorism through the use of the law.

The question of the sufficiency of the law in dealing with terrorism became of public concern at this time because of changes that the Republic made to their own terrorist law. They were in fact going to do much the same as we were doing in Northern Ireland and as John Whale wrote in the *Sunday Times* on 29 August: 'The new powers which the Irish government is to seek with some trepidation in the Dail on Tuesday are already available, with few differences, to the courts of the United Kingdom. Many people have been surprised by that discovery.' One of those who had not understood this was Harry West, who commented on a BBC programme that it showed a 'lack of will' on my part that we had not brought the law up to the standard of the South.

Much as I sympathised with the Irish government's difficulties about terrorism, I did not feel charitable towards them about their handling of their case to the European Commission on Human Rights, which reported on 2 September. There had rightly been an outcry about the interrogation techniques used on the introduction of internment in 1971, when the Irish government first took a complaint to the Commission, and in response the British government had initiated the Compton and Parker Reports. Ted Heath's prompt action then to stop any recurrence of the methods used had been supported by the Labour Party in Opposition and had since been reinforced by us in practice in government.

The British government's response had, however, not stopped the Irish government going ahead with its complaint. As Opposition spokesman on Northern Ireland I had been asked in 1971 to try to influence Jack Lynch's government to withdraw the case, but I had got nowhere: they felt that they represented the Catholics in the North. Their attitude had not changed since, although we had done all we could to change the situation in the North and the sixteen men cited by the Irish government to illustrate their case had been paid substantial compensation. It added salt to the wound that a week before the European Commission's Report was published, the Irish government issued a statement about it which they liberally handed out. I insisted that we protested to the Commission about this and we made sure that our views on the Report did not come out until it had been published.

What the Commission ruled was that the combined use of five deep interrogation techniques constituted inhuman treatment and torture, but it did not uphold torture in the sixteen individual cases chosen as illustration by the Irish government. On the issues of internment, detention and methods of trial, the Commission found no unjustified breach of the European Convention, and it also found no evidence that the powers of detention or internment had been applied with discrimination, or that the UK government was in breach of Article 1 of the European Convention concerning the duty of governments to secure rights and freedoms. Despite all this, as the Commission went on to report, the Irish government had stated that they were unable to regard the measures already taken by the UK government and those being considered by them for the future as satisfactory, and that they were not ready to discuss them with a view to settlement.

Here was the age-old problem of relations between 'England' and Ireland but, given the common enemy that our governments now faced, I did not think that history should be allowed to shackle our actions. I issued a carefully prepared press statement on 2 September:

> This case is about events which took place five years ago. It could have been settled long ago. I can see no justification for the Irish government's persistence in it. The fact is that the interrogation techniques which the Commission call 'torture', which were described by the Compton Report as 'physical ill-treatment' but not amounting to 'brutality', were stopped unilaterally by the British government of the day over four years ago, and relevant compensation awarded.
>
> On the question of ill-treatment, the Commission say that since December 1971 the United Kingdom government have taken 'important measures', which are set out in the Report, to secure the protection contemplated by the European Convention on Human Rights. These included fresh instructions to the security forces about the proper treatment of arrested persons, fresh disciplinary regulations for the RUC, and so on.

The Commission had said that internment and detention were 'strictly required by the exigencies of the situation in Northern Ireland', and I emphasised in the press statement that there was now nobody in detention: I was concerned that the Irish case would be presented abroad as if the grounds for their complaint still existed. I was also concerned that the Provisional IRA would use the Report for their own ends, and pointed out: 'The only people who can derive any satisfaction from all this are the terrorists. We should be concentrating our united energies on defeating the gunmen and bombers who menace the lives and well-being of peaceable citizens in both our countries.'

It was the lives of the security forces, not of the lawyers and politicians, which would be put at risk by the emotion engendered by the Report, and I emphasised their sacrifice.

> Of the 1,600 dead in Northern Ireland since 1969, some 400 are from the men and women of the security forces. They have been shot at, both on duty and in their homes, blown up by landmines, blown to pieces dismantling bombs aimed at the civilian population. Let us not forget that the Commission themselves describe the violence which the security forces have to face in Northern Ireland as being of 'extraordinary dimensions'. Without them, there can be no doubt that the violence would reach even more tragic dimensions in the divided society of Northern Ireland.

My anger was not connected with the Commission finding that torture had taken place in 1971. That was proper, and I had no doubt that it had been the result of a grave error of government. As I had repeated many times in the office, the interrogation methods had slipped through because there were two departments in charge – the Ministry of Defence and the Home Office, the former responsible for the army and the latter for Northern Irish affairs. Brian Faulkner and the Department of Home Affairs had wanted internment – and what a mess they had made of it! – but the request for 'interrogation measures' had come from the army, as Brian himself had said. It was no excuse that ministers in 1971 were advised that the measures fell within a 1965 Joint Intelligence Committee directive on interrogation which explicitly forbade brutality and inhuman or degrading treatment. It is the job of ministers to check carefully, particularly on such a serious issue.

Nevertheless, this was all in the past and everything possible had since been done by us to rectify the mistake. My anger lay with the Irish government for continuing, even in 1976, with their case. It finally came before the European Court on 18 January 1978 and in July of that year went to a Committee of Ministers: in essence there was then no change from the 1976 decision. During all this time, successive British governments faced bloody violence in Northern Ireland, where the Irish government's persistence with their complaint reinforced loyalist feelings about the perfidy of the South and gave respectability to the actions of the republican paramilitaries.

Although this whole issue roused my anger, it was not typical of my feelings towards the South in general. Our good relations were shown in particular by the improved security co-operation between the North and South. By September 1976 this had developed to the point that, when I suggested in the Northern Ireland Office and to the RUC another visit to the South to discuss security with Paddy Cooney, I was strongly advised that it could now be left to the professionals on both sides of the border. I readily agreed: the politicians should only come in if a change of policy was needed.

The days when my Stormont office was a hub of constant activity were now over. As I reported in my diary of 8 September, 'We have lowered the expectations of people politically, and although the security situation is not good, it is far removed from the old confrontation period of the British army against the IRA. I believe that this is the time to hand over. The policy of primacy of the police is working and this is the basis of a security policy which will develop in the future. We have moved forward from the Whitelaw/Rees situation of two years ago, with the constant involvement of the Secretary of State. And now there is, if not progress, at least a change.'

I was ready to move on. In early August, I had had a personal note from Jim about choosing a replacement Private Secretary to the Home Secretary – Roy Jenkins was taking his current Private Secretary with him to Brussels. I readily chose Bob Morris, whom I had known in the late sixties at the Home Office, but I advised him to be ready to work for somebody else because I was still not convinced that I would be the new Home Secretary. My doubts about the Home Office were strengthened when in the weeks that followed, the 'quality media mafia' decided that Shirley Williams was going to be appointed. I had overlooked that it was August, the month in which political correspondents are liable to 'make' news.

I was beginning to look forward to a life on the back-benches when the picture was changed for me. As I recorded in my diary of 10 September: 'I was leaving home for the Farnborough Air Show when Murray Stewart, my Private Secretary, telephoned to tell me that changes were taking place and would I go to see the Prime Minister. Colleen waited for me with Murray at the Northern Ireland Office. When I went into the Cabinet room at No 10 Jim explained that he could not leave the Home Office as it was, with Roy Jenkins as a lame duck incumbent. He looked at me in his characteristic way and said that he just wanted me to know that Shirley was to be Home Secretary. I responded, "You could not have done a better thing, Prime Minister. I will stay in Northern Ireland." Then, having had his little joke, he said "I would like you to be Home Secretary". I told him that I would be very pleased to accept.'

He would not reveal the other ministerial changes, except that Roy Mason would be going to Northern Ireland, and he warned me that nobody must know what he had just told me, not even the private offices, because he did not want any leaks. I said nothing to Murray or Colleen but they both knew something was afoot and I later told Colleen as we drove to Farnborough: she had kept enough secrets in Northern Ireland for this one to be perfectly safe with her. We met a lot of Northern Ireland people at the air show – and planned to see some of them the following week in Belfast! – but by 6.30 when we arrived back in London, our news was public knowledge.

Northern Ireland was behind me. Those days in the early 1970s of internment, Long Kesh, Diplock, culminating in Willie's breakthrough with his power-sharing Executive, seemed centuries away. Even the events of my day – the Ulster workers' strike, the Convention, the Sinn Fein talks, were disappearing into the past. Everything had gone full circle back to direct rule. As I had written to my Cabinet colleagues a few weeks before, this was for the moment not just the only policy to be followed but the only satisfactory policy.

In my farewell message to the province, I said: 'I am utterly convinced from what I have seen here that in the long term the good will triumph. It is for you, the community in Northern Ireland, to ensure that that comes about at the earliest possible opportunity.' But I knew that it would all take time, and my time had run out.

Part IV

IN RETROSPECT

Chapter 12

A PERSONAL REVIEW

I had always been aware in Northern Ireland that ministerial life there was different from thc lifc in Whitchall. Oncc I was Homc Sccretary everything would, I was sure, change. On my first night in the job, however, I came in for a surprise. I had gone to bed, with the security phone still at the bedside; there had been times in Northern Ireland when the phone had never seemed to stop ringing but I did not expect to hear it now. Then in the early morning a call came from the Home Office telling me that a hijacked plane was heading for Heathrow. I was soon in the Whitehall Operations Room with the General who had been Commander Land Forces in Northern Ireland and we spent the whole day there. As it turned out, the plane did not land but went on to Paris.

The incident was the nearest I was ever to get to a security operation while Home Secretary. I had been right in thinking that everything would change. I reflected in my diary at the beginning of my new job: 'It makcs mc rcalisc what a strangc lifc I havc lcd thcsc two and a half years. Almost incredibly, I have been home every evening. I have seen the family. Everything is much more relaxing. I still have detectives, but life is completely different.' Admittedly, Parliament was in recess at this time, but in Northern Ireland no notice would have been taken of that.

Office work was now more structured. The ever open door policy at Stormont could not be followed in practice at Westminster and, anyway, it was not relevant when decisions rarely had to be made quickly in response to changing events. The rhythm of work was much slower. There were all the pressure groups to consult and then all the paper-work to consider before making decisions on legislation. Even when there was an issue to decide on, the approach was different.

I was struck by this in my first days as Home Secretary when I had a discussion with ministers and civil servants in the office about the recent Notting Hill riots. It was not of the relaxed kind that we would have had in Northern Ireland over a meal or during the evening in our living quarters. The police view was put by John Harris, and Brynmor John talked of race relations; a paper was to be prepared for the following week. I did not, however, think that the public enquiry decided on by my predecessor was warranted and I informed the Commissioner of Police accordingly; if there were mistakes, it was his job to put them right.

I learned to respect the attributes and attitudes of the civil servants with whom I now worked; it was no use trying to operate as if I was still in Northern Ireland. Nevertheless, I could not shake off my thoughts about it, even though working there had not been easy. No one in charge of the province could ignore the violence, and criticism of UK politicians came easily to the lips of all the politicians in the North and even more easily to the lips of those in the South. As an outsider I had done my best to show my understanding of the people on both sides of the divide: the second-class status of the Catholic minority, brought home to me particularly as I looked over the walls of Derry into the Bogside, and the laager mentality of the loyalist working class, especially their fundamentalism and fear of peasant Catholicism. It seemed to do me little good, judging from the letters telling me that I was either pro-republican or pro-loyalist.

A typical example of the latter began, 'To a bigoted, anti-Protestant, Papist-loving bastard', and read:

> Many letters have appeared recently in our local newspapers condemning your love of the rebels here in Ulster, and what action should be taken against you for the blood on your hands. Well, as you have been warned before now, action is on the cards. Others who failed to be warned for their part in the loss of innocent lives, suffering and destruction, have paid the price. You are well to the fore on the list, so you cannot squeal like the bigoted pig you are. If RCs were being killed and maimed, you would be crying out in their defence, but Protestants and their property are suffering daily, yet you stand up for the murdering IRA and its supporters such as the SDLP, etc. So you are not getting away with your crimes much longer. All of Ulster has you in its sights for the filthy crimes you are guilty of.

From the same quarter I received during the Ulster workers' strike an Irish Free State coin, which circulate in the North, indented with the words 'Smash Rees', while my wife, whose Southern Irish Christian names identify one part of her family origins, received nasty letters about our sexual relationship! They revealed something of the gut feeling of some 'Prods' for the Catholics.

From the other side of the divide there came abusive and threatening letters alleging my allegiance to the loyalist cause and containing justification for violence. There was little to choose between the two sides except that more religious sectarianism was shown by the majority population and more anti-unionism by the minority.

Evil lies deep in Northern Ireland's history but it is not all-pervading. The troubles brought out the best as well as the worst in people and even in the areas where trouble predominated there were countless examples of people working against the grain of violence. As I had said in my farewell message, 'There is much that is good here. It cannot and should not be destroyed.' I felt the hope that lay beneath the surface and despite all the problems I was sad to leave.

I had grown to love the countryside: the lakes of Fermanagh, the Sperrins of Tyrone, the Mournes in County Down and the Glens of Antrim. Even in Armagh the sense of history in its cathedral city and the sight of its spreading orchards countered the atmosphere created by tit-for-tat murders. I would not easily be able to forget the province and its people. My experience there had left me with an abiding interest in Ireland and I would never have that sense of involvement in any other job.

The move to London did not mean that I would bow out of Irish affairs completely. I had views on the Irish question and I intended to play my part on the Cabinet Irish committee as Home Secretary, although I would not interfere with Roy Mason and his work. When I left the province, I wrote a long minute to the Prime Minister which I knew he would circulate to my successor and others on the Irish committee. In it I gave my perspective on Northern Irish problems and policies during my two and a half years as Secretary of State.

I began with a summary of present policy, which was, first, to continue with positive and fair direct rule for an indefinite period until a form of devolved government could be achieved which was acceptable to both parts of the community; and, second, to deal with violence through the rule of law applied by the police, with the support, as necessary, of the army. I then turned to the political situation during my term of office.

In February 1974, the power-sharing Executive created by William Whitelaw was still in existence but, as I told Harold Wilson soon after taking office, it would collapse before long, which happened in May. The next phase was to allow the people of Northern Ireland the opportunity to sort out their own affairs through the Constitutional Convention. Although this did not produce a constitutional solution, it demonstrated to the people the failure of the Northern Ireland politicians to rise above their squabbles and to reach agreements for the good of Ulster.

The Convention and the way in which it ended brought a substantial lowering of political tension in the province. There was clearly a sense of relief that direct rule, with the stability that that implied, was going to continue for a significant period. As I had said on 5 March 1976, 'This is not a time for new political initiatives.' It was a sign of the lowered tension that private talks between the Official Unionists and the SDLP were possible. They had lasted several months and although they had now broken down, there was no crisis. As I put it to Jim Callaghan:

> It is evident that there is no basis for agreement on the main issues yet, nor should we expect one to appear quickly. Future developments must come by some demonstration by the population at large of the recognition that for the political solution they wish to see, more compromise is necessary. I cannot forecast when the recognition that the way forward lies with compromise and not extremism will spread sufficiently widely. It is easy for the outsider to be deceived about the mood in the province as a whole. A change in mood might, however, be manifest in the local elections next year. We must be ready to recognise the moment when it comes.
>
> We should not take initiatives ourselves but we must be prepared to respond to local political movements and to make sure that agreements in principle are steered into practical constitutional form. We know from experience that we cannot expect talks within the Northern Ireland political parties to produce workable constitutional arrangements but the basic agreements must come from them.

I outlined the changes in security policy over the same period. Detention had continued to be the principal weapon against terrorism throughout 1974 but by the autumn, although violence was reduced from the peak years immediately following the introduction of internment, there was no prospect of it being extinguished. Despite large numbers in detention and even larger numbers of convicted prisoners, the basic IRA structure remained. The prison situation was dangerous: the accommodation was over-full and the service understaffed; indeed, in October 1974 the Maze was burnt down. The constant cry from all Catholic areas was of army harassment and there was extreme criticism of detention from all quarters, both within and without Northern Ireland. It was, and I am convinced remains, the hated symbol of a negative, repressive policy.

With this background there was no prospect whatsoever of political progress. The more extreme local politicians held sway and memories of the Ulster workers' strike still inflamed political passions on both sides of the community. Northern Ireland was in both a security and a political rut in 1974, and we had to break out of it.

Although the Provisional IRA had the capacity to continue violence, there were signs in late 1974 that the Army Council were conscious of a loss of public support, especially in the Republic, after the Birmingham bombings in November. Moreover, some members of the Council were thought to be coming to the view that violence was not advancing their cause. There seemed a possibility of manoeuvring them into a ceasefire which might last rather longer than the ten-day truce which William Whitelaw had achieved in 1972, but in the event it was the Provisionals who called a ceasefire on their own initiative in December.

I had taken this opportunity to begin bringing detention to an end and to establish a firm policy of proceeding by prosecution through the courts – the rule of law. The ceasefire gave people in Northern Ireland a taste of peace, which meant that they were likely to resent those who sought to break it. It was, I stressed, only by reducing positive public support for violence that the conditions could be created in which urban terrorism would finally be overcome.

The Provisional IRA ceasefire had lasted effectively until August 1975, although violence did not cease entirely during this period. There had been a steady stream of sectarian killings and inter-factional violence, rather more Protestant- than Catholic-inspired. I had been much concerned to restrain loyalist violence and to reduce the frustration on which that violence fed. Since last August there had been an increase in Provisional IRA attacks on the security forces and in bombing of commercial targets.

However, the success of the policy of police primacy to which we had committed ourselves two years ago was becoming apparent. I referred to the review we had made of the role of the army and the police in the light of this policy and pointed out that we were now well on the way to shifting the emphasis of our security force activities towards the police, and significant improvements were being made in police organisation under the new Chief Constable. I had removed the emotional shadows of detention and the political situation was gradually changing. The ability of the police, with the support of the army, to operate through the law had much improved, although the full benefits were yet to be seen, but most important of all we had driven a substantial wedge between the Provisional IRA and the Catholic population as a whole.

I put my strongly held view that it was very important not to over-react to security problems in Northern Ireland. The history of the nineteenth century, when communications were much less swift, showed only too clearly the tendency of British Cabinets to over-react, and the same tendency had been evident in 1971. The government then had faced the worsening situation with responsibilities for security divided between London and Stormont, and even within London no one minister had had a clear responsibility in Cabinet.

I assessed the co-operation with the Republic of Ireland which had been built up since 1974. I told the Prime Minister that the present Irish government realised that they could not absorb Northern Ireland with one million unwilling Protestants. They recognised that any political solution in the North must be acceptable to the Protestant majority and that to press for institutions such as a Council of Ireland would not at this stage be acceptable to that majority.

Much progress, I continued, had been made on certain aspects of security co-operation with the Republic; there was better control of explosives, some exchange of security information, and Garda co-operation with the RUC and army on some types of operations. What was lacking was day-to-day co-operation, due to the traditional anti-British feeling which still existed widely in the South. I repeated how angry I felt about the pursuit of the Irish state case against us with the European Commission on Human Rights but hoped that we would continue to keep in touch with the Taoiseach on all these matters.

The subject of Northern Ireland's economy formed a substantial section of the minute and I explained again that the province suffered with Scotland, Wales and the North-East all the problems of a peripheral area, aggravated by the additional transport costs involved in a sea crossing and more recently by the effects of the security situation. Energy costs were unusually heavy and unemployment – twelve per cent overall and over fifteen per cent outside Belfast – was very serious and likely to get worse.

The Quigley Economic Review and another review by the Central Policy Review Staff were being studied in the office and by the Economic Council but I told the Prime Minister that I was not optimistic that any easy solutions would be found. Failure to deal with the unemployment problem could, however, be the most important factor in destroying the improvements in the security and political situation, and the need for cuts in public expenditure would exacerbate this.

I finished with a brief section on relations with the Labour Party. I said that over the last five years we had made sure that the Parliamentary Labour Party, Transport House and the leaders of the main trade unions had been aware of government policy, and it had been of considerable value to have the support and understanding of the wider Labour movement.

This minute to Jim Callaghan was the last of the many papers that I had sent either direct to Cabinet colleagues or to the Prime Minister for onward transmission to them. Some dealt with particular policy issues for which I was asking approval; numerous others gave background information on the security and political situation in Northern Ireland. I knew that my colleagues living in London could not depend on the media for background information, as they might for international affairs, and in particular I did not want them to think that because Ulster was near, it was somehow British.

It was not just my Cabinet colleagues who were shown these papers. I discussed them with all my ministerial colleagues in the Northern Ireland Office before and after they were written. Admittedly, the discussions were sometimes ad hoc, but there was no question of the Northern Ireland ministers being kept in the dark about policy, as happens in some government departments. Indeed, when we felt we needed support, we talked to ministerial colleagues at Westminster to make sure that the main points of policy were understood. This was particularly so before a possibly difficult meeting of the Cabinet sub-committee or Cabinet itself. Before discussing, for example, the ending of detention in late 1975, I talked with the Prime Minister and a number of my close colleagues, while Stan Orme talked with Michael Foot and his particular colleagues. The result was a relevant meeting at which the right decision was I think reached. Because of our approach, ministers from other departments did not feel the need to talk on policies in which they had no previous involvement – unlike on some Cabinet committees – and our discussions were usually helpful and to the point.

During my years as Secretary of State I always had the full support of both the Prime Ministers under whom I served. I was, and am, much closer to Jim Callaghan whose friendship and wise advice I have always valued, but I appreciated also the personal support from Harold Wilson for me and my family, particularly during the Ulster workers' strike. An example of his consideration for us, which had unforeseen results, was in September 1975, when on finding out that Colleen and I had not been on holiday because of the difficult situation during the summer, Harold ordered us to go off immediately. At such short notice, we had little choice but there was a place available in Sorrento which we accepted, although I was not particularly keen on going there because I had been one of the first into the town in 1943 and had been on leave there a number of times subsequently during the war.

The Special Branch decided that there was no need for detectives to accompany us to Italy and they left us at the departure gate at Heathrow. On the plane I found myself sitting next to a voluble Dubliner who told me how to settle the whole Irish situation. There seemed no getting away from Ireland and it was a relief to reach Naples and drive off in a car along the autostrada to Sorrento.

The next morning at breakfast we were surprised that everybody seemed to know us and we decided that, rather than go on the organised hotel trip to Capri, we would travel under our own steam. We clambered on to the boat only to find it packed with hundreds of Catholics from Belfast! They were en route to Rome for the canonisation of the Irishman, the Blessed Oliver Plunkett. For the entire journey across to Capri, Colleen was asked to take photographs of me with groups of Irish people, and a queue was formed specially for the purpose. It was the same wherever we went on Capri, it was the same on the journey back, and in the next few days we seemed to do little but shake hands with Irish men and women.

On my return to Belfast, I went to the Upper Falls for an army briefing on events during my week's absence. The young Intelligence Officer looked me straight in the eye and told me that nothing much had occurred there, but West Belfast was full of postcards from holiday-makers reporting on my every movement! The Special Branch was not amused.

A senior colleague who was also constantly reassuring, in his typically diffident way, was Michael Foot. He possessed a fund of knowledge of eighteenth- and nineteenth-century Ireland and at one Cabinet meeting he passed me a note quoting the words of John Morley on, as he put it, 'the Merlyn Rees of his day': 'The new Viceroy [Spencer] attacked the formidable task before him with resolution, minute assiduity and an inexhaustible store of that steady-eyed patience which is the sovereign requisite of any man who, whether with coercion or without, takes it in hand to govern Ireland.'

The only real disagreement on Ireland that I had with my senior colleagues was over extra Westminster seats for the province. I had been against any increase in principle since 1972, when the subject reared its head after direct rule was introduced. I had then helped Willie Whitelaw head off this tack, commenting in my diary at the time: 'The Unionists have returned to the question of the twelve members at Westminster. We will have to be very firm. I am not very interested in the case for six more members but I am interested in the case for Northern Ireland: the Catholics see extra seats as a move to integration.' To talk about increased representation at Westminster when power sharing in the province was the main issue was to show a lack of understanding of the split nature of society in Northern Ireland.

While I was Secretary of State, I was able to maintain support for this view but when I became Home Secretary, I lost out. By that time the power-sharing argument was wearing thin and in 1977 continuing direct rule prompted Roy Mason, Michael Foot and then Jim Callaghan, with the support of the Cabinet, to agree to put the proposal to the Speaker's Conference, which was being set up to consider other issues. By the General Election of 1983, the number of Westminster seats in the province had been increased from twelve to seventeen, only two of which were then won by Catholics – John Hume of the SDLP and Gerry Adams of Provisional Sinn Fein, who was elected on a minority vote and did not take his seat. This reinforced the point I had put to Jim Callaghan in the spring of 1977 when I used the words of the 1975 White Paper on Scottish and Welsh devolution: '[Northern Ireland's] history and geography distinguish it from other parts of the United Kingdom, as does the presence of two separate communities. Its problems are not those of Scotland or Wales and therefore do not necessarily require the same treatment.'

I tried throughout my time in Ireland to keep in contact with the Parliamentary Labour Party in general over affairs in the province. I had regular discussions with the members of the back-bench committee on Northern Ireland and always listened carefully to their views and to those of my Scottish colleagues, in particular Willie Ross, the Secretary of State for Scotland, and Glasgow MP Gregor Mackenzie, an old friend. The West coast Scots knew all about the Orange and the Green, for it showed itself even within their constituency parties. Colleagues elsewhere who represented constituencies with many voters of Irish descent confirmed my view that the vast majority of the Irish settled in this country were against violence, but that if civil war broke out in Ireland, tribal blood would prove thicker than water.

There were always some members of the Party whose views on Northern Ireland ran counter to the policies developed with the support of the Labour Party Conference, but they were few in number. Some of the 'right-wing' liberals in the Party were, for example, rather wobbly in their support. They persisted in seeing the province as a colonial dependency which could be treated accordingly. The Tribune left was, however, always helpful; they had built up contacts in the province over the years and had no time for the paramilitaries.

I also kept in contact with the people working at Party headquarters. As I indicated in my minute to the Prime Minister on leaving the province, I had always made myself available to talk with the General Secretary of the Labour Party, while my research assistant had maintained contact with the relevant research section.

Much more important was for me to keep the House of Commons itself regularly and fully informed by statements and debates on Northern Ireland. My speeches were based firmly on Cabinet decisions and they were meant for the record. *Hansard* mattered. I intended it to be read by, for example, all those working in the government departments in Northern Ireland, and my statements in 1975 in particular were partly aimed at the Provisional Sinn Fein who were talking with my officials.

A significant point about all the speeches was that they did not contain the conventional Oxford Union anti-Tory flourishes; the subject was far too important to allow for such debate scoring. This helped maintain the bipartisan approach to Northern Ireland which had begun in 1972 and which continued after I became Secretary of State in March 1974, although not to the same extent. During this time the Opposition, particularly after Mrs Thatcher was elected the Conservative Party leader, became increasingly sceptical and was sometimes outright hostile to our policies. Their doubts about the ending of detention and our general security policy were made plain in the Commons, in letters to the press and in Northern Ireland itself.

I had no complaints about the Opposition's attitude, except on pairing arrangements, for politics is about policies and I accepted that the Tory front-bench disagreed about them – though since they came into government they have not pursued their previous policy line. There were always a number of Tory back-benchers who continued to support the general approach set by the Heath government and some of them spoke up in the Commons, which played a notable part in the development of Irish policy. The debates on Northern Ireland from that time are still worth reading and show the value of an individual MP's personal interest in the province.

Parliament, however, is only as good as the support it gets from the electorate and if my postbag was any basis for judgment, the people of Great Britain were as a whole sympathetic to the general thrust of our policy. The nasty pro-republican or pro-loyalist letters were of course always there, but they were not typical, and nor were many of the people who attended public meetings about Ireland, which tended to attract either left- or right-wing ultra-extremists.

Although most people whom I came across outside the realm of politics showed their understanding, there were a few who did not. Colleen and I had complaints about the constant police presence outside our London house, which was followed by attempts to get rates reduced on the grounds that this reduced property values. Floreat Suburbia! Colleen also had the experience of going into an off-license on arriving back from Ireland one Christmas Eve and inadvertently including some Irish coins when paying: 'I will not handle your rotten Irish money,' shouted the manager. She walked out empty-handed to go elsewhere.

In Northern Ireland, my ministerial colleagues played a valuable role and I tried to tap the detailed knowledge of the province which they had gained from running the various departments allocated to them. In return I made every effort to keep them informed on policy matters that did not come their way via the Northern Ireland Office. Working so closely together, we forged friendships deeper than those that normally arise from falling temporarily into the same political bed. Stan Orme, as my deputy and with his personal feel for Irish affairs, is the man I recall with most feeling. Although we came from different sides of the Labour Party spectrum, we trusted each other implicitly, a trust developed particularly during the Ulster workers' strike when, with Jack Donaldson, we stood alone. Jack came from another different background but the three of us complemented each other and, being in the province from the early and particularly difficult days of office, we built up a mutual respect.

Don Concannon I always found a tower of strength and full of common sense, while Roland Moyle had that mid-Wales caution that made me think a trifle longer before deciding how to proceed. As I wrote to Harold Wilson in August 1975, 'The four junior ministers . . . perform their tasks well. They spend much time in Northern Ireland and go about their business in all parts of the province. They know the people involved and have built up connections. It is for this reason that I ask that any ministerial changes in Northern Ireland should be kept to a minimum.'

It is as true now as then that Northern Ireland ministers should not be swapped around on the basis of 'Buggins' turn' but chosen carefully on the basis of their suitability for the job. Those asked to go there must consider not only the security implications but the physical and emotional stress of being separated from family and working anti-social hours which are involved in serving for long periods in the province. When Jim Callaghan reshuffled his ministerial team in 1976, the two new junior ministers for Northern Ireland were well chosen. Ray Carter worked with enthusiasm and an attention to the details of policy, and Jimmy Dunn was not just a statutory Catholic; he was able to get through to sections of the community denied to the rest of us. However, during the almost three years he served in the province, Jimmy Dunn suffered health problems, and at the end both he and Ray Carter lost their parliamentary seats at the polls, though for different reasons.

Careful choice of appointments applies equally to the civil servants. What suits London may not necessarily suit Belfast and, like ministers, the civil servants have to give more of their time to the job and be able to cope with the stress. Most of the senior UK civil servants who served with me in Northern Ireland were extraordinarily able – Frank Cooper, Brian Cubbon and Philip Woodfield. After the fall of the Executive, we were joined by Peter England as a Deputy Secretary. He was a powerful figure and his previous experience in the Ministry of Defence did not come amiss in Northern Ireland, nor his resourcefulness in less charted administrative fields. He was a hard taskmaster but at the same time he always showed concern for those working in the office. The new Deputy Under-Secretary who came in 1976, Douglas Janes, was from the Department of the Environment and his administrative skills were of increasing value the more direct rule became our main concern. I felt that the Northern Ireland civil servants appreciated his ability to express himself with precision, though I was not so sure that the army staff at Lisburn did.

My Private Secretaries served me no less well. They all guided me and often argued with me. I am no believer in the consensus approach to taking decisions and I wanted to hear all the counter-arguments. They and the not-so-senior servants have to remain nameless but there were those in the private offices in London and Belfast who worked extraordinarily hard at all hours of the day or night. They were first-rate, as were the Metropolitan Special Branch team and the RUC team of protection officers who, for other reasons, cannot be named.

I have no time for ex-ministers who blame their advisers for policy lapses while in government; if there are faults in general policy, the blame lies with the minister and no one else. In Northern Ireland I always found that once policy was set, or as it evolved, the UK civil servants stuck to their ministerial brief, however difficult this was given the speed of events. One advantage of Stormont was that we were able to discuss, argue and chat into the small hours of the morning and although we had formal meetings, by the time they took place we had often already decided on the direction in which we would move.

As well as the UK civil servants, there was of course the Northern Ireland Civil Service, which is locally recruited and whose members are quite different in background from those in Whitehall. Their offices at Stormont – a series of grandiose buildings from the 1920s with newer ones from the 1950s mushrooming down the hill – showed the growth in the number of civil servants since 1945, when the welfare state transferred from Great Britain took root in the province.

My first contact with the Northern Ireland senior civil servants had been in 1972 while in Opposition but from May 1974, after the Ulster workers' strike and the return to direct rule, I saw them on a daily basis. They had a detailed knowledge of the province and, not surprisingly in such a small population and area, they knew each other socially, often from schooldays. There was a religious imbalance in their membership, with few Catholics recruited – unlike in the lower clerical grades where over the years there had been a big change, particularly in the Department of Health and Social Security. I often talked to them about the need to correct this imbalance, and I did not doubt their willingness to act. There was, however, a reluctance among able Catholics to consider working at Stormont: the law and medicine were more attractive to them because the nature of these professions brooked less problem of promotion. The middle grades of the service concerned me most, for there lay the seed corn for the future: the Northern Ireland Civil Service is nothing if not meritocratic. Considerable effort was put into improving the situation at this level, but with only small returns.

I never saw any bias against the minority from the senior civil servants and they co-operated well with the SDLP members of the Executive in early 1974. It was, however, different down the line, where there was a strong innate tendency to lean towards the majority community, something which had developed from the nature and structure of Northern Ireland government over fifty years. Despite all the changes that have been made under direct rule, any political head of the government there has to correct this list. Left to itself, the Stormont rose bush goes back to its original brier.

In my early days of office the senior Northern Ireland civil servants did not show the political nous of their UK counterparts, possibly because the built-in Protestant majority in the province meant that they were unused to taking the impact of political decisions into consideration. One example of this was over the working of the Stormont legislation which provided payments to those injured or to the dependants of those killed as a result of criminal activities. Large sums were paid out; in 1975, from the £8-million fund, £2½ million went to members of the armed forces, the police and their dependants, and £5½ million to the rest of the community. My concern was that this latter figure included substantial benefits to paramilitaries and in April 1976 I was angry to read in the newspapers that the brother of Joe Cahill of the Provisional IRA had been awarded £20,000 for injuries received when he was shot during an Official/Provisional IRA feud. What I found startling was that this case had gone through the bureaucratic machine and reached the courts without anybody informing me.

As time went on and more Northern Ireland civil servants were brought into senior positions in the Northern Ireland Office, their outlook changed and they realised that there was a political – not party political – dimension to issues, of which ministers had to be informed. Our working relationships improved greatly, although I am not sure that in the summer of 1975 they all approved of the idea sprung from the fertile mind of Frank Cooper and a secretary in my office to transform the grounds immediately around Stormont Castle to allow a large party to be held with a mix of guests from the police, army and civil service, and dance music provided by army bands. Everyone, however, was won over on the day. It was a great success. We all relaxed and got to know each other outside our official business. I thought afterwards that Lord Brookeborough must have turned in his grave!

Inevitably in such a small community, the Northern Ireland civil servants and politicians knew each other and had much in common. It marked us out as different and, to some extent, outsiders. There was nothing either better or worse about this; it simply illustrated that Northern Ireland politics were, and are, different to those in Great Britain, with their own set of mores.

I cannot pretend that my meetings with the politicians, usually in large groups, showed many of them in a favourable light, for they often seemed to regard these occasions as an opportunity to impress each other. Looking back at individual politicians, I always had a high regard for Brian Faulkner as I realised his commitment not only to Ulster but to all its people, and William Craig won my increasing political respect despite his earlier populist involvement with the loyalist paramilitaries, particularly during the Ulster workers' strike. I recall the almost universal praise from the Northern Ireland civil servants for the administrative abilities of the SDLP members of the power-sharing Executive – John Hume, Austin Currie and Paddy Devlin – but I felt that they were haunted by the demise of the old constitutional Westminster nationalists who had succumbed too much to the embrace of the English. Gerry Fitt was in a class of his own, not so much because of his executive/ministerial responsibilities as Deputy Chief Executive, but because of his outstanding political feel for the province and his personal courage. Despite the fact that he brought down the Labour government of 1979, he and his wife Ann are friends of Colleen and myself for life.

Enoch Powell brought an incisive mind to the province when he was elected Westminster MP for South Down in 1974. I disagreed profoundly with his integrationalist outlook but his analysis of the security situation was valuable to me. He guided the Unionist Party at Westminster so that it became a more effective voice there and, knowing the ways of Whitehall and the House of Commons, he was a great help to Jim Molyneaux, a much underrated politician. Both Jim and Harold McCusker, MP for Armagh, who cared more about Stormont than Westminster and thus appealed to me, impressed the House of Commons far more than Harry West. I liked Harry as a person but he could, as I noted in my diary, 'drive more members to despair of Unionists than even the intransigence of Paisley'.

Of all the politicians I met, I disliked most the Rev Beattie, then Ian Paisley's deputy. He struck me as a naturally obnoxious man who gave a bad name to Christianity. Paisley himself I could never completely make up my mind about. He is able and he can speak to his tribe with golden phrases that touch the heart strings of their beliefs. Outside the political scene, I got on well with him and his wife, who were both courtesy itself. But I constantly wondered whether he could ever shake off the shackles of religious bigotry and his conspiratorial approach in order to be a man of government.

Paisley had links in the lower ranks of the civil service and obtained internal documents in this way. They were never important for documents of any import were closely controlled, but the leaks that came from him did cause problems. On one occasion in 1976 he got hold of a housing document, relating to the possible appointment of O'Hara, vice-chairman of the Housing Executive, to the position of chairman. Although Don Concannon had told me that O'Hara was just the man for the job, I wanted other suitable candidates to be considered. The old-boy network had been operating in the province for too long and we had been trying over the last two years to make sure that job selection was open and fair. We had, for example, wanted to encourage more women into jobs. The leaked document was an estimate of O'Hara's approach to the job should he be appointed and said that he would see his job as representing the Catholic minority but as chairman he would view it in a broad light. This Paisley managed to use, together with other information obtained by Westminster MP Jill Knight about so-called housing deals with the Provisional IRA, to impute pro-Catholic/IRA attitudes to the Northern Ireland Office. Because it was all aired at Westminster, the imputation was believed in the loyalist community.

This conspiracy theory of politics in Northern Ireland showed itself in many ways. The SDLP, for example, seemed to believe from our arrival in the province in 1974 that the British were going to pull out. As I commented in my diary of the time, 'No doubt there are people in the South and in the SDLP who believe that there is a clever plot on the part of Harold Wilson and myself to fight the forthcoming election on "pull out". This is not the case and in no circumstances would I ever stand for this, and neither would Harold Wilson.' Paddy Devlin was still at it in August 1983, when he made the astonishing claim that the major reason for the fall of the Executive was the ambition of Harold Wilson, who wanted to destroy the Executive to discredit Edward Heath whose popularity could thus be weakened before the October 1974 General Election!

It was not only the constant belief in conspiracy that affected my general view of the politicians but also their behaviour during the sitting of the Assembly and the Convention. The House of Commons can be childish but, thankfully, only in small doses. In Northern Ireland the political exchanges were more often than not of this type, with ill-informed discussions about, for example, the Rev Arlow's allegations about the ceasefire and denigration of successive Secretaries of State. In my darkest moments I commented to my Cabinet colleagues on the general low level of the Northern Irish politicians, but this was not giving credit to the special nature of politics in Northern Ireland.

There were two major differences between elected representatives at Westminster and at Stormont. First, just to be in public life in Northern Ireland is to run a continuous risk of violence, not only for the individual but for his or her family. The Northern Irish politicians were, and are, operating against a background unknown in Great Britain and we who operate at Westminster should never forget it. Second, the elected representatives in the province are far more directly the creatures of the electorate: look what happened to Brian Faulkner when he deviated from the loyalist tribal line. The political arithmetic of Ulster people and hence their politicians is bounded by the six counties. These differences explain to a large degree why the Convention broke down and why the concept of the voluntary coalition did not emerge then as an acceptable compromise. The Unionists were not prepared to move in front of their own troops by working with the SDLP, and certainly not while Dr Paisley was around.

I was constantly told by people in Northern Ireland who had chosen to go into business or the professions rather than politics that what the province needed was a new generation of politicians. Opting out of politics was nothing new. Forster, Secretary of Ireland, had written to Lord Ripon in 1881, 'The greatest of all Irish evils is the cowardice or at best the non-action of the moderate men who let things alone and let them get from bad to worse because they know that at a certain point the English will step in and prevent utter anarchy.' In the security situation of the 1970s and 1980s, 'cowardice' would be an unfair accusation, but the middle classes did keep their heads low. I still think, however, that there might well have been a change in the attitudes of the existing politicians if the power-sharing government had continued. Long periods of opposition at Westminster lead to irresponsibility, and in Northern Ireland responsibility for government could well have conditioned the politicians' rhetoric.

Politics and religion are inextricably linked in Northern Ireland and any consideration of the former has to take into account the influence of the Church leaders, who are closer to the political scene than their counterparts in Great Britain. They knew their Ireland and just to listen to them was an education in itself. On one occasion, Cardinal Conway and Dr Jack Weir of the Presbyterian Church talked to me about the ebb and flow of violence in their country over the years, with the Whiteboys, Rockites, Threshers and Blackfeet, through to the Irish Brotherhood and the Fenians. They posed the question whether in 1976 'the pike was not now going back into the thatch' – temporarily.

The Church leaders always spoke out against violence but their words had little effect on the murderers and bombers for whom religion is anyway only a cloak. Organised religion is nevertheless a factor, though not the only one, in reinforcing the divide in the province. This was illustrated by the issue of integrated schooling, which has long been put forward as a way to help solve the problem of Northern Ireland's divided society. The first government grant for integrated schooling was made available in 1817, and Unionists over the years had spoken in favour of the idea, although in practice Unionist governments had made generous grants to Catholic schools. The cry for integration was, however, seen by the Catholic Church as a means to weaken their influence on their own community.

As Secretary of State I watched with interest when during the short life of the power-sharing Executive Basil McIvor, the Unionist member responsible for Education, put forward a proposal whereby schools would be set up with representatives of the Catholic and Protestant Churches on the governing bodies. Modest though this proposal was, the SDLP showed political bravery in supporting it in the face of strong Church feelings on the subject. However, before it could be taken any further, the Executive fell.

The issue of integrated education surfaced again at the British/Irish Conference in July 1976, when Lady Patricia Fisher, former Northern Ireland Westminster MP, spoke of the many people in support of the idea. I agreed in my summing up that if that was the case, there should be a meeting of all those interested in Northern Ireland to consider progress on the matter. The BBC Northern Ireland correspondent, Billy Flackes, did no more than report the possibility of a conference but in the province that was escalated to mean that integrated schools were to be set up immediately.

I returned to Belfast ready to welcome the next day Jim Callaghan on his first visit to the province as Prime Minister, a visit only known about in advance by a handful of people for security reasons. I invited the Cardinal to Stormont, without telling him about Jim's presence, and he arrived in my office ashen-faced. When I explained the reason for the invitation, he exclaimed, 'Thank God! I thought you were going to tell me that we had to integrate our schools.' In the short discussion that followed, he made it clear that the Catholic Church would fight the idea all the way.

Our conference seemed unlikely to get far but Roland Moyle arranged a meeting with Cardinal Conway, Bishop Philbin and Bishop

Daly about it, explaining that the issue of shared schools had once more become a focus of public interest and that there was now pressure for the setting up of a conference; he said that no decisions had been taken and he was only taking preliminary soundings among interested parties. As a note of the meeting reveals, the Cardinal's attitude was one of complete intransigence:

> He dismissed the idea as trivial, irrelevant and without popular support; he would not participate in any conference on the matter, which would be set up by liberals for liberals and would be so constructed as to put the Catholic hierarchy 'in the dock'; he described Lady Fisher's scheme as an 'ambush'. He affirmed that his Church attached the very highest importance to Catholic children continuing to be educated in Catholic schools – this was embodied in Canon Law, had been endorsed by the Vatican Council, and was the only way in which a stable environment could be created where children could learn about the meaning of life and the rules of principled human conduct.
>
> He thought that to take a child from a Catholic home and educate that child in a non-Catholic school would create tension between the home and school environment which could only be harmful to the child. This might not be the case in middle-class areas such as Holywood – a kind of North Down Hampstead – but it certainly applied in the big housing estates, where Catholic schools were a great force for peace, teaching love, non-violence and the importance of the family. It would be folly to destroy this and replace it by an unwanted and disruptive system of shared schools.

In his summary, the Cardinal said that the Catholic Church would not attend an open conference to discuss the subject and would wage a campaign to fight any proposals which set out to relax the hold of the Church on the education of its children; he was sure that all his clergy supported his views.

With that veto, the idea of the conference and any scheme for integrated schools ran into the ground. I wished that such an educational experiment could have begun but I never believed that it would transform the situation in Northern Ireland. It would help, and no more. The reality of life in the province has to be accepted; all that we could do was to encourage the mixing of young people in sixth-form activities and at colleges of further education.

This view was part of my overall philosophy on Northern Ireland: we have to accept the divided nature of its society and work to bring the two sides together. There was little hope of this while violence continued, which is the reason why security policy came top of the agenda, alongside but not ahead of political change, and why I had highlighted the problem of security in my final minute to the Prime Minister when I looked back at the previous two and a half years.

Looking back at that period now, I am even more convinced that I was right to end the use of detention and to have used the Provisional IRA ceasefire as an instrument of policy; to have ended detention while the security situation was deteriorating would have been well-nigh impossible. Part of the art of government is to use events to one's own purpose and this is what I had endeavoured to do – not only to end detention but to achieve eventually the primacy of the police which had been foreshadowed in the July 1974 White Paper. This needed time, just as our policy of ending special category status did. The introduction of that had been a mistake and those 'liberals' who later favoured it and the hunger strikers did not know Northern Ireland or the nature of its violence. Nor could they have appreciated that the whole system of compound prisons made life – literally – difficult for the prison officers, who came from within the community and faced with their families great personal dangers.

Even after the ending of detention and special category status, there was still the special legislation of the Emergency Provisions Act in the province. Harcourt, the late nineteenth-century Liberal statesman, said of the 'coercion' law of his day, 'It is like caviare. It is unpleasant at first but you acquire a taste for it.' I never acquired a taste for special laws but I could not dismiss the activities of paramilitary murderers able to use modern machine guns and explosives. As long as violence was there, the state had the right to react and I could not ignore reality by sitting in my office as if it were an ivory tower from which I could occasionally descend to make elegant speeches in the Commons.

Whenever any of the normally accepted freedoms are modified, there must be regular questioning of the necessity for it. This was the purpose of the Gardiner Committee and its recommendations were very important to me. There was, however, no question of thinking that it was enough to shovel off difficult issues to independent committees and we constantly considered in the office whether our special powers continued to be needed and what changes might be made to them. One aspect of this which the Gardiner Committee recognised was the need for juryless courts in Northern Ireland. Impartial juries were not a possibility in a divided society where terrorism continued, and jury members would anyway be at risk from violence. The judges sitting alone were already putting their lives at risk, as the murder statistics showed.

A very much larger group of people who risked death daily were the members of the RUC and their families. When I arrived in the province, police morale was still low after the events of the late 1960s and early 1970s but it improved during the years I was there, along with the force's efficiency as it took the lead in the fight against violence. The overall credit for this goes to the men and women of the RUC but for the leadership that brought the change about, the credit must go to both the Chief Constables who served in the province in my time. Sir James Flanagan and Sir Kenneth Newman were first-class policemen who worked well together as Chief and Deputy until Jamie's retirement, when Ken was appointed to replace him by the Police Authority. The allegation that I had sacked Jamie was another piece of conspiratorial nonsense.

My contact with them was necessarily close, particularly in my early days in the province, but it was understood that their job was to carry out the law and that I would not interfere. It was important to build on this, for it had not always been the case in Northern Ireland. In my meetings with senior officers as I travelled round the province, I hardly needed to be told that the police had been against detention from the beginning. It had been imposed on them in 1972 when the RUC was supporting the army and not the other way round.

After the Ulster workers' strike, I tried gradually to use the Police Authority in the way it was originally intended. It was important to have such a body when there was no real local or regional government and its questioning role was of particular value in a split community. This was shown, for example, by Donal Murphy, a Catholic lawyer on the Authority, who to his credit often spoke out on police matters affecting the minority community. I was glad, too, that I had personally appointed – not with the approval of some of my advisers – Jack Hassard, an independent councillor from Dungannon. He was a thorn in the flesh of some Authority members but he knew his area inside out and regarded many of the local police as friends.

The policy of police primacy is easy enough to talk about but it was individuals in the RUC who put it into practice. Those who put their lives most at risk were the detectives who obtained and collated evidence and interrogated alleged terrorists in preparation for the courts, a much harder task than providing information for an interim custody order to be put to the Secretary of State. They have been the victims of propaganda claims by the paramilitaries outside the interrogation centres, helped by those being questioned inside alleging intimidation or inflicting wounds on themselves in order to protect themselves from the charge of giving information. This is not of course the full story; given the deaths and maiming of policemen and their families, it would be idle to pretend that there has not been police violence in the course of questioning. Whatever the scale of it, it was wrong. The police must be superior to the paramilitaries in everything that they do. I made my views clear to both Chief Constables and I and my staff regularly visited the interrogation centre at Castlereagh to show our interest and concern.

I also kept in close contact with the Police Federation of the province, whose members whether in public or private always discussed issues that concerned them in a civilised manner, in contrast to the later boorish behaviour of some of their British colleagues in London and Scarborough when I was Home Secretary. The harsh reality of policing in Northern Ireland did not encourage such silliness.

The fact that I felt so strongly about police primacy was not a reflection on the army. Policing must be a matter for civilians in uniform who know the people of their area. The police are trained to piece evidence together; the army tends to collect too much irrelevant information, which clogs the minds of those trying to solve the many jigsaws. Soldiers, quite simply, can never be policemen; their role is different and of most relevance in the long-term to the security situation in the rural border areas, a situation which needs much more cross-border co-operation if the army's role is to be reduced.

I was never in any doubt about how much I depended on the army, particularly in the early days and certainly during the Ulster workers' strike. I have never adopted a flag-waving attitude to the armed services, and mistakes were made by them, but no words of mine can express how much we and the people of Ulster owe to them. Without the army, far more local people would have been killed or maimed from the activities of the paramilitary groups.

I made it my job to visit as many of the battalions in the province as possible, within the constraints of time and geography. As with my visits to the RUC, the aim was to listen and learn, and to be seen by all ranks, so that I did not seem a remote figure up at Stormont taking decisions without thought for those at the sharp end. I of course had regular meetings, both formal and informal, with the two GOCs who served in Northern Ireland during my time, Frank King and David House, and I always felt that our personal relationships were good. We discussed and evaluated security policy in the light of the fast-moving events in the province and they rightly pressed their views but always accepted that overall the security decisions were mine. Both of them, for example, questioned my policy on the timing of the ending of detention but after I had listened carefully to their arguments, they did not demur at my decision. There was no disagreement over detention itself, and indeed the young commanding officers on the ground consistently put to me the need to end it; they knew at first hand the propaganda value of detention to the Provisional IRA. Never was I advised, even remotely, that the paramilitaries of any hue could be defeated. There was no Luneburg Heath on the horizon, to be followed by a victory march.

Although differences of opinion arose from time to time with my security advisers, they did not stand in the way of my general policy – contrary to any impression given by the 'revelations' in *The Times* of February 1976, which published 'army' documents criticising my policies on power sharing and releases of detainees. The documents came from an ex-army information officer who had been stationed at Lisburn, and such army personnel were never brought into policy discussions at Stormont nor, as I understood, at Lisburn. Perhaps they should have been, if only to avoid uninformed publications.

In the early period of my office, security discussions with soldiers, policemen, civilian security staff and my Northern Ireland ministerial colleagues would sometimes go on by night as well as by day, but our nightly discussions became rarer as the nature of violence changed and the police began to take the lead on security. With time also, support for the paramilitaries waned, at least on the loyalist side of the divide.

Given my own working-class background I found the changing attitudes of the loyalist working class particularly interesting. The various paramilitary groups among it had thought that the success of the Ulster workers' strike was a sign that they would be able to make future political advance but, despite later help from Stan Orme, this did not materialise. The people had been prepared to support the paramilitaries when Sunningdale had seemed to threaten their existence but not afterwards.

This was shown in the Paisley strike of 1977 when Jim Smyth of the UWC and active again in this later stoppage, said in the *Belfast Telegraph*, 'We won the propaganda battle in 1974 but the government won it hands down in 1977 because of their special department set up with their own operational room at Stormont where they were putting out false propaganda.' The special operation department which Peter England was largely responsible for setting up after 1974 was certainly an important factor, but it was not 'propaganda' that mattered but that in 1977 there was no Sunningdale issue: the people did not give their mass support and the stoppage was thus on a smaller scale. Moreover, by this time the RUC was organised to step in at an early stage.

Despite the lack of political support for the loyalist paramilitaries, they have not given up their political aims for an independent Ulster. Groups to achieve this seem to come and go but the constant theme of all of them is betrayal, going back to 1922 and Carson, to the Tories in 1972 with the introduction of direct rule, and the loyalist politicians in 1974 after the Ulster workers' strike. As a loyalist working man put it in

1974: 'We are a hybrid race descended from men who colonised Northern Ireland from Scotland in the seventeenth century. For four hundred years we have known nothing but uprising, murder, destruction and repression. We ourselves have repeatedly come to the support of the British Crown, only to be betrayed within another twenty years or so by a fresh government of that Crown . . . second-class Englishmen, half-caste Irishmen . . . how can we be expected to beat the world revolutionary movement?'

That self-assessment could largely be borne out by history, except for its conclusion. The loyalist paramilitaries believe that their republican counterparts are nurtured by foreign revolutionaries and although some such outside influence is constantly revealed, it is on a small scale. Even the financial contributions from the North American Irish do not alter this fact; the Boston Irish are hardly left-wing, let alone revolutionaries. The basic support for the republican paramilitaries comes from within Ireland itself.

The Provisional IRA or Provisional Sinn Fein failed in my day to make any real political advance and even its later concern with community politics has made little difference. Its overall political strength compared to that of the Fianna Fail, Fine Gael and the Irish Labour Party in the South, and the SDLP in the North, remains small. The talks between my officials and the Provisional Sinn Fein would have had different results if this weakness had not been apparent.

While its philosophy depends so much on armed strength, the Provisional IRA/Sinn Fein will not make any significant political advance. The nationalism which it advocates rests on a campaign of death against the security forces and the loyalists, and the new generation in control in recent years has reinforced this by rejecting the old federal solution, which at least recognised the reality of a loyalist community in the North, and has espoused the cause of British withdrawal accompanied by a disarmed RUC and UDR. This reveals a naivety of political thinking both in not understanding that Ulster Protestants are not tools of the British but people native to Ireland, and in an urge to find a 'final solution' – there is a strong grain of fascism in all ultra-nationalist parties.

The Official IRA, unlike the Provisional IRA, gave up violence against the security forces and the loyalists, if not against the Provisionals, after 1972. I was much taken later with the words of one of their men in the Maze: 'In turn the Catholic community must reject those who offer only violence as a solution to our political problems. The Protestant community must also reject purveyors of religious hatred. This is not a solution in itself, but it can create the situation and atmosphere in which the community can pursue a proper solution. The alternative to talking together is dying together.'

This statement illustrated the line of thought behind the emergence in the North of the Republican Clubs and of the Workers' Party in the South, and marked the Official IRA out as morally superior to the Provisional IRA, which broke away from the old IRA for straight nationalist reasons, or to the later Irish National Liberation Army, who broke from the Official IRA for twisted Marxist reasons. As yet the political parties of the Official IRA have drawn little support away from the strongly established Catholic parties in the North and South.

What I learned over the years in opposition and in government, from observations in the Maze, from the talks between my officials and the Provisional Sinn Fein, from my own talks with the UDA, was that the paramilitaries shared a common belief in victory through violence. None of them could see that there would never be a victory for any armed group or their supporters, only a brutal stalemate.

To understand Northern Ireland is difficult for outsiders. You have to listen, to observe, and to read the large numbers of locally produced newspapers, most of which reveal the all-pervading tribal attitudes of the province; an exception is the excellent evening paper, the *Belfast Telegraph*. Which paper one reads in Northern Ireland is an identity tag, however named – Fermanagh's *Impartial Reporter* to me has a particular touch of irony.

Although the local papers of course reported violence, it was not the only aspect of Northern Ireland's news to concern them. Most of the British national newspapers, on the other hand, seemed interested only in what the late Professor Lyons called the 'journalism of catastrophe'. Scenes of violence were the subject of instant reporting, with banner headlines and pictures, but little attention was paid to the other issues in the province and there was scant analysis of security or economic problems.

In reporting violence, the media in general and the press in particular too often ignored the effect of the publicity on the paramilitaries themselves, who basked in the attention. It was alleged in one of the leaked army documents to *The Times* in 1976 that the British press overemphasised the personal views of the men of violence and even 'doctored' the news to be 'actively destructive' of the army's activities. The last point was foolish but there was certainly a tendency to glamorize the paramilitaries.

The Gardiner Committee had suggested in 1974 that the Press Council should closely examine the 'reconciliation of the reporting of terrorist activities with the public interest'. I feel strongly that the media must be self-regulating, and the Council made this principle clear in its reply to the Committee. It was 'confident that in publishing reports about terrorist activities, editors will continue to have regard to overriding considerations of the public interest, the dangers of glamorizing such incidents in a way which may encourage support for them and of providing a platform for propaganda in favour of the criminal'.

Violence has to be reported, and without any censorship. However, I was not willing to suppress my anger when I thought that the BBC was erring in its judgment. Its role during the Ulster workers' strike had been less than impartial but when in 1979 it screened an interview with a representative of INLA just after one of this paramilitary group had murdered Airey Neave, I wrote in protest to Sir Ian Trethowen, the Director General of the BBC:

> As a minister, I never attempted to dictate or interfere in BBC programmes. Indeed, it is my view that the BBC has a duty to allow a wide spectrum of political opinions to be voiced. Ideas and opinions will never subvert our society. Nevertheless, in my view it was a grave error to show on television a man claiming to be an organiser of a murder gang. I can only hope that details of the man and his activities have been passed to the Irish Garda and to the Metropolitan Policy Special Branch.

In his reply, Sir Ian accepted that 'in this case there was a special sensitivity for those close to the tragedy of Airey Neave's murder and however clear we may be about the journalistic principle, we clearly misjudged the emotional impact on those particularly involved, not least in the House, and this we much regret'. He pointed out that there was nothing new about reporting terrorism, and that newspapers talked to and quoted individual terrorists in the process:

> On television, however, such interviews have far greater impact, which is why over Northern Ireland the BBC has only done it four times in ten years. We saw this particular case as one of those very rare occasions when the public in Britain should be able to judge directly the nature of these terrorists. . . . You are good enough to recognise that it is the BBC's duty 'to allow a wide spectrum of opinions to be voiced', but it is inevitable that occasionally those opinions will shock. What matters is not the messenger (although being human, he will no doubt sometimes err) but the message, and the way it is received. We believe that the common sense of the public will lead it to recognise very clearly the nature of the message from interviews like this, and that in the process its democratic resolve will be strengthened, not weakened.

He said, too, that the BBC had made it clear to the terrorists from the outset that it would give the police any assistance they sought, which had been happening for some days.

Despite its reasonableness, the Director-General's letter did not satisfy me. The programme was not reporting the nature of terrorism, it was giving publicity to someone associated with a particular murder, and at the wrong time. The programme could have been broadcast at a later date. I felt that it had not heeded another recommendation of the Gardiner Committee, which was that 'the governors of the BBC and IBA should re-examine the guidance they give to programme controllers or companies about contact with terrorist organisations and the reporting of their views and activities'.

The question of media reportage of Northern Ireland is not easy to resolve. There is no comparison to be made with the Second World War, as some people in the province believed, suggesting even that if the modern media had been reporting the last war, they would have interviewed Hitler and Goering! Of course the media should explain the nature of terrorism and comment on the views of those who kill for political ends, but the line has to be drawn somewhere. I could never support the law in the Republic which proscribes broadcast interviews with members of illegal organisations. On the other hand, people in the media ruling from plush offices at a safe distance from the violence should show sensitivity to the feelings of those whose relatives and friends have been killed or maimed, or who themselves are in the firing line.

Journalists coming in to Northern Ireland to report events should also realise that one short visit to the province provides little more than the beginning of wisdom. The Annan Report on Broadcasting of 1977 noted: 'In our talk in Northern Ireland we heard criticism not so much of Ulster Television or of BBC Northern Ireland, but of the BBC and Independent Television teams who come over from London. We were told that these teams will not take guidance from those who live with the situation and either by their actions in Northern Ireland or by the programmes which they produce, not merely give deep offence to people of varied political or religious persuasions, but distort the truth by their superficial treatment of the issues.'

No doubt those criticised would reply that people too close to the action imperceptibly cover up or are unwilling to face facts which visitors to the province expose. Broadcasters, like newspaper journalists, must tell the truth as they see it and no government, through politicians or civil servants, should exercise control over their work. Nevertheless, a little self-generated humility would not come amiss.

I knew and respected many of the journalists working in the province. Their job was not an easy one; they faced not only the dangers of violence but also the famous Ulster reticence. As Seamus Heaney, the Northern Irish poet, put it: 'To be saved you must only save face; and whatever you say, you say nothing.' Some journalists responded to these difficulties by taking in each other's washing in the Europa Hotel. Others lapped up the cloak-and-dagger approaches of the paramilitaries and enjoyed a new-found sense of self-importance which even led to fantasies of their phones being tapped. Others, to their credit, went around the province and wrote perceptively about the problems which they encountered. I learned much from them and took account of the information they provided and their views on future policy. They bothered to check their facts, unlike the London-based scissors-and-paste practitioners who created their own picture of events and made the same factual errors over and over again in their 'investigative' pieces.

Even in day-to-day reporting, the press would often not provide the full facts behind an event. The ghastly Armagh murders in January 1976 were an example of this. Given a free press and the sense of outrage at the murders, it was almost inevitable that editors, and MPs, would put their own solutions forward and find the government and the army wrong, but the issues behind the murders were not analysed carefully by the journalists writing the articles and they certainly were not properly considered by the headline-writers.

The press also got the story of the Price sisters wrong. My disillusionment came out in my diary of the time: 'It is quite incredible how the papers piece bits together to get these so-called inside stories. It worries me as someone who used to look at newspapers for ideas and information. They pick up little bits, snippets from the press offices in the departments. I don't know where they get most of it from but they end up telling a story that is plainly wrong.'

It was less surprising, given the secrecy surrounding them, that the ceasefire and the talks with the Provisional Sinn Fein should have been misreported. One newspaper, however, managed a particularly high flight of fancy when it alleged that government industrial policies had been altered to suit the Provisional IRA. In fact, in the autumn of 1974 – before the talks with the Provisional Sinn Fein had even been thought of – I had informed Tony Benn, the Secretary of State for Industry, that I did not want Harland and Wolff or Short and Harland brought within the ambit of the nationalisation plans for British shipyards and the aircraft industry. Stan Orme had explained to Tony that these firms were a Northern Ireland responsibility and that I wanted them kept entirely separate from those in Britain. This was because of my belief that our ultimate aim should be a devolved government for Northern Ireland, which would be responsible for the province's industry. It was not a sign of a policy of disengagement from Northern Ireland and had nothing to do with the talks. Today, Harland and Wolff employees should be grateful that the firm was not absorbed into British shipbuilding; by now it would have been closed.

Sometimes inaccurate reporting of security issues arose because of a lack of understanding of the operational difficulties of soldiers or policemen. In July 1981, Dick Francis, BBC Director of News and Current Affairs and former BBC Controller in Northern Ireland, stated in a speech made to the Royal Television Society: 'Although our reporters take the greatest pains to point out the illegality of men in paramilitary uniforms and masks firing volleys over the coffins, they also point out that the security forces normally choose to stay well clear rather than make immediate arrests.' The implication was that the army condoned the actions of the Provisional IRA; it did not seem to be appreciated that to send soldiers in to such a scene would lead to further shootings, and worse. As I concluded in my own speech to the Royal Television Society, 'Such an action could make the Derry Bloody Sunday of nine years ago look like a picnic.' When in the early days of office, I had asked for the army to stop the paramilitary funeral ceremonies, Frank King had quickly pointed out to me that this was not feasible because of the risk of injuries and death. That he was right was borne out by the incident in August 1984 when the RUC was put in a position of having to attempt the arrest of an unimportant American fund-collector for the IRA, which led to the death of a demonstrator.

Perhaps we in the Northern Ireland Office should have done more to explain policy to the media, and there were certainly weaknesses in our information service during the Ulster workers' strike, which we had afterwards done our best to rectify. We had, for example, carefully explained our policy on the ending of detention to newspaper editors. This was not, however, typical and there is a limit to what can be done. There must always be a distance between any government and the media: too much contact only breeds suspicion and scepticism among journalists and commentators.

Despite my strong feelings amounting occasionally to downright anger against the press, they never led me to want to control it. From their investigations in the province, the Gardiner Committee recognised that the advertisements from paramilitary groups accepted by some newspapers could provide propaganda platforms for those whose aim was the violent overthrow of lawful government and although they said that there could be no question of introducing censorship in a free society in time of peace, they recommended that in Northern Ireland it be made a summary offence for editors, printers and publishers of newspapers to publish anything which purported to be an advertisement for an illegal organisation. Even this limited form of control was something that I was not prepared on principle to pursue; it would in any case have soon been circumvented.

The same principle applied when, as Home Secretary, I proposed in the light of the Annan Report a loosening of government control over the BBC in a time of emergency. I also made it clear to my Cabinet colleagues, some of whom were often angry at aspects of BBC reporting, that I would not make representations to the BBC about policy questions for which they had ministerial responsibility. They were free to make their own representations but I was not going to act as a sieve for their complaints. Any representations should, I thought, be no more than an attempt to ensure that the BBC was seized of a legitimate point, and I would expect to be informed of these.

The problems in Northern Ireland between the media and the government went deeper than disagreements on facts and policies. During the Ulster workers' strike, the information arrangements at Stormont and at the army and police headquarters were undoubtedly poor, and we were rightly criticised for them. That does not, however, invalidate my criticism of the BBC's so-called impartial role in the strike. I did not want the BBC to be the voice of government, but nor did I want it to be the voice of the UWC. The later problem that arose over the Maire Drumm affair was in my view an example of press confusion about the protection of source argument: if words spoken on a public occasion are reported, the press should be able to substantiate them.

There were also the difficulties shown up by a leak of official documents by a Ministry of Defence civil servant to Robert Fisk of *The Times* in early 1975, which led the Law Officers to consider a prosecution because of a breach of the Official Secrets Act. I was consulted about whether I thought this was merited 'in the public interest' but, as I said in my diary of the time, 'It is my view that we should not act under Section 2. If there were any really serious documents, it might be different.'

We had found out about the leaks only because some of the documents were delivered by hand through Fisk's letter-box and the lady who cleaned for him had found them and passed them to the police. There was of course a full enquiry. Robert Fisk was questioned in Belfast by the police, and in Dublin it was put to him by a member of the British Embassy that the documents ought to be returned. The source of the leaks was identified and appropriate action taken.

Subsequently, Jim Kilfedder, the Unionist MP for North Down, tabled a parliamentary question about why, and on whose instructions, Robert Fisk had been questioned, to which I replied that it was on the instructions of senior officers of the RUC, that police enquiries were continuing and I could make no further comment. Robert Fisk himself described the details of his questioning in Belfast and of the request in Dublin for the return of the documents. He revealed too that he had asked Stan Orme, who happened to be in Dublin, about 'the government's change of information policy' and had been 'met with denials'. These so-called changes in government information policy were what Robert Fisk had been investigating, and he wrote:

> The reports in Belfast concern a committee which is said to have drawn up a new policy for giving information to the press. According to the reports, which have been strenuously denied by official sources at Stormont Castle, the committee is chaired by Mr Michael Cudlipp, the Secretary of State's public relations consultant, and has decided among other things that details about the personal lives of extremist leaders may be used by the army and police in order to discredit them in the eyes of their supporters. British army officers are believed to have been called to a briefing at military headquarters at Lisburn, in County Antrim, where the policy has been explained.
>
> Government sources say that no such committee exists in Stormont and they seem unaware of any military briefing. Mr Cudlipp confirms that he is head of a committee in Northern Ireland, but categorically refuses to say what its function or business is, on the ground that this is a private matter. Apparently those involved include a Foreign Office official seconded to the Northern Ireland Office, the Chief Army Information Officer at Lisburn, a Royal Ulster Constabulary press officer, a senior police officer, and a number of civil servants involved in security matters. Asked whether such a committee existed, an RUC spokesman said: 'I am not aware of what you are talking about; you cannot expect me to tell you the details of committees at Stormont Castle.'
>
> The policy seems to be that a more 'aggressive' approach should be adopted towards public relations and that items of information about extremist leaders might be given in private to newspapermen in the hope of sowing distrust among various paramilitary groups.

I was astonished by all this, and particularly by his further claim that we were 'accusing' him of possession of government documents because of the subject of his investigations. We had only got to know of the leaked documents by accident, after which there had inevitably been full enquiries. If we chased journalists because they were investigating supposed changes of policy, we would never have stopped! Equally untrue was the later allegation that the papers were 'planted'.

Robert Fisk was right that a committee existed under the chairmanship of Michael Cudlipp. It was the Information Policy Co-ordinating Committee, which met regularly and consisted of representatives of the army, the RUC, the Northern Ireland Office, both in London and Belfast, and the Northern Ireland Civil Service. Its aim was to co-ordinate government information policy in the province which, because there were three information departments, tended to go off in different directions.

The information policy which I wished to see followed by the Committee had been firmly laid down. Because I had been extremely concerned about what I regarded as freelance attempts by the army information people to use 'black propaganda', which could have blow-back effects, I had emphasised that such methods should not be used. I wanted, however, to ensure that positive policy was produced and to control rash statements made in the heat of the moment. In late 1974/ early 1975 Michael Cudlipp had prepared a paper on these lines, which I had approved. It set down the more 'vigorous and attacking' policy that I had been aiming for, which meant providing not only information on day-to-day policy but emphasising our long-term aims for primacy of the police.

Information policy was an important subject in which the media quite properly were interested, although I would have preferred it if journalists had discussed it openly with me rather than take a cloak-and-dagger approach. Other important subjects appeared on the press agenda only fitfully, for example, there was little in-depth reporting of affairs in the Irish Republic. This put the media in good company with British governments, which until the early 1970s had largely ignored the Republic for nearly fifty years. It was as if a century of Irish political trauma at Westminster had ended in 1922 with a feeling of good riddance: at last the place was no longer our concern. Yet of course the Irish Republic should be of concern to us. It is a close neighbour, part of the EEC, with large numbers of its citizens residents in Great Britain; above all, what goes on there is relevant to Northern Ireland.

When I had become Secretary of State in 1974, I had continued my efforts from opposition to learn about the twenty-six counties. To live and work at Stormont did not in itself make one knowledgeable about the Republic but it was a better vantage point for education than Great Britain, where Irish comedians vie with school history books as the bench-mark of comprehension and where universities are concerned more with Africa than Ireland.

The journals and newspapers of the South, especially the *Irish Times*, gave me a feel for the changing independent country of today. On my regular visits to Dublin I found a small state still dominated by history and the Catholic Church but with an emerging modern identity. Its industry was developing and, with the aid of EEC funds, its agriculture was being restructured. These changes were creating a different outlook, particularly amongst young people, who looked more to the future than the past. Northern Ireland continues to matter – the Catholics there are seen to belong to the South – but despite all the talk of unification and the impact of the Northern troubles, I judged that the people in the South, whatever their emotions, had turned their back on the 'black' North.

No Southern government in my period of office had put its mind to what it would do if the North ever fell into its lap, let alone considered unilateral action to take it over by force. In discussions, the economic cost of the North to Whitehall was often brought up, with the assumption that one day the burden of this cost would lead to a cutting of our ties with the North, but at the same time that the British would willingly continue to pick up the tab for a republican government when reunification was achieved. The reasoning was that we would do anything to get rid of the North!

This kind of wishful thinking by Southern governments was accompanied by expressions of blame on successive British governments and particularly that of 1922. Deep-down, however, the Southern politicians understood the reality: the loyalists would fight incorporation with the South and without their co-operation, Dublin could not govern the North. All Irish governments have recognised, and continue to recognise, this – consequently their repeated use of the phrase 'unity by consent', which was not a concept that first arose at Sunningdale in 1974. De Valera, for example, had said in August 1921 that the Dail had not the power to use force with Ulster. Nor did the main political parties of the South have the inclination to use it. Fianna Fail and Fine Gail were born of civil war and they wanted no repeat performance of recent painful history. They were, and are, firmly opposed to paramilitary organisations of whatever kind and they continue to see the North as the tip of an iceberg which could wreck their own ship of state.

I and Stan Orme kept in close contact with the leaders of all the Southern political parties and particularly with friends in the Labour movement in Dublin. There was always a warmth of spirit to our discussions even when we disagreed and even if the press briefing of our formal meetings showed that it was easy to have two versions of the same event. We were never left in doubt that Ireland was an independent state and that Gladstone, Parnell and Redmond were long dead.

My visits to Dublin, sometimes arranged so that I could also enjoy watching an international rugby match at Lansdowne Road, were mainly concerned with security matters. It was vital to prevent the flow of arms and explosives, and to exchange information. The meetings were very productive and the co-operation that developed was praised by Harold Wilson on 12 January 1976 at the time of the Armagh atrocities. It was not, however, complete. There was still a lack of co-operation between our armies, even when the Irish army became increasingly involved in the border areas, and still the problem of no full extradition agreement: the 'joint' legislation following Sunningdale did not work effectively. The best co-operation was between the two police forces, which had become so established by September 1976 that politicians were better kept out of the regular meetings. When I left the province, there was still, however, room for improvement, particularly on the exchange of information on the whereabouts of terrorists.

Our security discussions with the South would have been counter-productive unless there were also discussions on constitutional issues. Most of these took place in meetings with the Taoiseach, although there were occasions at the British Ambassador's residence in Dublin when the informal talk about wider political issues went on till the early hours with Southern ministers. I recall the anger of Conor Cruise O'Brien and Garret Fitzgerald on one such occasion in May 1976 when the subject of the talks with the Provisional Sinn Fein cropped up. I explained our reasons for holding them and said that although the IRA might not be particularly meaningful in the South, it was holding down large numbers of soldiers and policemen in the North. I also told them that the Southern government was watching from the touchline and still treating the Provisional IRA and INLA murders as politically motivated if the 'action' was in the North. We were not, I said yet again, negotiating with the Provisionals. By this time the talks were anyway in effect over, which I assumed that Garret knew from his own security sources.

My personal relations with Irish ministers were always good. I was sometimes irritated by Garret, for example, over his radio remarks about the SAS border-crossing incident in May 1976 and his critical press briefing after the South Armagh atrocities earlier in the year, when it was reported that he was concerned that South Armagh should be properly policed: army patrols were non-existent after dark. In South Armagh? It was, however, an irritation between friends. He is a very able man who knows what he wants for Ireland and, unlike most other Southern politicians, goes to the North to see for himself the situation.

Although my relations with the Southern politicians were good, I sensed that both the Fianna Fail and Fine Gail parties preferred the

British Tories, and still do. This was not because I had authorised talks with the Provisional Sinn Fein or because Harold Wilson and I had talked with Provisional Sinn Fein members when in Opposition; after all Willie Whitelaw had done this twice when in government. It was because the Sunningdale conference had occurred when Edward Heath's government was in office and we in the Labour government had not sustained the agreement made then nor put down the Ulster workers' strike. It was also not well received that I kept emphasising that the North was where the problem was and where it had to be tackled, not in London or Dublin.

Until the late 1960s politicians in both capitals had ignored the North. Since then the talk about it has too often been based on wishful thinking rather than reality, and many Southern politicians have never been there despite its closeness. If they had, they would have found that fifty years of de facto independence and the effects of the Second World War had cemented an Ulster identity. This is what I had encountered during the Ulster workers' strike and referred to as Ulster nationalism. It is not something that can be ignored.

A major surprise for me was to find this feeling expressed in the wider field of the arts in both communities, if in rather different form. Ulster's cultural development since the war years, particularly in literature and music, is extraordinary and even more striking when compared to that in London where the arts are cosmopolitan. The poets of the North, for example Seamus Heaney and Paul Muldoon, or Michael Longley from the other side of the divide, speak for their people, revealing aspects of the community that no sociological tome could ever reach. The urban tribal instinct, reinforced by the killing and maiming of the last decade, finds direct expression in their work; Longley's poem 'Wounds' could only stem from the Shankill but its gut feeling is essentially no different to that found in another context in the nearby Falls Road:

> Here are two pictures from my father's head –
> I have kept them like secrets until now:
> First, the Ulster Division at the Somme
> Going over the top with 'Fuck the Pope!'
> 'No Surrender!'; a boy about to die
> Screaming 'Give 'em one for the Shankill!'

However real Northern Ireland's problems, and rooted as they are in history, recent and past, and in a mythology which counts as much as reality, there is much that the paramilitaries have to answer for. They are no freedom fighters, as some people in the safety of their British and American homes seem to believe; there is a ballot box in the North, as there is in the South. Gunmen from either side may call in aid the word socialism, but their activities show as much socialism as those of Hitler's National Socialists did. A philosophy is needed to cover the degeneration since 1969 of their stand as defenders of their communities to a vested interest in criminal murder. Anyone who has seen the results of their actions knows the spurious nature of their acquired beliefs, which are accompanied by feelings of betrayal either by Dublin or London. These are part of a common Ulster outlook, straddling the divide.

I had no doubt in 1976, and have none now, that our commitment to the province is long-term. Those who advocate pull-out are ignoring its implications. Ulster is part of an island whose problems have defeated us for centuries; the Boyne, the Lagan and the Bann are not the Zambezi, the Nile or the Ganges. Northern Ireland does not pose a classical colonial question. There is no government there and to pull out quickly would mean handing over to an ad hoc loyalist administration; even if a period were allowed for a government to be formed before pulling out, the result would simply be an elected loyalist administration.

Charles Haughey of Fianna Fail has put forward the view to visiting groups of British MPs to Ireland that a pull-out by Britain would be accepted by the loyalists and all would be well. It is a view that would be stopped in its tracks if he made frequent visits to all parts of the North and talked to the UDA rather than to the Northern industrialists whom he calls in aid. I had not in any case noticed any pro-Dublin feelings among the latter in May 1974.

Whether pull-out occurred by design or by accident, it would lead to bloodshed on a scale far greater than exists now in Northern Ireland and would wash over into Glasgow, Merseyside, Birmingham and London. The paramilitaries would come into their own as defenders of their communities and in this last-ditch situation, one does not have to guess on which side the local and only remaining security forces would be, nor what the response of the security forces in the South would have to be. The fighting would be ruthless, and at the end of the day the Northern Ireland state would still be there but smaller in size as the illogicality of the border was rectified by military reality.

For this reason alone, the British have a continuing role in Northern Ireland. Direct rule must not, however, be allowed to set into a rut; it must be approached positively, without the wearisome colonial attitude to the job expressed by Sir George Trevelyan as Secretary for Ireland in the 1880s: 'I get along because I regard it in a dogged semi-sulky way, as if one had to walk uphill against the rain and wind, in a fog, for an indefinite number of miles, being certain of nothing except that you are walking in what you believe to be the right direction, and renouncing all ideas of finding pleasure in the landscape.' Ministers must play a positive role and be appointed not because they are in line for a job but because they are willing and able to commit themselves to the province.

Northern Ireland has to be governed in a non-sectarian way, with special attention paid to unemployment, which cannot be left to the working of free market forces alone, and to housing, which is an affront to decency in parts of Belfast, particularly the Divis Flats area – a monument to the foolishness of planners in the fifties and sixties. An improved industrial and social economy would not solve the problem of violence but it would have a marginal effect on it. More important, economic measures to help the province would indicate Westminster's commitment. Joint economic development with the South, particularly in the western border areas, would be sensible, and funding for projects might come not only from the EEC but also from Irish-Americans, whose money at the moment is used to buy weapons and thus to commit murder by proxy.

The difficult problem of discrimination has also to be faced. It was a state of mind acquired over the centuries and reinforced by myth as well as reality. I learned quickly that the loyalists blamed the Catholics for it. They asserted that Catholics never tried to play a full part in the North but were always crying that they did not have a part because of discrimination against them. To the loyalists, the Catholics were the enemy within. The Catholics saw it otherwise: they were discriminated against by name, school and religion. The problem was not connected with class struggle; working-class Protestants, however poor, did not feel discriminated against because, in the Irish sense of the term, they were not.

Various government actions had been taken in the 1970s to help deal with discrimination in the province and I had asked the Standing Advisory Committee on Human Rights to consider the question of a Bill of Rights, which was being mooted in the province. When the Committee reported in 1977, it pointed out that there was already an 'impressive body of law' in force, with a Parliamentary Commissioner for Administration, a Complaints Commission, and a Fair Employment Agency which 'should not be underrated'. It concluded that a Bill of Rights for Northern Ireland would be inappropriate and not generally welcomed at the time – although one for the UK as a whole was a different matter! I myself had grown increasingly sceptical of the need for such a Bill and although I have no doubt that positive government action through the law is valuable in tackling discrimination, it is only time that can bring real changes in attitudes.

Continuing direct rule has to include co-operation between the governments in Dublin and London, building on the relationships formed over the last decade. Those in the North who disparage and distrust this co-operation need to be reminded of the origin of the six counties and the nationalist veto which followed their establishment; the nationalists in the South were left with a sense of almost parental duty towards their Northern kith and kin, and the violence that has gone on over the years since has to be pointed out. Talks and action on security problems are a vital part of inter-governmental co-operation, and might include the setting up of a joint committee, as the South has suggested, although no such committee can legally control the RUC and the Garda. It would, however, bring to the fore such questions as whether the South would allow the RUC to operate in Monaghan, though I doubt such an idea would get far.

The South has to convince its fellow-Irishmen in the North, loyalist/Protestant though they may be, that it is serious about stopping the hit-and-run murders in South Armagh. As anyone who has been involved in talks with Southern ministers and politicians knows, there is no doubt of their horror at the murders by the Provisional IRA and INLA, but this is simply not accepted by the loyalist community, which does not believe the South's commitment to do something about it. I was constantly told that the 'gombeen' politicians in Dublin could not be trusted; they only pretended to be against the IRA. How often, I was asked, were murderers sent back to the North? How often were protest marches organised against the killing of loyalists?

While republican murderers still escape across the border and until positive action is taken about it, all talk of political change is moonshine. Although I have never seen a redrawing of the border as a means of aiding political change, I think it foolish for the UK to continue to be responsible for South Armagh either administratively or for security. A redrawing of the border there would save lives, and I think it is at least worth discussing with the South. Inevitably the question of the Protestants in Monaghan would follow.

I think that it is also time to discuss again the problem of extradition and the second-best arrangement implemented as a result of Sunningdale. A joint court should be considered, but the law that it would administer would need to be much clearer on the definition of terrorism and there would have to be another look at whether such a joint activity would be allowable under the Irish constitution.

Other, wider security issues for the agenda of inter-governmental talks would include ways of stemming the flow of money and arms to the Provisional IRA. The major source of money is from bank and post office robberies in all parts of Ireland but the 'welfare' money received from the USA is also a gap that needs to be sealed, along with the arms coming in from the Middle East. The impressive speed with which the Irish government and its Dail recently acted to block laundered funds coming into Ireland is one of the most important moves against terrorism for years. I had suggested the need for this in the House of Commons on 20 December 1984 and I have little doubt that the Irish government's act was prompted by the search in Ireland for the funds of the British National Union of Miners.

The talks should of course go further than security issues and cover all constitutional possibilities for the North, however remote the chance of implementation. It would be apparent very early on that there is no solution waiting to be put into elegant prose in a White Paper and followed by a speech of high tone in the Commons or the Dail. Public acceptance of this reality would, however, be a step forward.

The talks could profitably be based on the agenda put forward by the New Ireland Forum of 1984, which had been set up to collect the voices of nationalist opinion on both sides of the border. One of the Forum's implications was a continuing role for the British government: above all the Irish government does not want a withdrawal – yet. It may be that such discussions would soon end because those with no responsibility in both parts of Ireland would propose the unattainable. If so, it would be nothing unusual in Irish history. However, they would be a way of testing the feeling expressed in the Forum Report that the Irish state has to become more pluralistic before it can be acceptable to the North. They would also strengthen the hand of the few Southern politicians who visit the North and focus attention on that section of the Report which shows an understanding of the loyalist feeling for Britain. It is the loyalists and not the British who are the veto on unification, just as the republican Northern Irish are the veto on an Ulster Protestant state for a Protestant people. Because it would highlight the real source of the veto, I would agree with the demand put forward over the years, and implied in the Forum Report, to end the UK constitutional guarantee for the North.

Although the talks would be important, I do not believe that the answer to Northern Ireland's problems lies with the Westminster or Dublin governments. Grandiose Anglo/Irish solutions will not work. The only way forward from the talks lies in Northern Ireland itself. As Charles James Fox said nearly two centuries ago, 'We ought not to presume to legislate for a nation with whose feelings and affections and interests, opinions and prejudices, we have no sympathy.' His words are still as relevant today in the context of both communities in Northern Ireland.

The aim of a Westminster government must be to bring a devolved administration back to the province. This was the one point of agreement in the Convention. The fundamental disagreement was on its form, and once more the idea of a voluntary coalition must be pursued. This policy would of course have to be approved by Parliament at Westminster, as the body responsible for Northern Ireland, and afterwards would need to be discussed with the government of the South. How and when to proceed must be left to a Secretary of State aware of the local issues of the time, but he would have the 1982 Northern Ireland Act on the statute book, which provides for devolution by stages.

One way out of the dilemma of finding a chief executive in the province would be to adapt the idea of a 'resident minister', which was a proposal made in one of the option papers put to Cabinet during my term of office. The chief executive, from Great Britain but committed to Northern Ireland, could build a small executive from the main parties, as opposed to the large unwieldy body built up in 1973, which would take over the powers last exercised in 1974. In time the chief executive would be someone from the province and not Great Britain.

The Secretary of State for Northern Ireland in a Westminster Cabinet would still be responsible for finance, the courts and emergency legislation but would be supported by fewer UK ministers. It would be important this time to transfer responsibility for the police to the executive, which would now be possible, as it was not in the past, because of the continuing reduction in the role of the army. Ideas in some military circles that the established army camps in the province should remain when the troubles end should be resisted: swift response from Great Britain would be very easy because of efficient air transport.

The UDR, carefully monitored, would still be required to carry out such roles as guarding public buildings; its long-term future would need much deeper consideration. Although people in its ranks have acted illegally, it should not be forgotten that members of the UDR have died and been injured carrying out their duties. Overall, it has to be remembered that the alienation of the minority from the forces of law and order has been a major reason why the fight against terrorism has taken so long. The security forces in Northern Ireland will not be fully effective until they are wholeheartedly supported by both sides of the community.

These are not proposals to set hearts beating with hope; I do not believe that any realistic scheme could do so. The problems that have emerged since 1969 are embedded in history and all of my experience in Northern Ireland showed that any move to solve them must be slow and accompanied by the expectation of constant setbacks and resistance from the paramilitaries. Time is of the essence.

The dream of a united Ireland will long remain a dream. A devolved government in the North is the only basis on which the people in the two parts of the island will one day talk to each other. The hope of finding a successful solution lies with the Northern Irish people, not with outsiders in Dublin and London talking by proxy. Northern Ireland has been the scene of battle; only there can peace slowly be forged.

INDEX